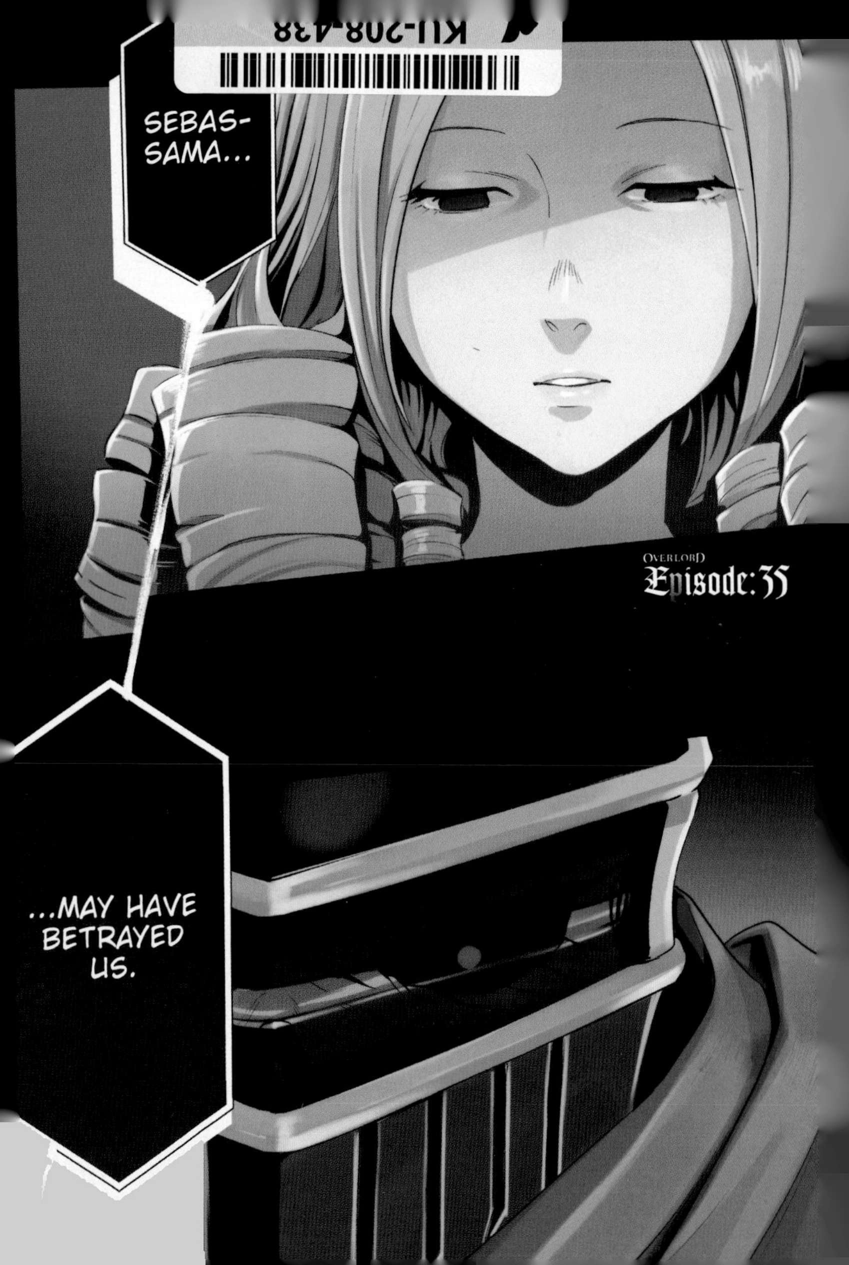
SEBAS-SAMA...
OVERLORD
Episode:35
...MAY HAVE BETRAYED US.

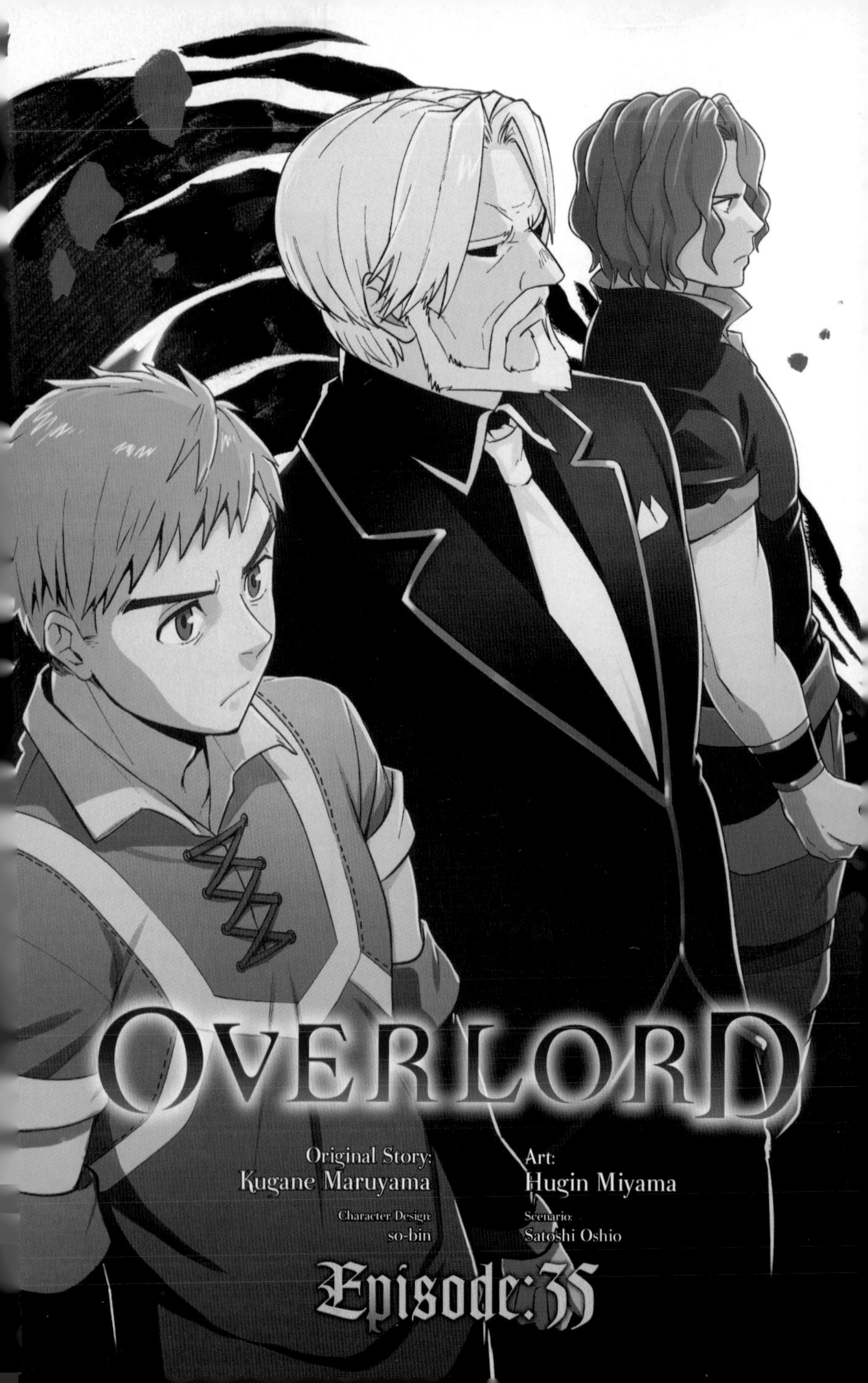
OVERLORD
Original Story:
Kugane Maruyama
Art:
Hugin Miyama
Character Design:
so-bin
Scenario:
Satoshi Oshio
Episode:35

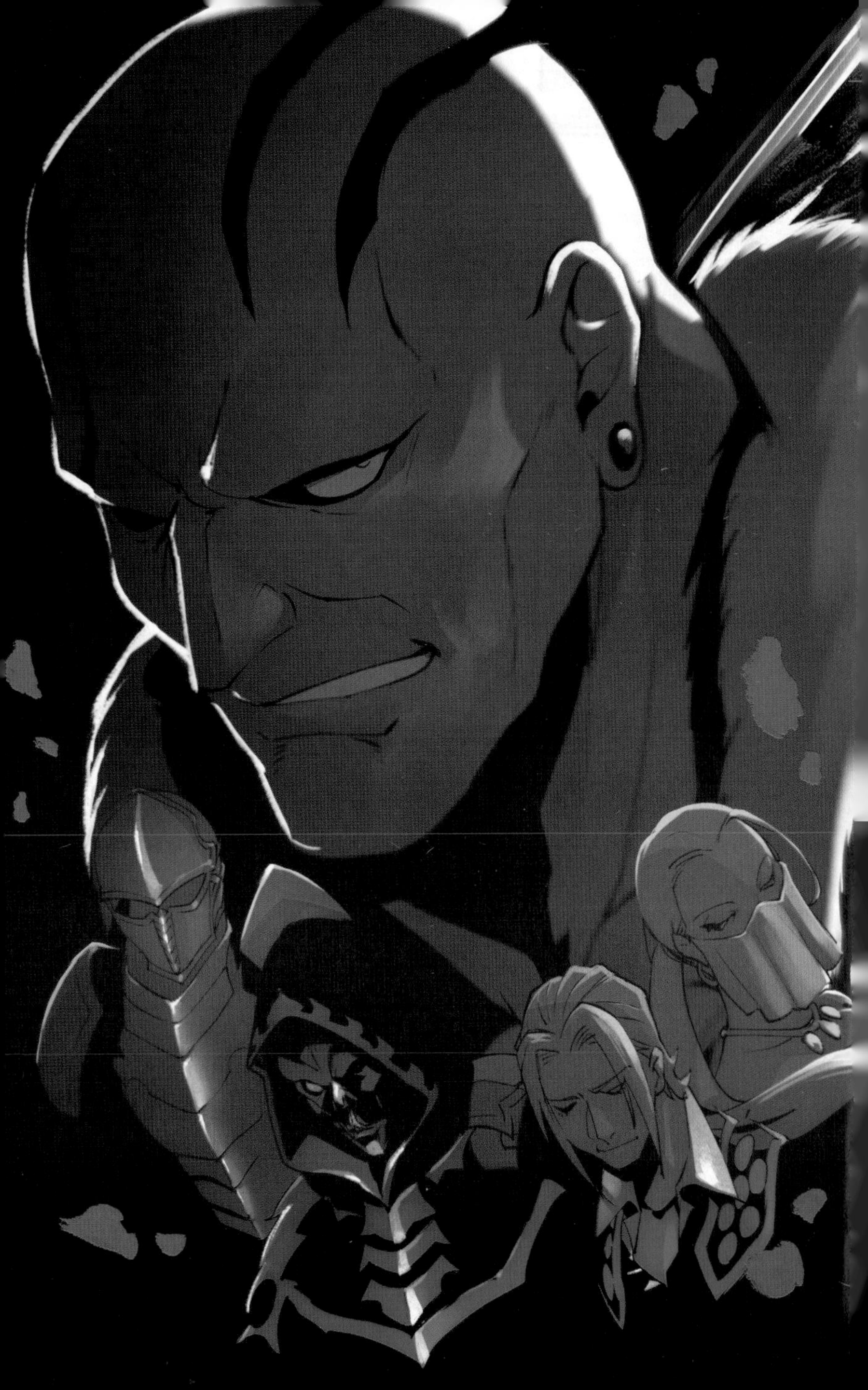

OVERLORD

10

Original Story:
Kugane Maruyama

Art:
Hugin Miyama

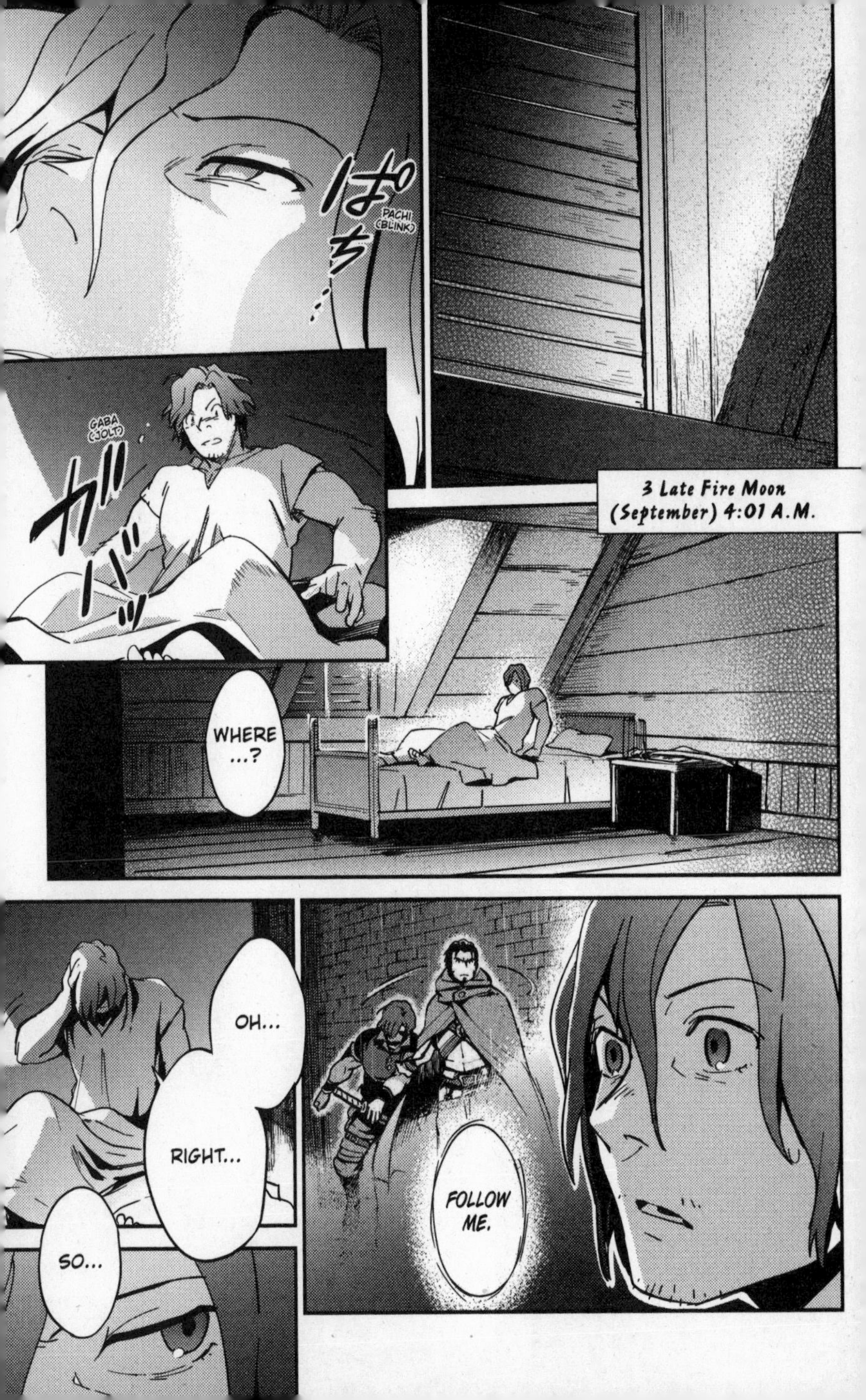
ぱち…
PACHI (BLINK)
ガバッ
GABA (JOLT)
3 Late Fire Moon (September) 4:01 A.M.
WHERE ...?
FOLLOW ME.
OH...
RIGHT...
SO...

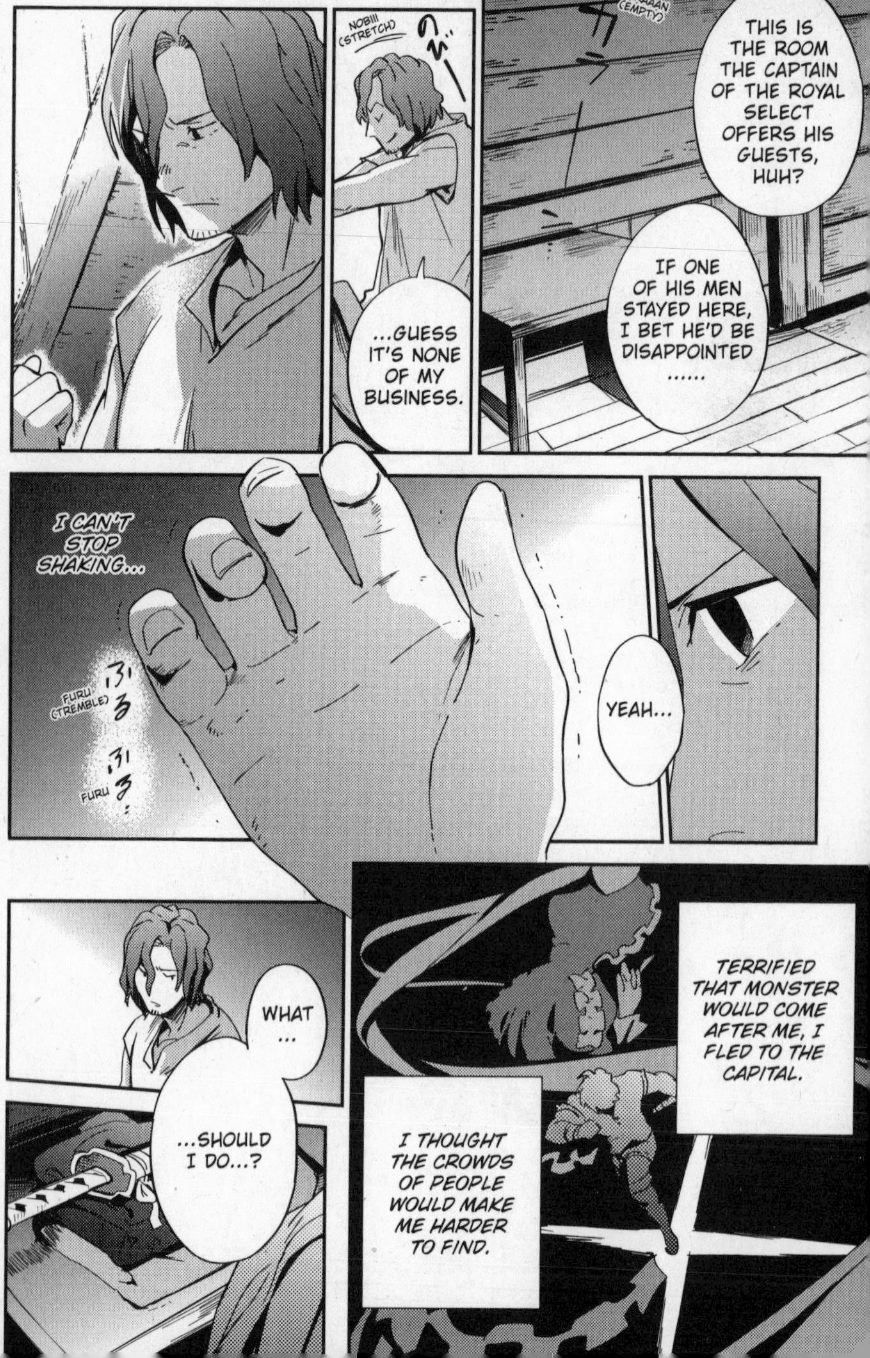
KARAAAN (EMPTY)
THIS IS THE ROOM THE CAPTAIN OF THE ROYAL SELECT OFFERS HIS GUESTS, HUH?
IF ONE OF HIS MEN STAYED HERE, I BET HE'D BE DISAPPOINTED ......
NOBIII (STRETCH)
...GUESS IT'S NONE OF MY BUSINESS.
YEAH...
I CAN'T STOP SHAKING...
FURU (TREMBLE)
FURU
TERRIFIED THAT MONSTER WOULD COME AFTER ME, I FLED TO THE CAPITAL.
I THOUGHT THE CROWDS OF PEOPLE WOULD MAKE ME HARDER TO FIND.
WHAT ...
...SHOULD I DO...?

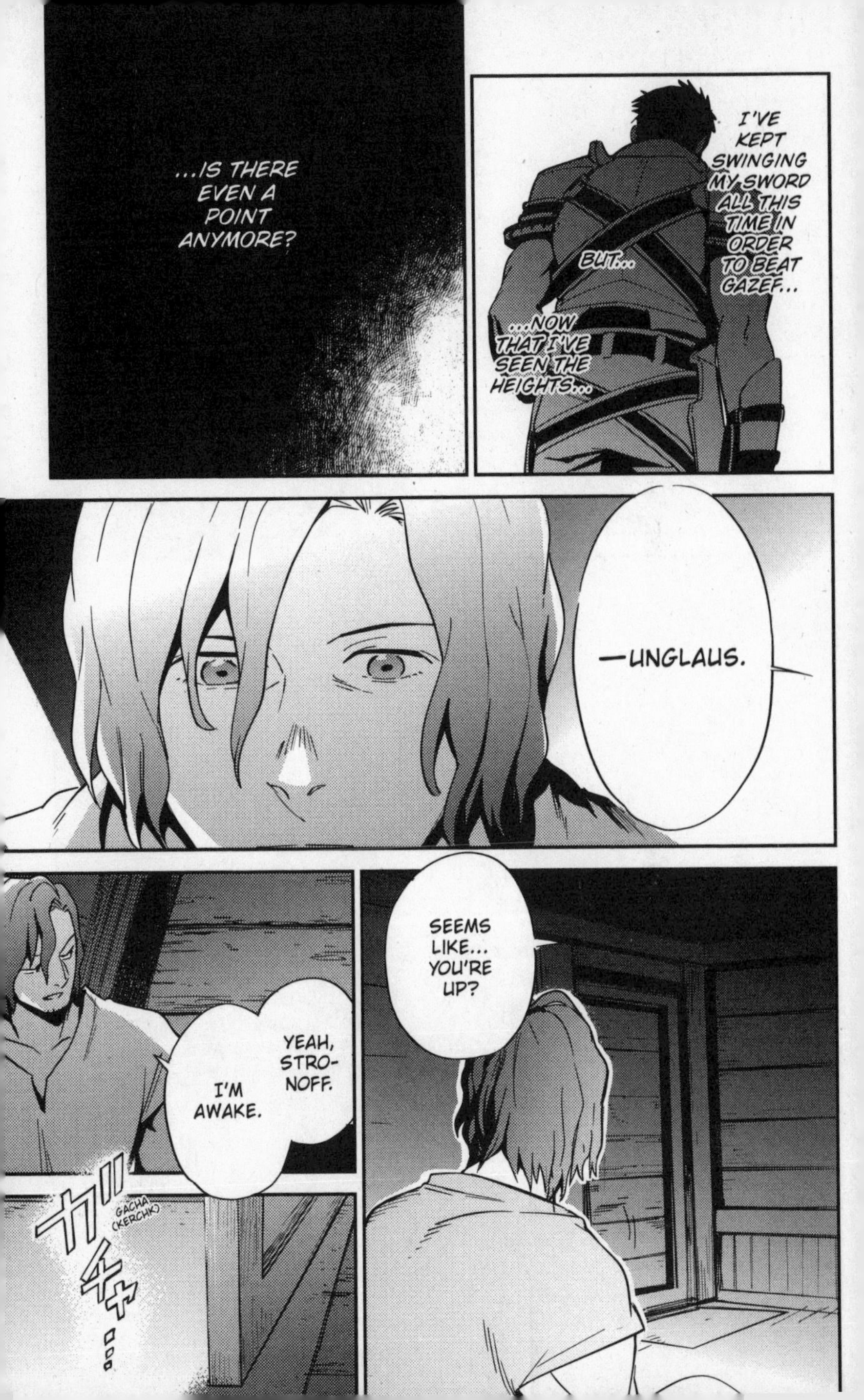
I'VE KEPT SWINGING MY SWORD ALL THIS TIME IN ORDER TO BEAT GAZEF...
BUT...
...NOW THAT I'VE SEEN THE HEIGHTS...
...IS THERE EVEN A POINT ANYMORE?
—UNGLAUS.
SEEMS LIKE... YOU'RE UP?
YEAH, STRO-NOFF.
I'M AWAKE.
GACHA (KERCHK)

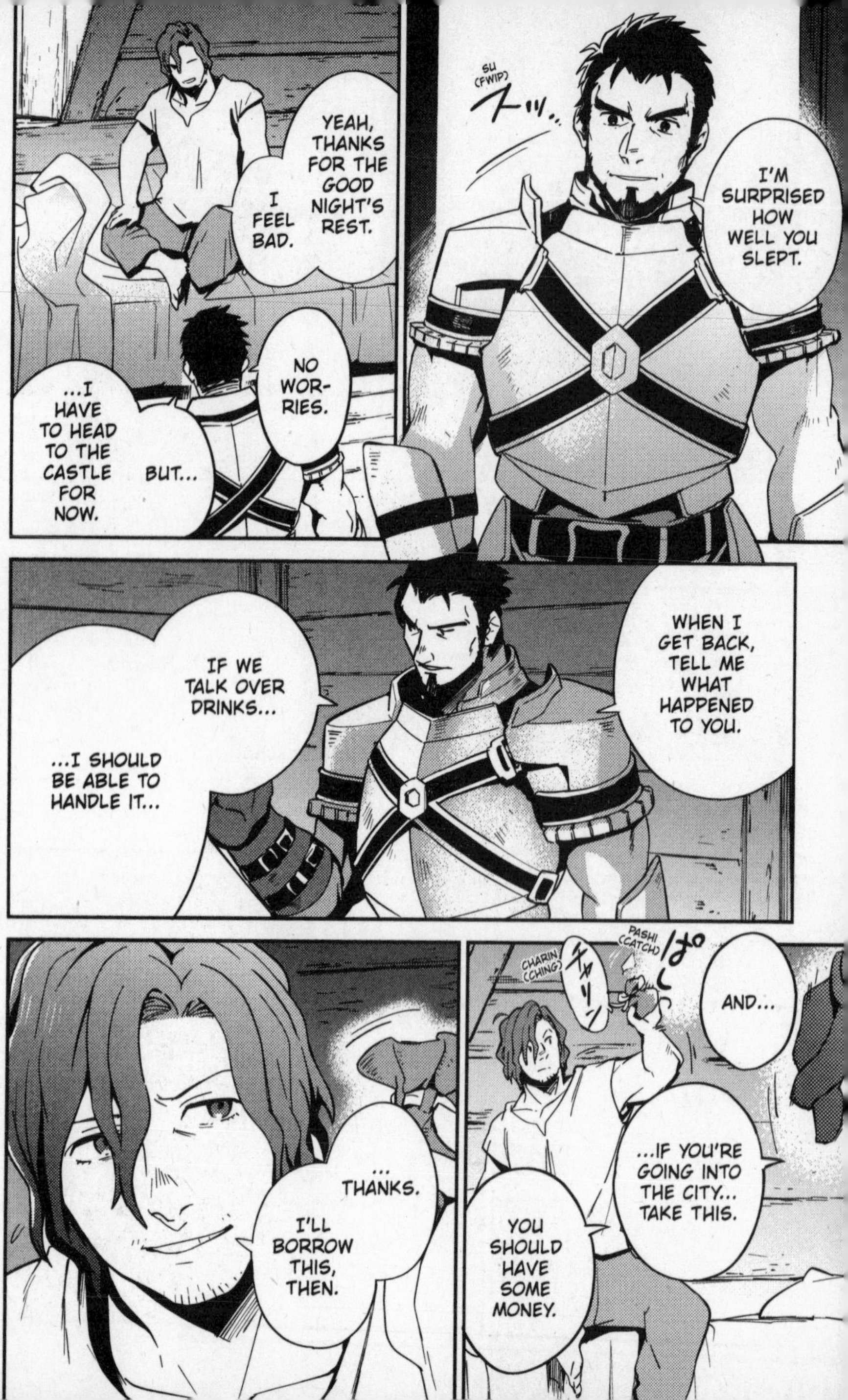
SU (FWIP)
I'M SURPRISED HOW WELL YOU SLEPT.
YEAH, THANKS FOR THE GOOD NIGHT'S REST.
I FEEL BAD.
NO WORRIES.
BUT...
...I HAVE TO HEAD TO THE CASTLE FOR NOW.
WHEN I GET BACK, TELL ME WHAT HAPPENED TO YOU.
IF WE TALK OVER DRINKS...
...I SHOULD BE ABLE TO HANDLE IT...
PASHI (CATCH)
CHARIN (CHING)
AND...
...IF YOU'RE GOING INTO THE CITY... TAKE THIS.
YOU SHOULD HAVE SOME MONEY.
...THANKS.
I'LL BORROW THIS, THEN.

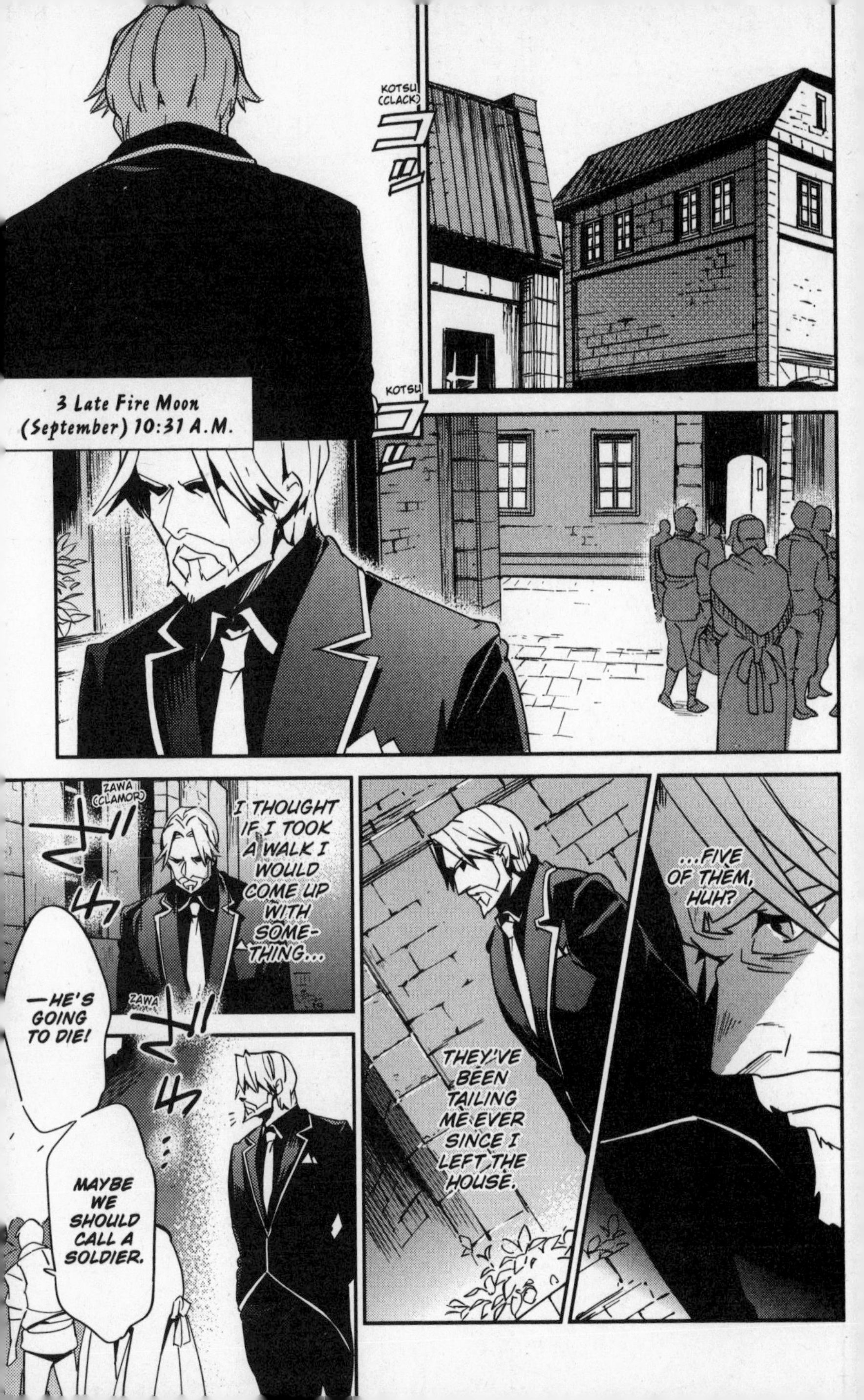
KOTSU (CLACK)
KOTSU
3 Late Fire Moon (September) 10:31 A.M.
...FIVE OF THEM, HUH?
THEY'VE BEEN TAILING ME EVER SINCE I LEFT THE HOUSE.
I THOUGHT IF I TOOK A WALK I WOULD COME UP WITH SOME-THING...
ZAWA (CLAMOR)
—HE'S GOING TO DIE!
ZAWA
MAYBE WE SHOULD CALL A SOLDIER.

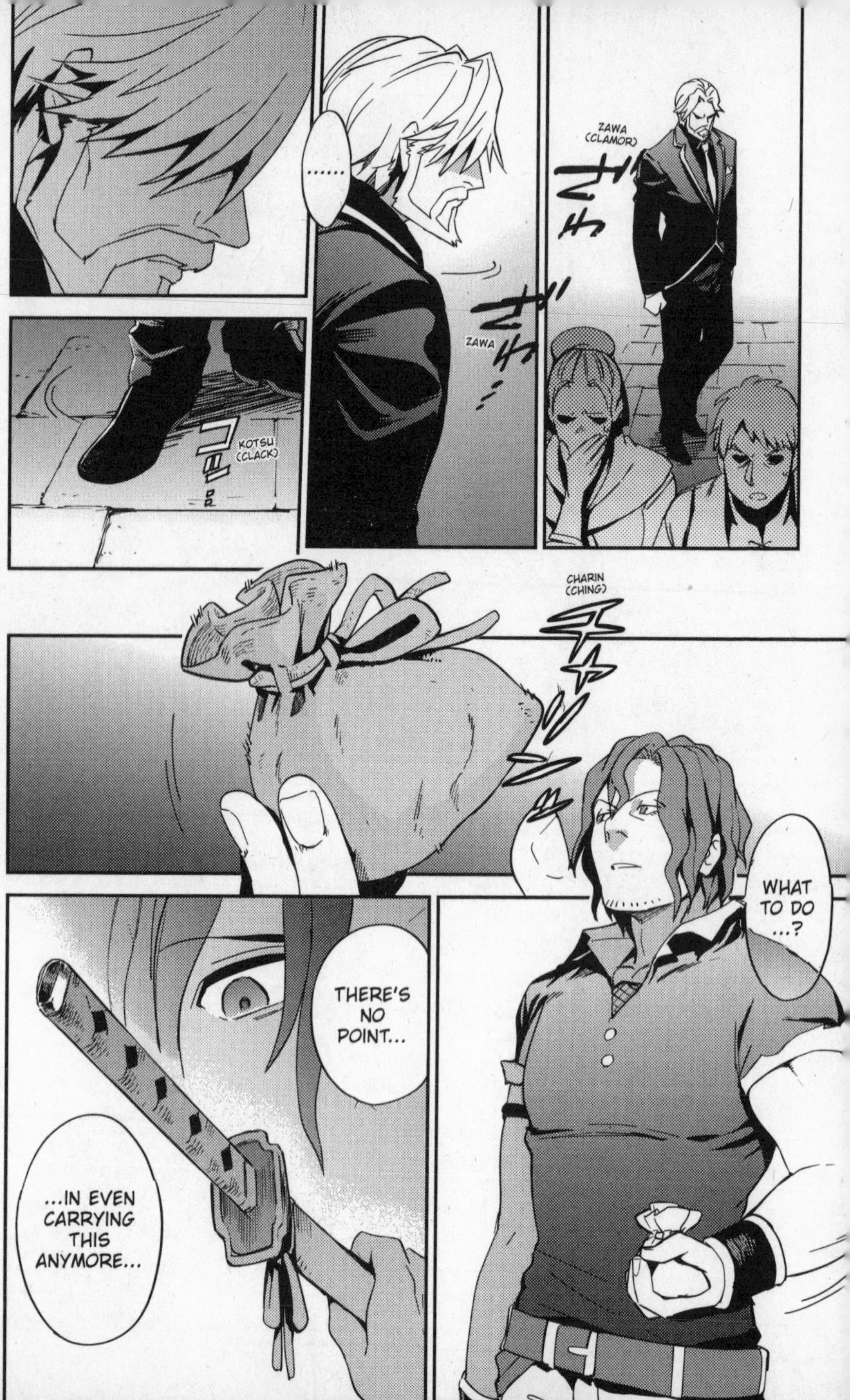
ZAWA (CLAMOR)
......
ZAWA
KOTSU (CLACK)
CHARIN (CHING)
WHAT TO DO ...?
THERE'S NO POINT...
...IN EVEN CARRYING THIS ANYMORE...

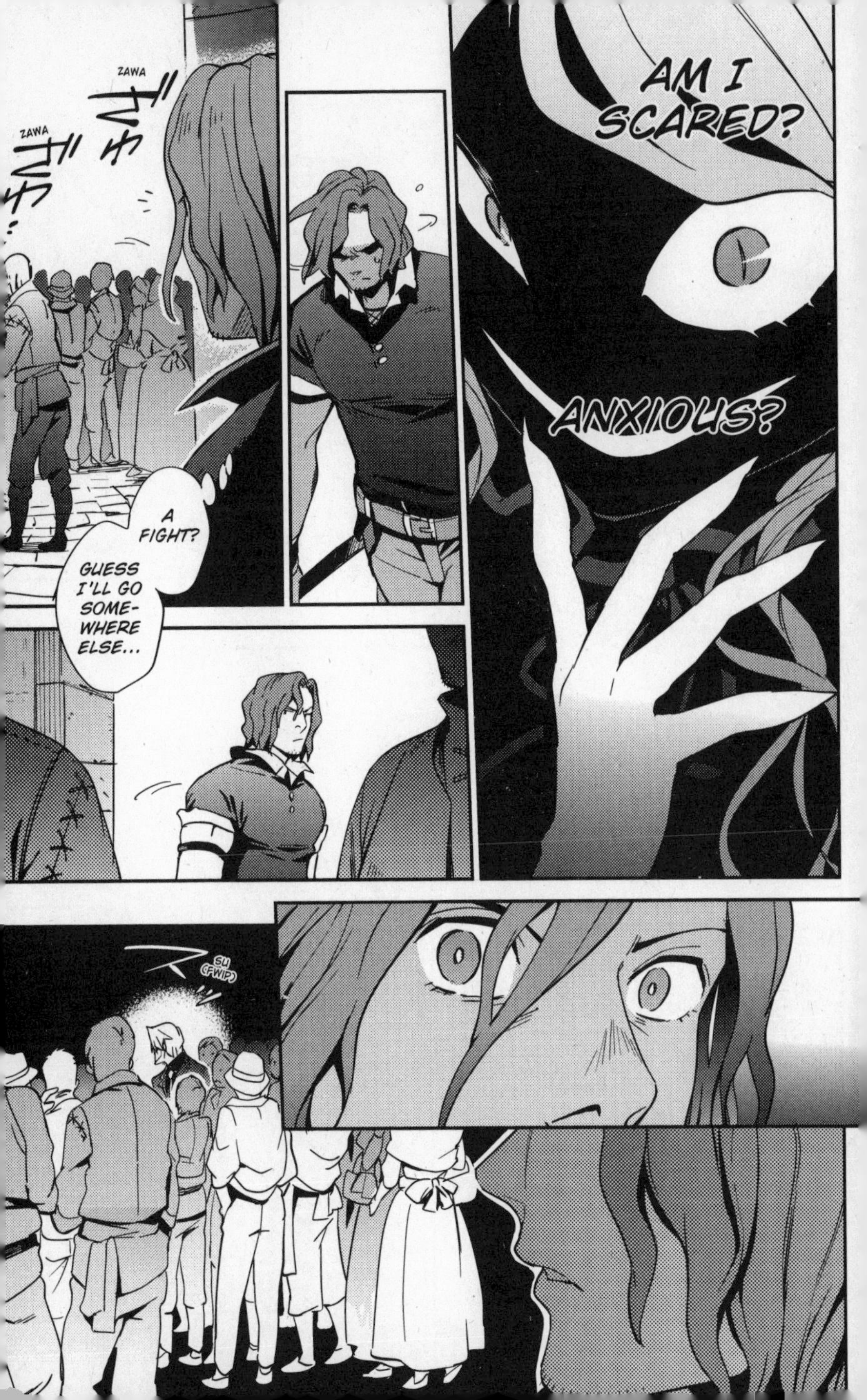
AM I SCARED?
ANXIOUS?
ZAWA
ZAWA
A FIGHT? GUESS I'LL GO SOMEWHERE ELSE...
SU (FWIP)

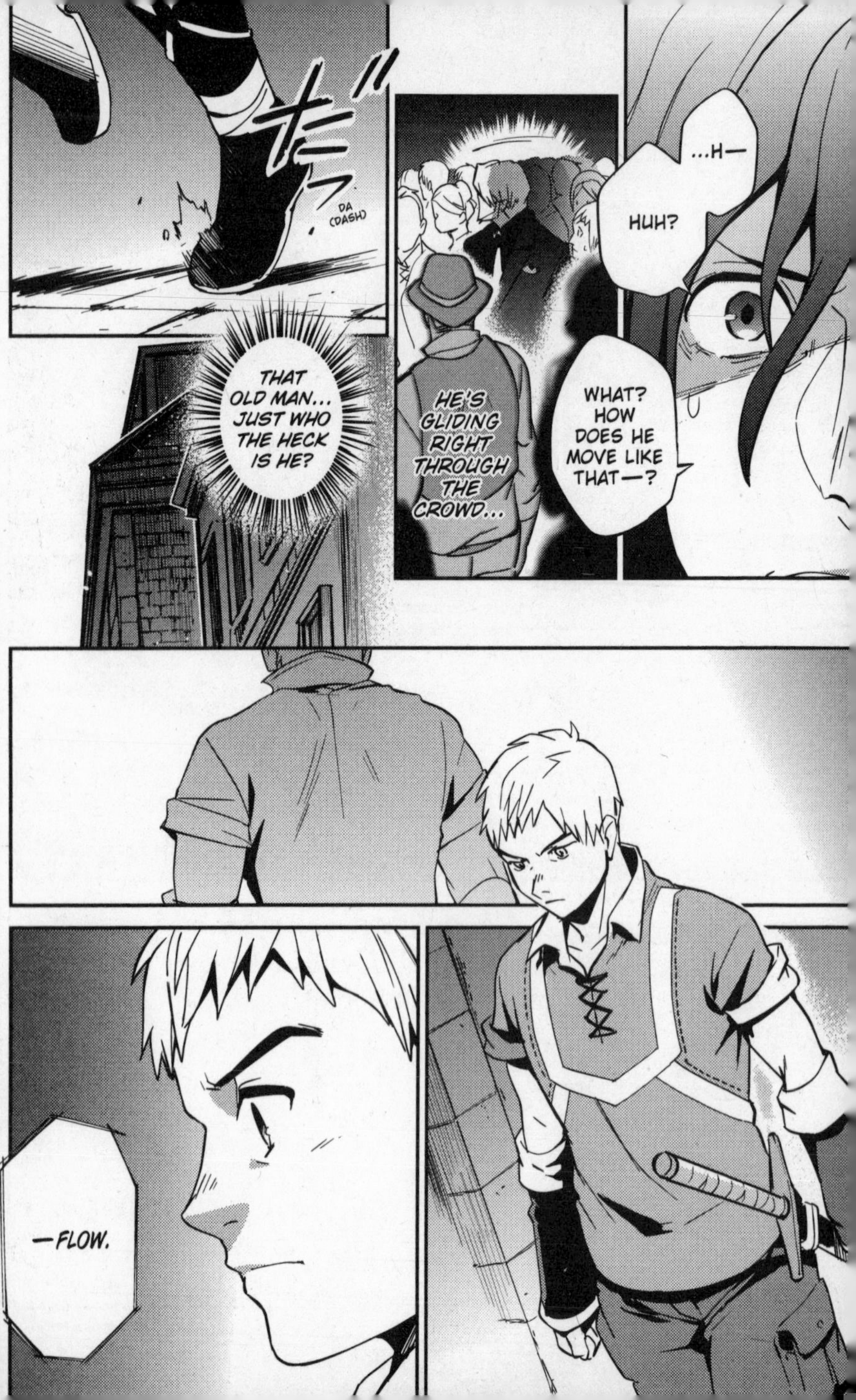
...H—
HUH?
WHAT? HOW DOES HE MOVE LIKE THAT—?
HE'S GLIDING RIGHT THROUGH THE CROWD...
DA (DASH)
THAT OLD MAN... JUST WHO THE HECK IS HE?
—FLOW.

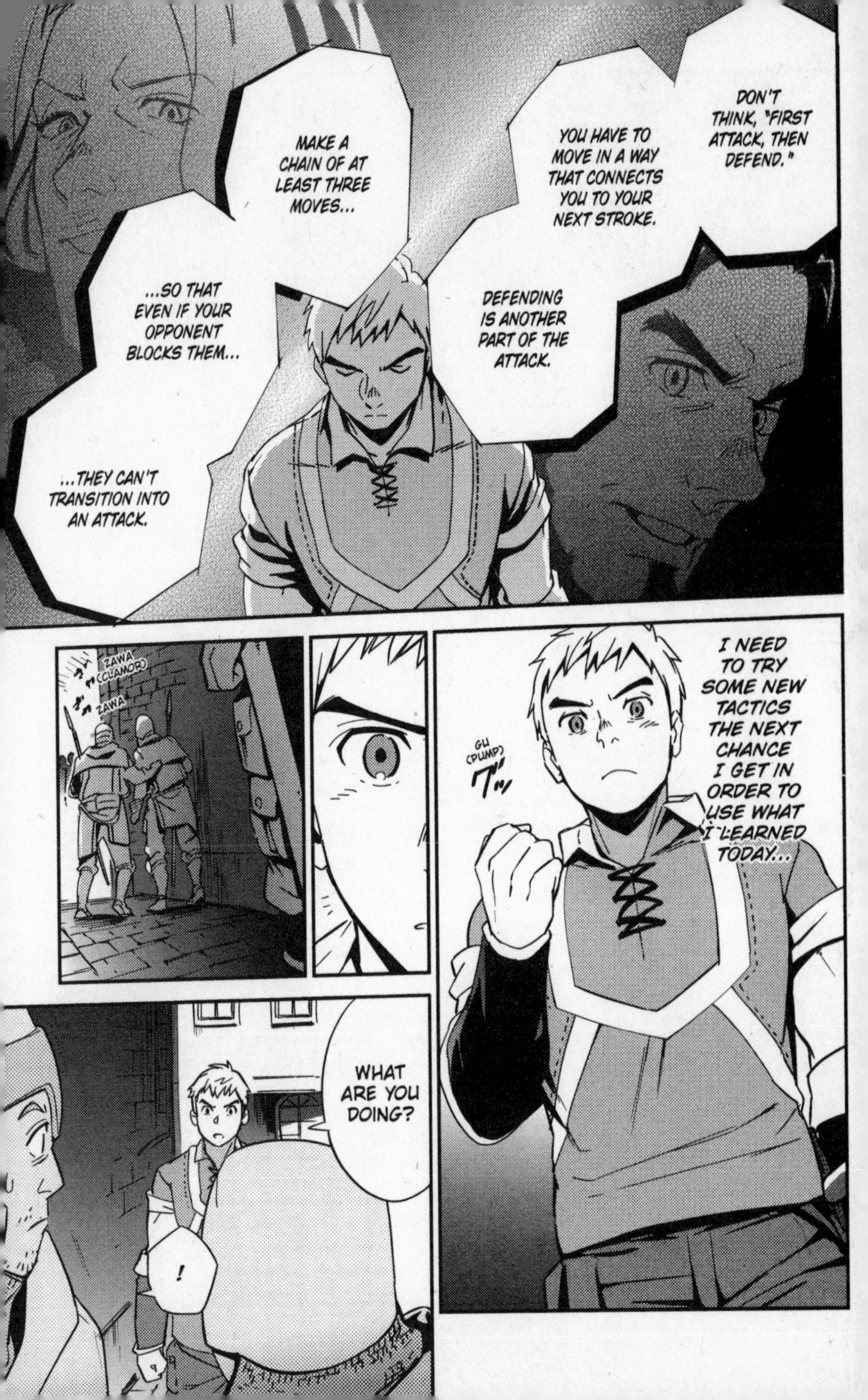
DON'T THINK, "FIRST ATTACK, THEN DEFEND."
YOU HAVE TO MOVE IN A WAY THAT CONNECTS YOU TO YOUR NEXT STROKE.
DEFENDING IS ANOTHER PART OF THE ATTACK.
MAKE A CHAIN OF AT LEAST THREE MOVES...
...SO THAT EVEN IF YOUR OPPONENT BLOCKS THEM...
...THEY CAN'T TRANSITION INTO AN ATTACK.
I NEED TO TRY SOME NEW TACTICS THE NEXT CHANCE I GET IN ORDER TO USE WHAT I LEARNED TODAY...
GU (PUMP)
ZAWA (CLAMOR)
ZAWA
WHAT ARE YOU DOING?
!

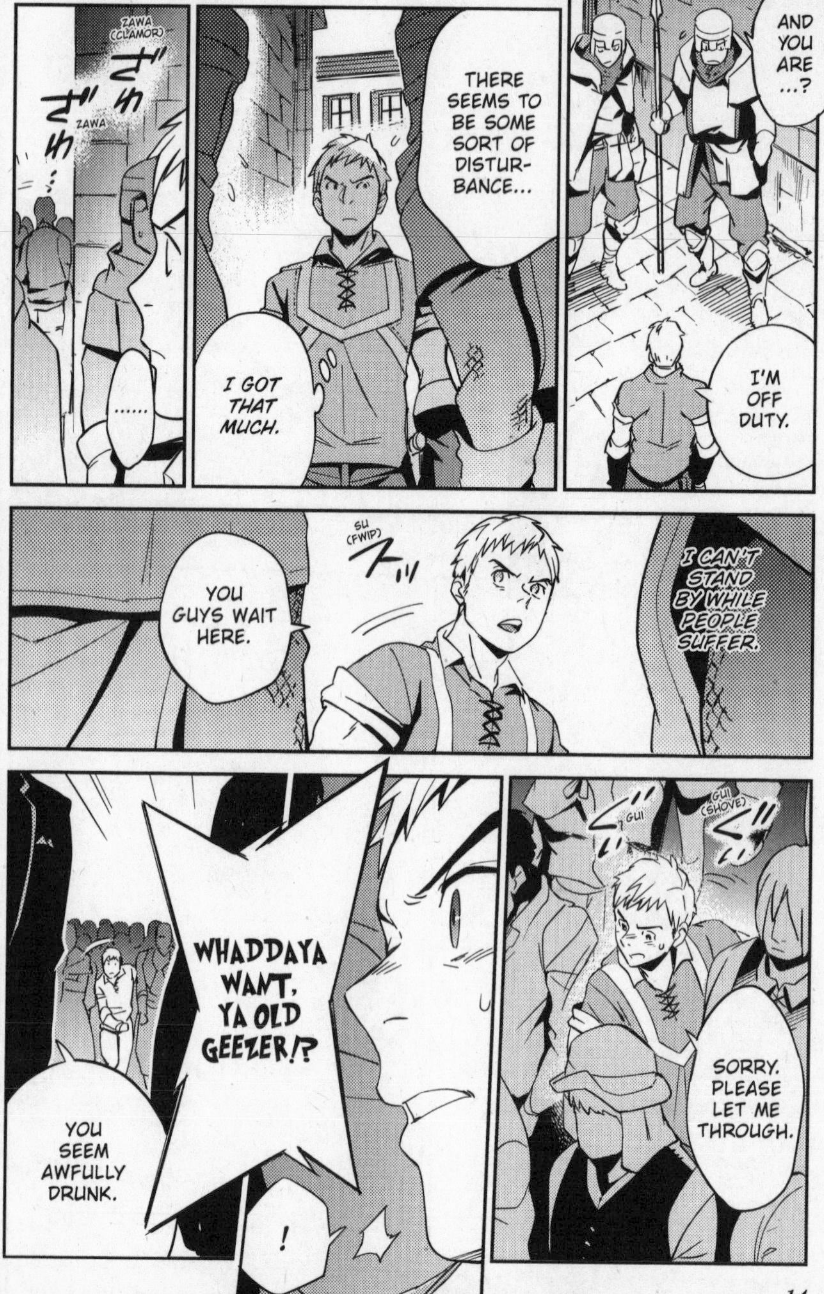
AND YOU ARE ...?
I'M OFF DUTY.
THERE SEEMS TO BE SOME SORT OF DISTURBANCE...
I GOT THAT MUCH.
ZAWA (CLAMOR)
ざわ
ざわ
ZAWA
......
I CAN'T STAND BY WHILE PEOPLE SUFFER.
SU (FWIP)
スッ
YOU GUYS WAIT HERE.
GUI (SHOVE)
ぐい
GUI
ぐい
SORRY. PLEASE LET ME THROUGH.
WHADDAYA WANT, YA OLD GEEZER!?
YOU SEEM AWFULLY DRUNK.
!

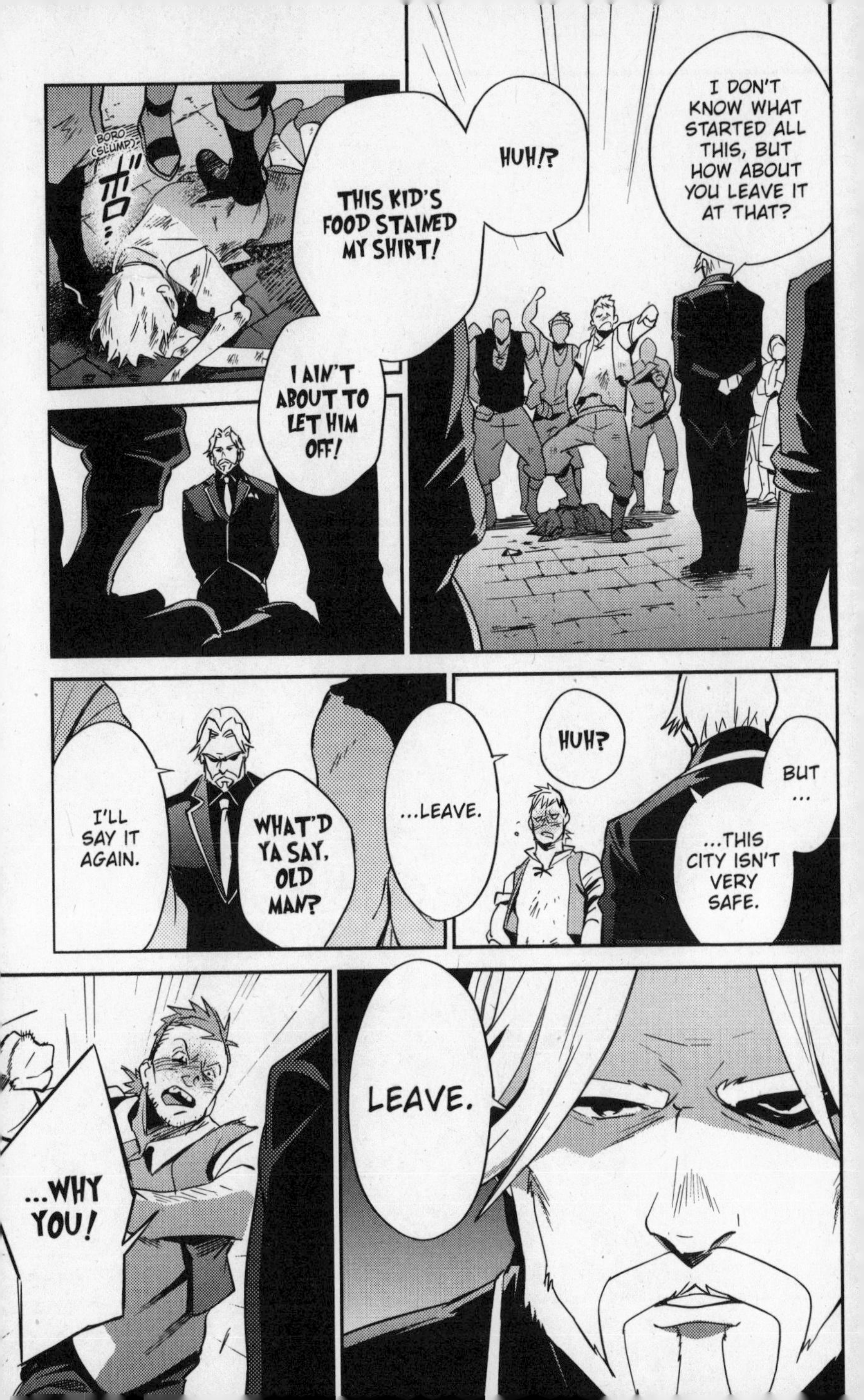
I DON'T KNOW WHAT STARTED ALL THIS, BUT HOW ABOUT YOU LEAVE IT AT THAT?
HUH!?
THIS KID'S FOOD STAINED MY SHIRT!
I AIN'T ABOUT TO LET HIM OFF!
BORO (SLUMP)
ボロ…
HUH?
BUT…
…THIS CITY ISN'T VERY SAFE.
…LEAVE.
WHAT'D YA SAY, OLD MAN?
I'LL SAY IT AGAIN.
LEAVE.
…WHY YOU!

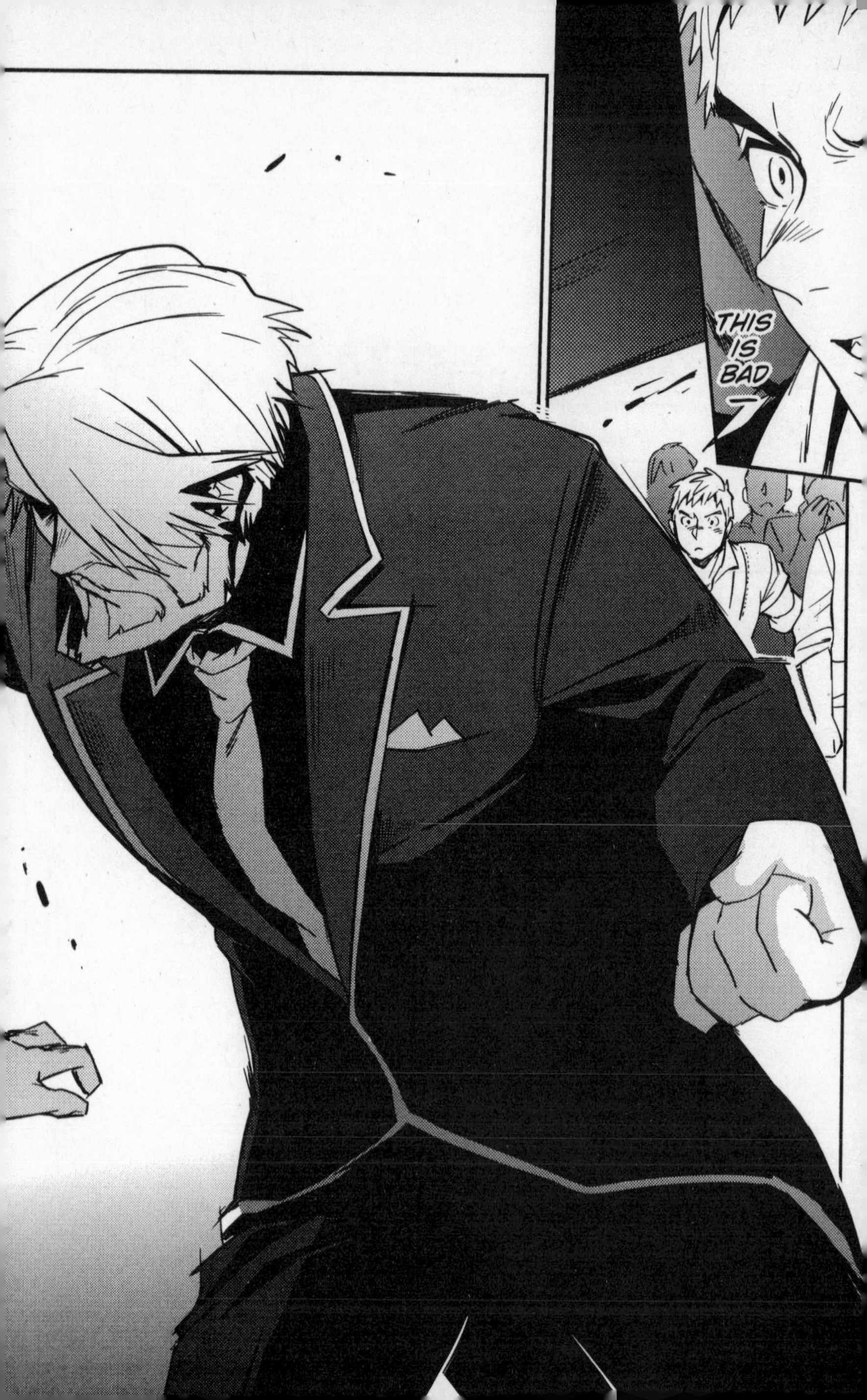
THIS IS BAD —

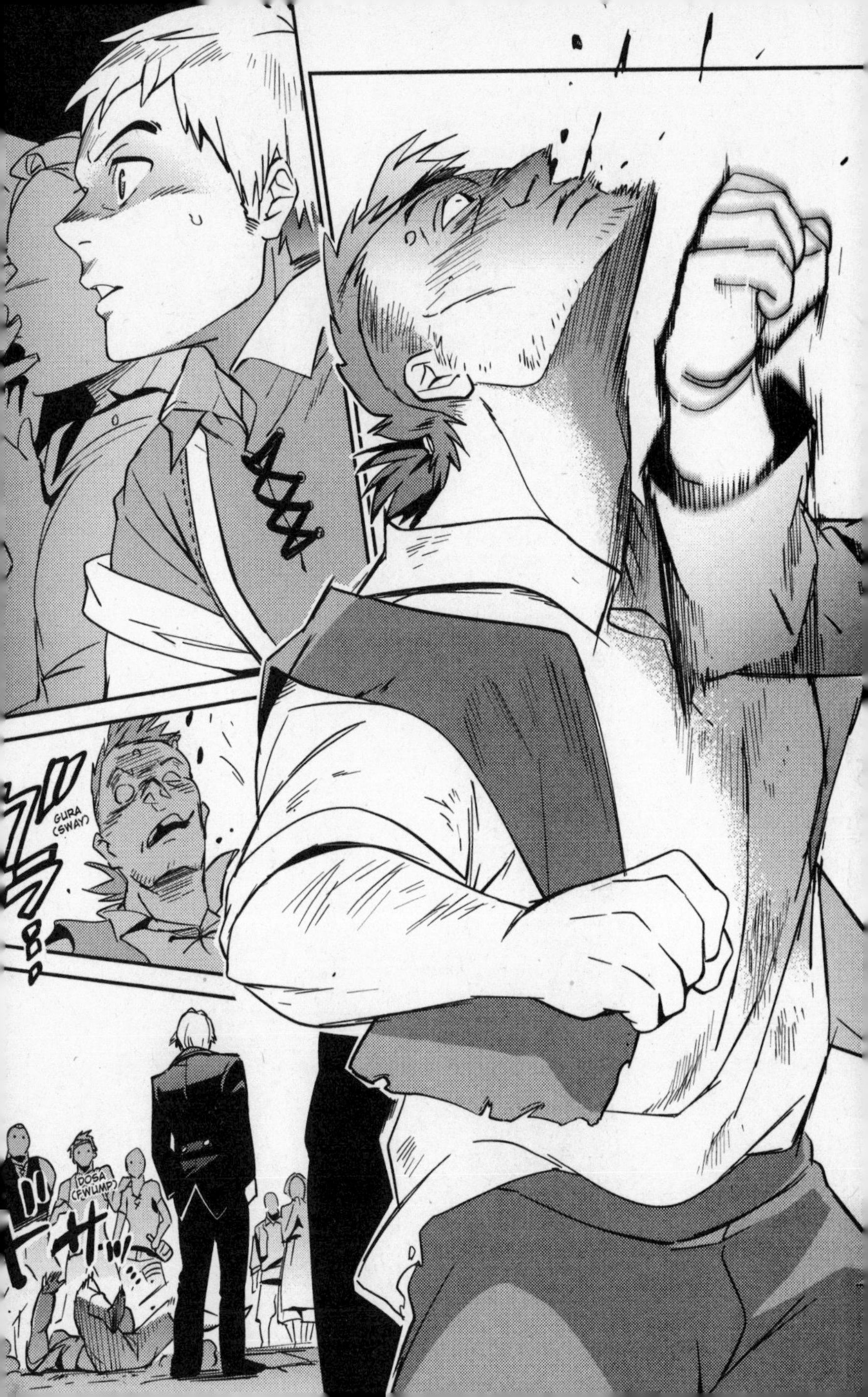
GURA (SWAY)
DOSA (FWUMP)

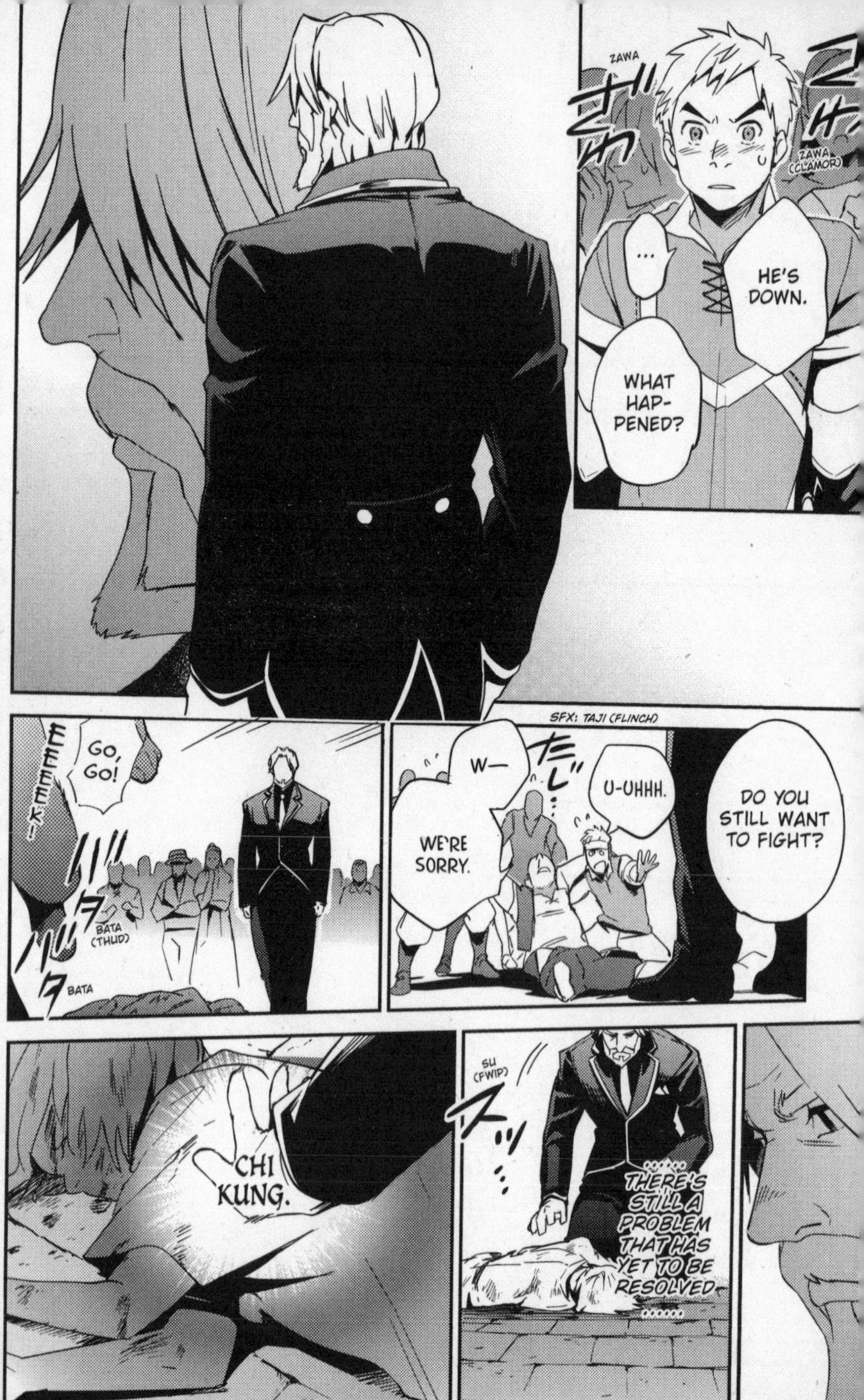
ZAWA
ZAWA (CLAMOR)
HE'S DOWN.
...
WHAT HAPPENED?
SFX: TAJI (FLINCH)
DO YOU STILL WANT TO FIGHT?
U-UHHH.
W—
WE'RE SORRY.
GO, GO!
BATA (THUD)
BATA
SU (FWIP)
......THERE'S STILL A PROBLEM THAT HAS YET TO BE RESOLVED......
CHI KUNG.

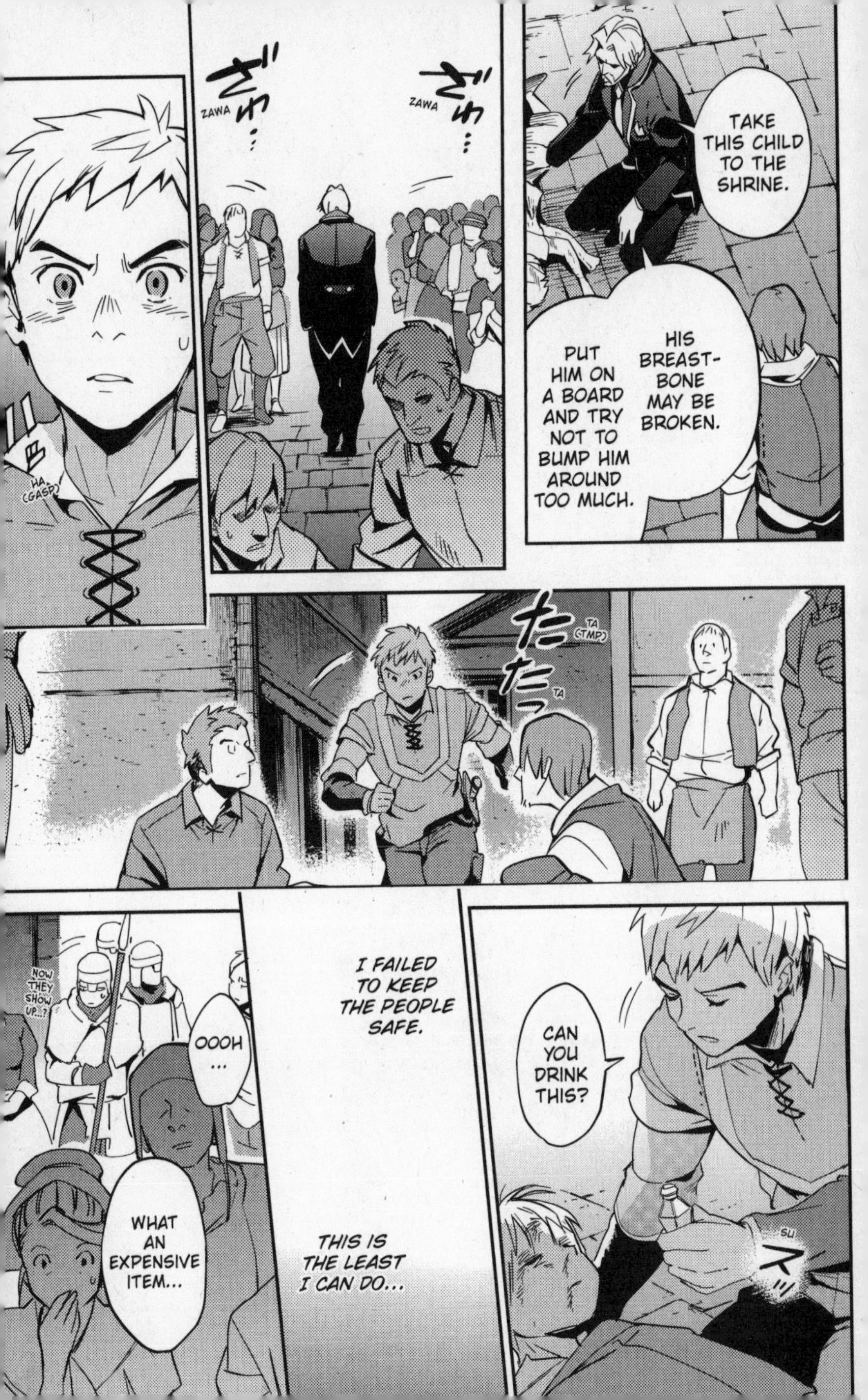
TAKE THIS CHILD TO THE SHRINE.
HIS BREAST-BONE MAY BE BROKEN.
PUT HIM ON A BOARD AND TRY NOT TO BUMP HIM AROUND TOO MUCH.
ざわ…
ZAWA
ざわ…
ZAWA
HA (GASP)
たたっ
TA (TMP)
TA
CAN YOU DRINK THIS?
ス…
SU
I FAILED TO KEEP THE PEOPLE SAFE.
THIS IS THE LEAST I CAN DO...
NOW THEY SHOW UP...?
OOOH...
WHAT AN EXPENSIVE ITEM...

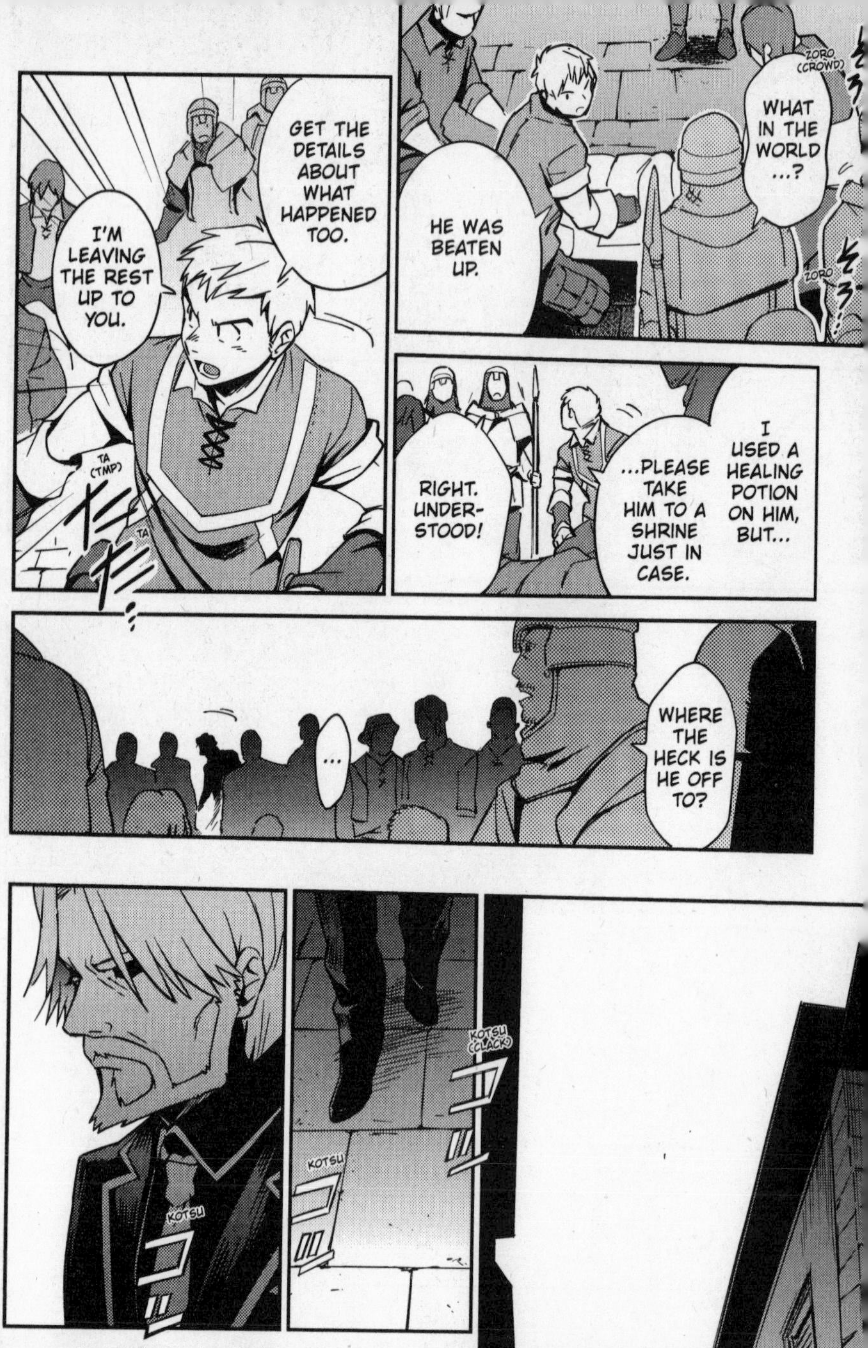
ZORO (CROWD)
WHAT IN THE WORLD ...?
HE WAS BEATEN UP.
ZORO
I USED A HEALING POTION ON HIM, BUT...
...PLEASE TAKE HIM TO A SHRINE JUST IN CASE.
RIGHT. UNDERSTOOD!
GET THE DETAILS ABOUT WHAT HAPPENED TOO.
I'M LEAVING THE REST UP TO YOU.
TA (TMP)
TA
WHERE THE HECK IS HE OFF TO?
...
KOTSU (CLACK)
KOTSU
KOTSU

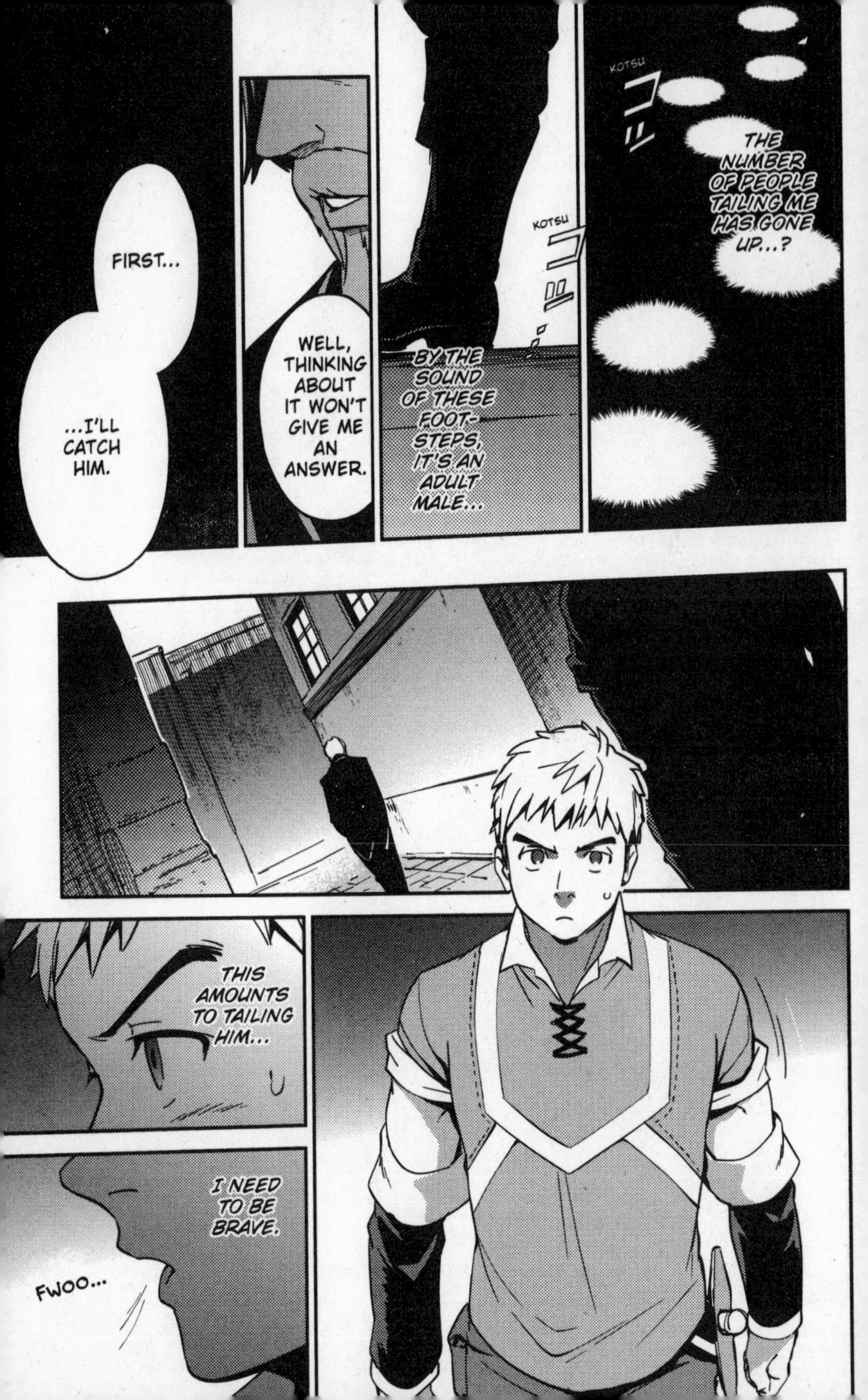
KOTSU
THE NUMBER OF PEOPLE TAILING ME HAS GONE UP...?
KOTSU
BY THE SOUND OF THESE FOOTSTEPS, IT'S AN ADULT MALE...
WELL, THINKING ABOUT IT WON'T GIVE ME AN ANSWER.
FIRST...
...I'LL CATCH HIM.
THIS AMOUNTS TO TAILING HIM...
I NEED TO BE BRAVE.
FWOO...

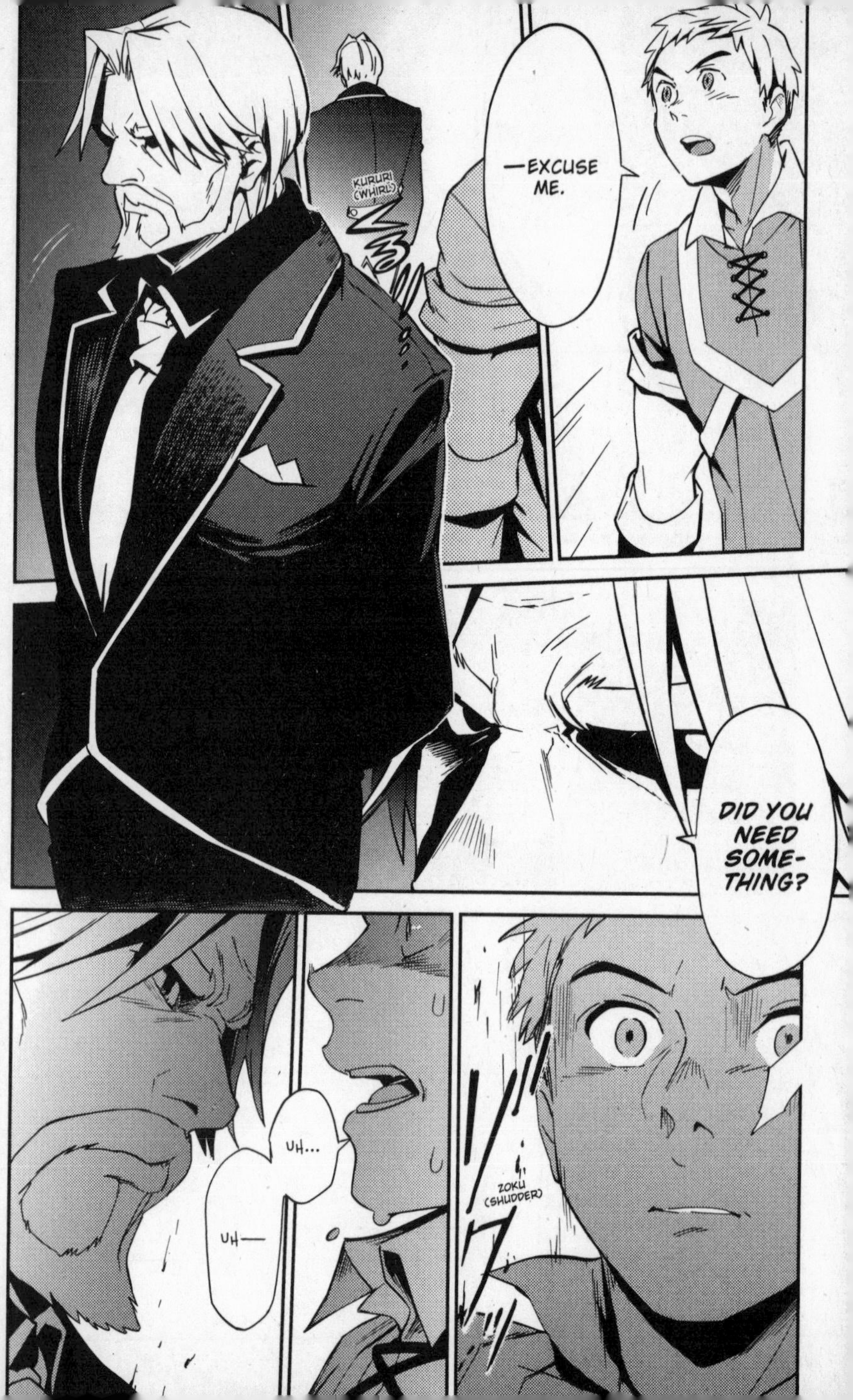
—EXCUSE ME.
DID YOU NEED SOME-THING?
KURURI (WHIRL)
ZOKU (SHUDDER)
UH...
UH—

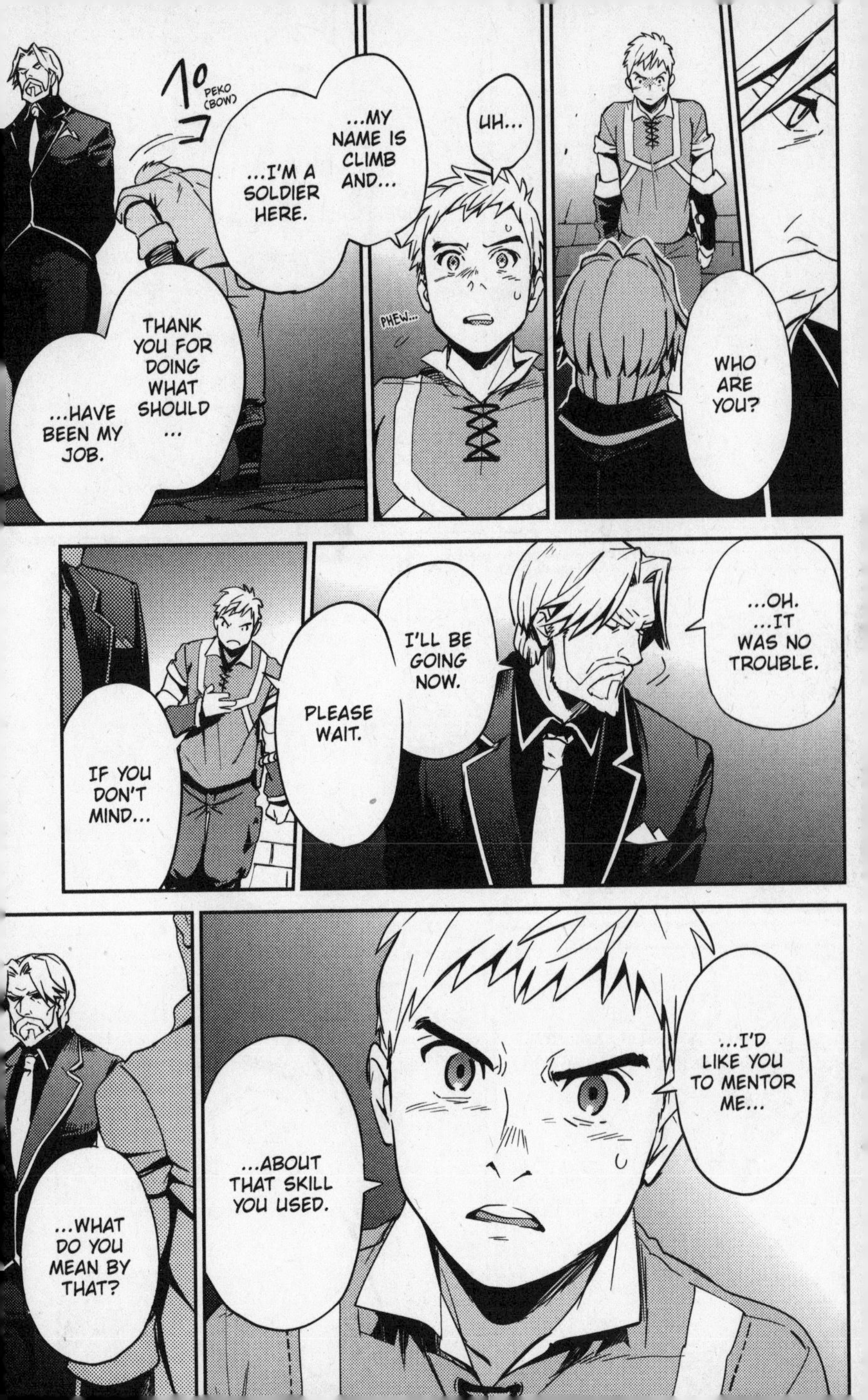
WHO ARE YOU?
UH...
PHEW...
...MY NAME IS CLIMB AND...
...I'M A SOLDIER HERE.
PEKO (BOW)
THANK YOU FOR DOING WHAT SHOULD ...
...HAVE BEEN MY JOB.
...OH. ...IT WAS NO TROUBLE.
I'LL BE GOING NOW.
PLEASE WAIT.
IF YOU DON'T MIND...
...I'D LIKE YOU TO MENTOR ME...
...ABOUT THAT SKILL YOU USED.
...WHAT DO YOU MEAN BY THAT?

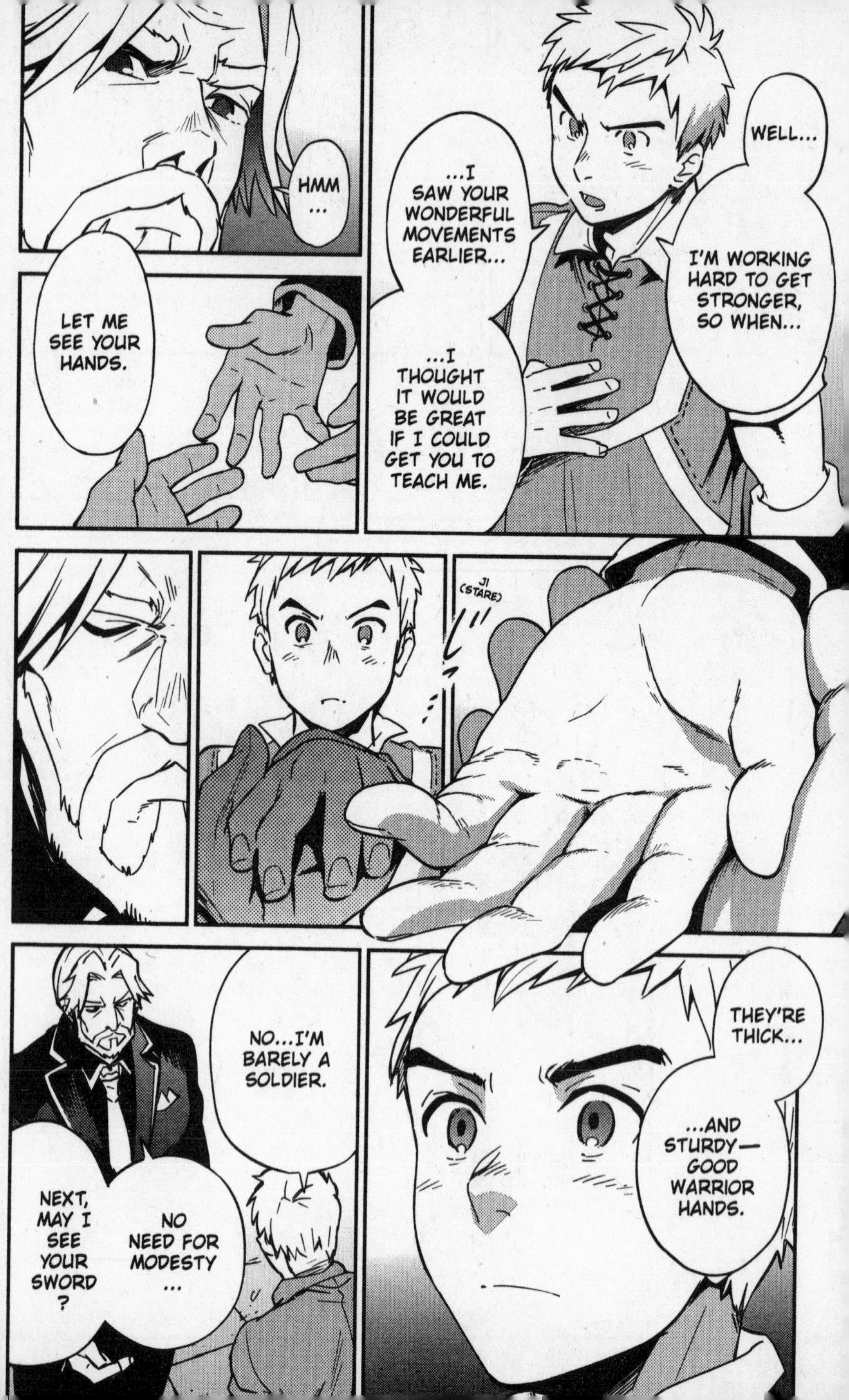
WELL...
I'M WORKING HARD TO GET STRONGER, SO WHEN...
...I SAW YOUR WONDERFUL MOVEMENTS EARLIER...
...I THOUGHT IT WOULD BE GREAT IF I COULD GET YOU TO TEACH ME.
HMM...
LET ME SEE YOUR HANDS.
JI (STARE)
THEY'RE THICK...
...AND STURDY—GOOD WARRIOR HANDS.
NO...I'M BARELY A SOLDIER.
NO NEED FOR MODESTY...
NEXT, MAY I SEE YOUR SWORD?

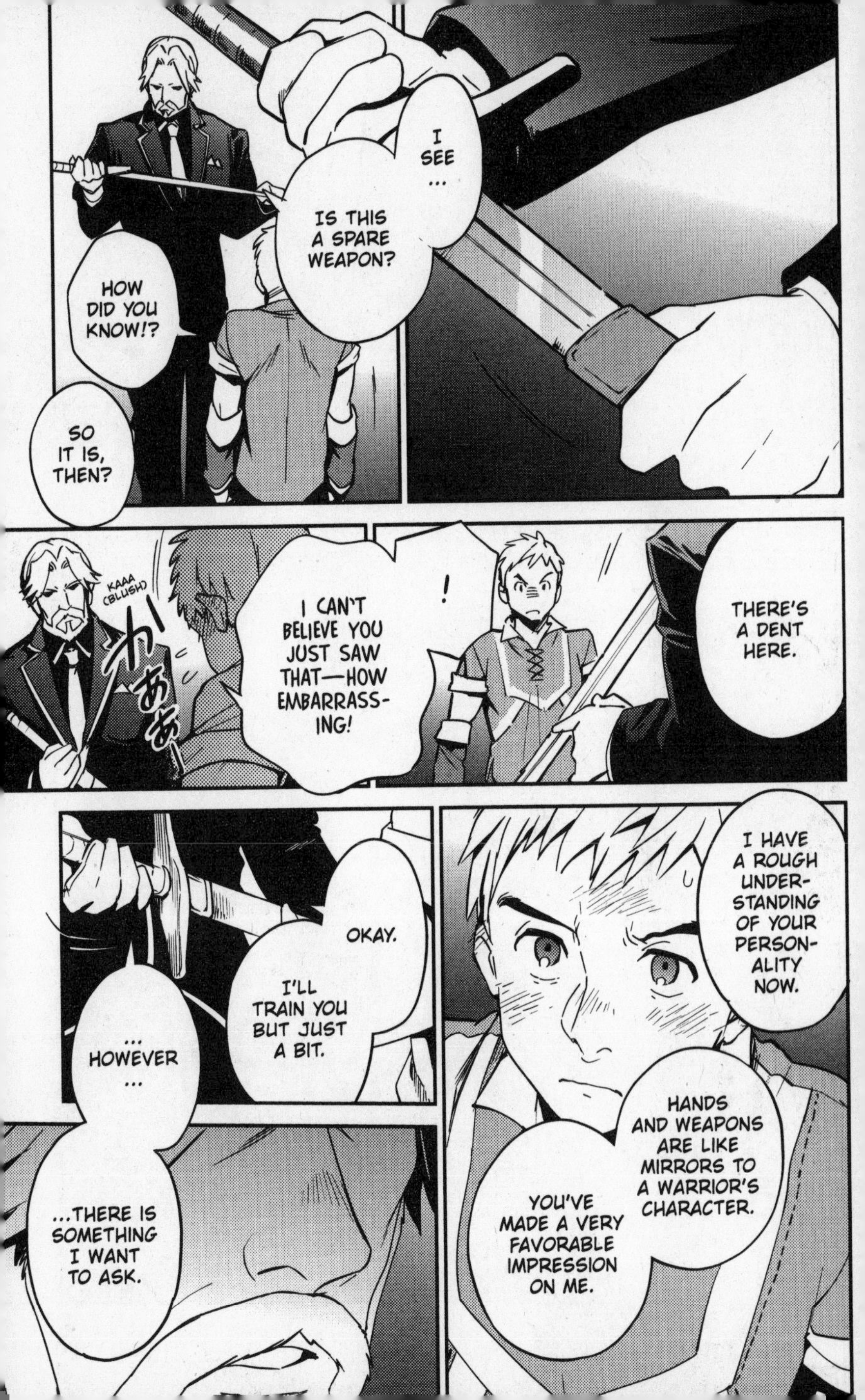
I SEE ...
IS THIS A SPARE WEAPON?
HOW DID YOU KNOW!?
SO IT IS, THEN?
THERE'S A DENT HERE.
!
I CAN'T BELIEVE YOU JUST SAW THAT—HOW EMBARRASSING!
KAAA (BLUSH)
I HAVE A ROUGH UNDERSTANDING OF YOUR PERSONALITY NOW.
HANDS AND WEAPONS ARE LIKE MIRRORS TO A WARRIOR'S CHARACTER.
YOU'VE MADE A VERY FAVORABLE IMPRESSION ON ME.
OKAY.
I'LL TRAIN YOU BUT JUST A BIT.
... HOWEVER ...
...THERE IS SOMETHING I WANT TO ASK.

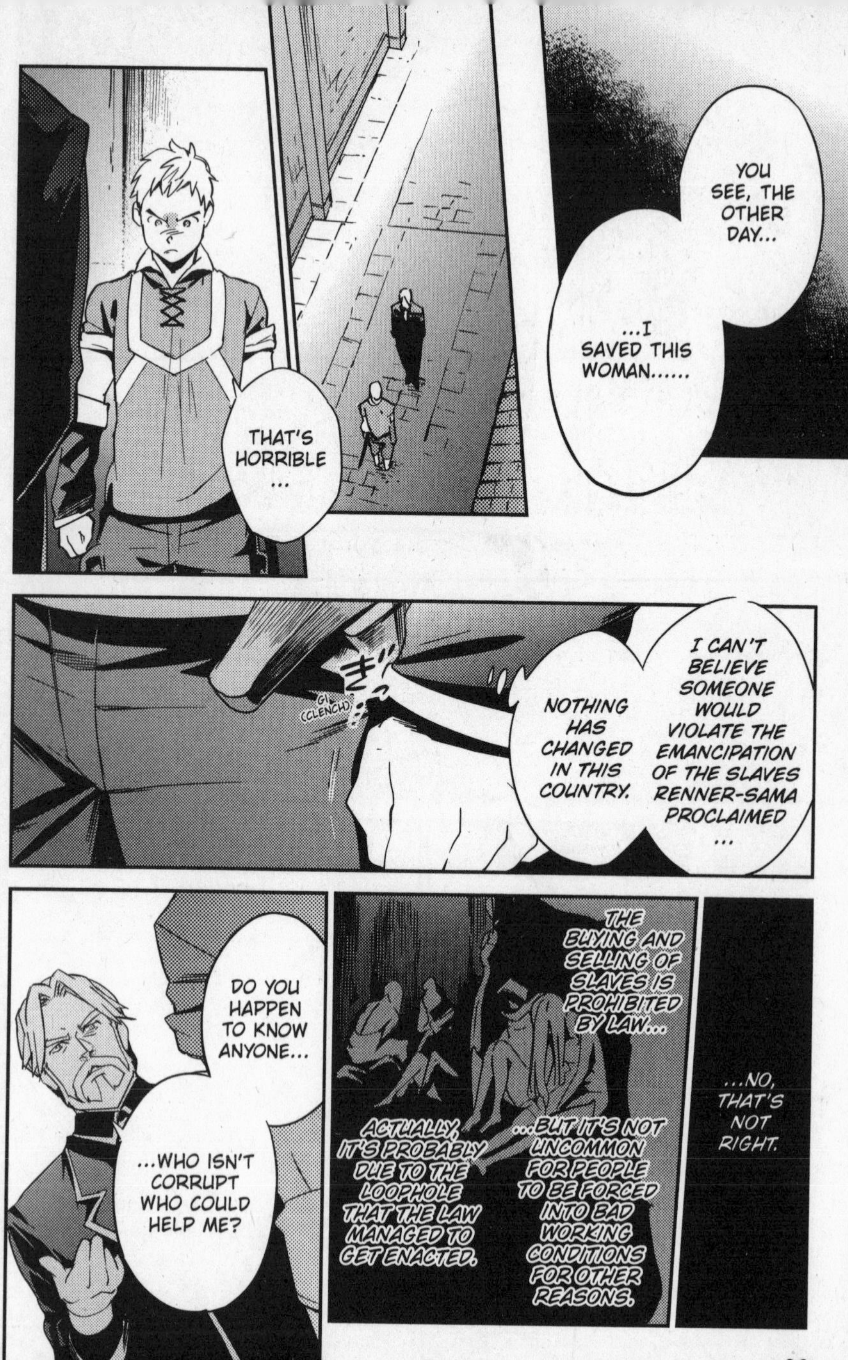
YOU SEE, THE OTHER DAY...
...I SAVED THIS WOMAN......
THAT'S HORRIBLE ...
I CAN'T BELIEVE SOMEONE WOULD VIOLATE THE EMANCIPATION OF THE SLAVES RENNER-SAMA PROCLAIMED ...
NOTHING HAS CHANGED IN THIS COUNTRY.
GI (CLENCH)
...NO, THAT'S NOT RIGHT.
THE BUYING AND SELLING OF SLAVES IS PROHIBITED BY LAW...
...BUT IT'S NOT UNCOMMON FOR PEOPLE TO BE FORCED INTO BAD WORKING CONDITIONS FOR OTHER REASONS.
ACTUALLY, IT'S PROBABLY DUE TO THE LOOPHOLE THAT THE LAW MANAGED TO GET ENACTED.
DO YOU HAPPEN TO KNOW ANYONE...
...WHO ISN'T CORRUPT WHO COULD HELP ME?

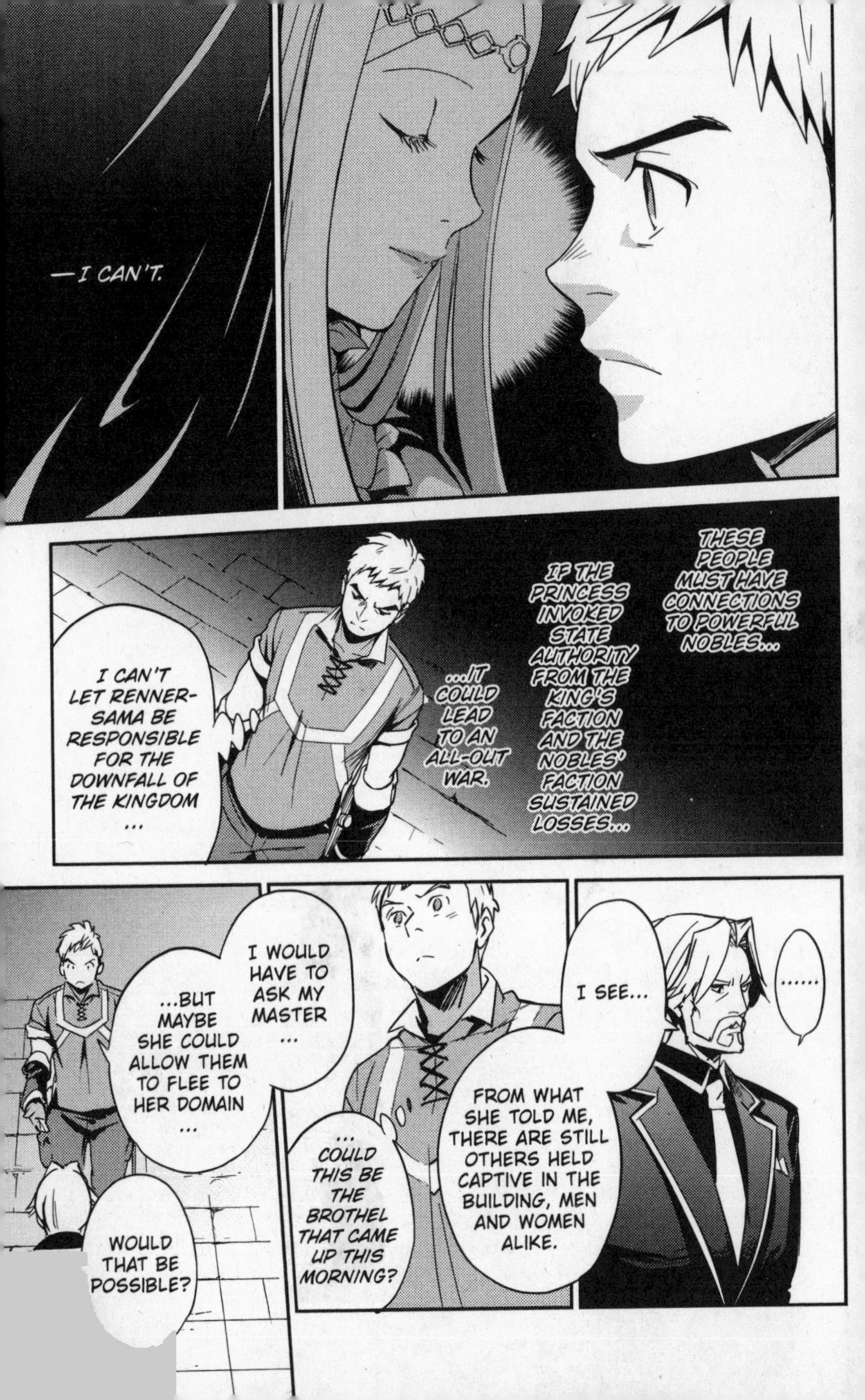
—I CAN'T.
THESE PEOPLE MUST HAVE CONNECTIONS TO POWERFUL NOBLES...
IF THE PRINCESS INVOKED STATE AUTHORITY FROM THE KING'S FACTION AND THE NOBLES' FACTION SUSTAINED LOSSES...
...IT COULD LEAD TO AN ALL-OUT WAR.
I CAN'T LET RENNER-SAMA BE RESPONSIBLE FOR THE DOWNFALL OF THE KINGDOM ...
......
I SEE...
FROM WHAT SHE TOLD ME, THERE ARE STILL OTHERS HELD CAPTIVE IN THE BUILDING, MEN AND WOMEN ALIKE.
... COULD THIS BE THE BROTHEL THAT CAME UP THIS MORNING?
I WOULD HAVE TO ASK MY MASTER ...
...BUT MAYBE SHE COULD ALLOW THEM TO FLEE TO HER DOMAIN ...
WOULD THAT BE POSSIBLE?

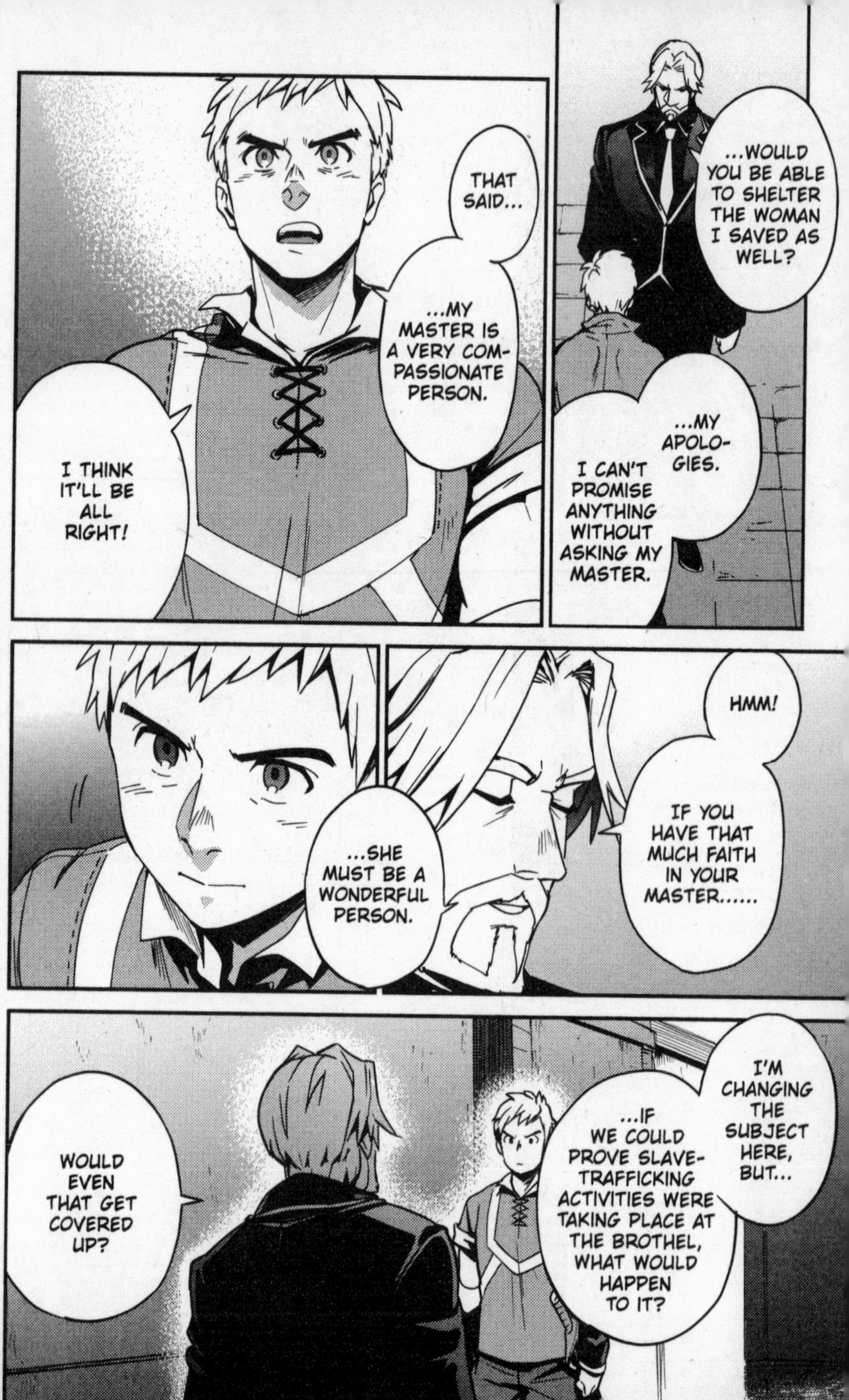
...WOULD YOU BE ABLE TO SHELTER THE WOMAN I SAVED AS WELL?
...MY APOLOGIES.
I CAN'T PROMISE ANYTHING WITHOUT ASKING MY MASTER.
THAT SAID...
...MY MASTER IS A VERY COMPASSIONATE PERSON.
I THINK IT'LL BE ALL RIGHT!
HMM!
IF YOU HAVE THAT MUCH FAITH IN YOUR MASTER......
...SHE MUST BE A WONDERFUL PERSON.
I'M CHANGING THE SUBJECT HERE, BUT...
...IF WE COULD PROVE SLAVE-TRAFFICKING ACTIVITIES WERE TAKING PLACE AT THE BROTHEL, WHAT WOULD HAPPEN TO IT?
WOULD EVEN THAT GET COVERED UP?

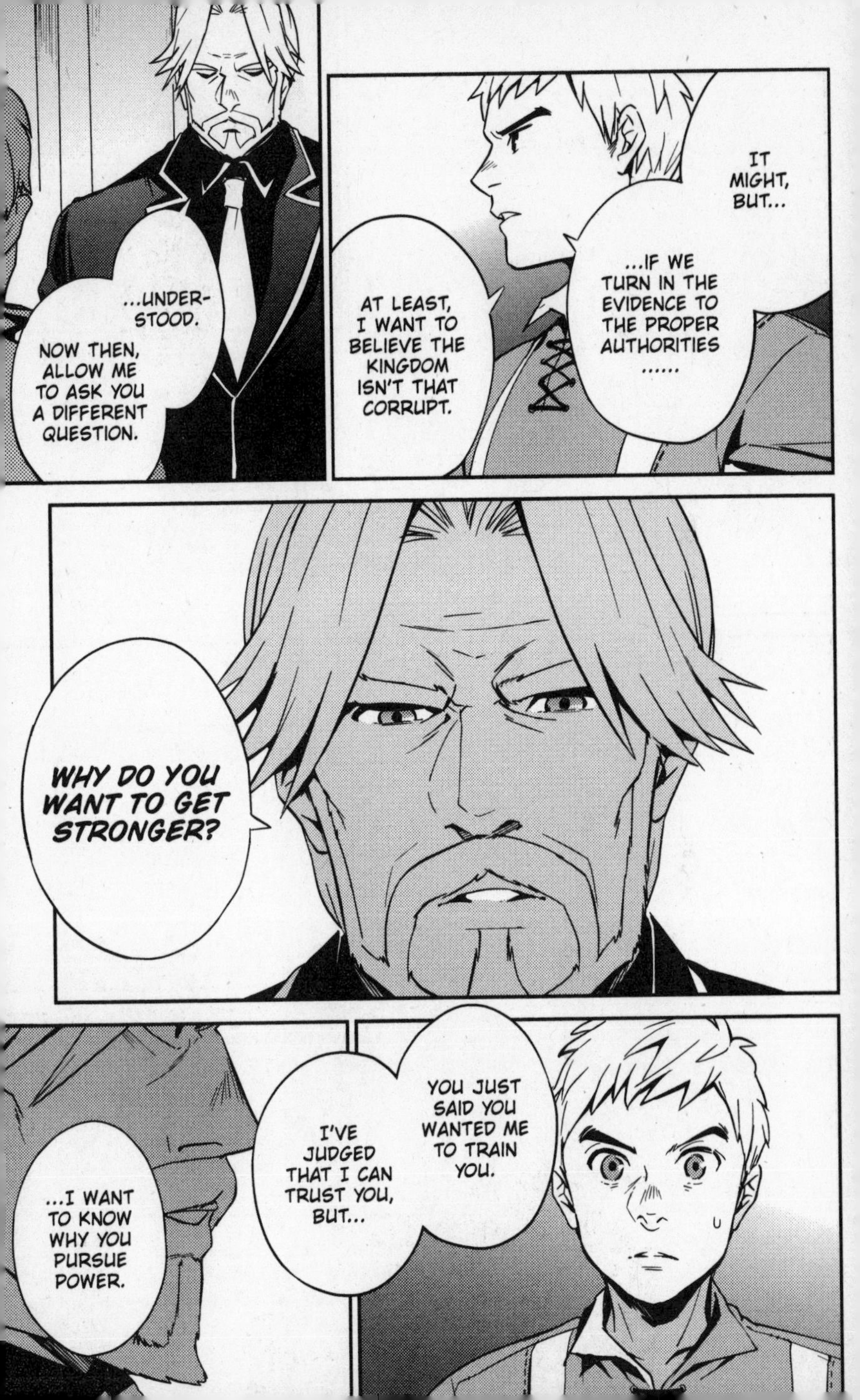
IT MIGHT, BUT...
...IF WE TURN IN THE EVIDENCE TO THE PROPER AUTHORITIES......
AT LEAST, I WANT TO BELIEVE THE KINGDOM ISN'T THAT CORRUPT.
...UNDER-STOOD.
NOW THEN, ALLOW ME TO ASK YOU A DIFFERENT QUESTION.
WHY DO YOU WANT TO GET STRONGER?
YOU JUST SAID YOU WANTED ME TO TRAIN YOU.
I'VE JUDGED THAT I CAN TRUST YOU, BUT...
...I WANT TO KNOW WHY YOU PURSUE POWER.

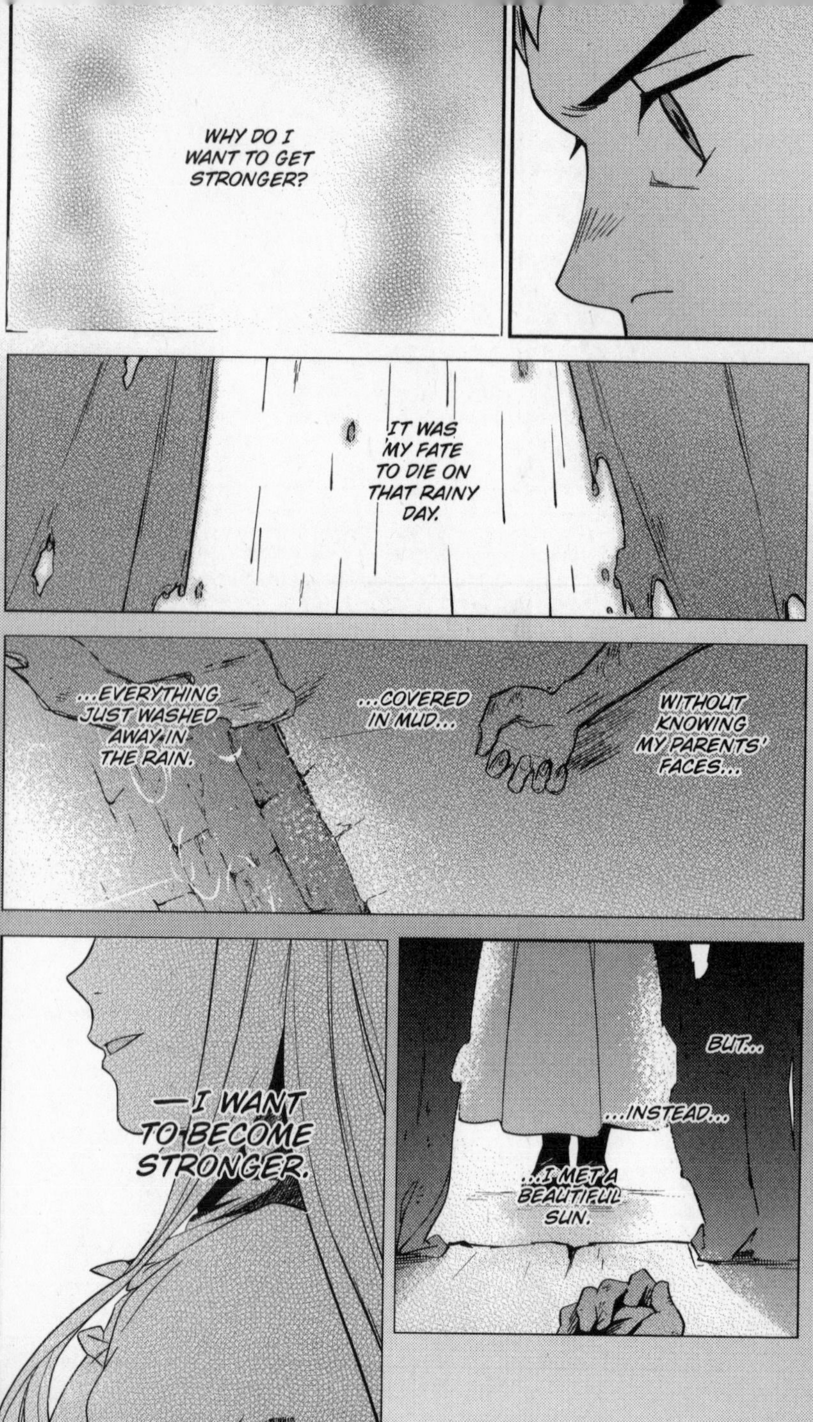
WHY DO I WANT TO GET STRONGER?
IT WAS MY FATE TO DIE ON THAT RAINY DAY.
WITHOUT KNOWING MY PARENTS' FACES...
...COVERED IN MUD...
...EVERYTHING JUST WASHED AWAY IN THE RAIN.
BUT...
...INSTEAD...
...I MET A BEAUTIFUL SUN.
—I WANT TO BECOME STRONGER.

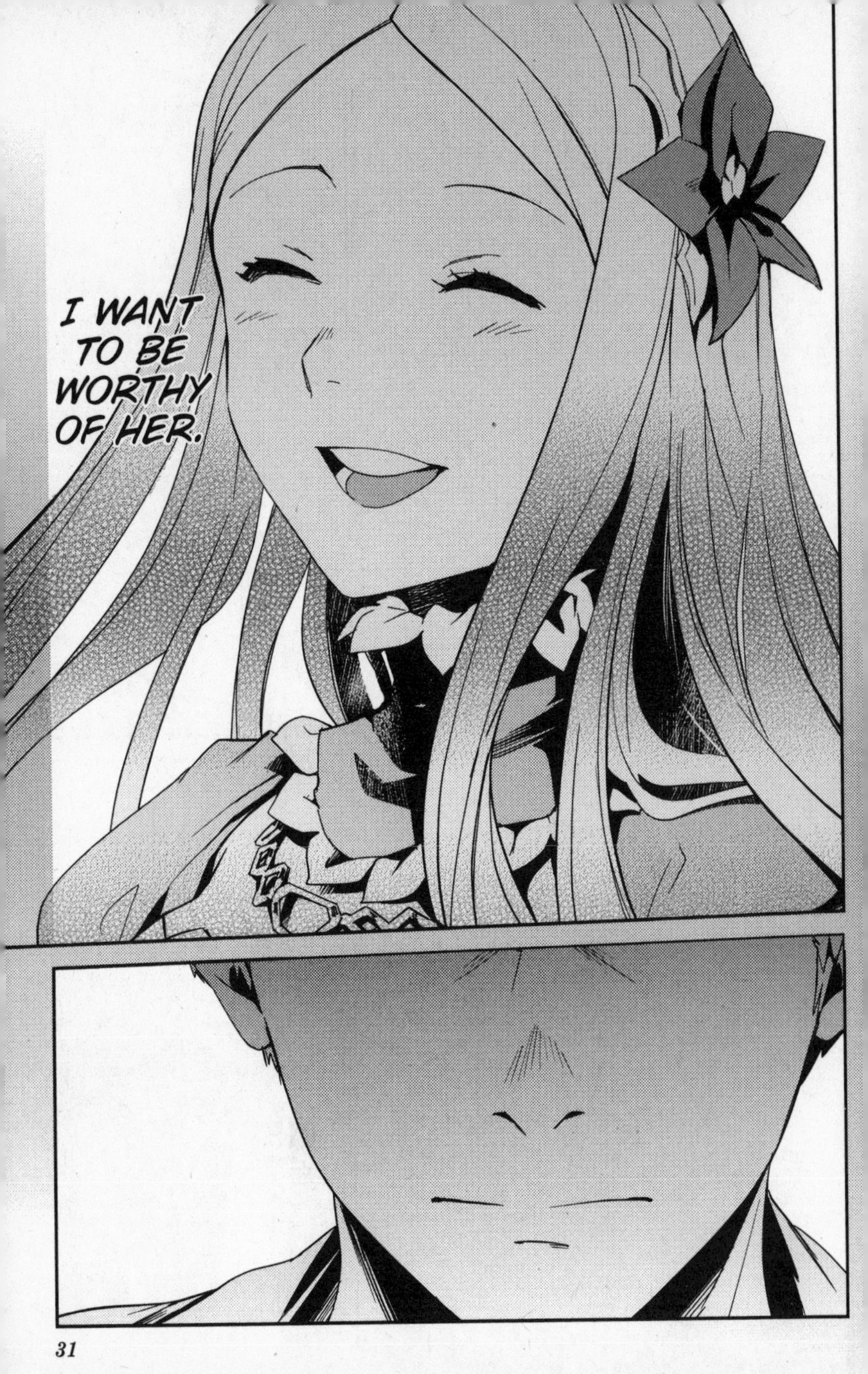
I WANT TO BE WORTHY OF HER.

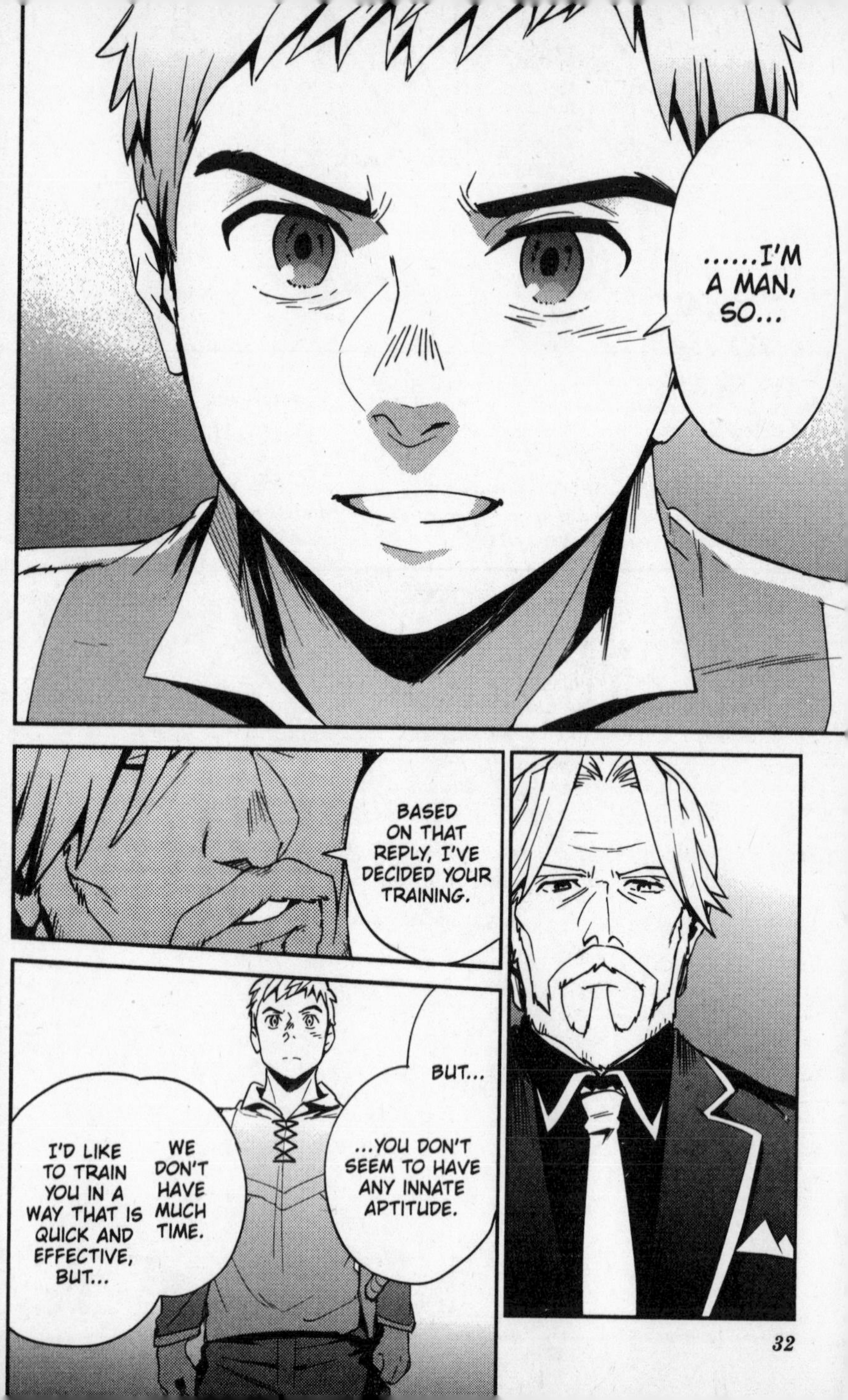
......I'M A MAN, SO...
BASED ON THAT REPLY, I'VE DECIDED YOUR TRAINING.
BUT...
...YOU DON'T SEEM TO HAVE ANY INNATE APTITUDE.
WE DON'T HAVE MUCH TIME.
I'D LIKE TO TRAIN YOU IN A WAY THAT IS QUICK AND EFFECTIVE, BUT...

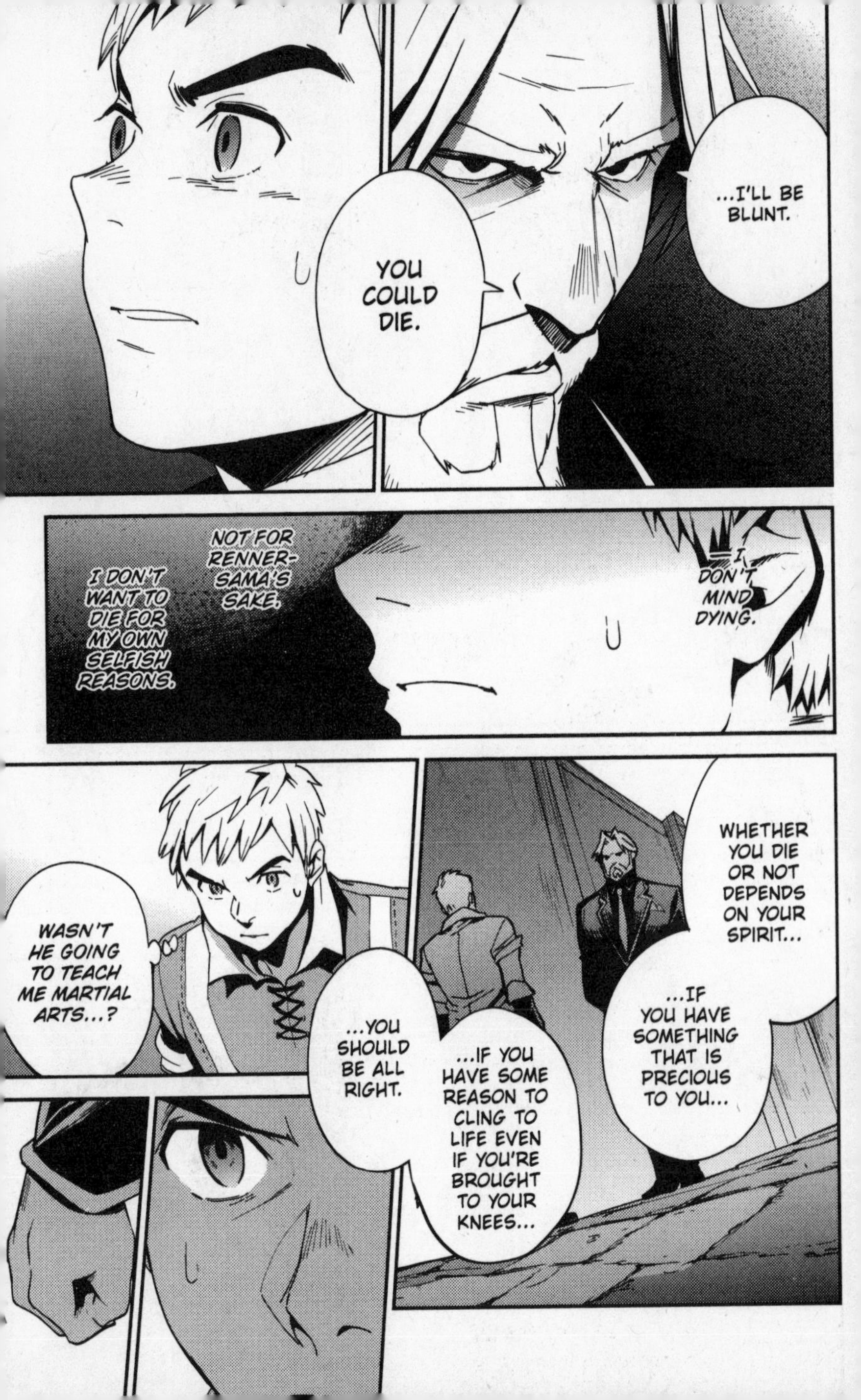
...I'LL BE BLUNT.
YOU COULD DIE.
I DON'T MIND DYING.
NOT FOR RENNER-SAMA'S SAKE.
I DON'T WANT TO DIE FOR MY OWN SELFISH REASONS.
WHETHER YOU DIE OR NOT DEPENDS ON YOUR SPIRIT...
...IF YOU HAVE SOMETHING THAT IS PRECIOUS TO YOU...
...IF YOU HAVE SOME REASON TO CLING TO LIFE EVEN IF YOU'RE BROUGHT TO YOUR KNEES...
...YOU SHOULD BE ALL RIGHT.
WASN'T HE GOING TO TEACH ME MARTIAL ARTS...?

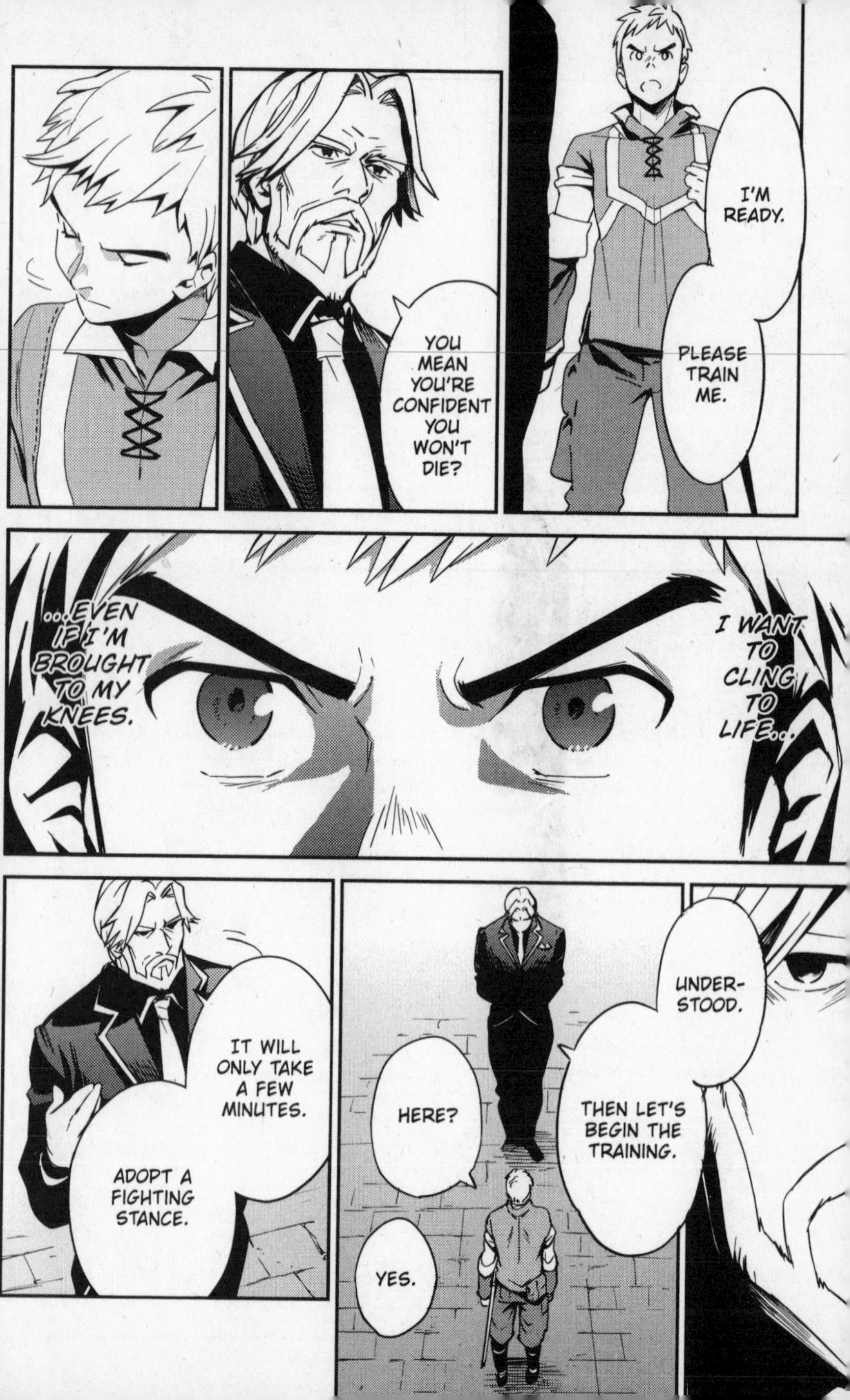
I'M READY.
PLEASE TRAIN ME.
YOU MEAN YOU'RE CONFIDENT YOU WON'T DIE?
I WANT TO CLING TO LIFE...
...EVEN IF I'M BROUGHT TO MY KNEES.
UNDER-STOOD.
THEN LET'S BEGIN THE TRAINING.
HERE?
YES.
IT WILL ONLY TAKE A FEW MINUTES.
ADOPT A FIGHTING STANCE.

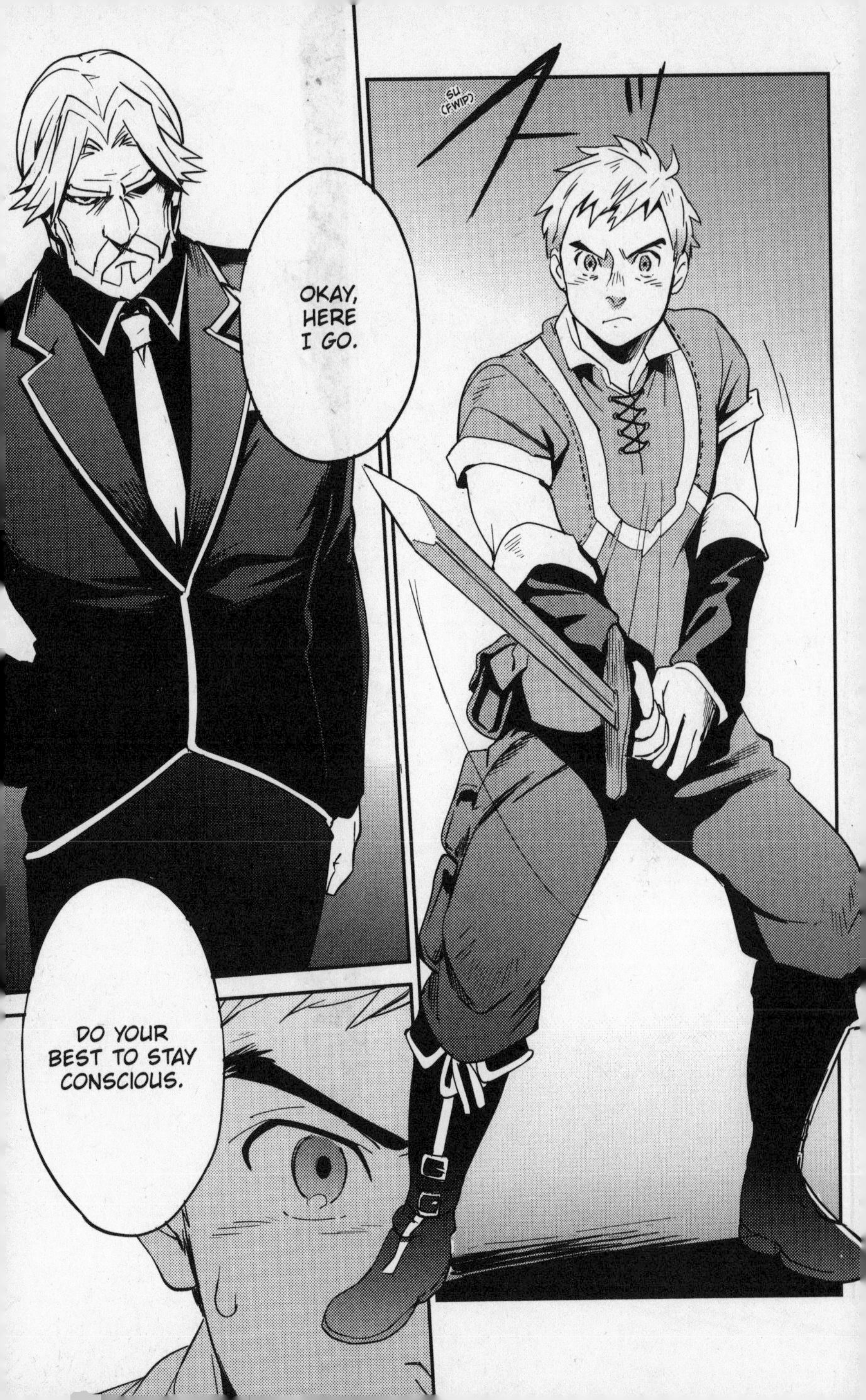
SU (FWIP)
OKAY, HERE I GO.
DO YOUR BEST TO STAY CONSCIOUS.

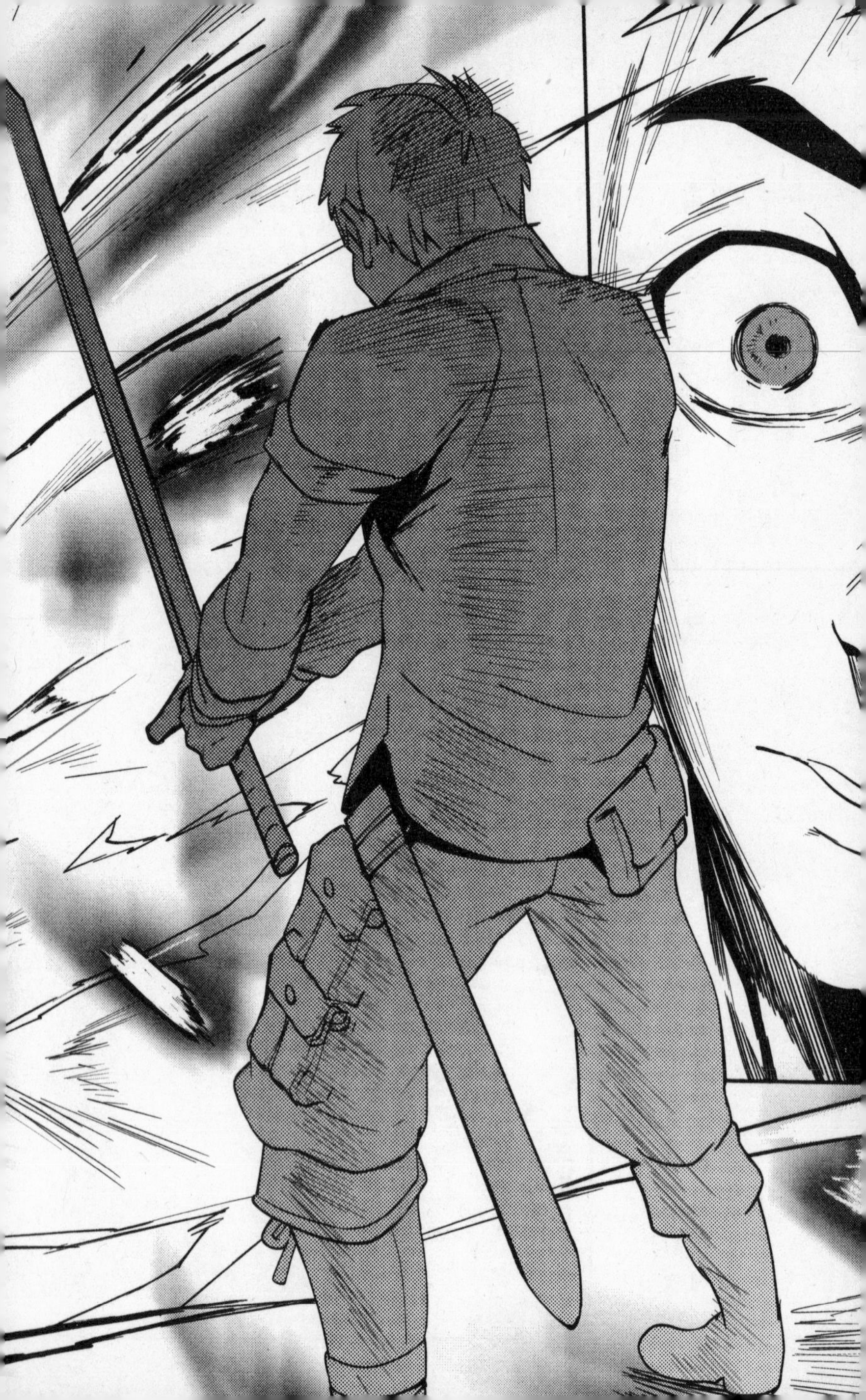

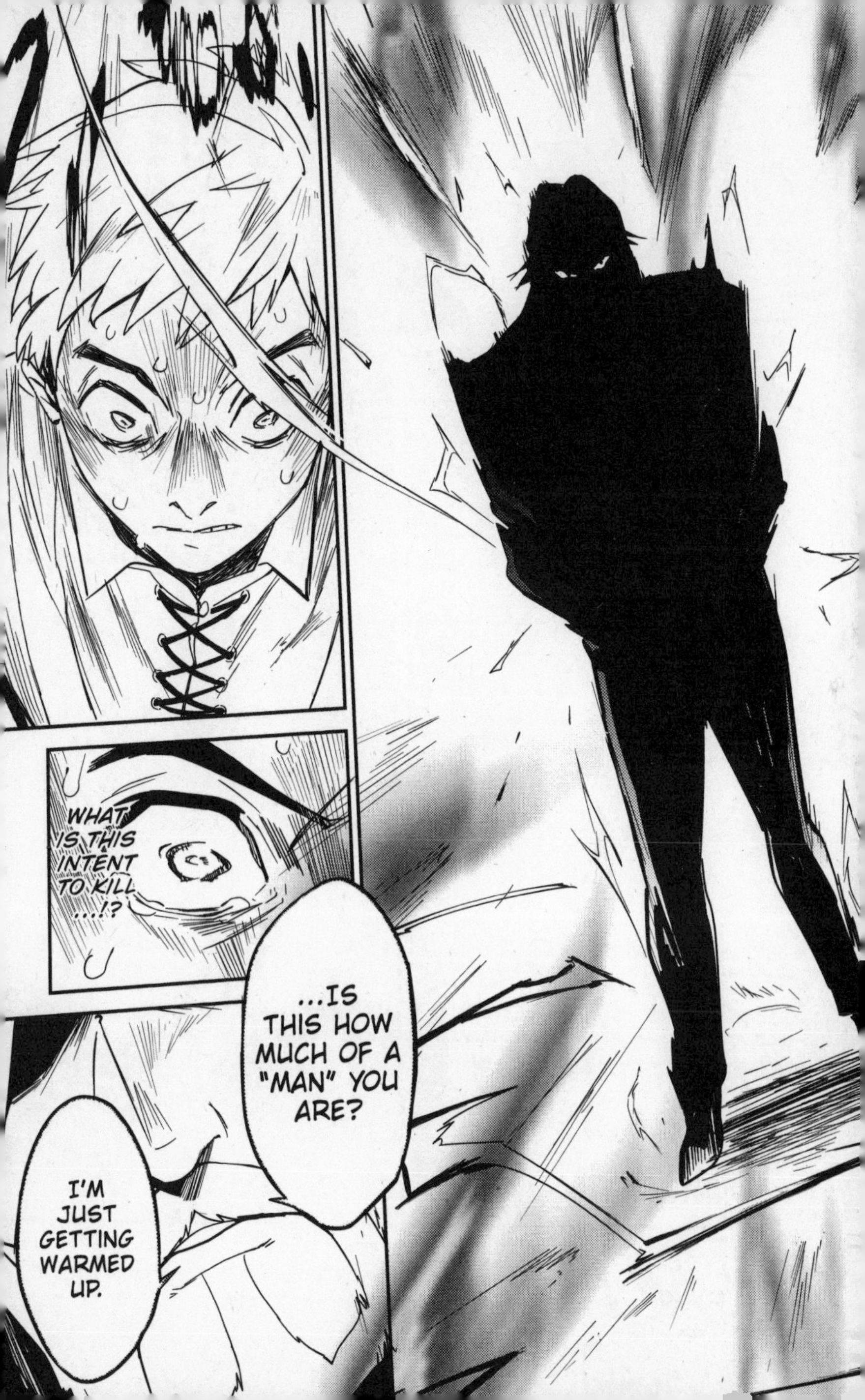
...IS THIS HOW MUCH OF A "MAN" YOU ARE?
WHAT IS THIS INTENT TO KILL ...!?
I'M JUST GETTING WARMED UP.

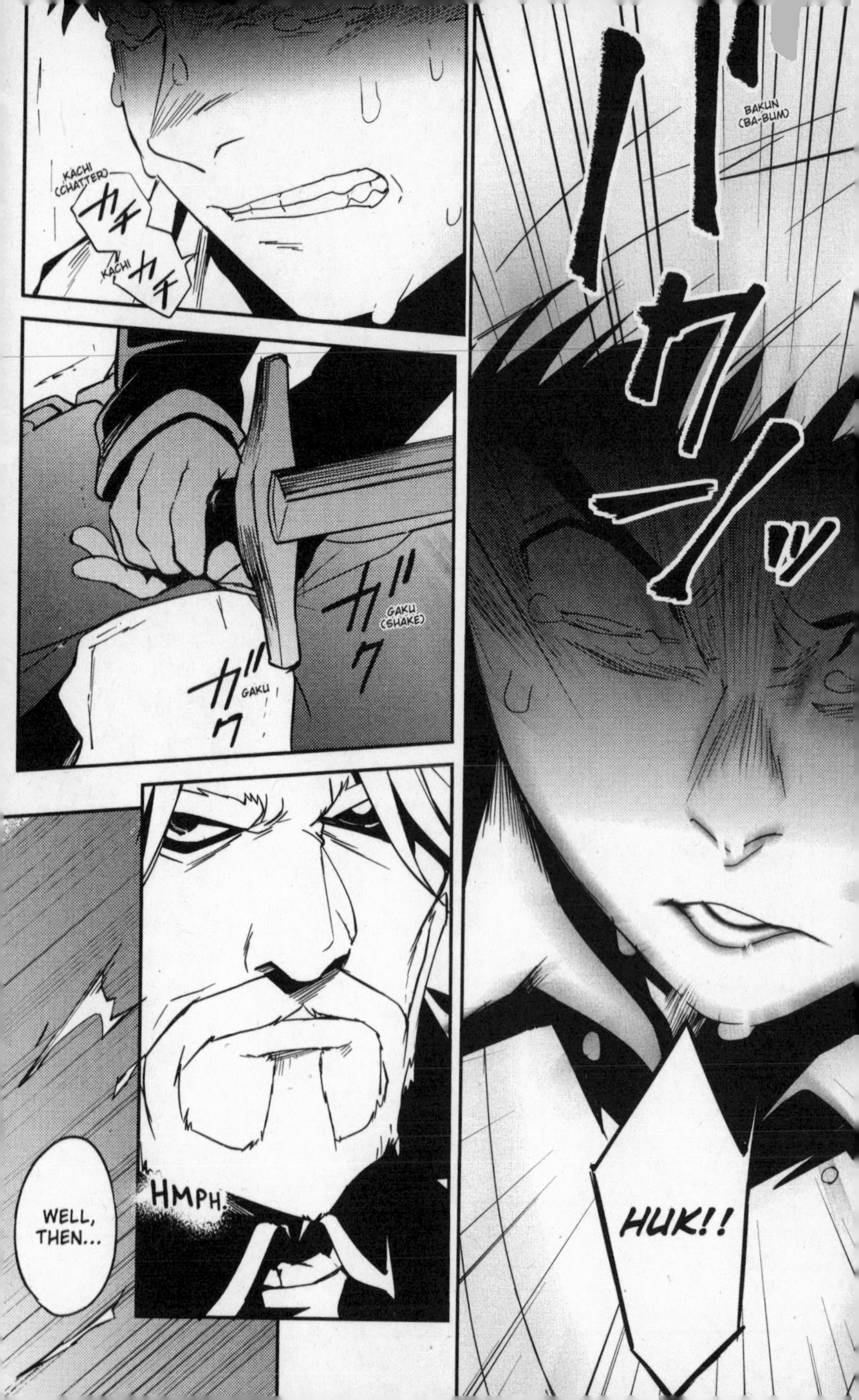

BAKUN (BA-BUM)
ドクンッ
HUK!!
KACHI (CHATTER)
カチ
KACHI
カチ
GAKU (SHAKE)
ガク
GAKU
ガク
HMPH.
WELL, THEN...

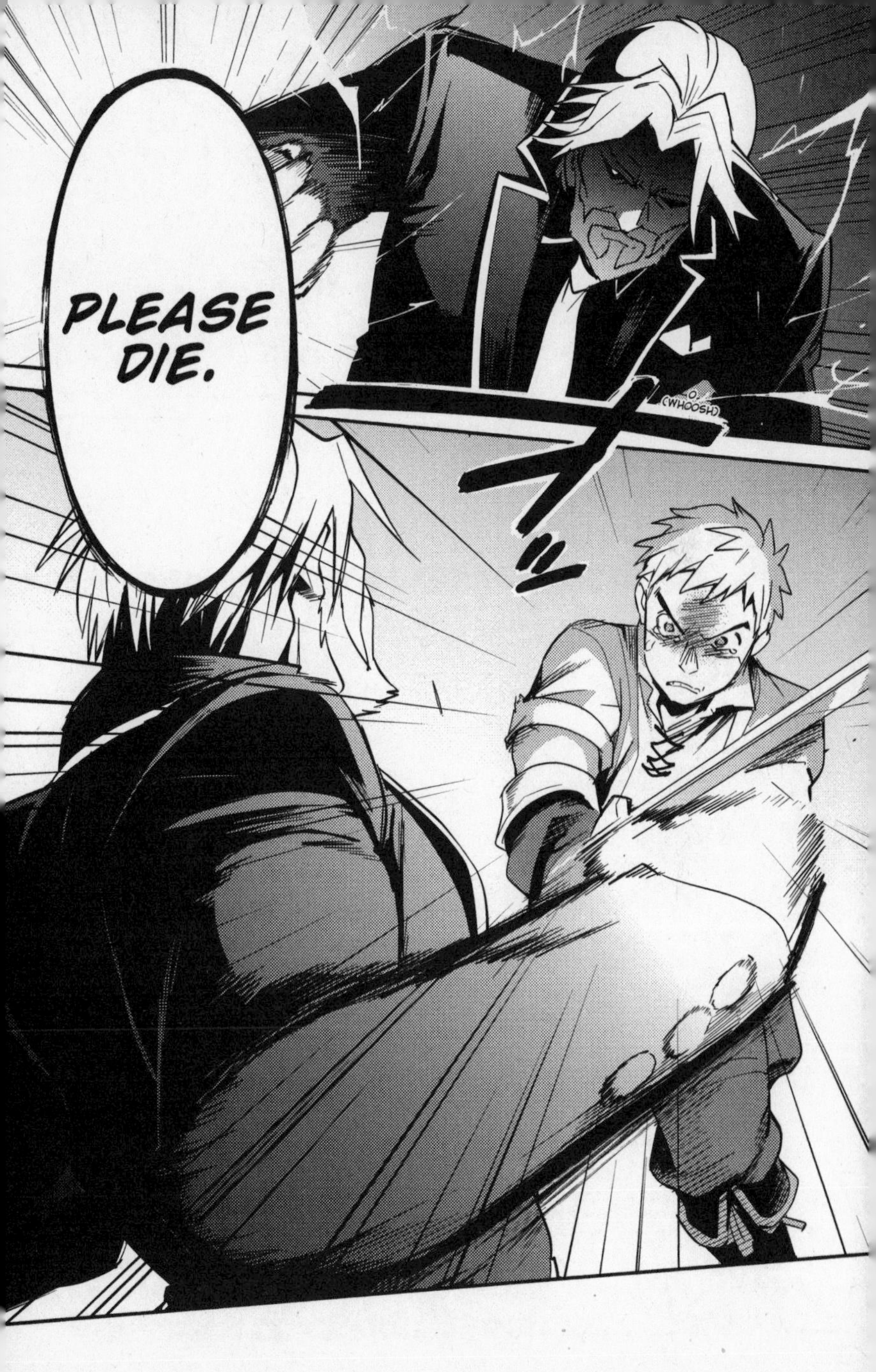
PLEASE DIE.
(WHOOSH)

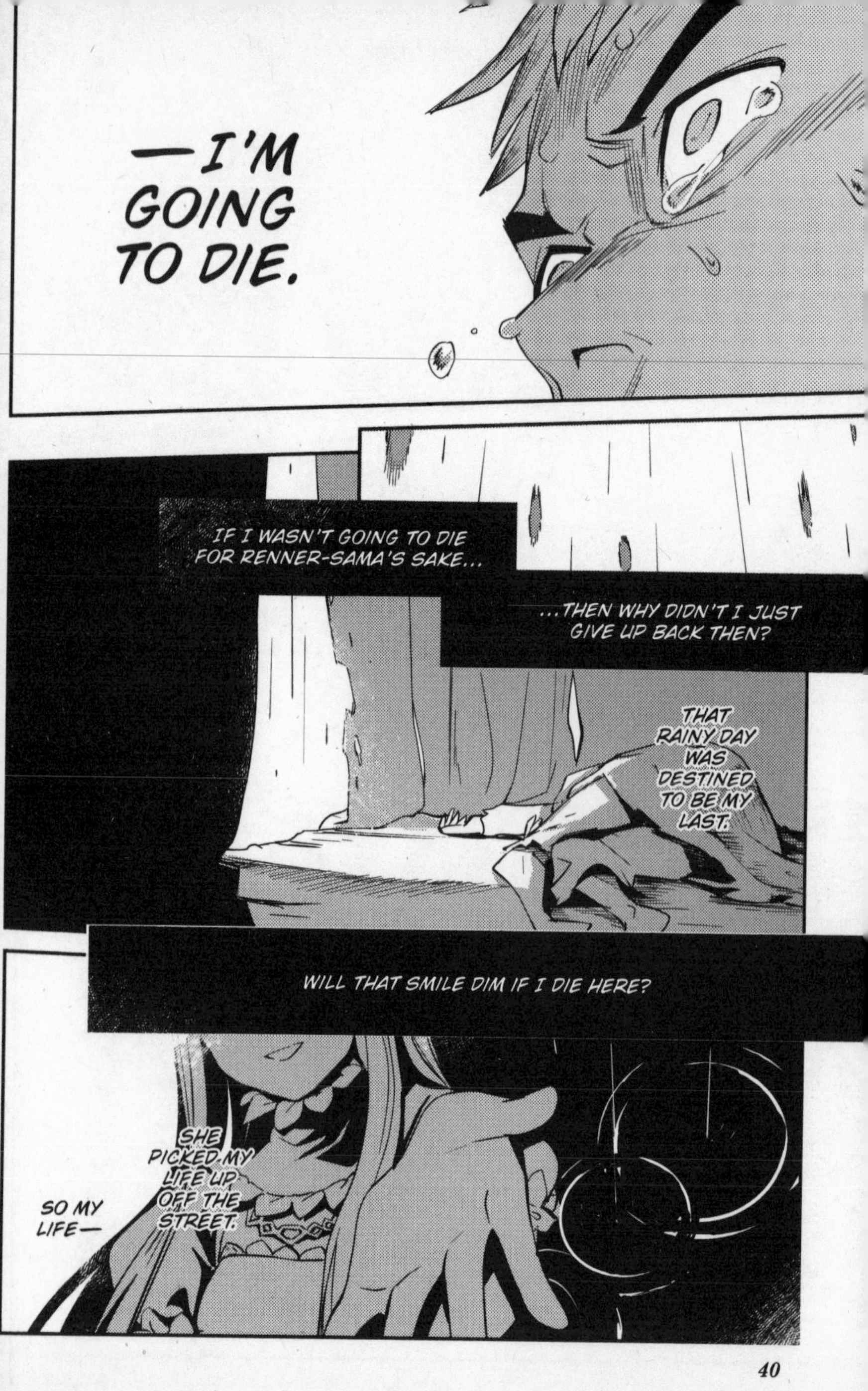
—I'M GOING TO DIE.
IF I WASN'T GOING TO DIE FOR RENNER-SAMA'S SAKE...
...THEN WHY DIDN'T I JUST GIVE UP BACK THEN?
THAT RAINY DAY WAS DESTINED TO BE MY LAST.
WILL THAT SMILE DIM IF I DIE HERE?
SHE PICKED MY LIFE UP OFF THE STREET.
SO MY LIFE—

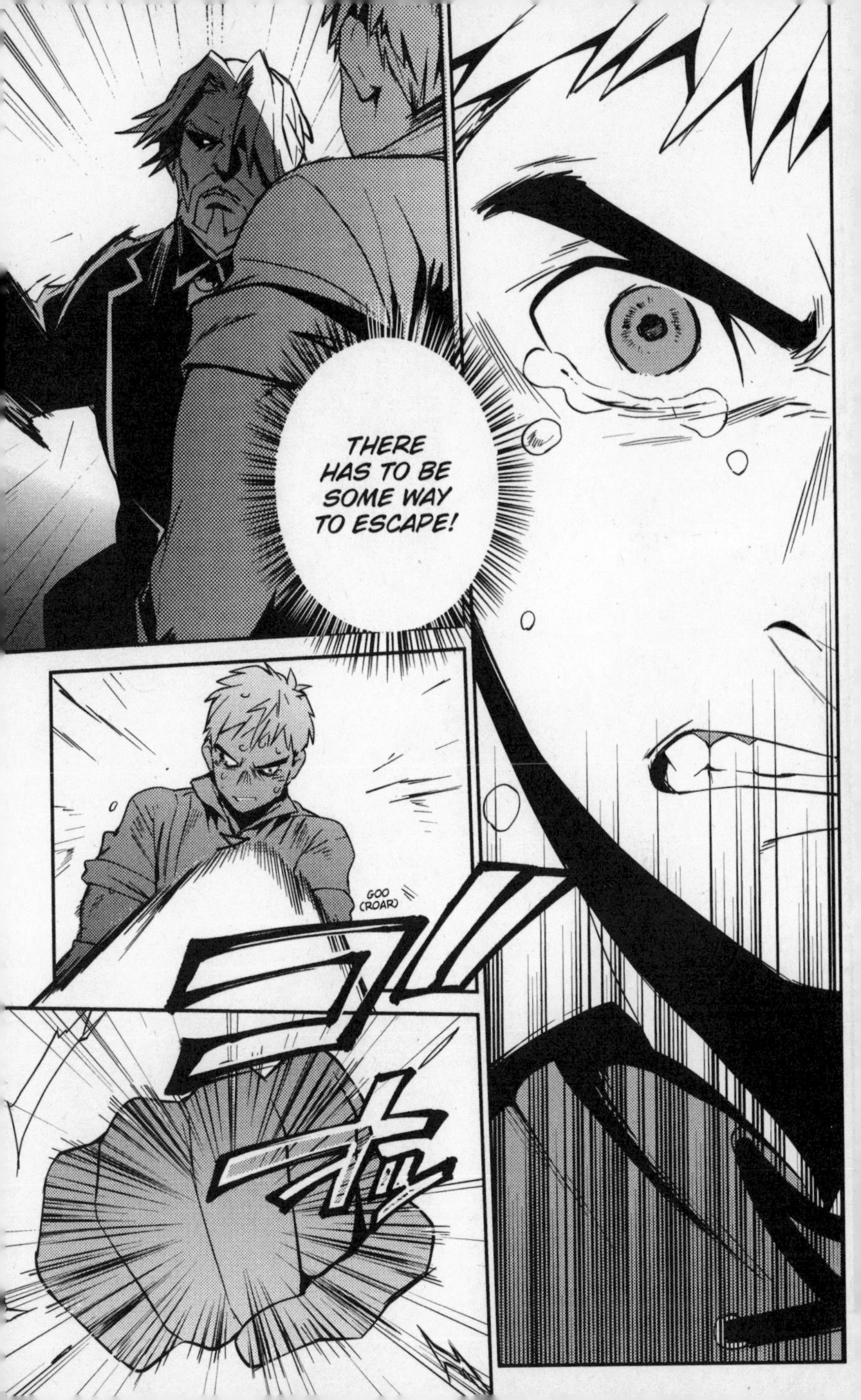
THERE HAS TO BE SOME WAY TO ESCAPE!
GOO (ROAR)

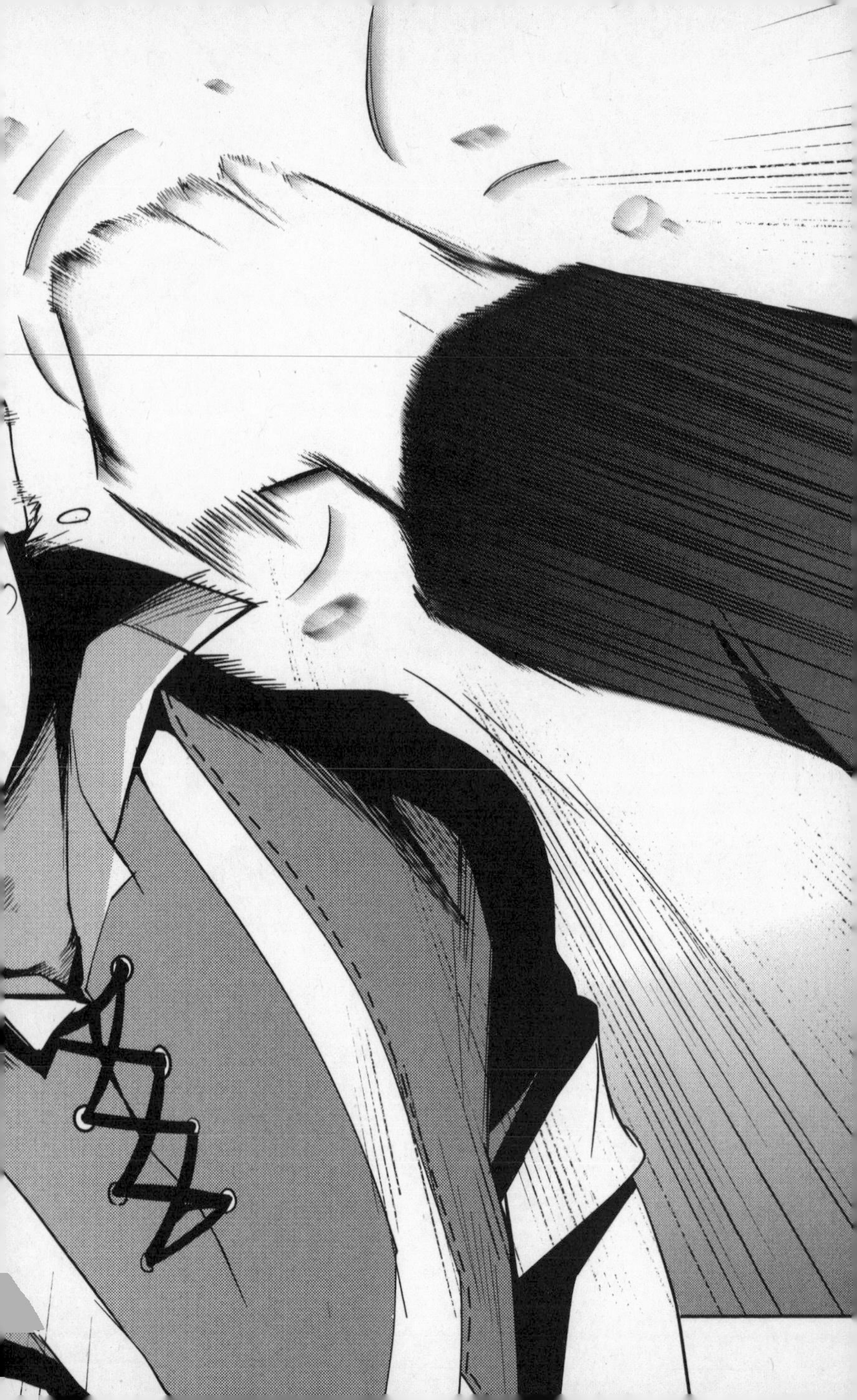

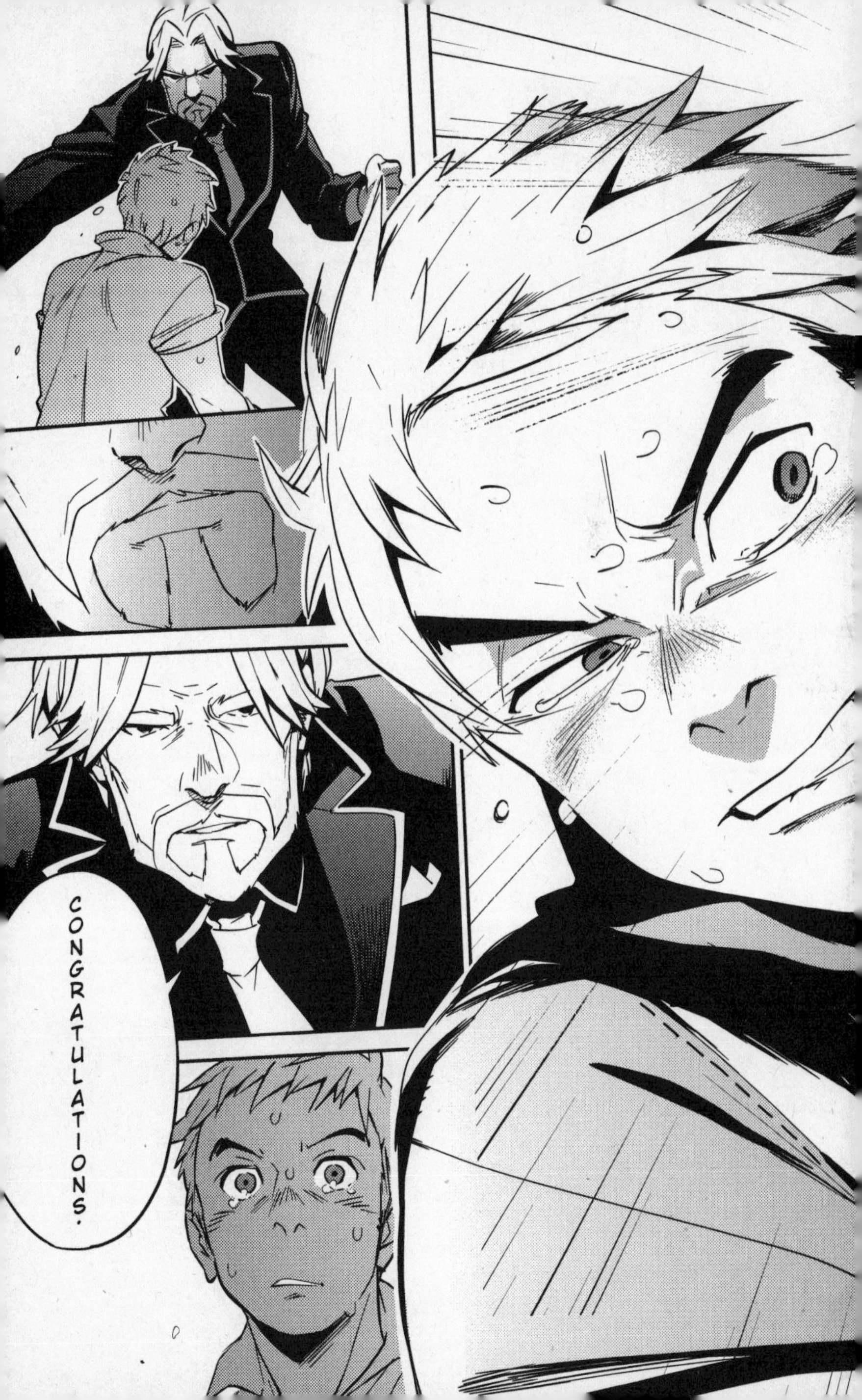
CONGRATULATIONS.

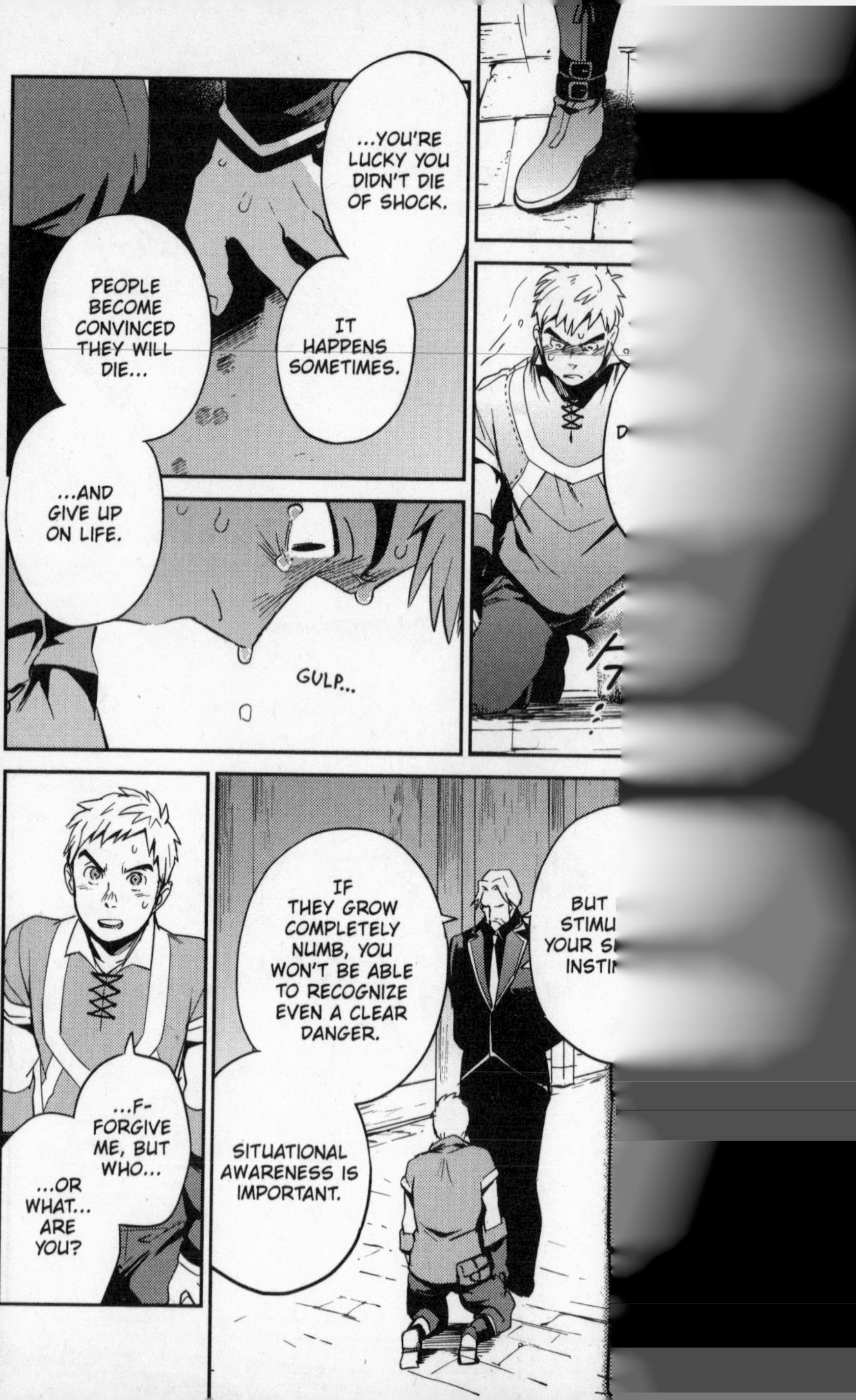
...YOU'RE LUCKY YOU DIDN'T DIE OF SHOCK.
IT HAPPENS SOMETIMES.
PEOPLE BECOME CONVINCED THEY WILL DIE...
...AND GIVE UP ON LIFE.
GULP...
IF THEY GROW COMPLETELY NUMB, YOU WON'T BE ABLE TO RECOGNIZE EVEN A CLEAR DANGER.
SITUATIONAL AWARENESS IS IMPORTANT.
...F-FORGIVE ME, BUT WHO...
...OR WHAT... ARE YOU?

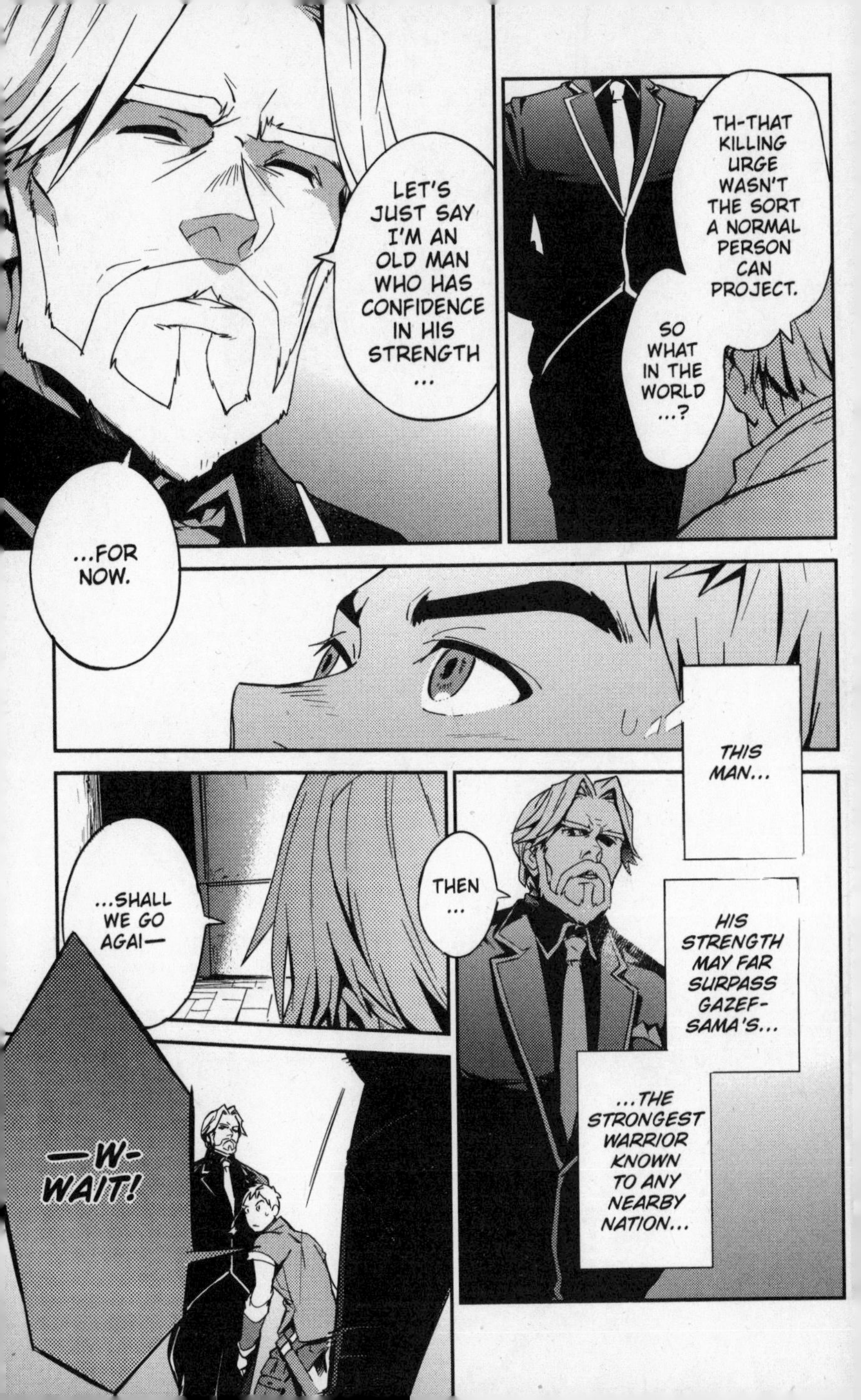
TH-THAT KILLING URGE WASN'T THE SORT A NORMAL PERSON CAN PROJECT.
SO WHAT IN THE WORLD ...?
LET'S JUST SAY I'M AN OLD MAN WHO HAS CONFIDENCE IN HIS STRENGTH ...
...FOR NOW.
THIS MAN...
THEN ...
HIS STRENGTH MAY FAR SURPASS GAZEF-SAMA'S...
...THE STRONGEST WARRIOR KNOWN TO ANY NEARBY NATION...
...SHALL WE GO AGAI—
—W-WAIT!

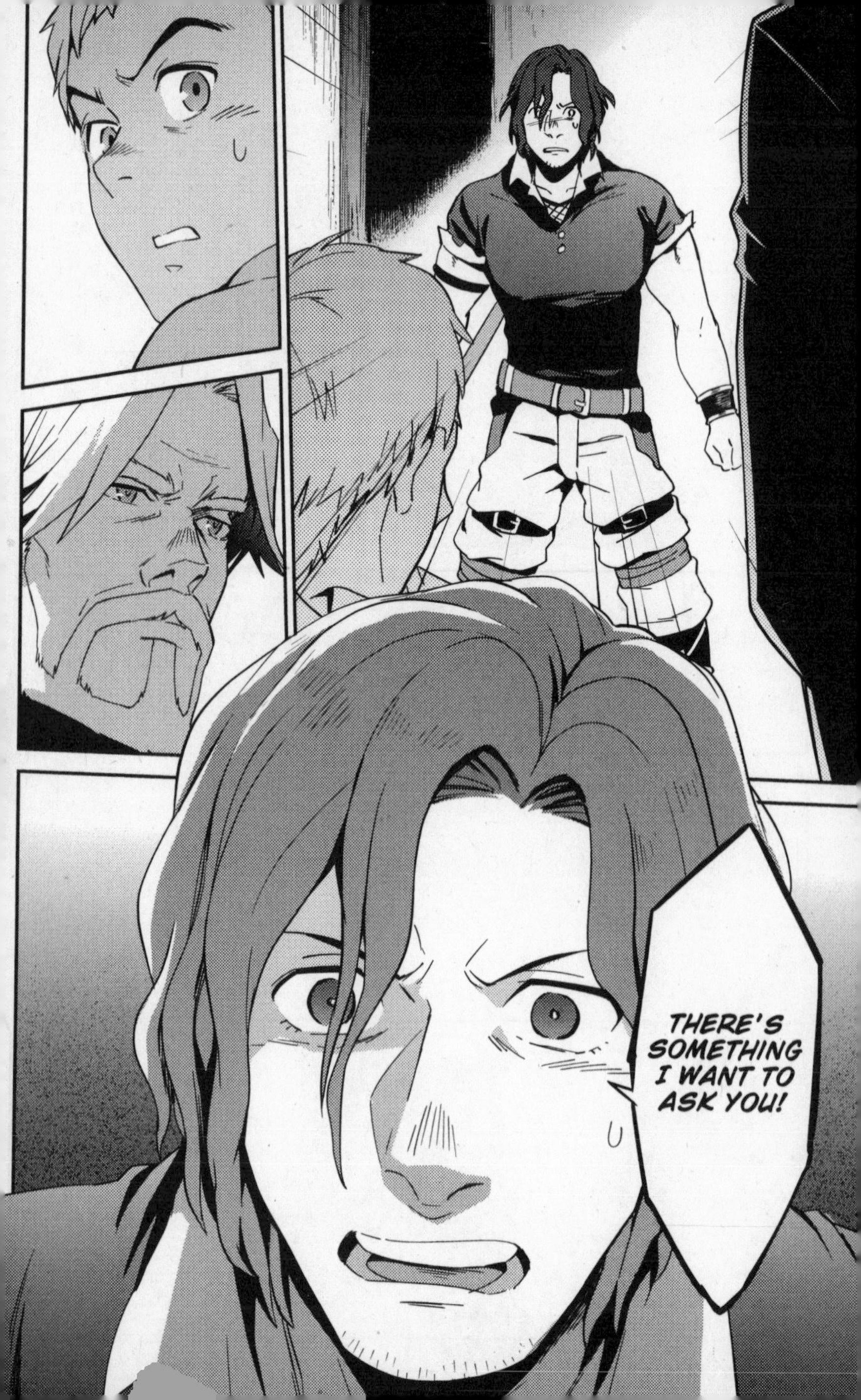
THERE'S SOMETHING I WANT TO ASK YOU!

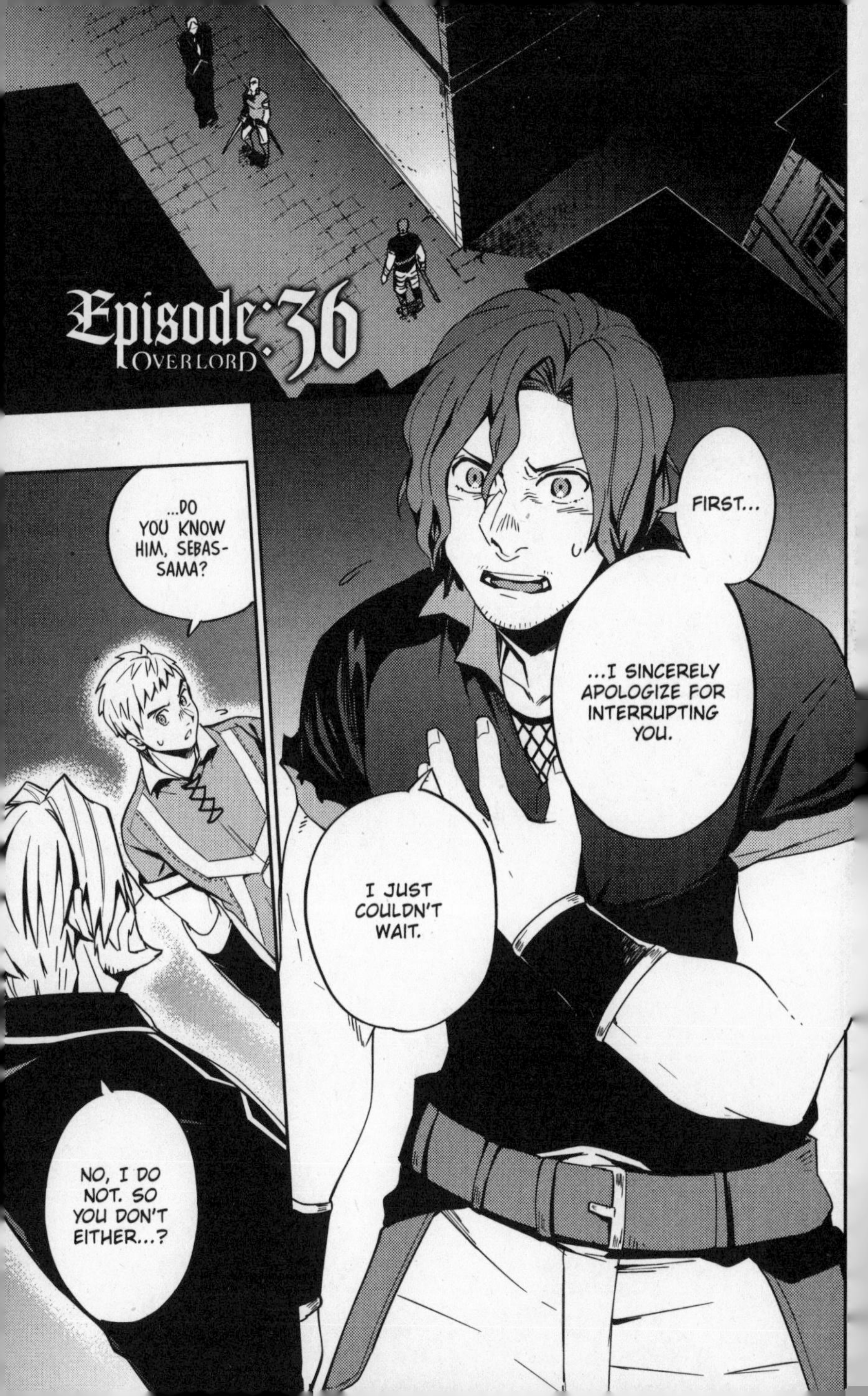
Episode: 36
OVERLORD
FIRST...
...I SINCERELY APOLOGIZE FOR INTERRUPTING YOU.
I JUST COULDN'T WAIT.
...DO YOU KNOW HIM, SEBAS-SAMA?
NO, I DO NOT. SO YOU DON'T EITHER...?

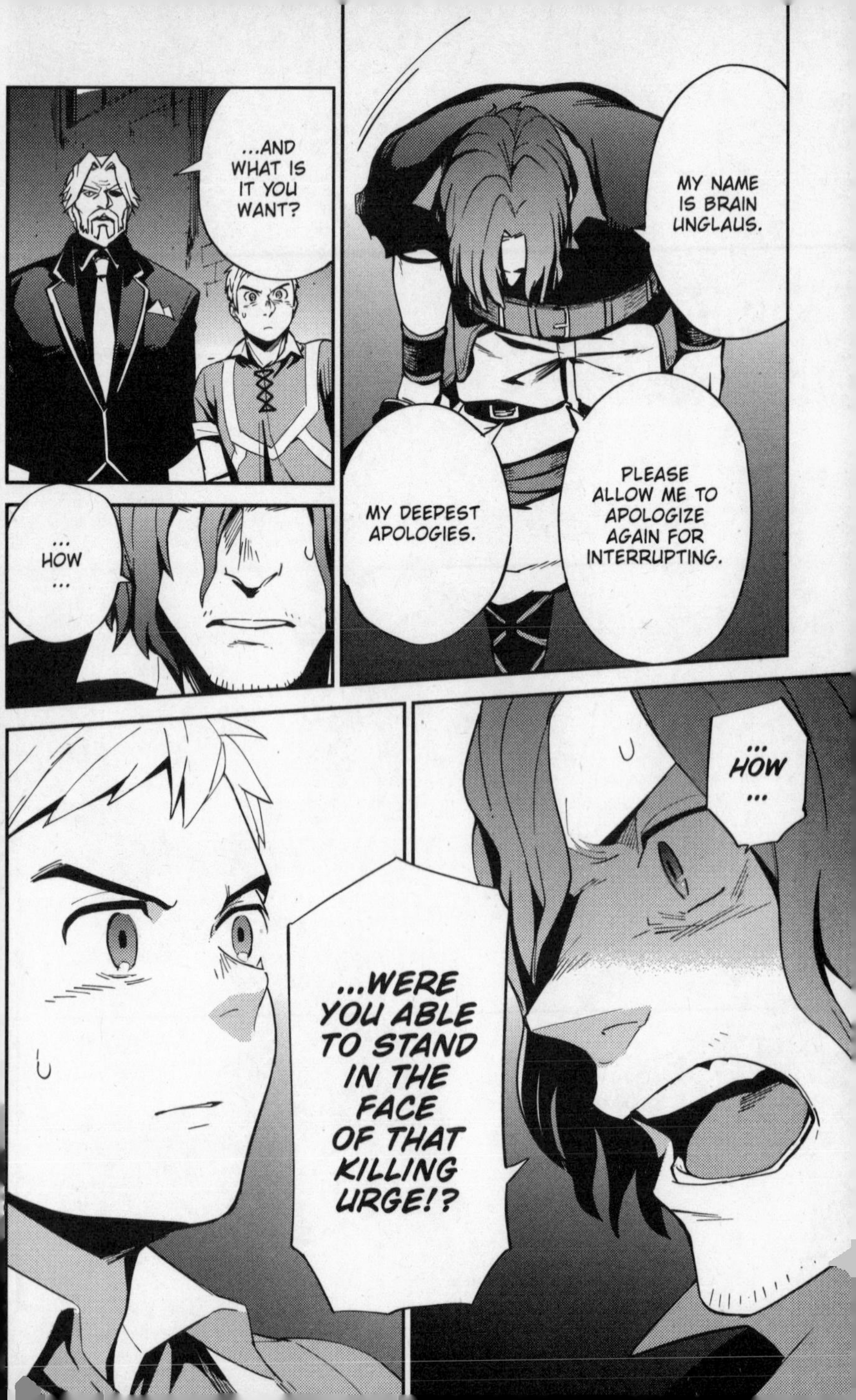
MY NAME IS BRAIN UNGLAUS.
PLEASE ALLOW ME TO APOLOGIZE AGAIN FOR INTERRUPTING.
MY DEEPEST APOLOGIES.
...AND WHAT IS IT YOU WANT?
... HOW ...
... HOW ...
...WERE YOU ABLE TO STAND IN THE FACE OF THAT KILLING URGE!?

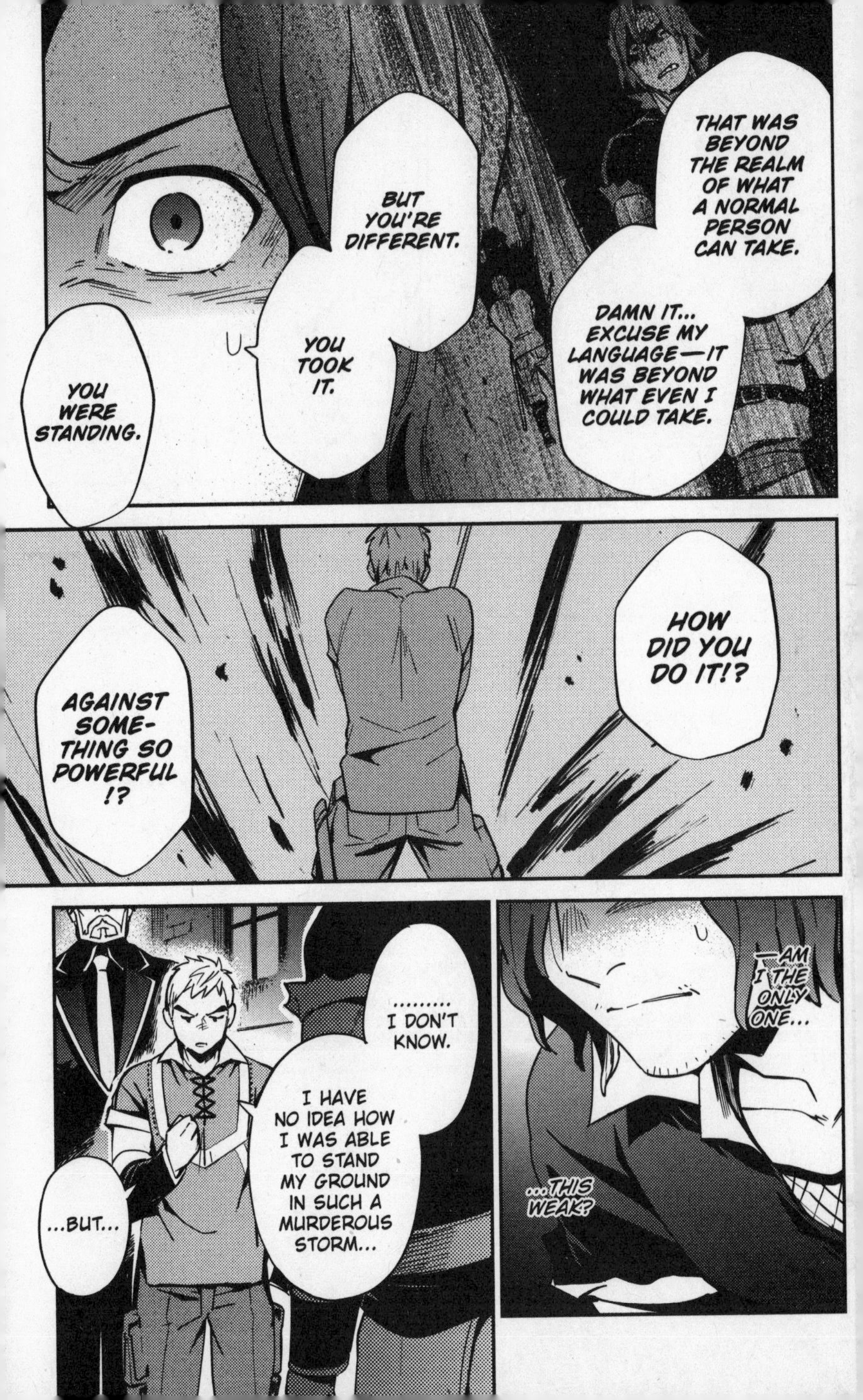
THAT WAS BEYOND THE REALM OF WHAT A NORMAL PERSON CAN TAKE.
DAMN IT... EXCUSE MY LANGUAGE—IT WAS BEYOND WHAT EVEN I COULD TAKE.
BUT YOU'RE DIFFERENT.
YOU TOOK IT.
YOU WERE STANDING.
HOW DID YOU DO IT!?
AGAINST SOME-THING SO POWERFUL!?
—AM I THE ONLY ONE...
...THIS WEAK?
.... I DON'T KNOW.
I HAVE NO IDEA HOW I WAS ABLE TO STAND MY GROUND IN SUCH A MURDEROUS STORM...
...BUT...

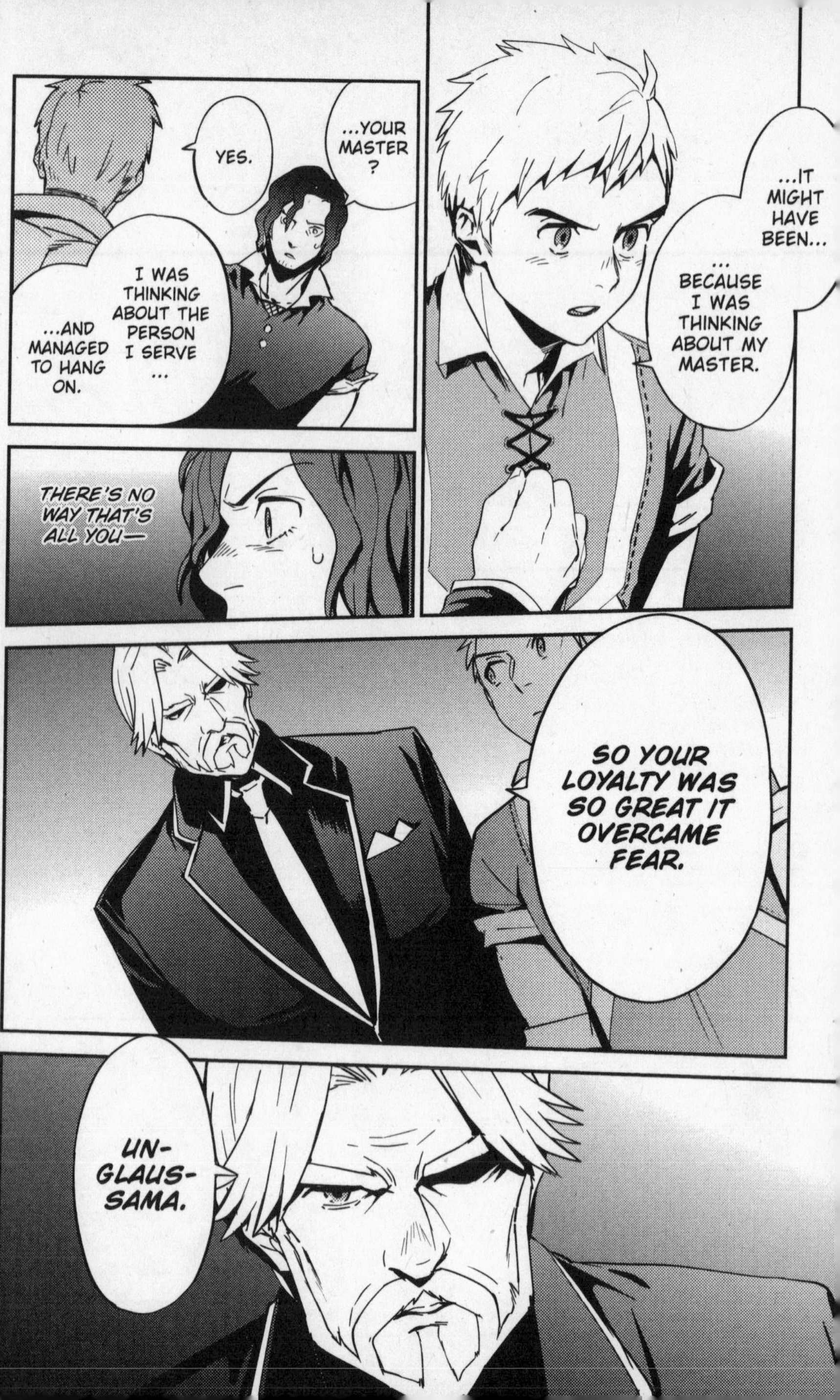
...IT MIGHT HAVE BEEN...
...BECAUSE I WAS THINKING ABOUT MY MASTER.
...YOUR MASTER?
YES.
I WAS THINKING ABOUT THE PERSON I SERVE...
...AND MANAGED TO HANG ON.
THERE'S NO WAY THAT'S ALL YOU—
SO YOUR LOYALTY WAS SO GREAT IT OVERCAME FEAR.
UN-GLAUS-SAMA.

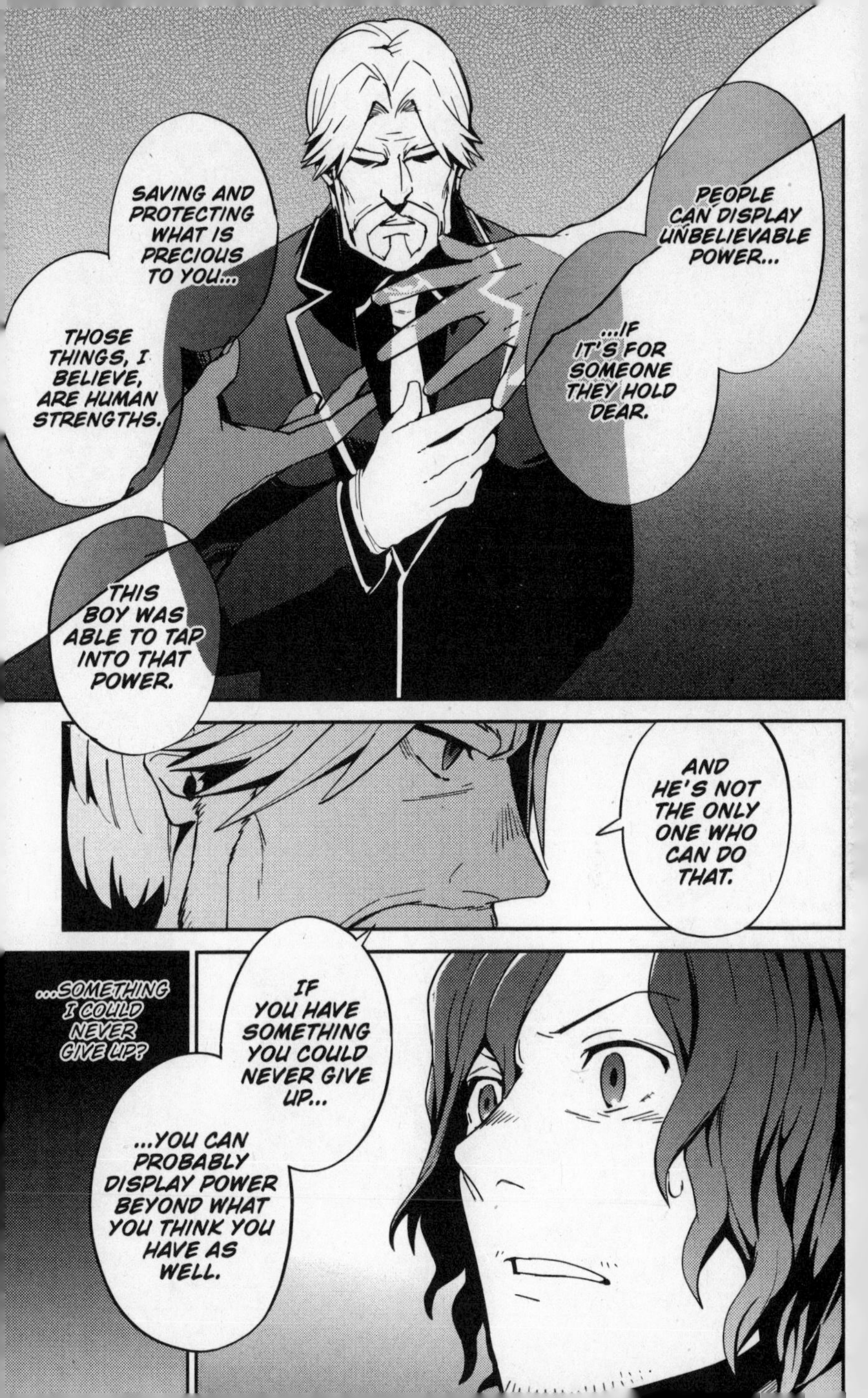
PEOPLE CAN DISPLAY UNBELIEVABLE POWER...
...IF IT'S FOR SOMEONE THEY HOLD DEAR.
SAVING AND PROTECTING WHAT IS PRECIOUS TO YOU...
THOSE THINGS, I BELIEVE, ARE HUMAN STRENGTHS.
THIS BOY WAS ABLE TO TAP INTO THAT POWER.
AND HE'S NOT THE ONLY ONE WHO CAN DO THAT.
IF YOU HAVE SOMETHING YOU COULD NEVER GIVE UP...
...YOU CAN PROBABLY DISPLAY POWER BEYOND WHAT YOU THINK YOU HAVE AS WELL.
...SOMETHING I COULD NEVER GIVE UP?

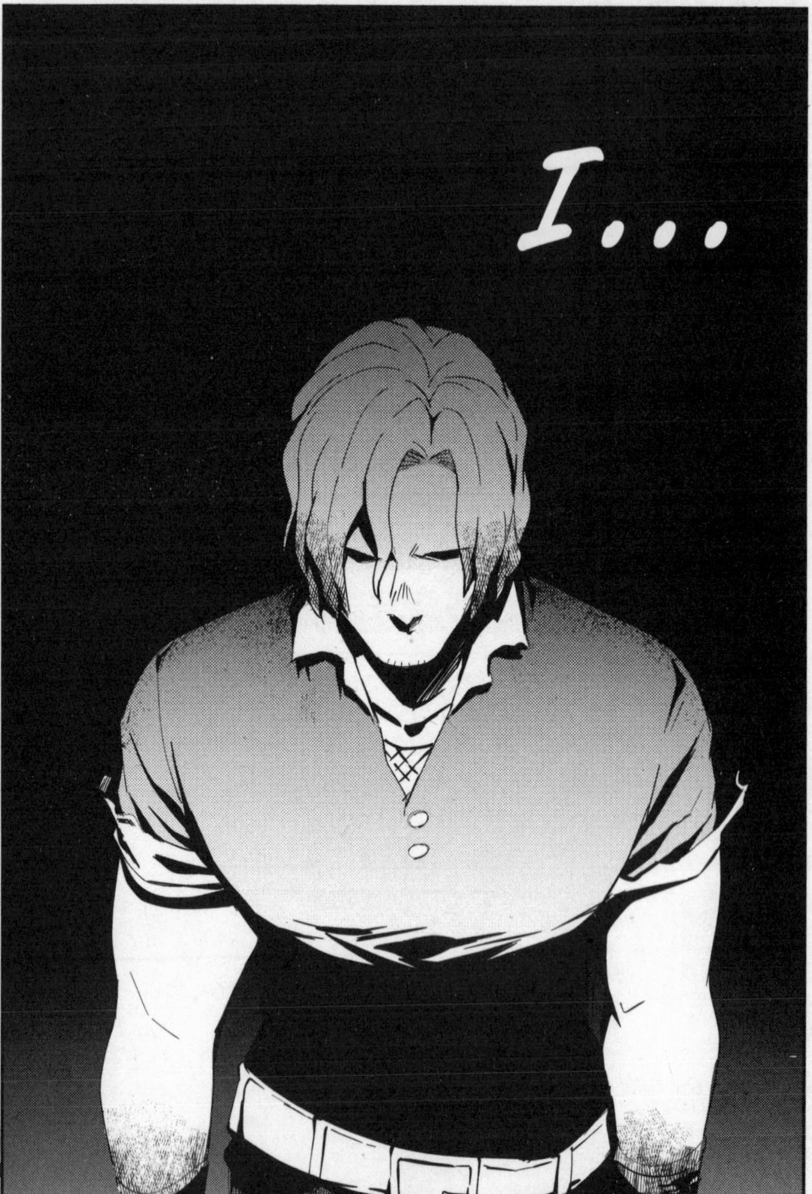
I...

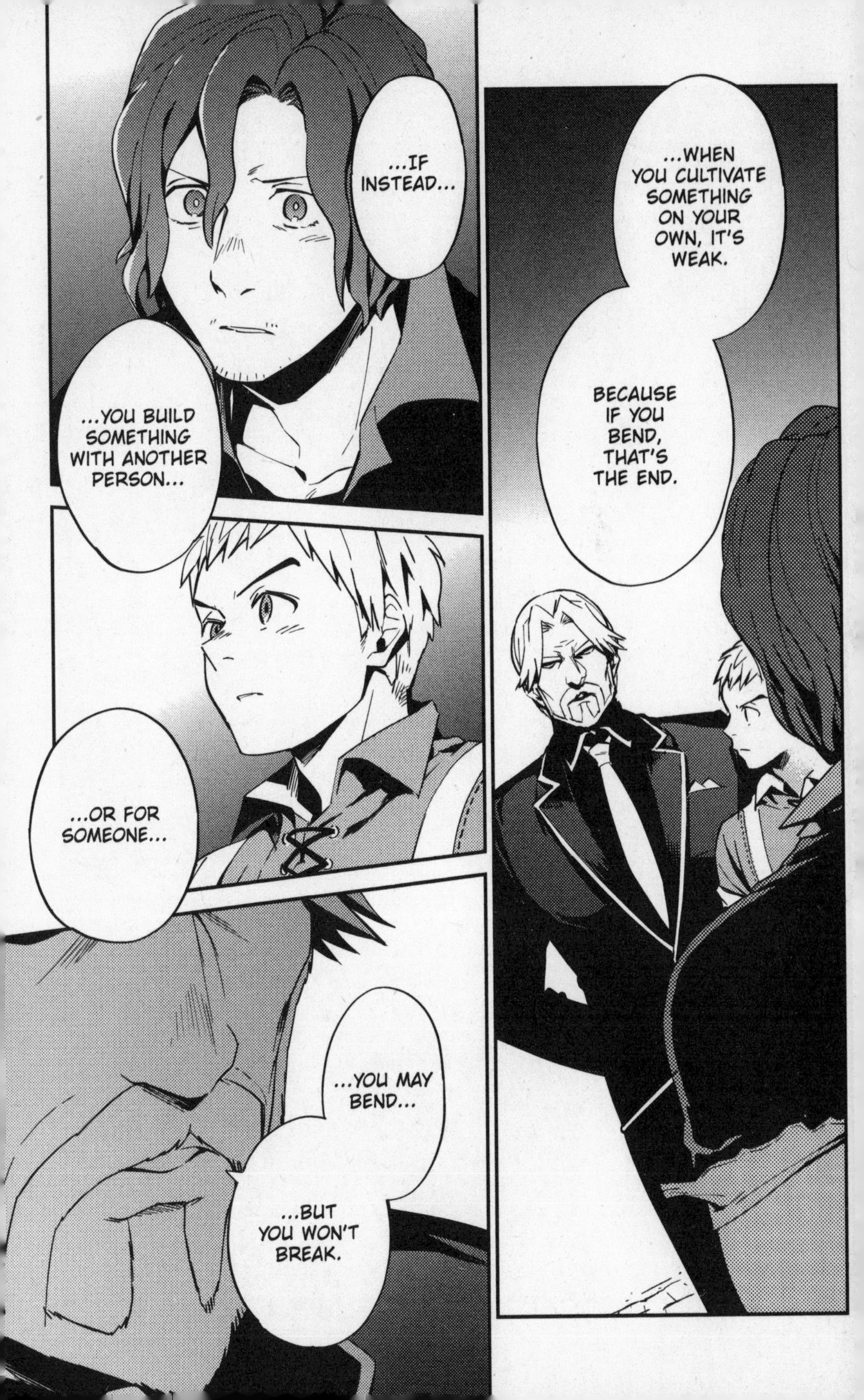
...WHEN YOU CULTIVATE SOMETHING ON YOUR OWN, IT'S WEAK.
BECAUSE IF YOU BEND, THAT'S THE END.
...IF INSTEAD...
...YOU BUILD SOMETHING WITH ANOTHER PERSON...
...OR FOR SOMEONE...
...YOU MAY BEND...
...BUT YOU WON'T BREAK.

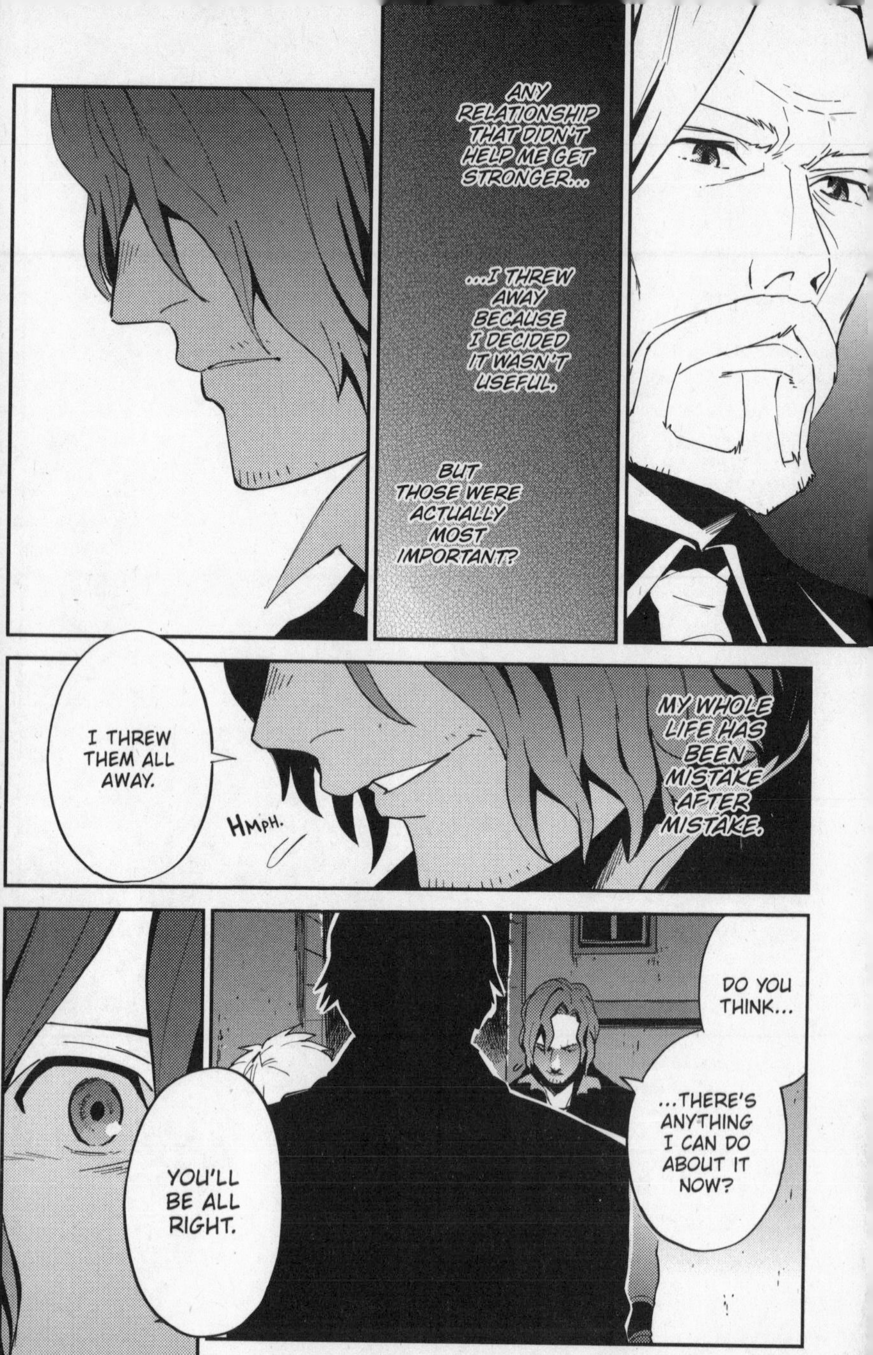
ANY RELATIONSHIP THAT DIDN'T HELP ME GET STRONGER...
...I THREW AWAY BECAUSE I DECIDED IT WASN'T USEFUL.
BUT THOSE WERE ACTUALLY MOST IMPORTANT?
MY WHOLE LIFE HAS BEEN MISTAKE AFTER MISTAKE.
I THREW THEM ALL AWAY.
HMPH.
DO YOU THINK...
...THERE'S ANYTHING I CAN DO ABOUT IT NOW?
YOU'LL BE ALL RIGHT.

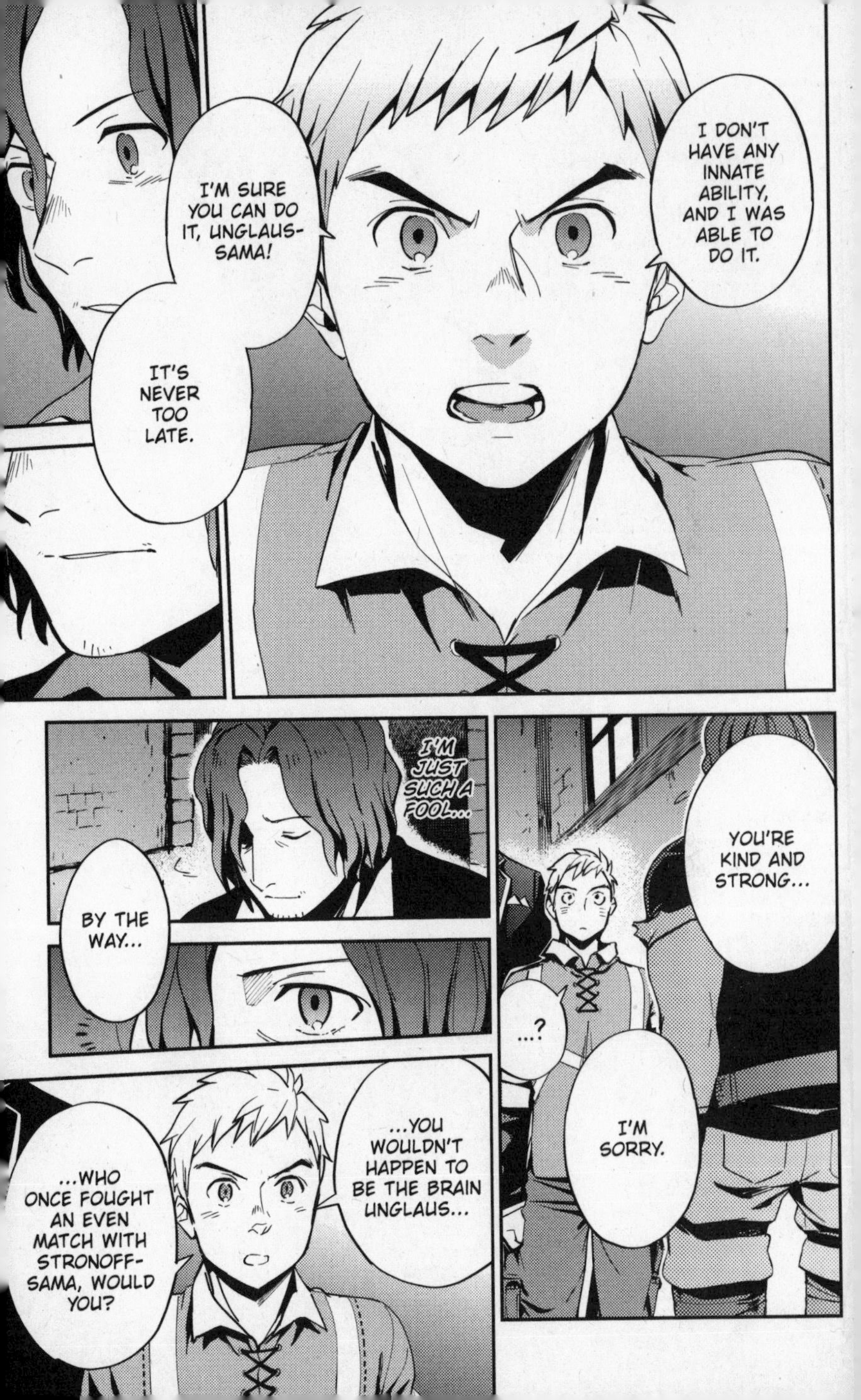
I DON'T HAVE ANY INNATE ABILITY, AND I WAS ABLE TO DO IT.
I'M SURE YOU CAN DO IT, UNGLAUS-SAMA!
IT'S NEVER TOO LATE.
YOU'RE KIND AND STRONG...
...?
I'M SORRY.
I'M JUST SUCH A FOOL...
BY THE WAY...
...YOU WOULDN'T HAPPEN TO BE THE BRAIN UNGLAUS...
...WHO ONCE FOUGHT AN EVEN MATCH WITH STRONOFF-SAMA, WOULD YOU?

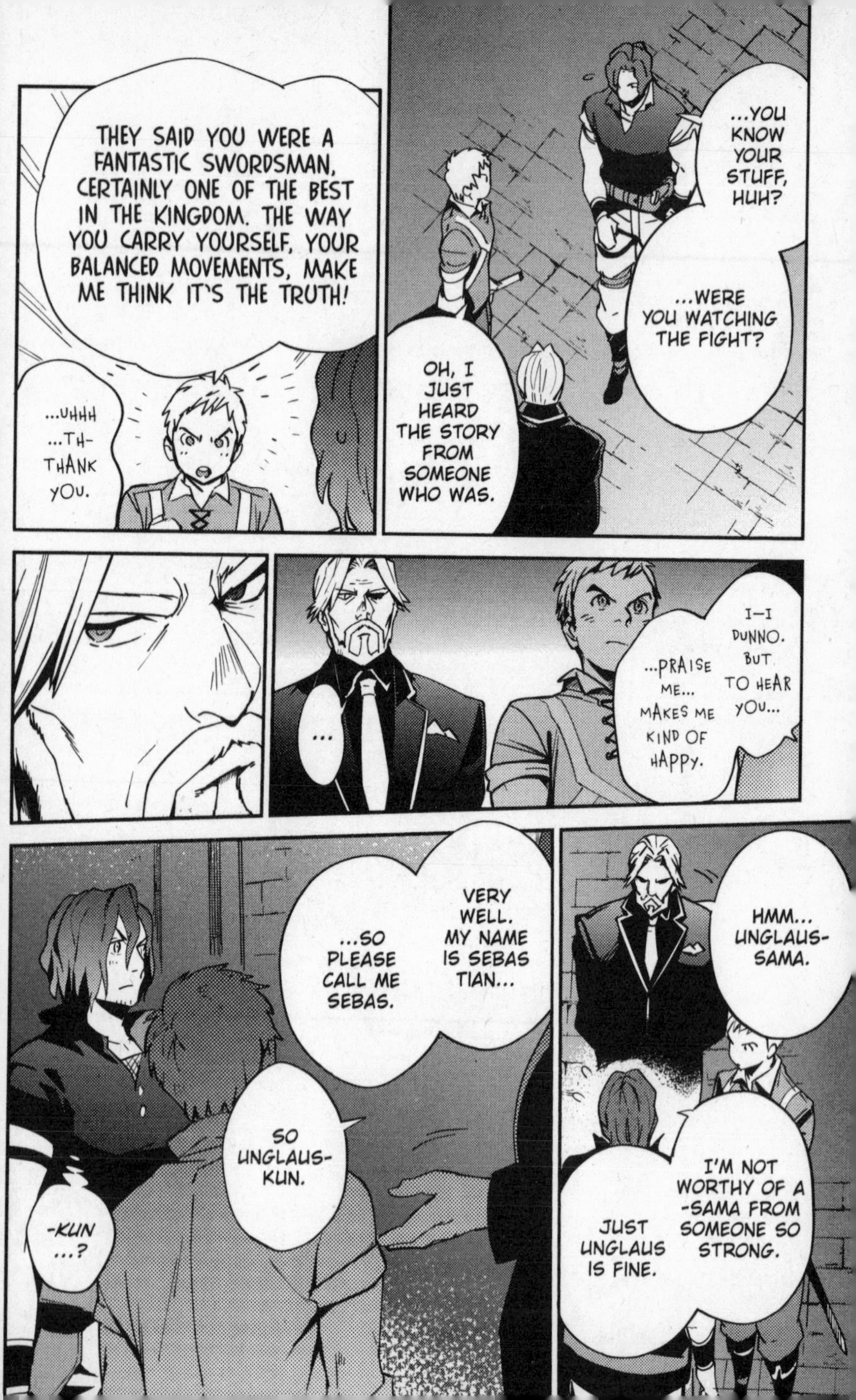
...YOU KNOW YOUR STUFF, HUH?
...WERE YOU WATCHING THE FIGHT?
OH, I JUST HEARD THE STORY FROM SOMEONE WHO WAS.
THEY SAID YOU WERE A FANTASTIC SWORDSMAN, CERTAINLY ONE OF THE BEST IN THE KINGDOM. THE WAY YOU CARRY YOURSELF, YOUR BALANCED MOVEMENTS, MAKE ME THINK IT'S THE TRUTH!
...UHHH ...TH-THANK YOU.
I—I DUNNO. BUT TO HEAR YOU...
...PRAISE ME... MAKES ME KIND OF HAPPY.
...
HMM... UNGLAUS-SAMA.
I'M NOT WORTHY OF A -SAMA FROM SOMEONE SO STRONG.
JUST UNGLAUS IS FINE.
VERY WELL. MY NAME IS SEBAS TIAN...
...SO PLEASE CALL ME SEBAS.
SO UNGLAUS-KUN.
-KUN ...?

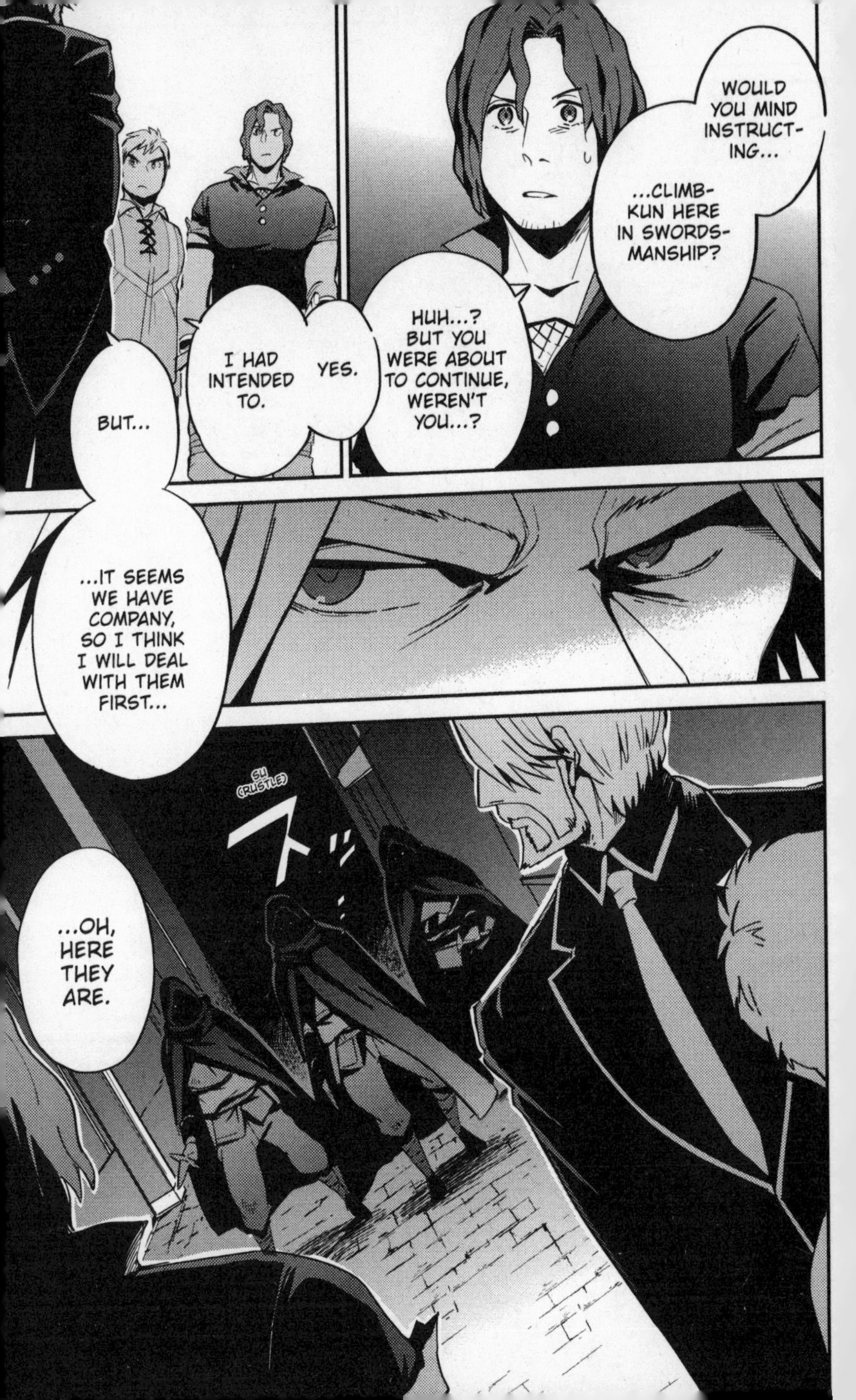
WOULD YOU MIND INSTRUCTING...
...CLIMB-KUN HERE IN SWORDSMANSHIP?
HUH...? BUT YOU WERE ABOUT TO CONTINUE, WEREN'T YOU...?
YES.
I HAD INTENDED TO.
BUT...
...IT SEEMS WE HAVE COMPANY, SO I THINK I WILL DEAL WITH THEM FIRST...
SU (RUSTLE)
スッ
...OH, HERE THEY ARE.

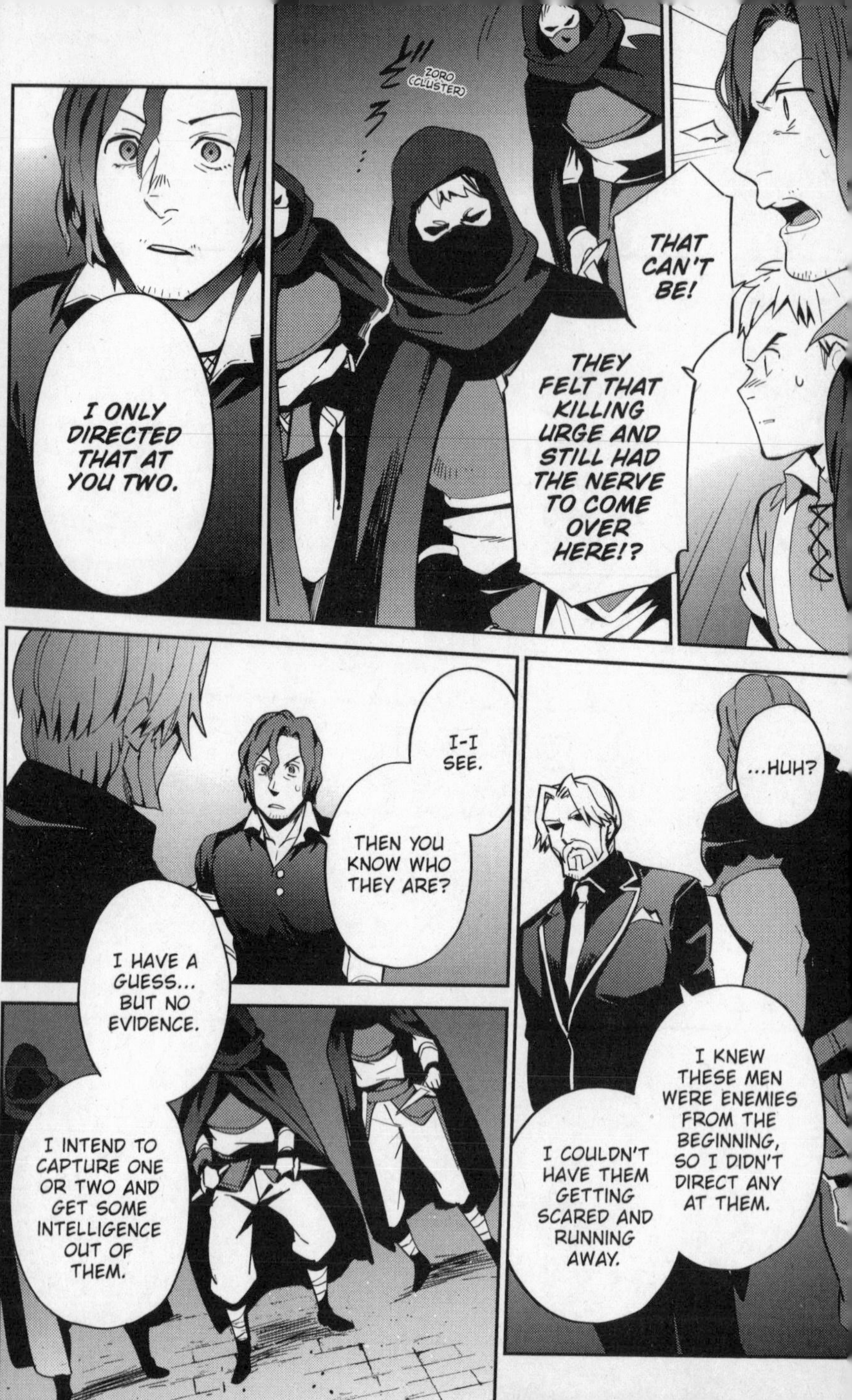
THAT CAN'T BE!
THEY FELT THAT KILLING URGE AND STILL HAD THE NERVE TO COME OVER HERE!?
ZORO (CLUSTER)
I ONLY DIRECTED THAT AT YOU TWO.
...HUH?
I KNEW THESE MEN WERE ENEMIES FROM THE BEGINNING, SO I DIDN'T DIRECT ANY AT THEM.
I COULDN'T HAVE THEM GETTING SCARED AND RUNNING AWAY.
I-I SEE.
THEN YOU KNOW WHO THEY ARE?
I HAVE A GUESS... BUT NO EVIDENCE.
I INTEND TO CAPTURE ONE OR TWO AND GET SOME INTELLIGENCE OUT OF THEM.

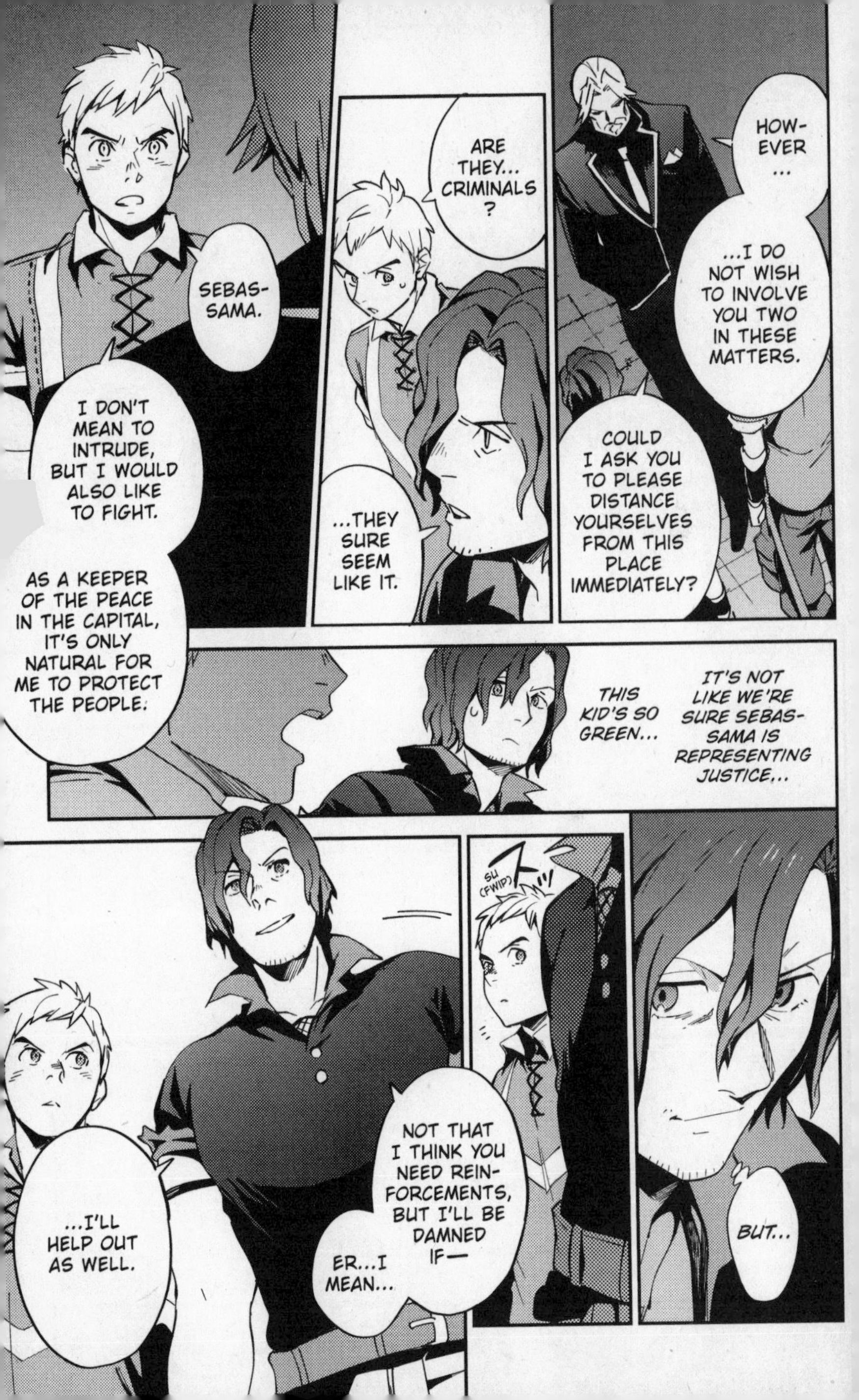
HOW-EVER...
...I DO NOT WISH TO INVOLVE YOU TWO IN THESE MATTERS.
COULD I ASK YOU TO PLEASE DISTANCE YOURSELVES FROM THIS PLACE IMMEDIATELY?
ARE THEY... CRIMINALS?
...THEY SURE SEEM LIKE IT.
SEBAS-SAMA.
I DON'T MEAN TO INTRUDE, BUT I WOULD ALSO LIKE TO FIGHT.
AS A KEEPER OF THE PEACE IN THE CAPITAL, IT'S ONLY NATURAL FOR ME TO PROTECT THE PEOPLE.
IT'S NOT LIKE WE'RE SURE SEBAS-SAMA IS REPRESENTING JUSTICE...
THIS KID'S SO GREEN...
BUT...
SU (FWIP)
NOT THAT I THINK YOU NEED REIN-FORCEMENTS, BUT I'LL BE DAMNED IF—
ER...I MEAN...
...I'LL HELP OUT AS WELL.

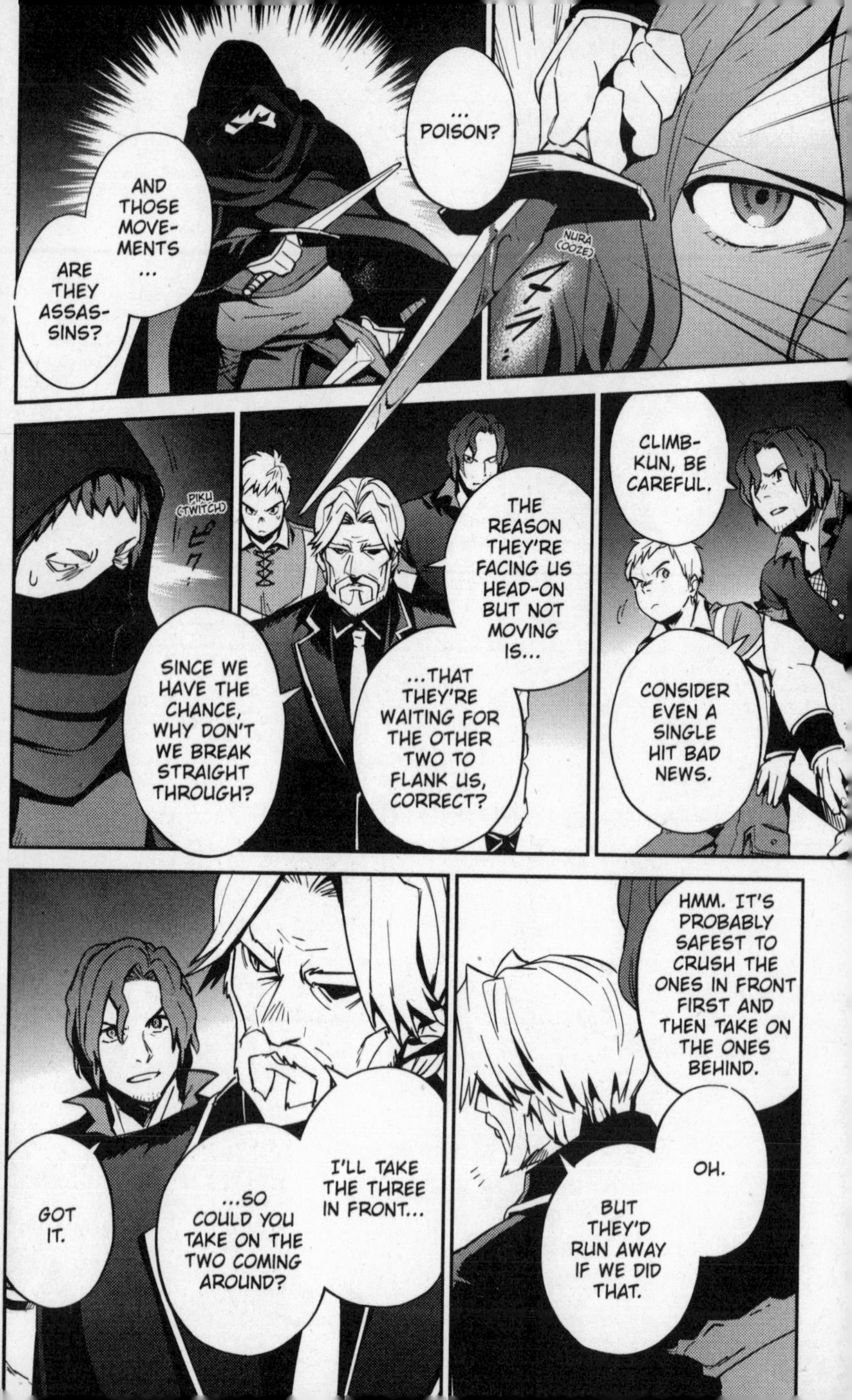
...POISON?
NURA (OOZE)
AND THOSE MOVE-MENTS...
ARE THEY ASSAS-SINS?
CLIMB-KUN, BE CAREFUL.
CONSIDER EVEN A SINGLE HIT BAD NEWS.
THE REASON THEY'RE FACING US HEAD-ON BUT NOT MOVING IS...
...THAT THEY'RE WAITING FOR THE OTHER TWO TO FLANK US, CORRECT?
SINCE WE HAVE THE CHANCE, WHY DON'T WE BREAK STRAIGHT THROUGH?
PIKU (TWITCH)
HMM. IT'S PROBABLY SAFEST TO CRUSH THE ONES IN FRONT FIRST AND THEN TAKE ON THE ONES BEHIND.
OH.
BUT THEY'D RUN AWAY IF WE DID THAT.
I'LL TAKE THE THREE IN FRONT...
...SO COULD YOU TAKE ON THE TWO COMING AROUND?
GOT IT.

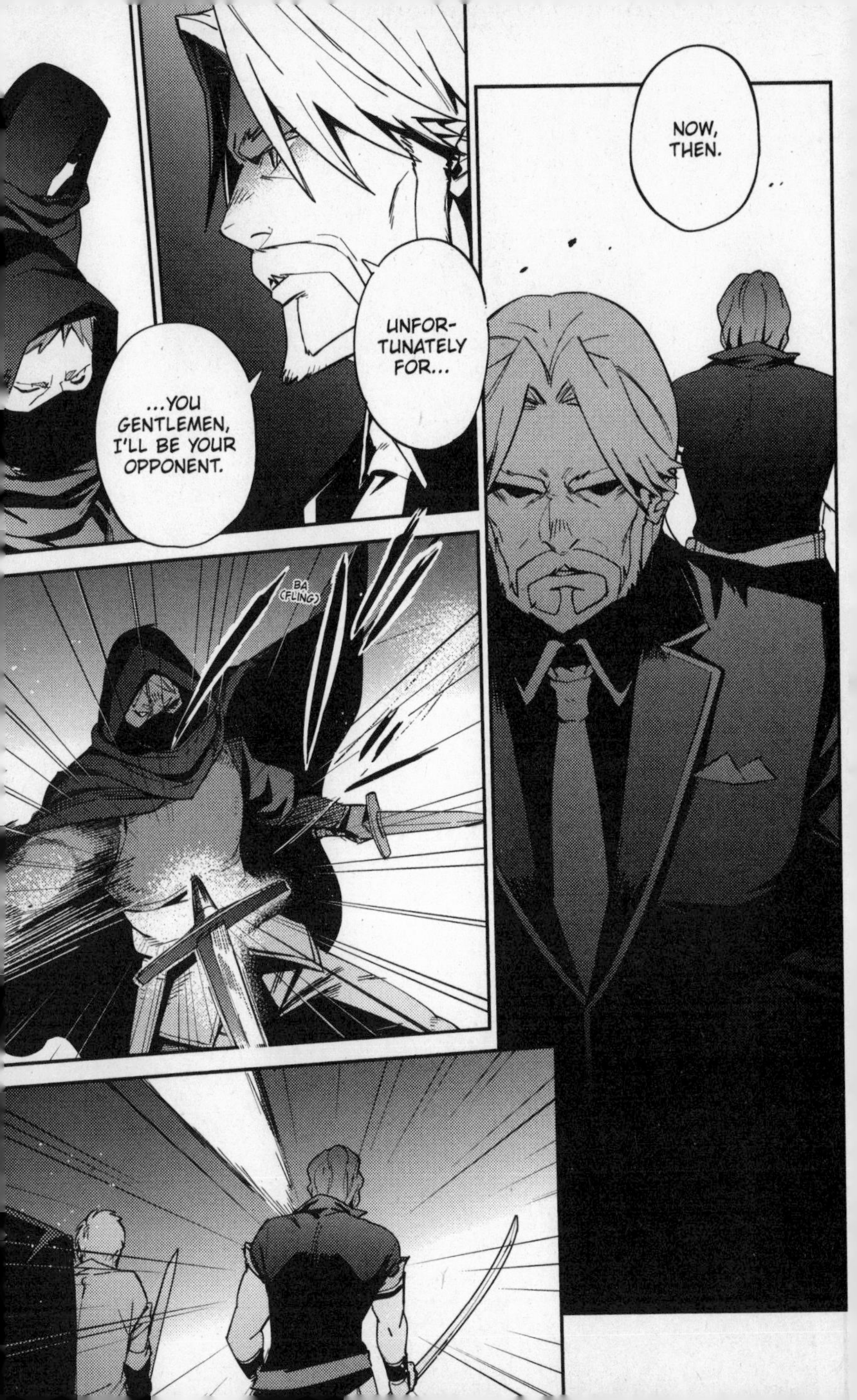
NOW, THEN.
UNFORTUNATELY FOR...
...YOU GENTLEMEN, I'LL BE YOUR OPPONENT.
BA (FLING)

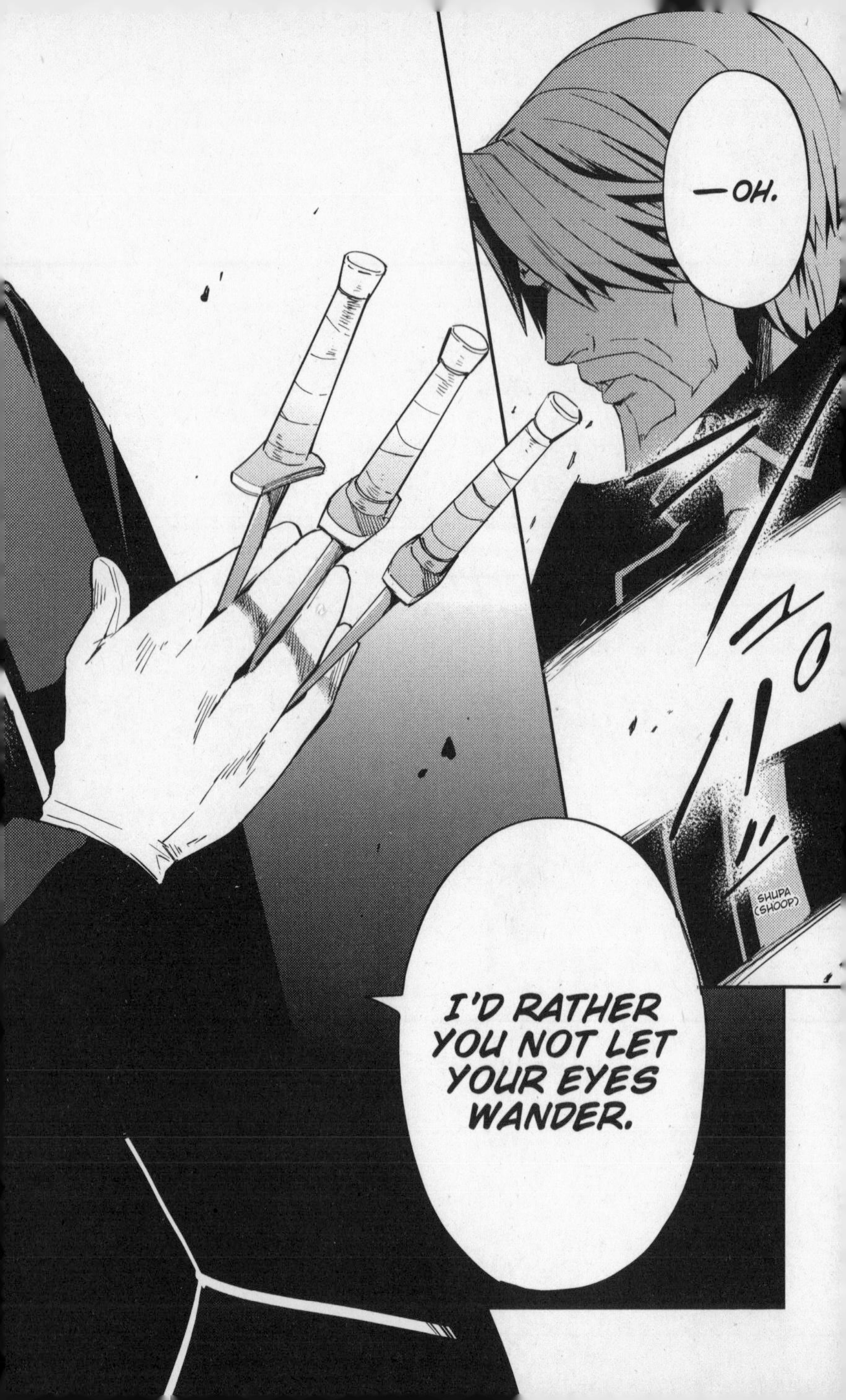
—OH.
SHUPA (SHOOP)
I'D RATHER YOU NOT LET YOUR EYES WANDER.

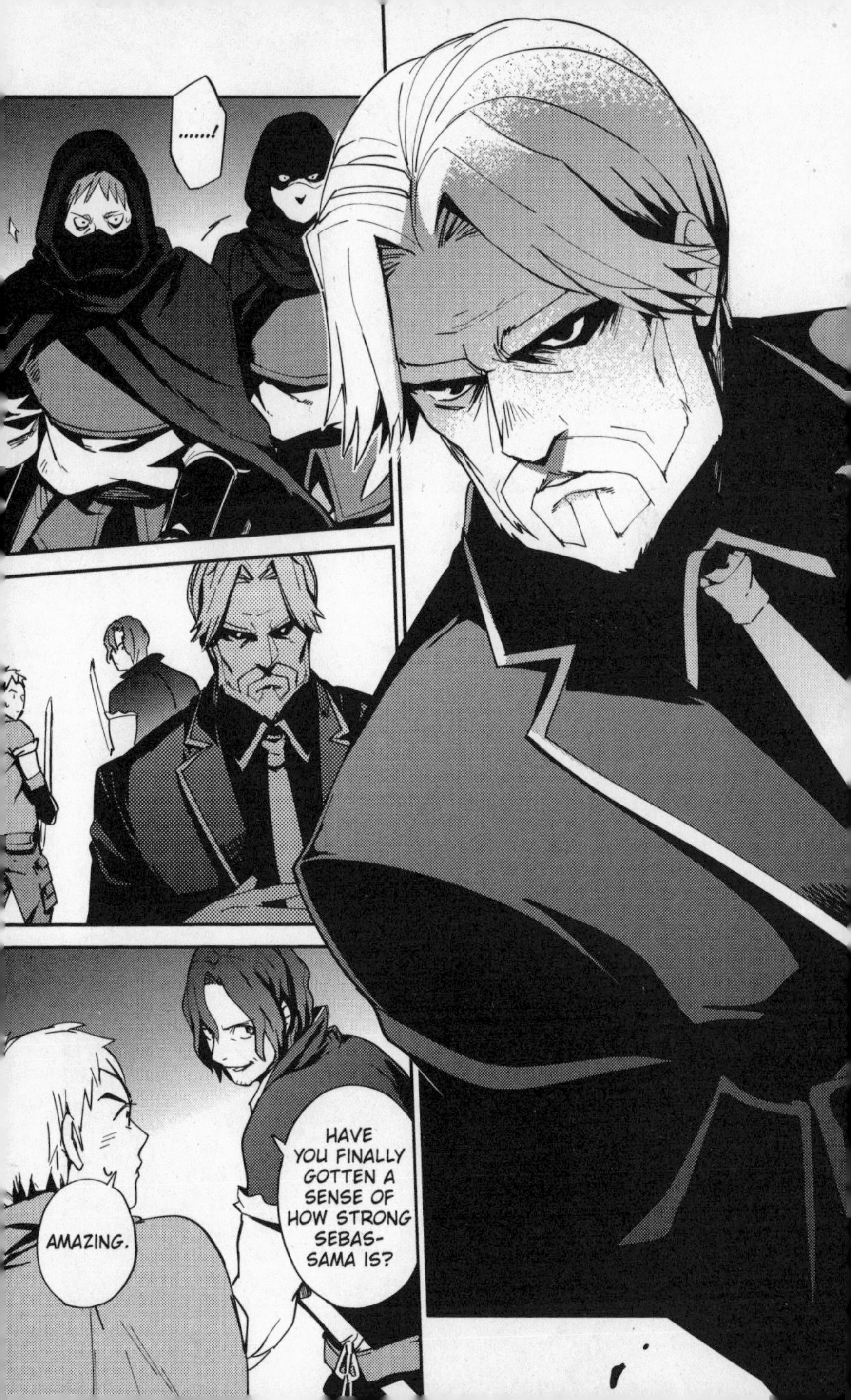
......!
HAVE YOU FINALLY GOTTEN A SENSE OF HOW STRONG SEBAS-SAMA IS?
AMAZING.

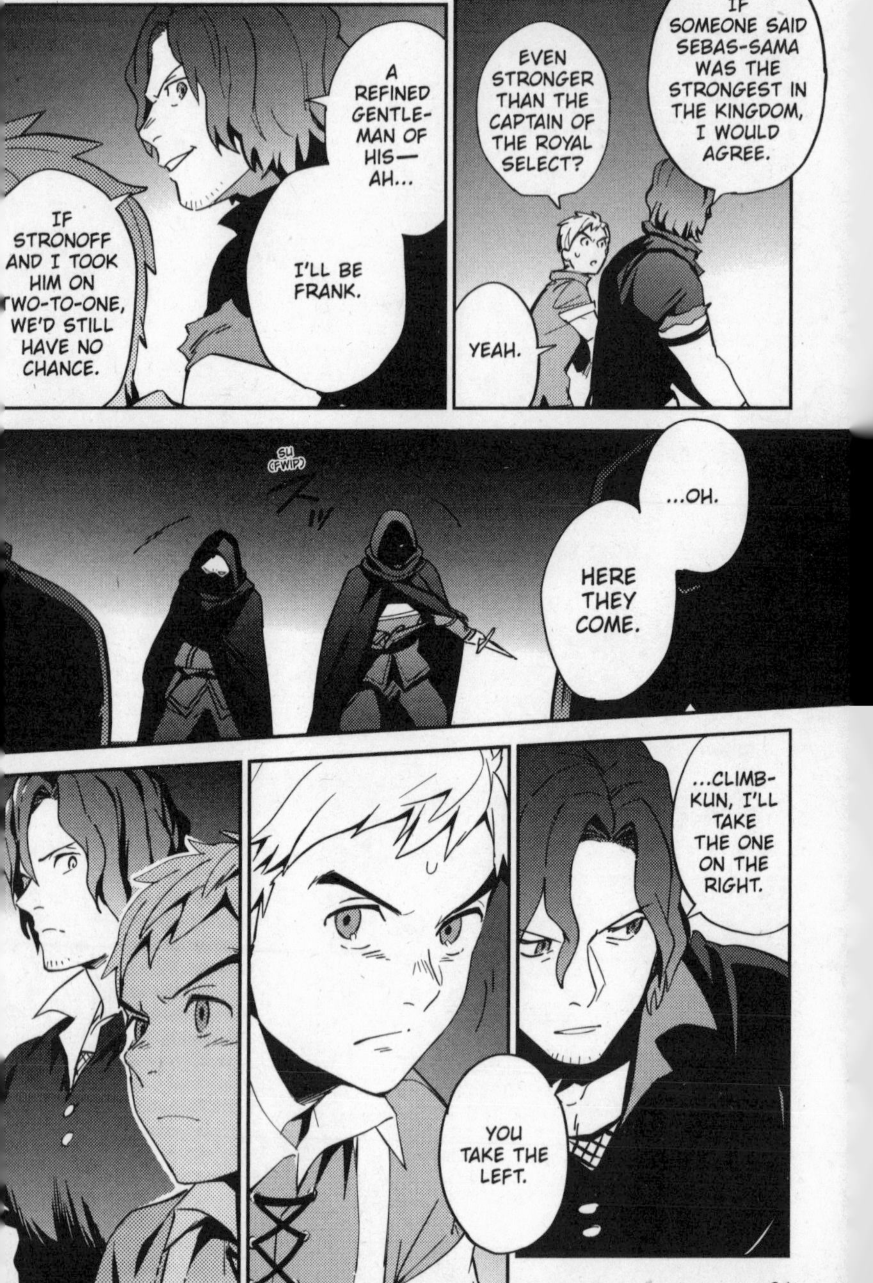
IF SOMEONE SAID SEBAS-SAMA WAS THE STRONGEST IN THE KINGDOM, I WOULD AGREE.
EVEN STRONGER THAN THE CAPTAIN OF THE ROYAL SELECT?
YEAH.
A REFINED GENTLE-MAN OF HIS— AH...
I'LL BE FRANK.
IF STRONOFF AND I TOOK HIM ON TWO-TO-ONE, WE'D STILL HAVE NO CHANCE.
...OH.
HERE THEY COME.
SU (FWIP)
...CLIMB-KUN, I'LL TAKE THE ONE ON THE RIGHT.
YOU TAKE THE LEFT.

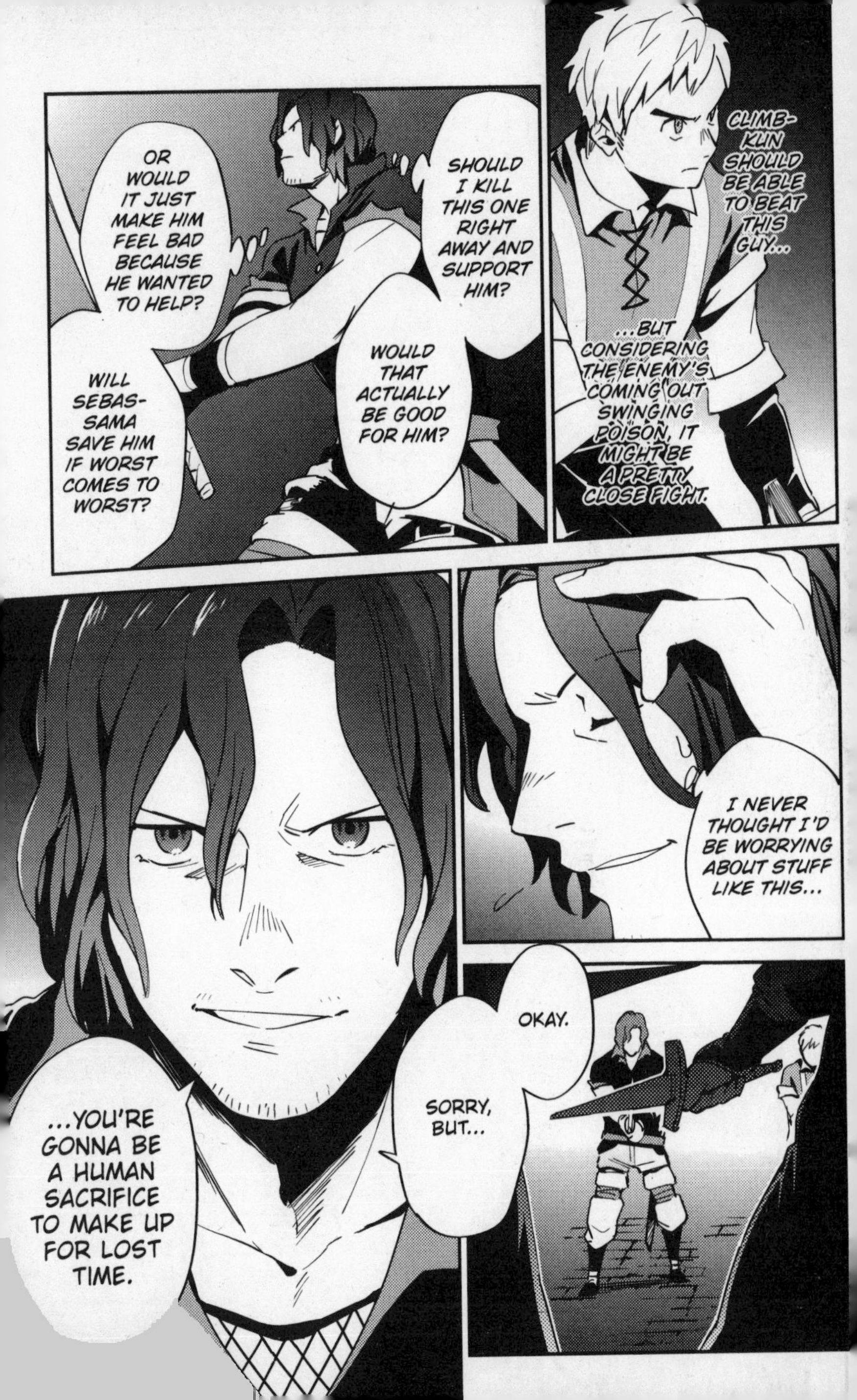
CLIMB-KUN SHOULD BE ABLE TO BEAT THIS GUY...
...BUT CONSIDERING THE ENEMY'S COMING OUT SWINGING POISON, IT MIGHT BE A PRETTY CLOSE FIGHT.
SHOULD I KILL THIS ONE RIGHT AWAY AND SUPPORT HIM?
WOULD THAT ACTUALLY BE GOOD FOR HIM?
OR WOULD IT JUST MAKE HIM FEEL BAD BECAUSE HE WANTED TO HELP?
WILL SEBAS-SAMA SAVE HIM IF WORST COMES TO WORST?
I NEVER THOUGHT I'D BE WORRYING ABOUT STUFF LIKE THIS...
OKAY.
SORRY, BUT...
...YOU'RE GONNA BE A HUMAN SACRIFICE TO MAKE UP FOR LOST TIME.

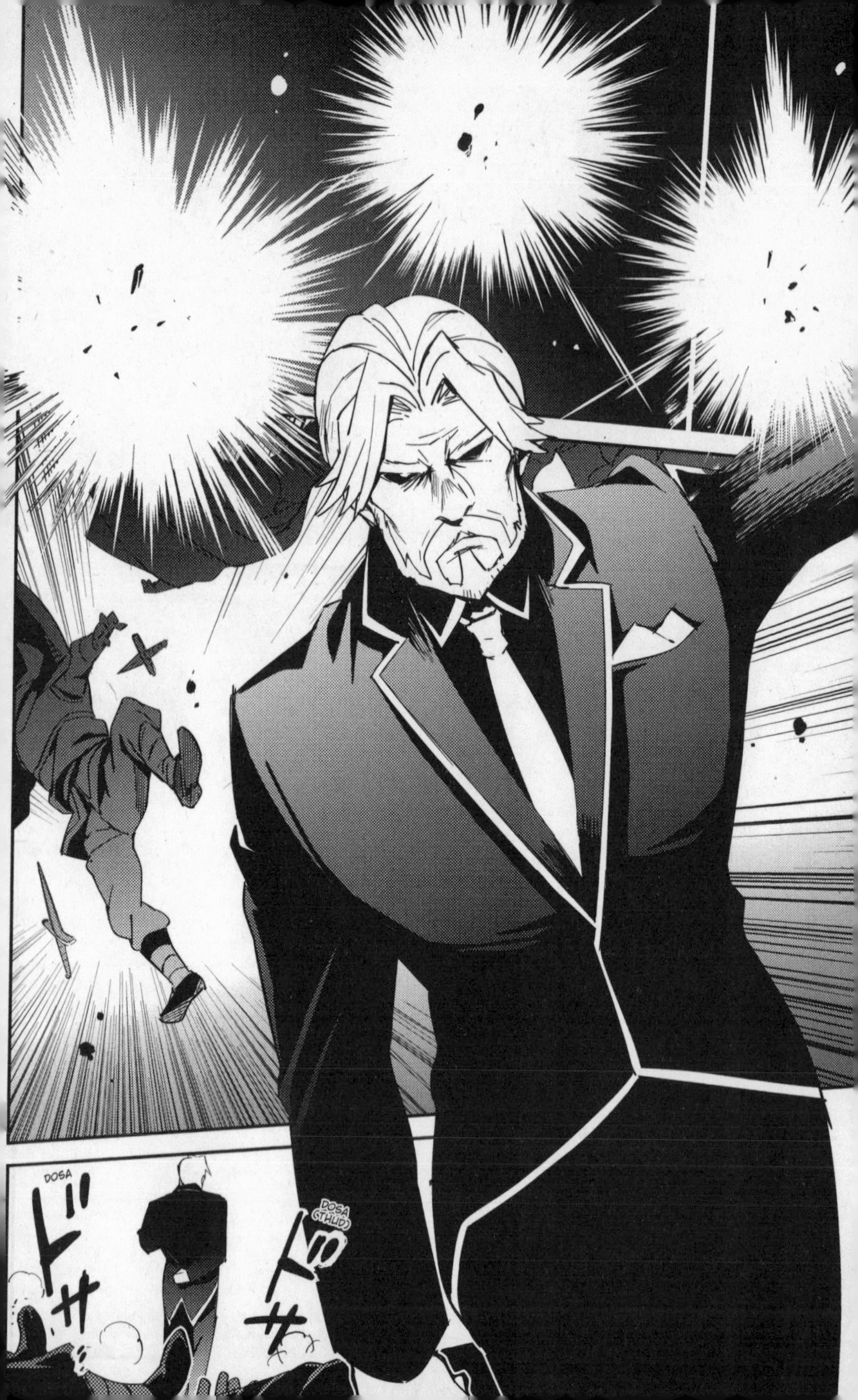
DOSA
(THUD)
DOSA

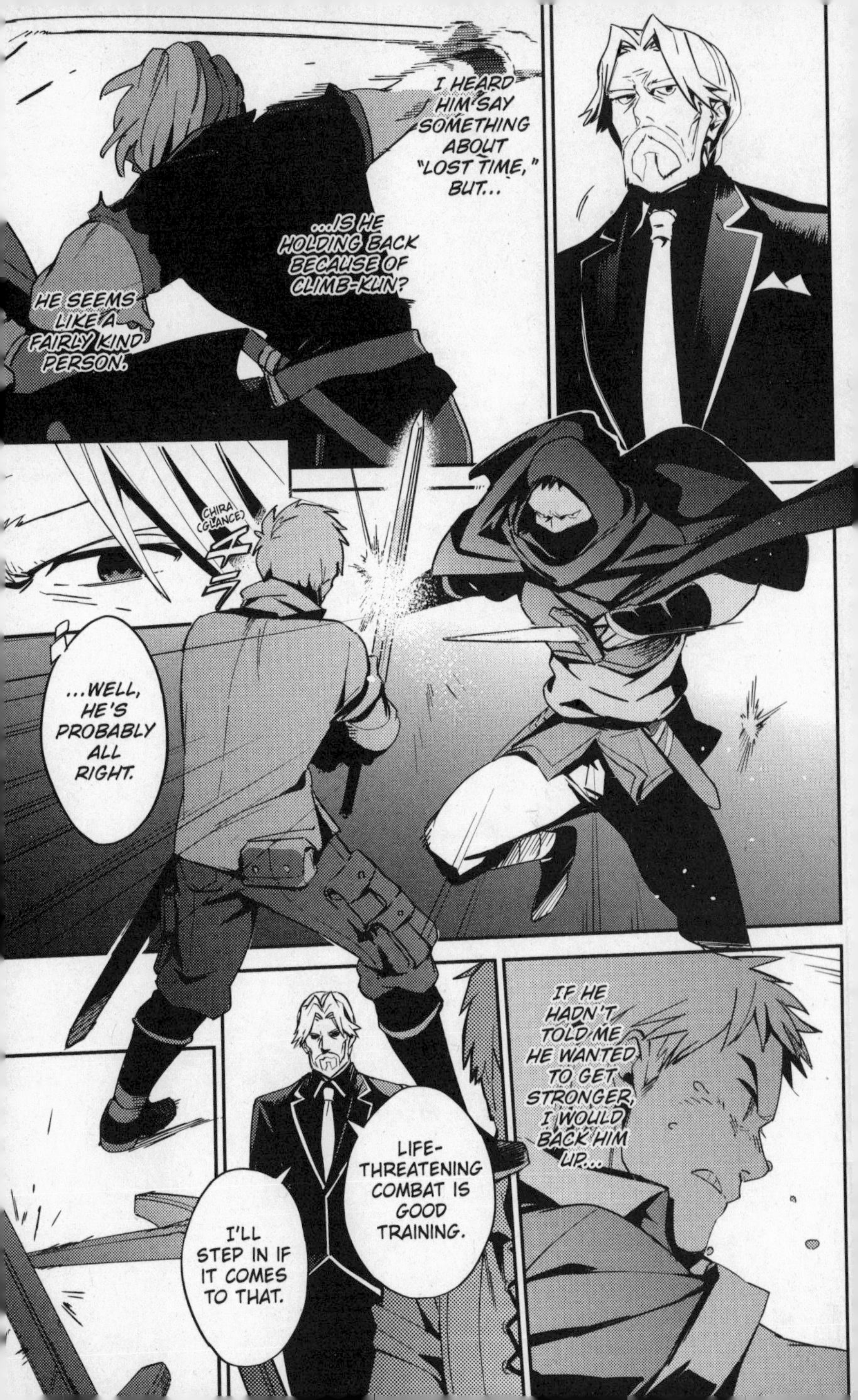
I HEARD HIM SAY SOMETHING ABOUT "LOST TIME," BUT...
...IS HE HOLDING BACK BECAUSE OF CLIMB-KUN?
HE SEEMS LIKE A FAIRLY KIND PERSON.
CHIRA (GLANCE)
...WELL, HE'S PROBABLY ALL RIGHT.
IF HE HADN'T TOLD ME HE WANTED TO GET STRONGER, I WOULD BACK HIM UP...
LIFE-THREATENING COMBAT IS GOOD TRAINING.
I'LL STEP IN IF IT COMES TO THAT.

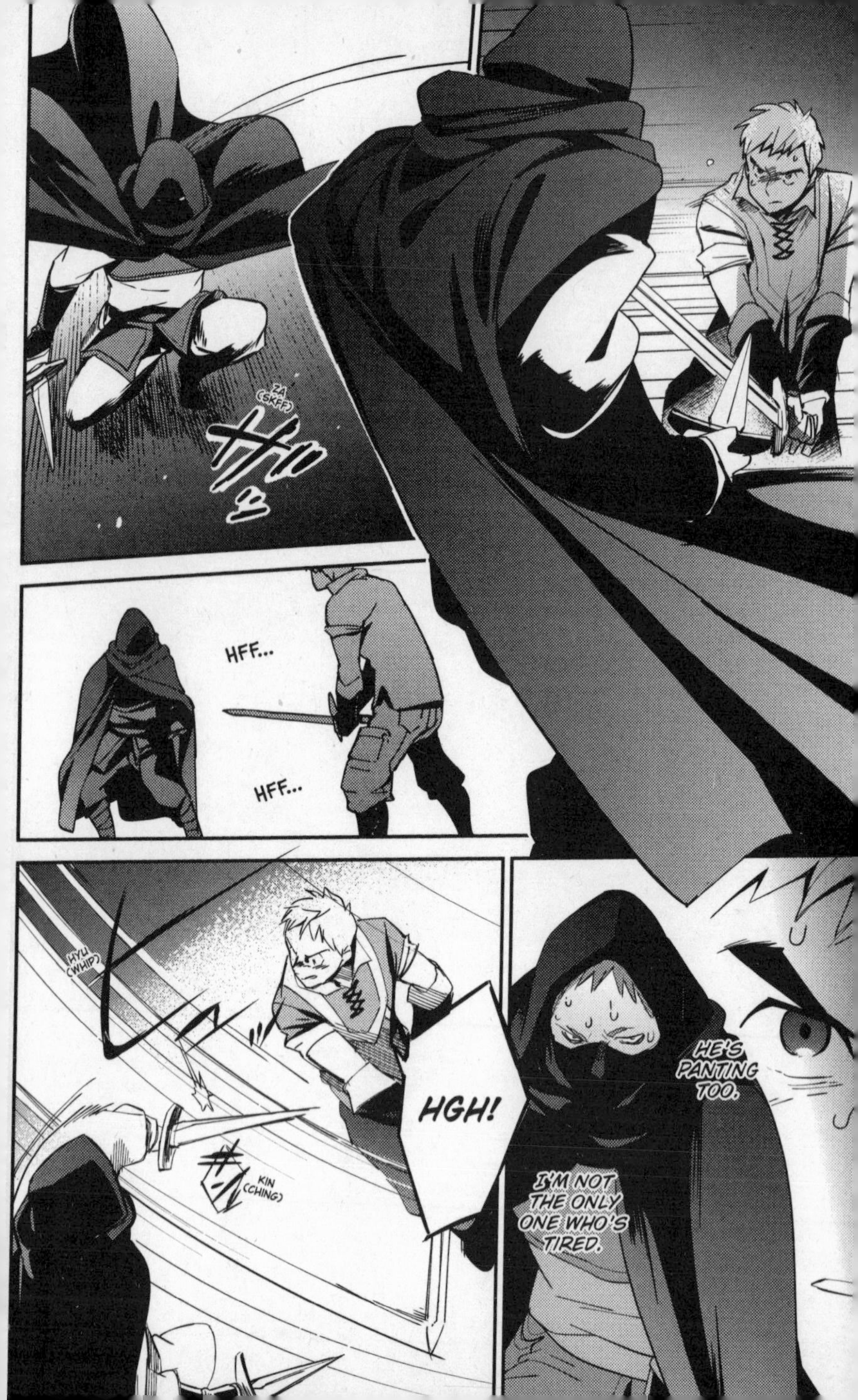
ZA (SKFF)
HFF...
HFF...
HE'S PANTING TOO.
I'M NOT THE ONLY ONE WHO'S TIRED.
HGH!
HYU (WHIP)
KIN (CHING)

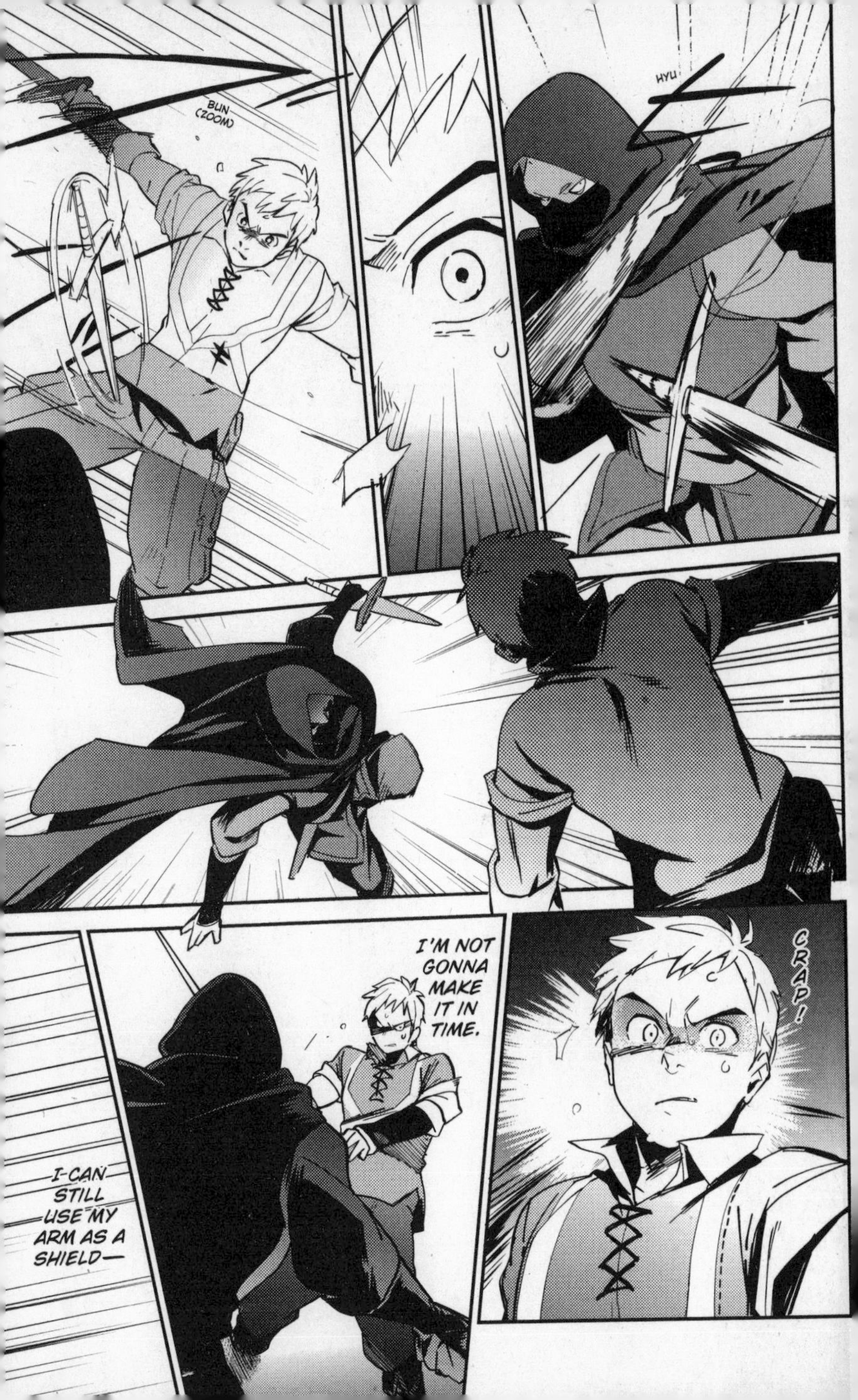
HYU
BUN (ZOOM)
CRAP!
I'M NOT GONNA MAKE IT IN TIME.
I-CAN STILL USE MY ARM AS A SHIELD—

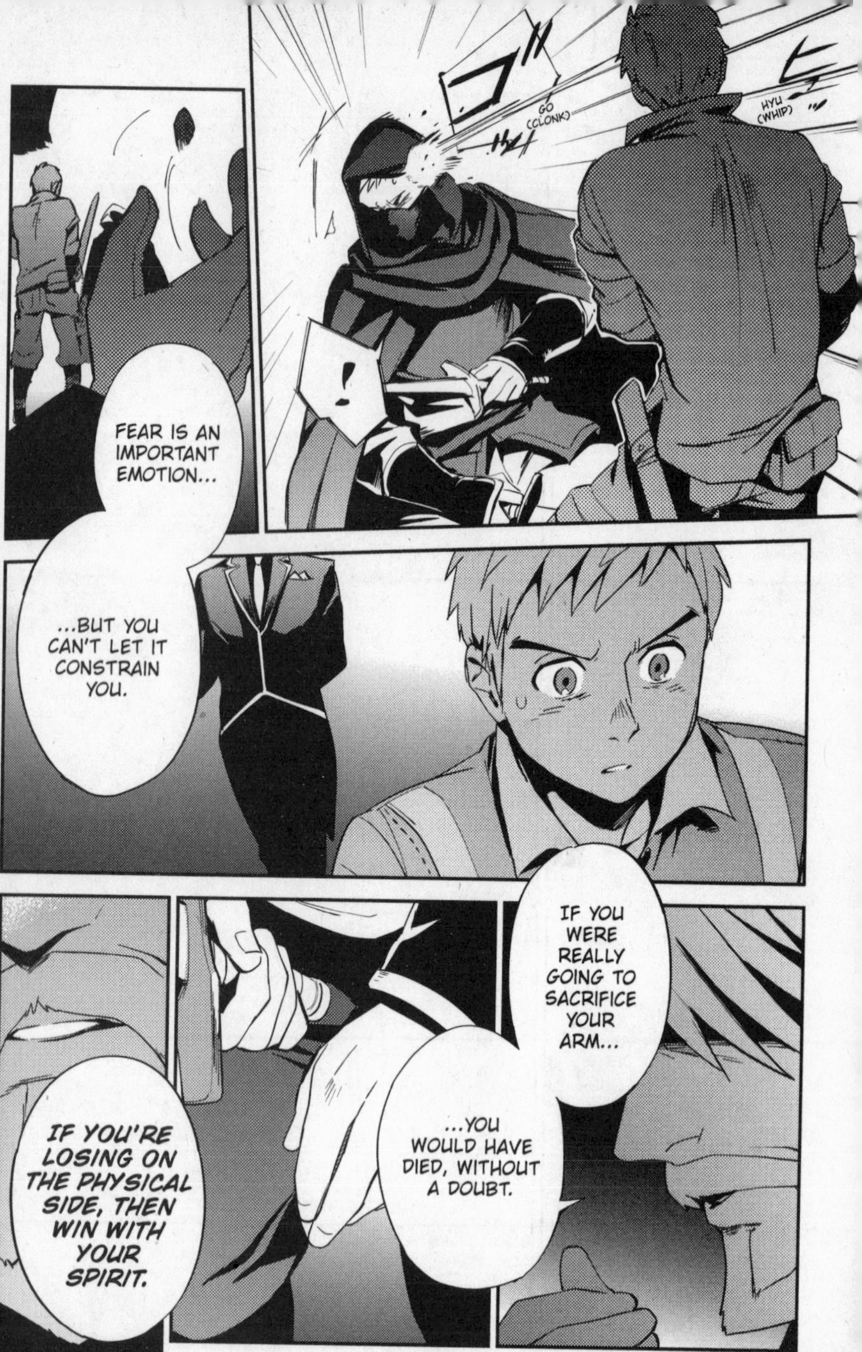
HYU (WHIP)
GO (CLONK)
!
FEAR IS AN IMPORTANT EMOTION...
...BUT YOU CAN'T LET IT CONSTRAIN YOU.
IF YOU WERE REALLY GOING TO SACRIFICE YOUR ARM...
...YOU WOULD HAVE DIED, WITHOUT A DOUBT.
IF YOU'RE LOSING ON THE PHYSICAL SIDE, THEN WIN WITH YOUR SPIRIT.

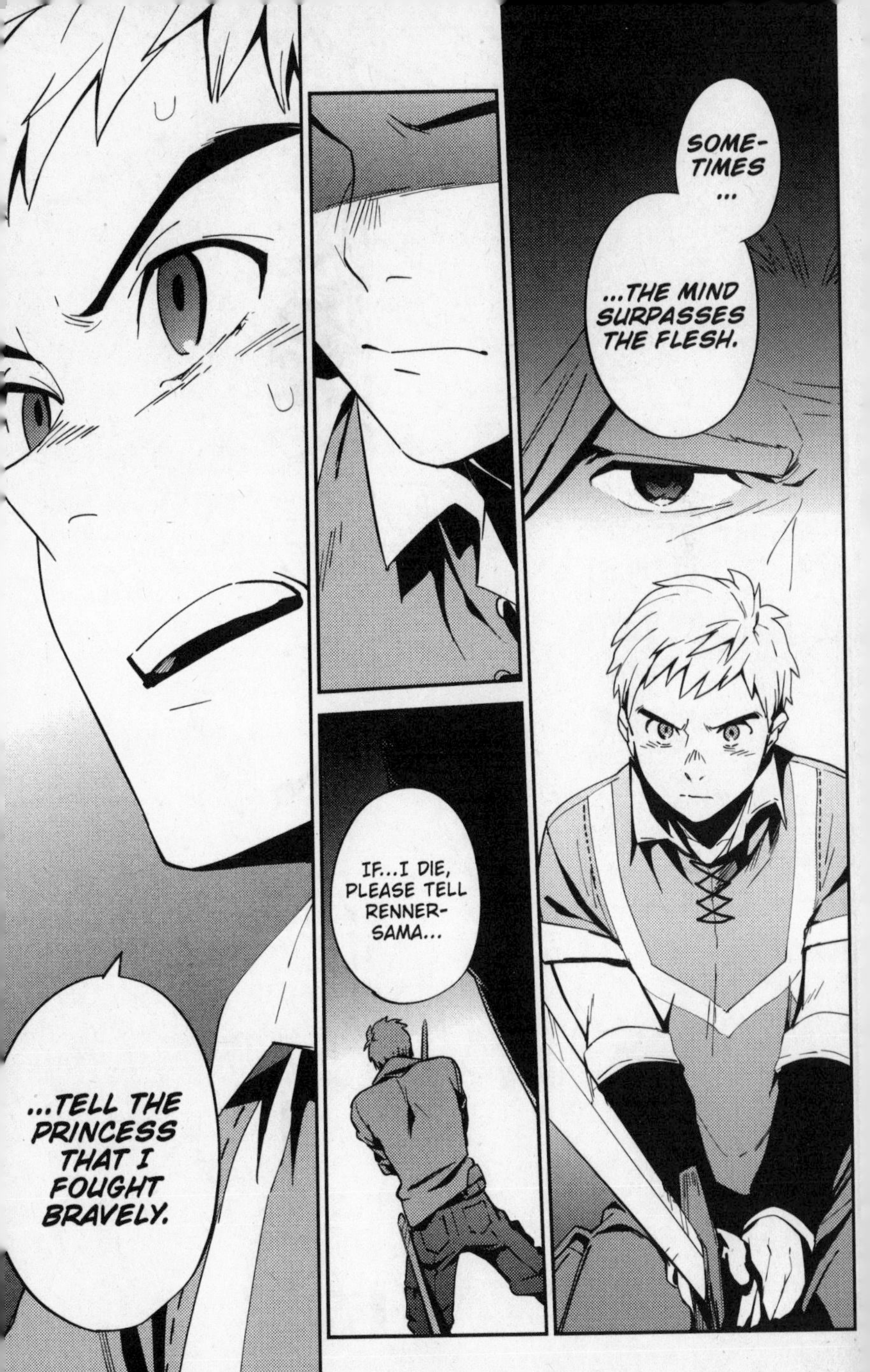
SOME-TIMES...
...THE MIND SURPASSES THE FLESH.
IF...I DIE, PLEASE TELL RENNER-SAMA...
...TELL THE PRINCESS THAT I FOUGHT BRAVELY.

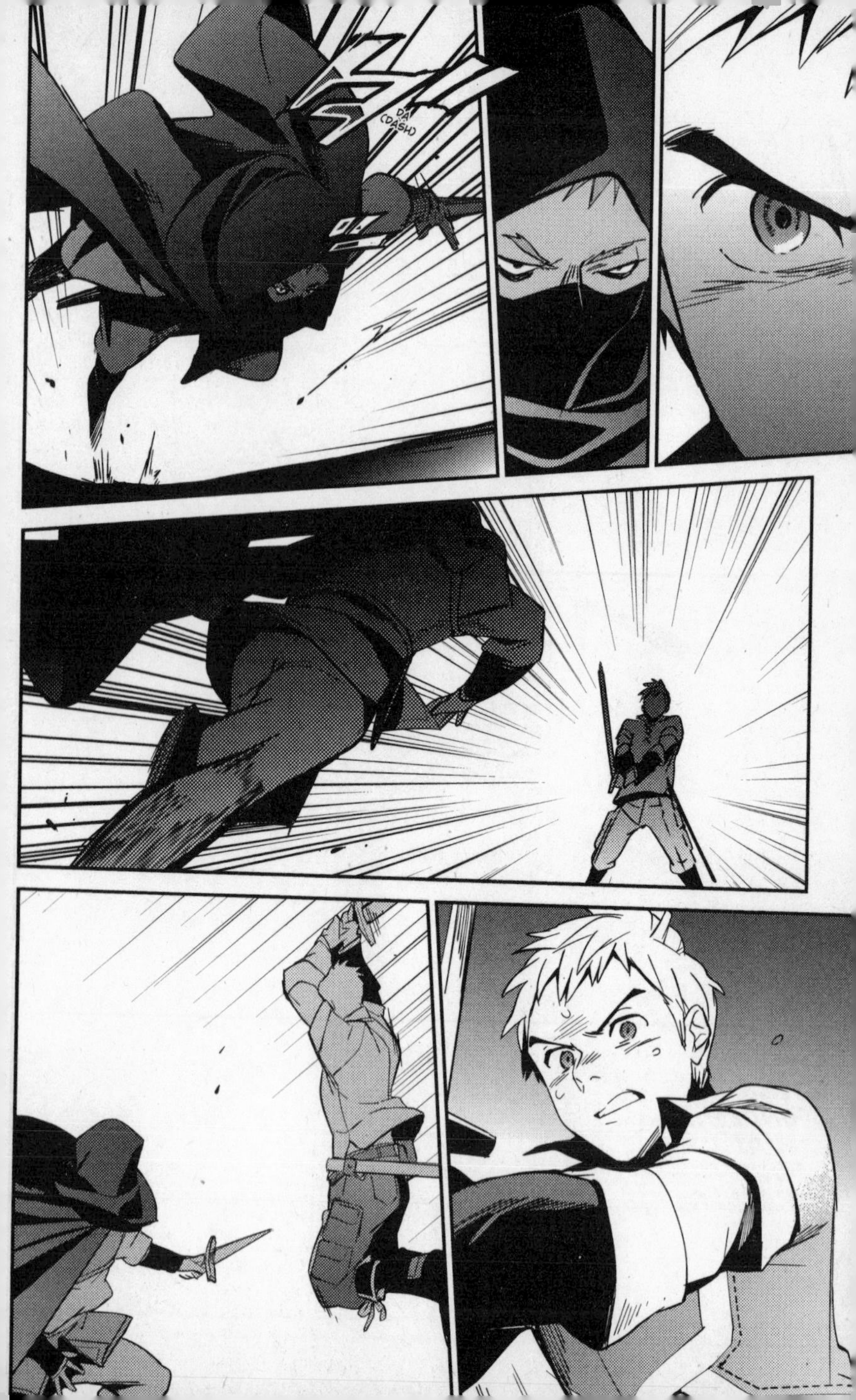
DA
(DASH)

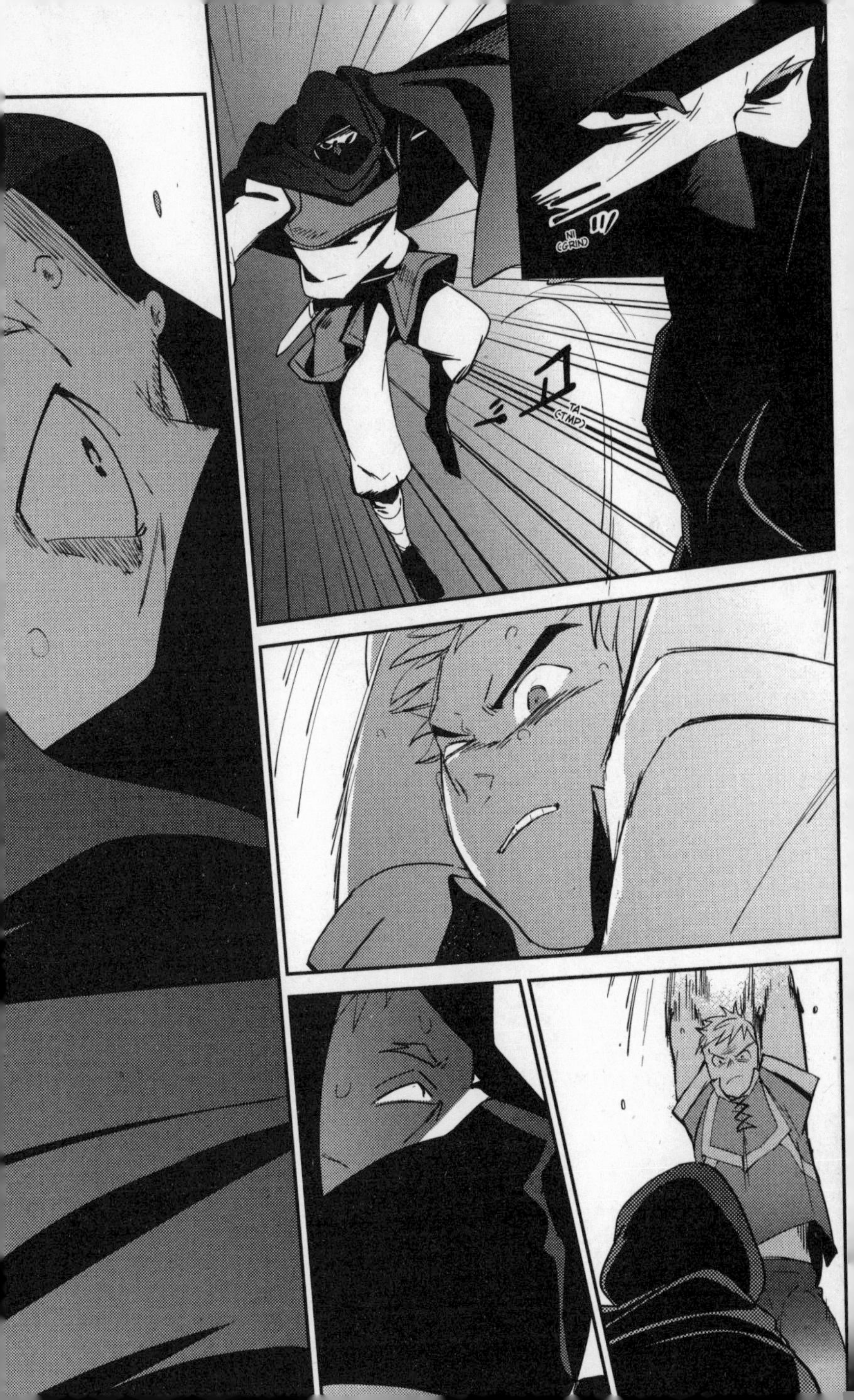
NI (GRIN)
TA (TMP)

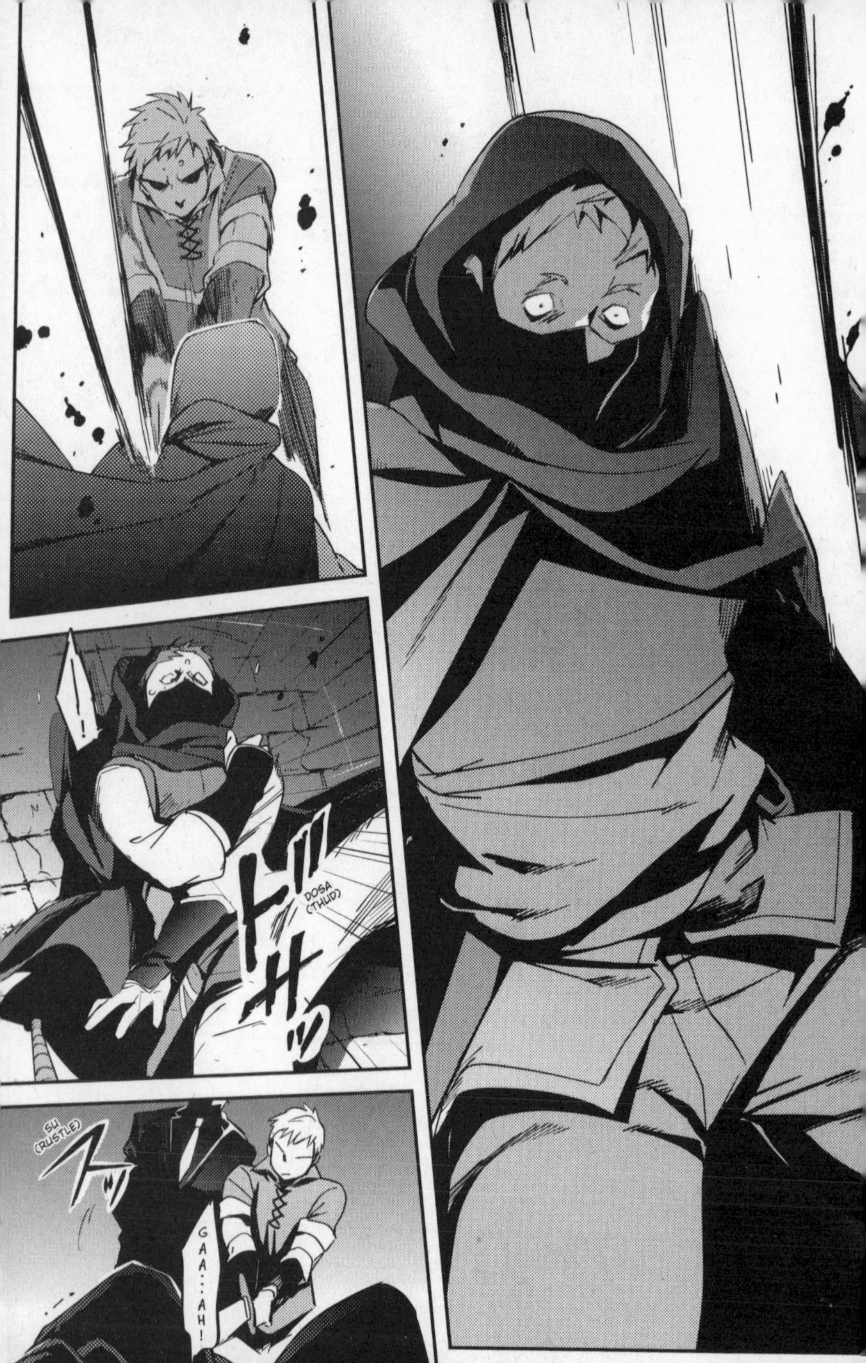
DOSA (THUD)
SU (RUSTLE)
GAA...AH!

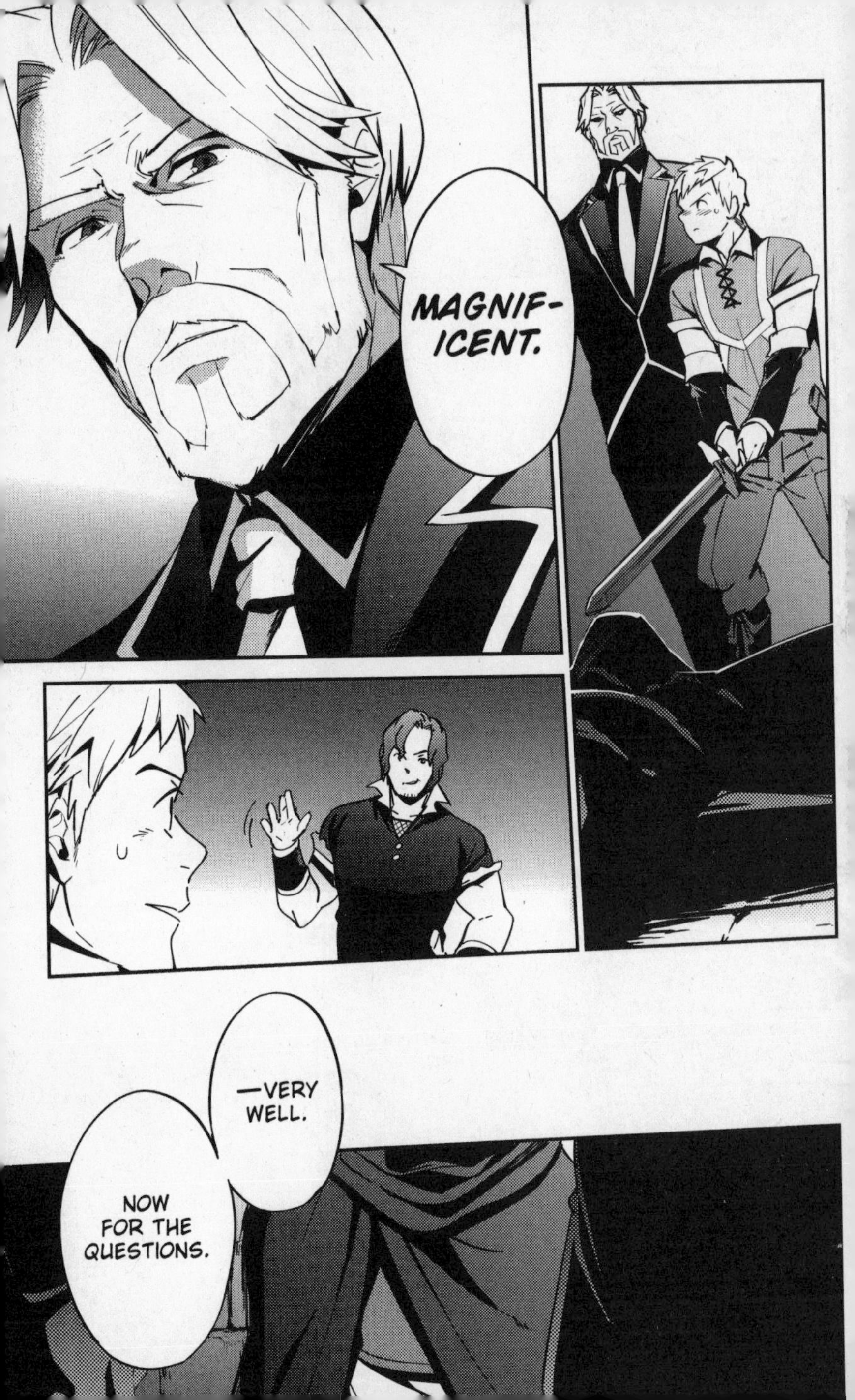
MAGNIF-
ICENT.
—VERY
WELL.
NOW
FOR THE
QUESTIONS.

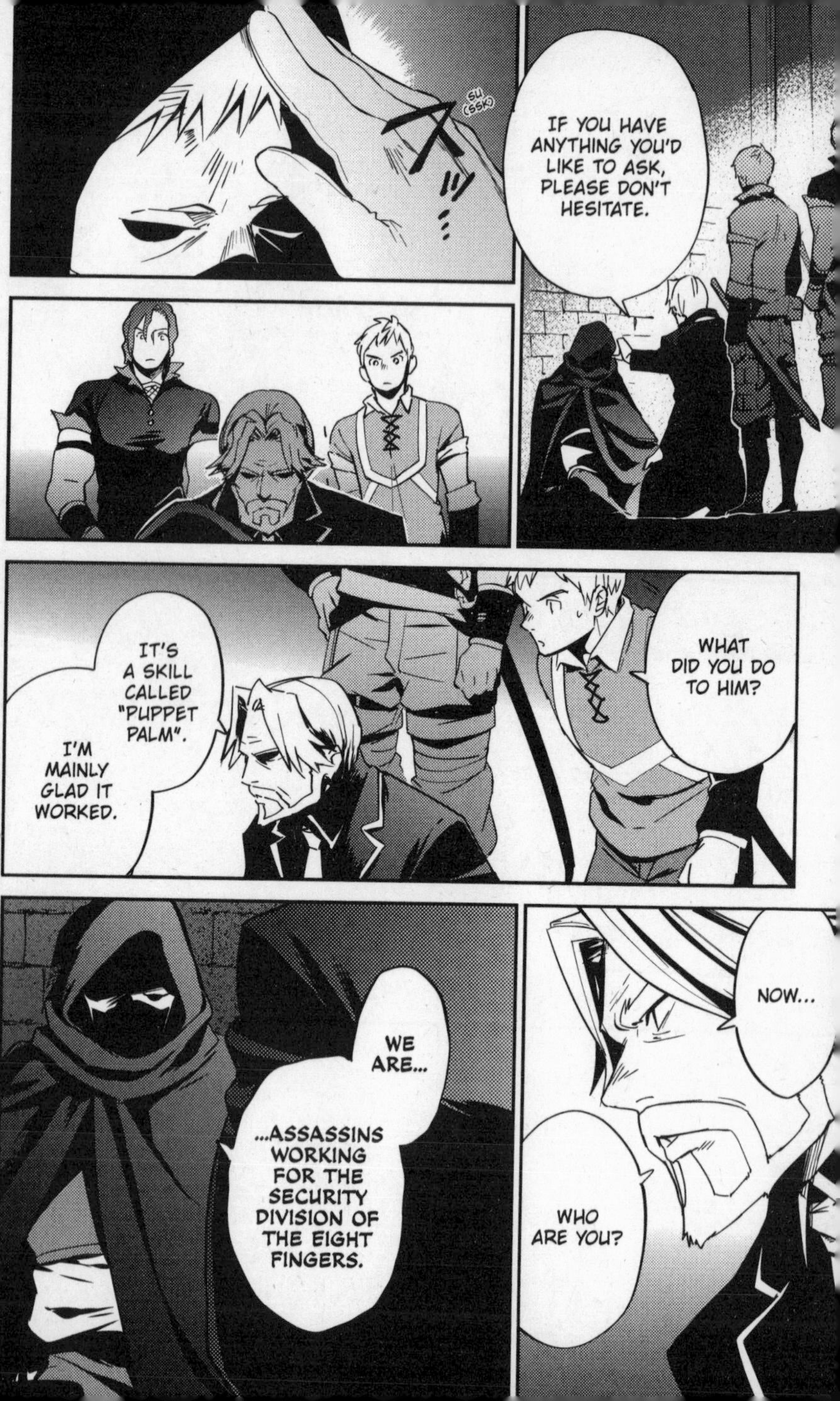
IF YOU HAVE ANYTHING YOU'D LIKE TO ASK, PLEASE DON'T HESITATE.
SU (SSK)
WHAT DID YOU DO TO HIM?
IT'S A SKILL CALLED "PUPPET PALM".
I'M MAINLY GLAD IT WORKED.
NOW...
WHO ARE YOU?
WE ARE...
...ASSASSINS WORKING FOR THE SECURITY DIVISION OF THE EIGHT FINGERS.

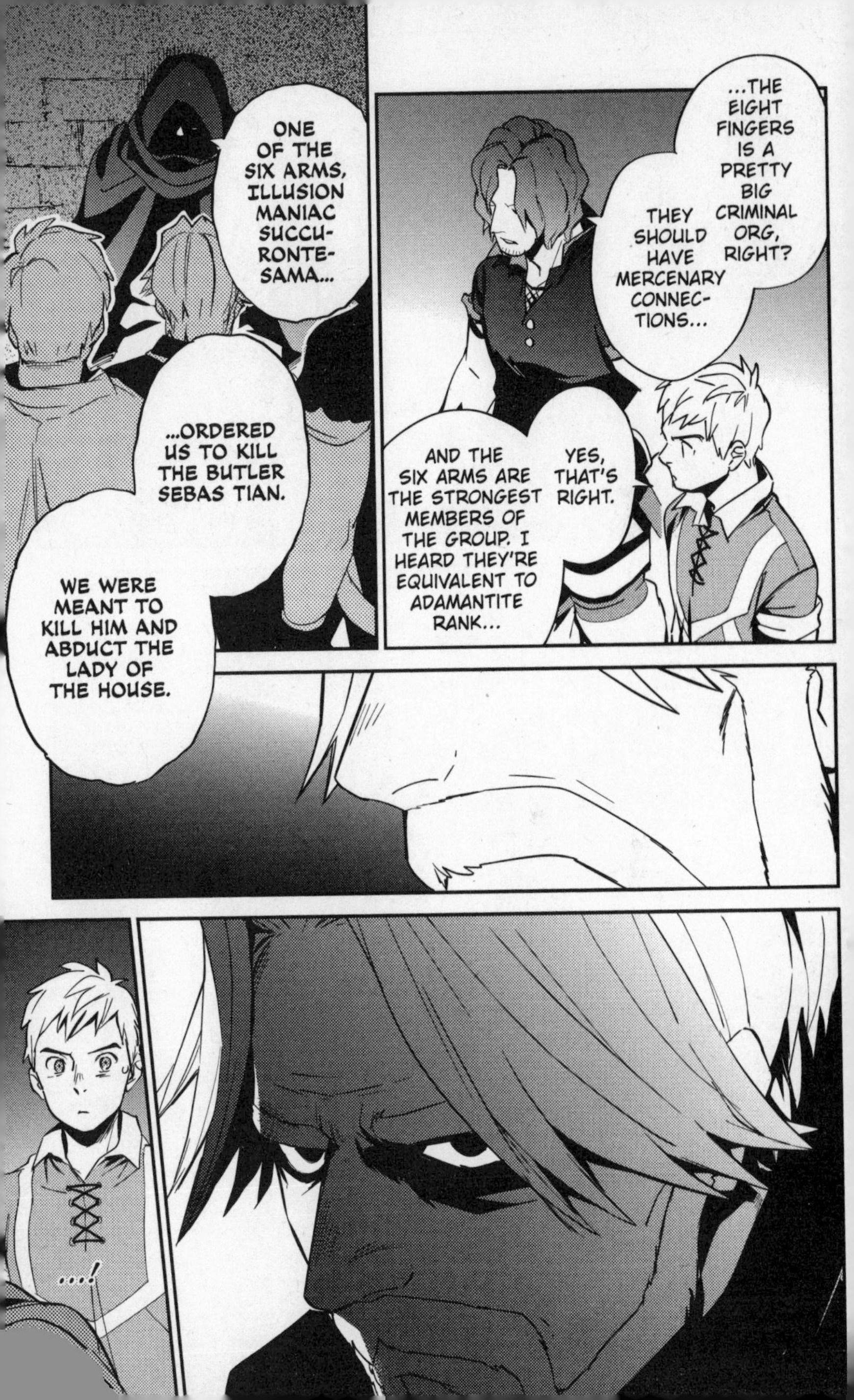
...THE EIGHT FINGERS IS A PRETTY BIG CRIMINAL ORG, RIGHT?
THEY SHOULD HAVE MERCENARY CONNECTIONS...
YES, THAT'S RIGHT.
AND THE SIX ARMS ARE THE STRONGEST MEMBERS OF THE GROUP. I HEARD THEY'RE EQUIVALENT TO ADAMANTITE RANK...
ONE OF THE SIX ARMS, ILLUSION MANIAC SUCCURONTE-SAMA...
...ORDERED US TO KILL THE BUTLER SEBAS TIAN.
WE WERE MEANT TO KILL HIM AND ABDUCT THE LADY OF THE HOUSE.
...!

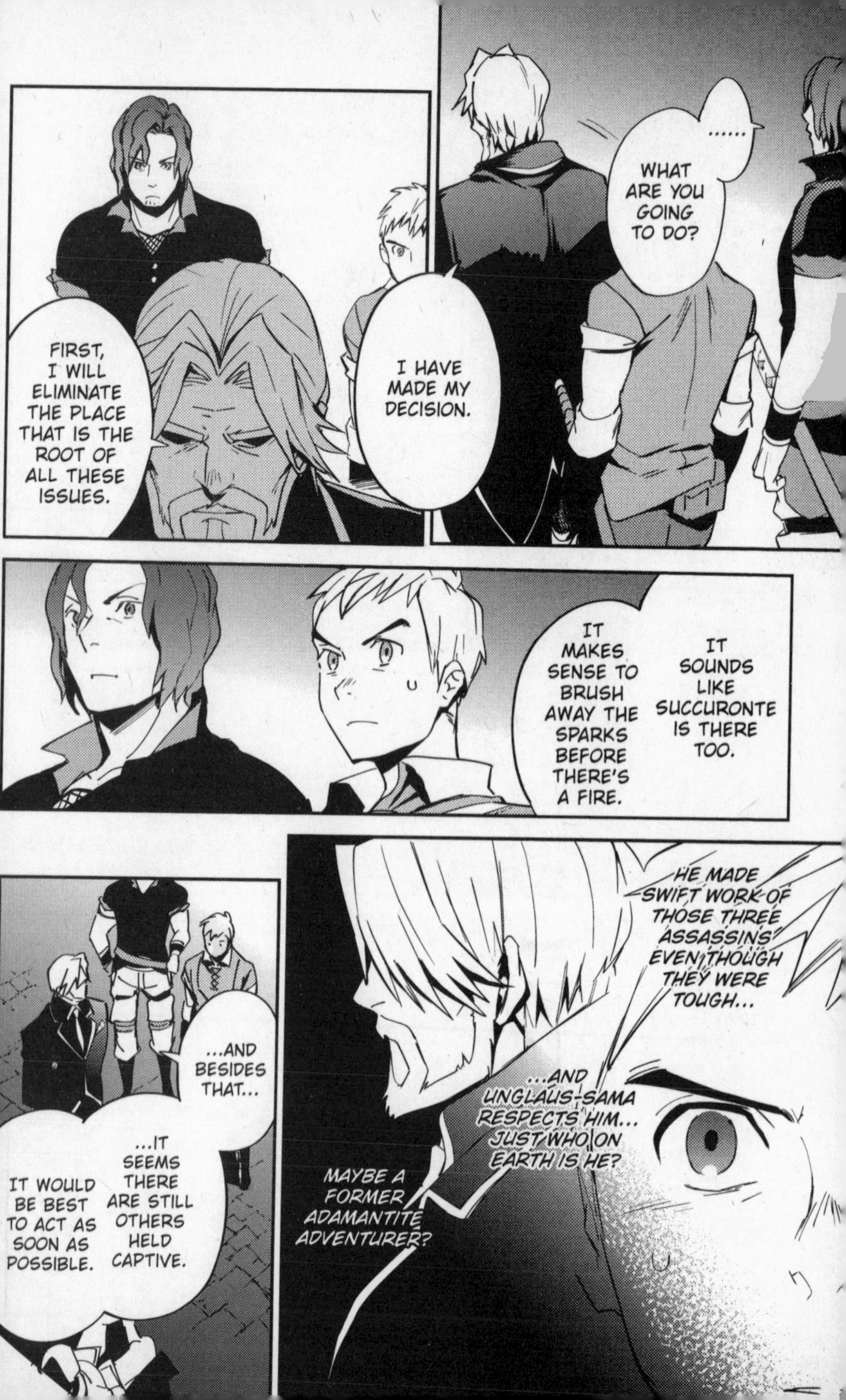
......
WHAT ARE YOU GOING TO DO?
I HAVE MADE MY DECISION.
FIRST, I WILL ELIMINATE THE PLACE THAT IS THE ROOT OF ALL THESE ISSUES.
IT SOUNDS LIKE SUCCURONTE IS THERE TOO.
IT MAKES SENSE TO BRUSH AWAY THE SPARKS BEFORE THERE'S A FIRE.
HE MADE SWIFT WORK OF THOSE THREE ASSASSINS EVEN THOUGH THEY WERE TOUGH...
...AND UNGLAUS-SAMA RESPECTS HIM... JUST WHO ON EARTH IS HE?
MAYBE A FORMER ADAMANTITE ADVENTURER?
...AND BESIDES THAT...
...IT SEEMS THERE ARE STILL OTHERS HELD CAPTIVE.
IT WOULD BE BEST TO ACT AS SOON AS POSSIBLE.

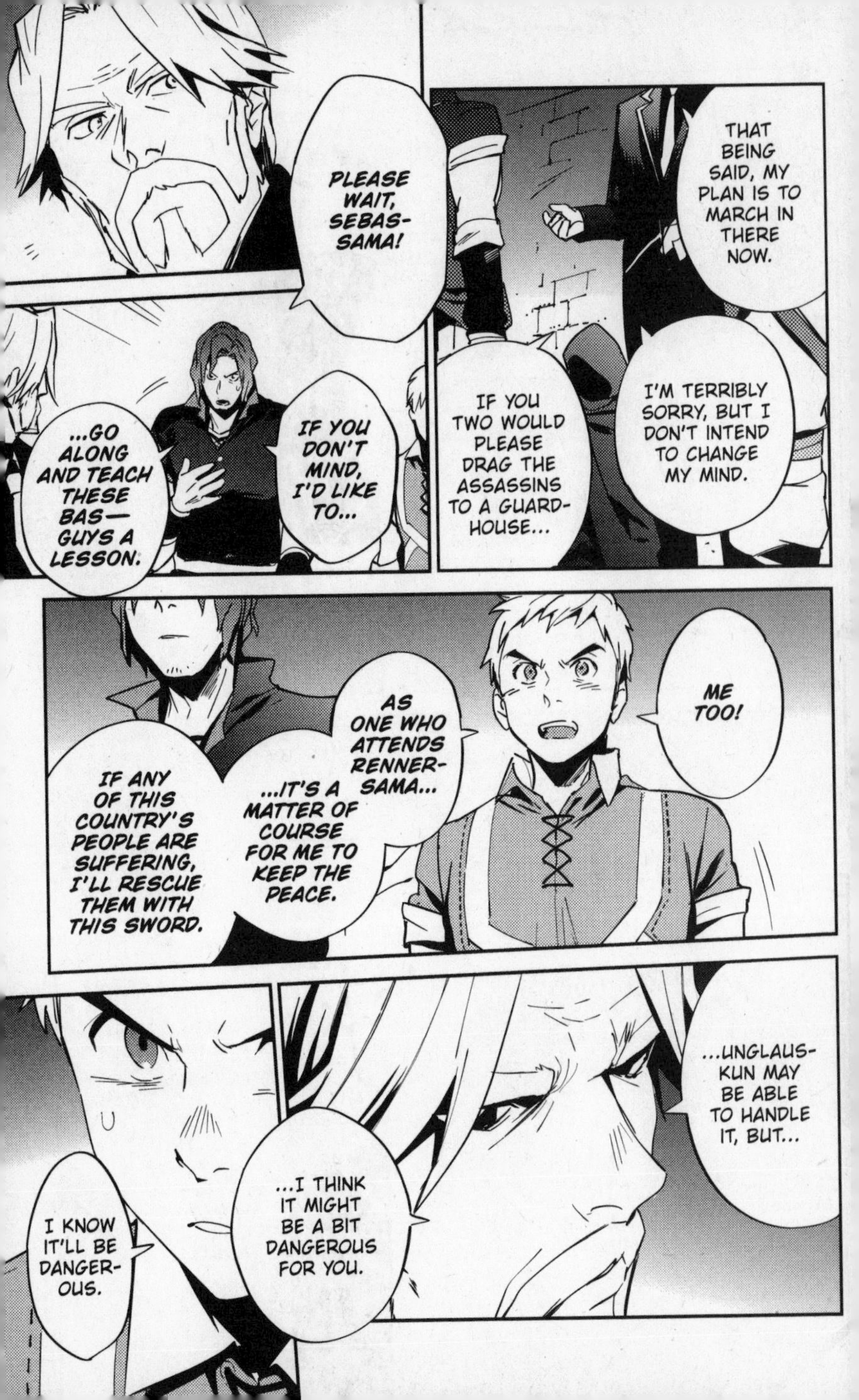
THAT BEING SAID, MY PLAN IS TO MARCH IN THERE NOW.
PLEASE WAIT, SEBAS-SAMA!
I'M TERRIBLY SORRY, BUT I DON'T INTEND TO CHANGE MY MIND.
IF YOU TWO WOULD PLEASE DRAG THE ASSASSINS TO A GUARD-HOUSE...
IF YOU DON'T MIND, I'D LIKE TO...
...GO ALONG AND TEACH THESE BAS—GUYS A LESSON.
ME TOO!
AS ONE WHO ATTENDS RENNER-SAMA...
...IT'S A MATTER OF COURSE FOR ME TO KEEP THE PEACE.
IF ANY OF THIS COUNTRY'S PEOPLE ARE SUFFERING, I'LL RESCUE THEM WITH THIS SWORD.
...UNGLAUS-KUN MAY BE ABLE TO HANDLE IT, BUT...
...I THINK IT MIGHT BE A BIT DANGEROUS FOR YOU.
I KNOW IT'LL BE DANGER-OUS.

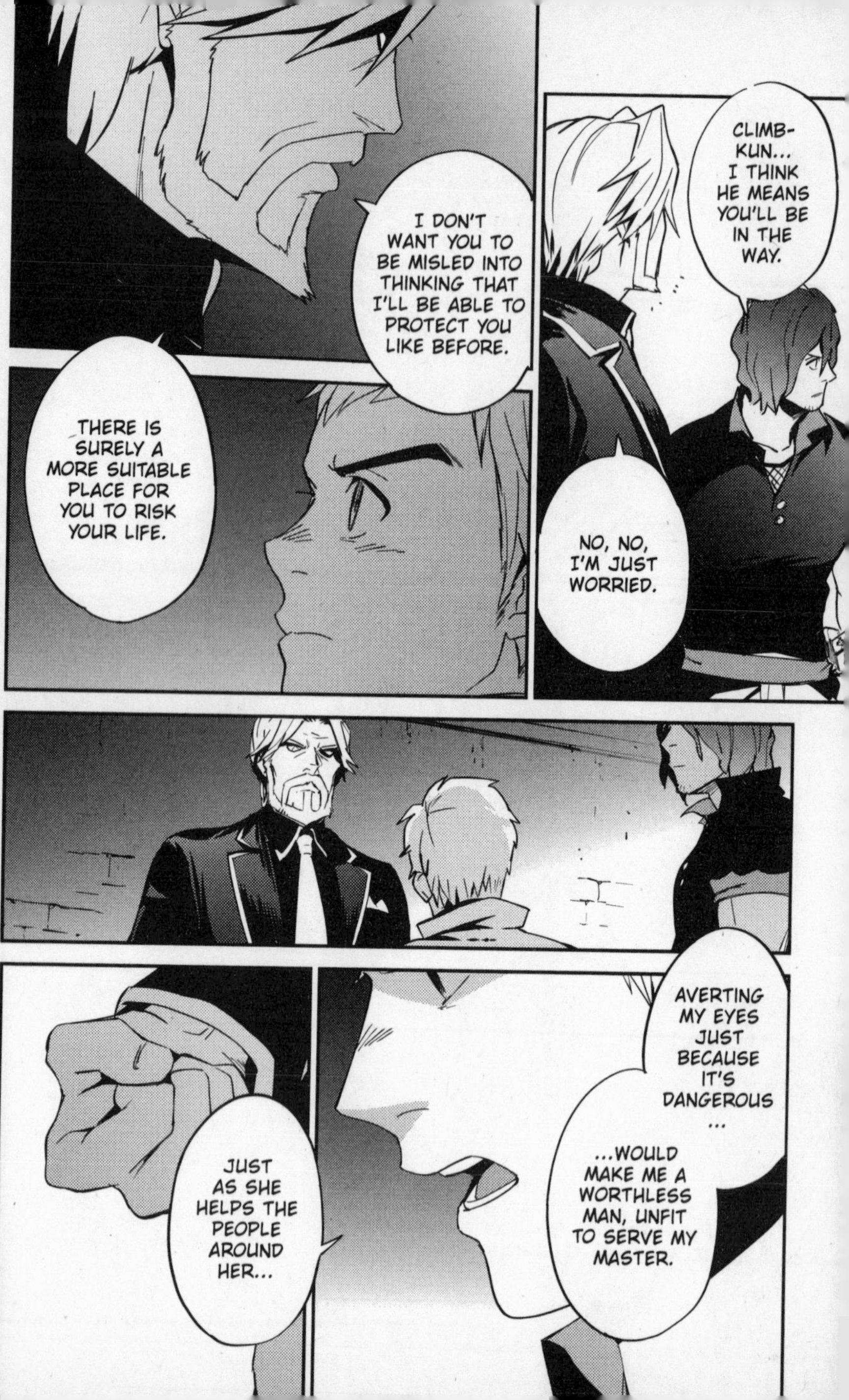
I DON'T WANT YOU TO BE MISLED INTO THINKING THAT I'LL BE ABLE TO PROTECT YOU LIKE BEFORE.
CLIMB-KUN... I THINK HE MEANS YOU'LL BE IN THE WAY.
NO, NO, I'M JUST WORRIED.
THERE IS SURELY A MORE SUITABLE PLACE FOR YOU TO RISK YOUR LIFE.
AVERTING MY EYES JUST BECAUSE IT'S DANGEROUS...
...WOULD MAKE ME A WORTHLESS MAN, UNFIT TO SERVE MY MASTER.
JUST AS SHE HELPS THE PEOPLE AROUND HER...

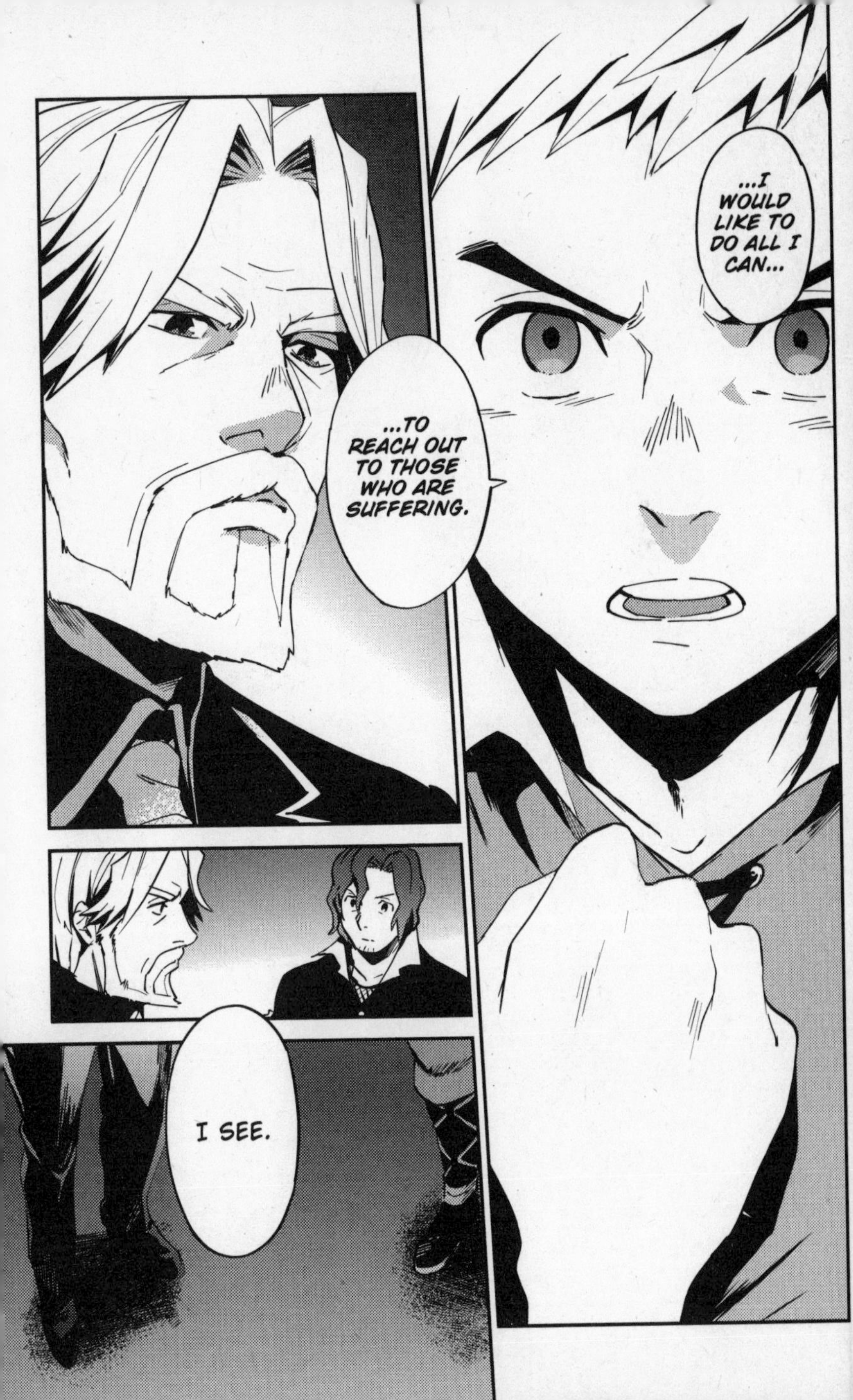
...I WOULD LIKE TO DO ALL I CAN...
...TO REACH OUT TO THOSE WHO ARE SUFFERING.
I SEE.

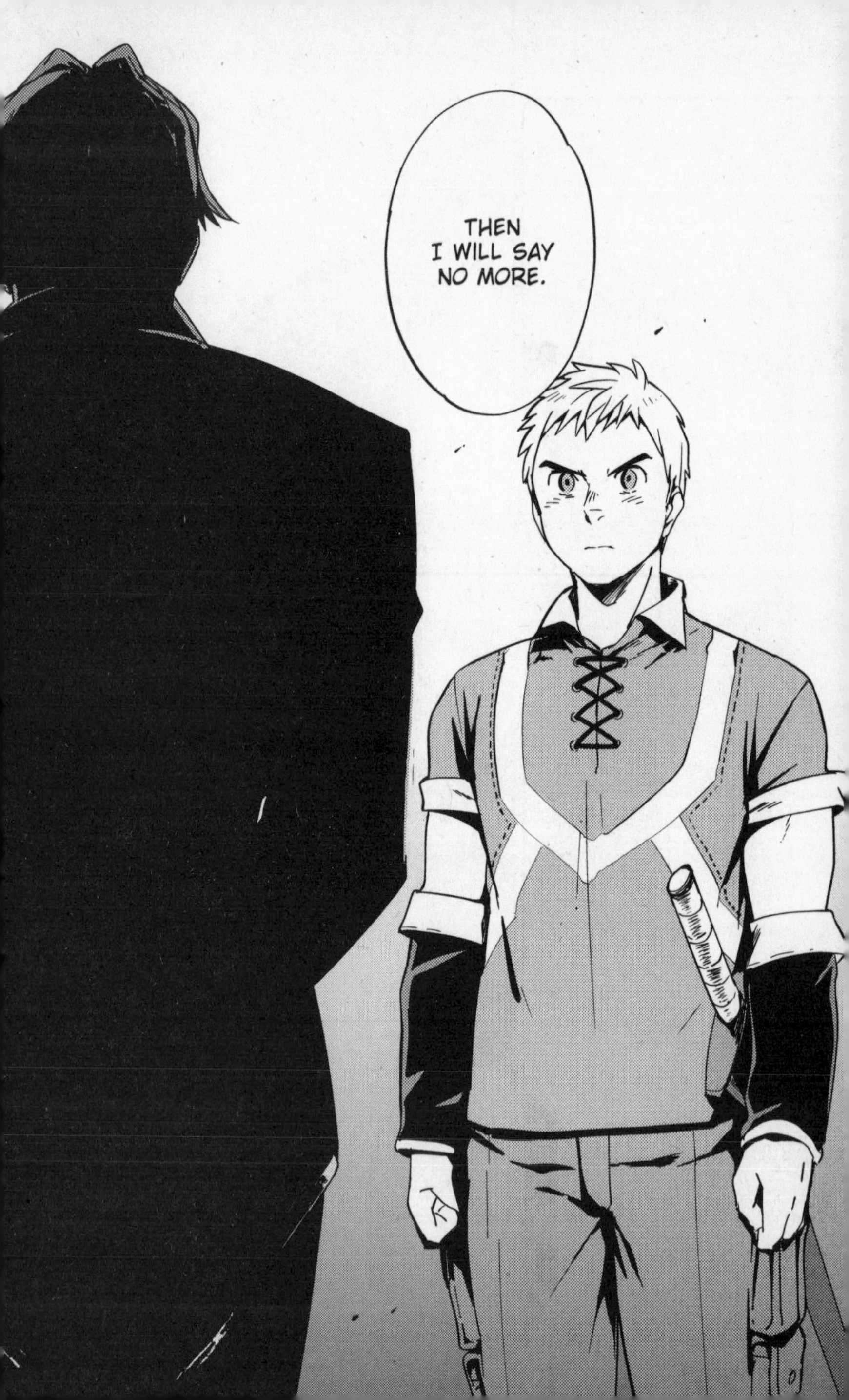
THEN I WILL SAY NO MORE.

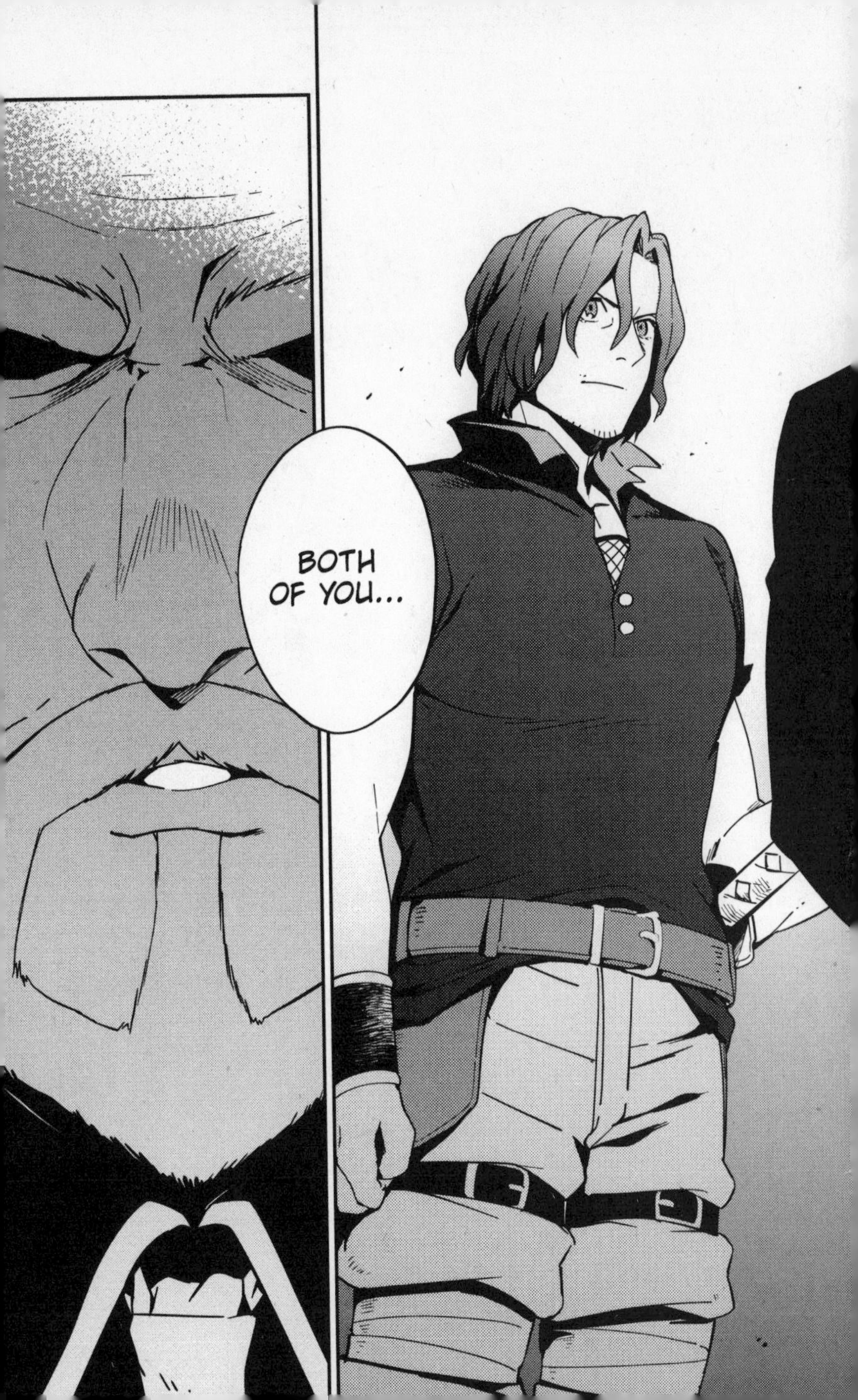
BOTH OF YOU...

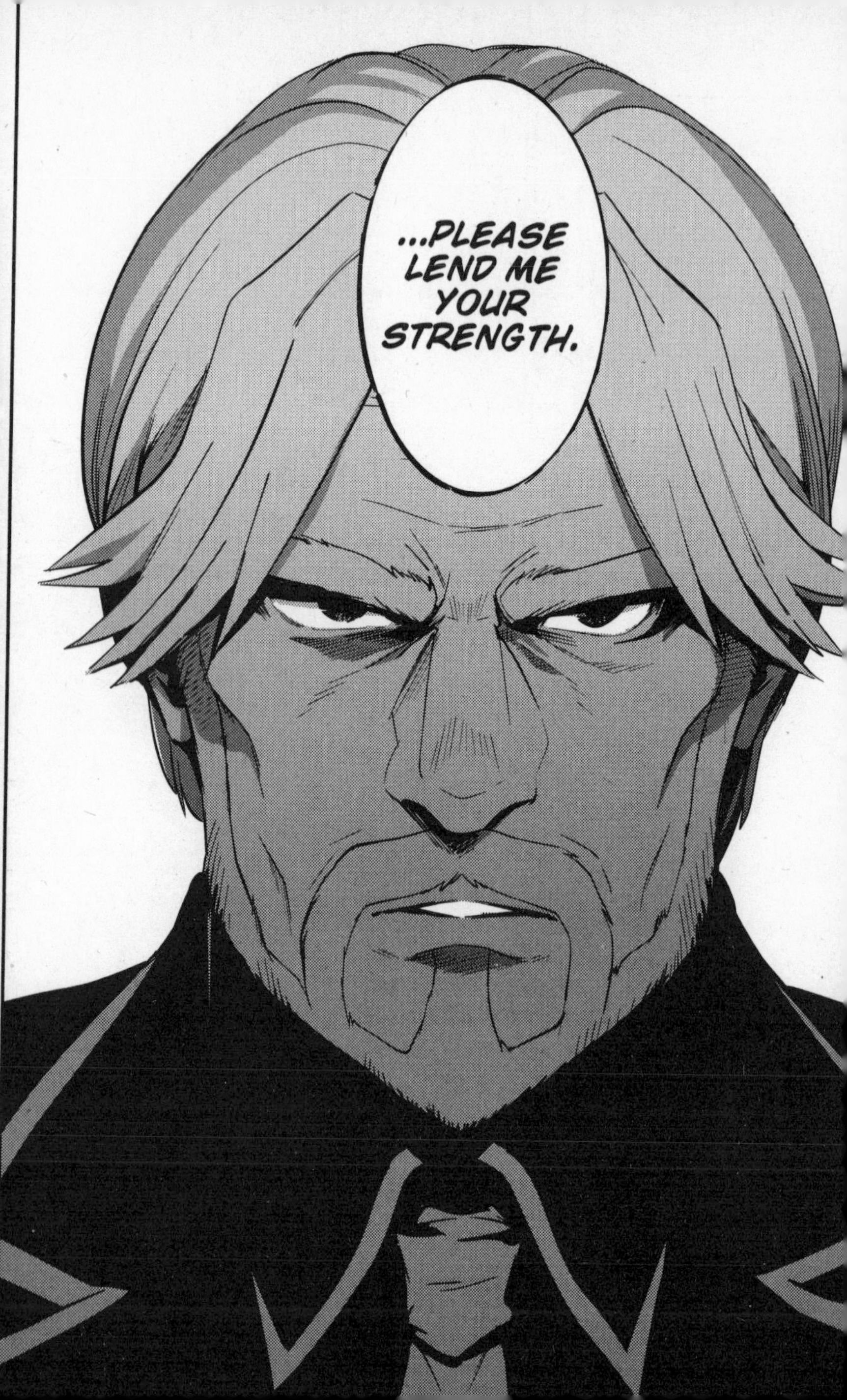
...PLEASE LEND ME YOUR STRENGTH.

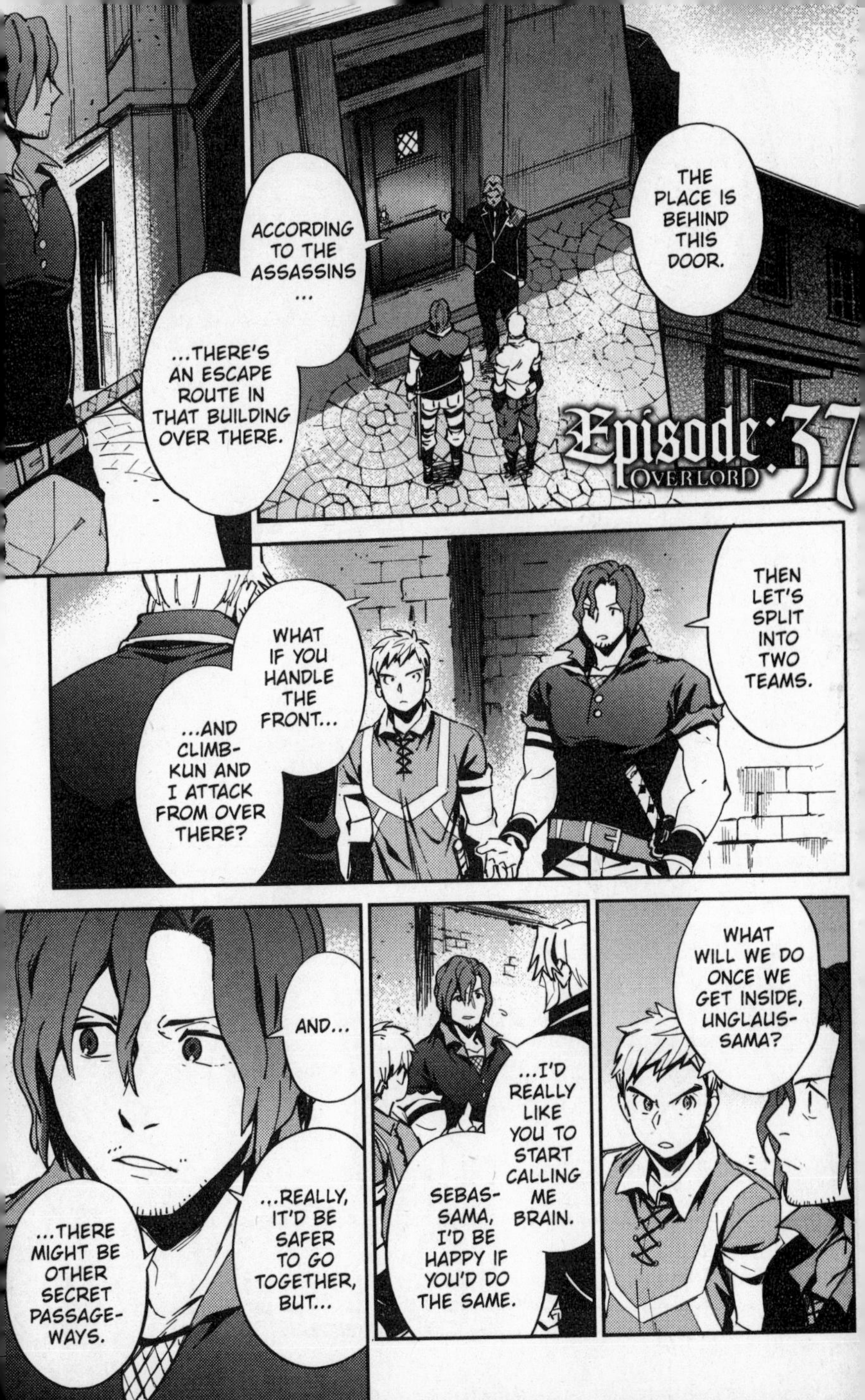
THE PLACE IS BEHIND THIS DOOR.
ACCORDING TO THE ASSASSINS...
...THERE'S AN ESCAPE ROUTE IN THAT BUILDING OVER THERE.
Episode:37
OVERLORD
THEN LET'S SPLIT INTO TWO TEAMS.
WHAT IF YOU HANDLE THE FRONT...
...AND CLIMB-KUN AND I ATTACK FROM OVER THERE?
WHAT WILL WE DO ONCE WE GET INSIDE, UNGLAUS-SAMA?
...I'D REALLY LIKE YOU TO START CALLING ME BRAIN.
SEBAS-SAMA, I'D BE HAPPY IF YOU'D DO THE SAME.
AND...
...REALLY, IT'D BE SAFER TO GO TOGETHER, BUT...
...THERE MIGHT BE OTHER SECRET PASSAGE-WAYS.

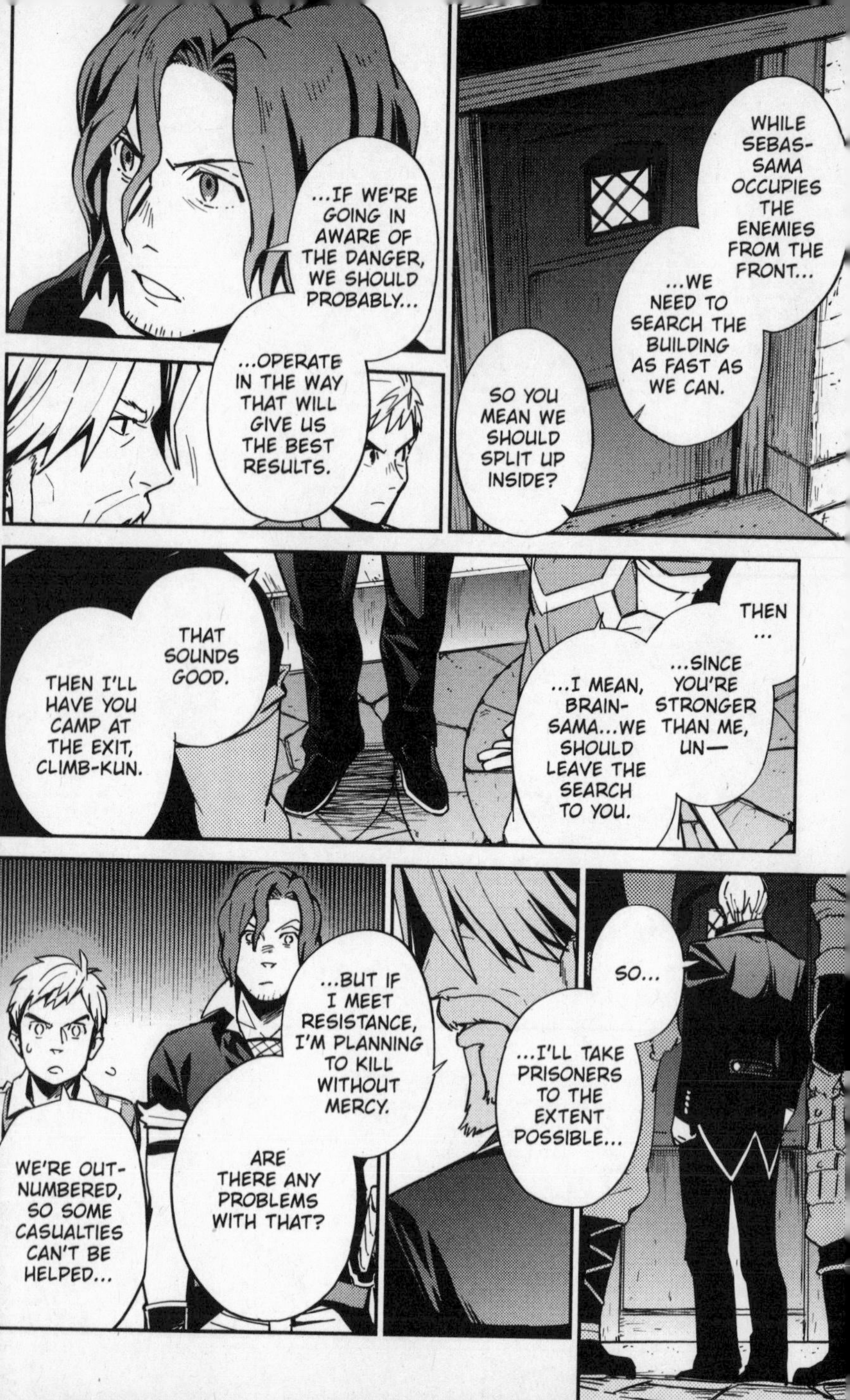
WHILE SEBAS-SAMA OCCUPIES THE ENEMIES FROM THE FRONT...
...WE NEED TO SEARCH THE BUILDING AS FAST AS WE CAN.
SO YOU MEAN WE SHOULD SPLIT UP INSIDE?
...IF WE'RE GOING IN AWARE OF THE DANGER, WE SHOULD PROBABLY...
...OPERATE IN THE WAY THAT WILL GIVE US THE BEST RESULTS.
THEN...
...SINCE YOU'RE STRONGER THAN ME, UN—
...I MEAN, BRAIN-SAMA...WE SHOULD LEAVE THE SEARCH TO YOU.
THAT SOUNDS GOOD.
THEN I'LL HAVE YOU CAMP AT THE EXIT, CLIMB-KUN.
SO...
...I'LL TAKE PRISONERS TO THE EXTENT POSSIBLE...
...BUT IF I MEET RESISTANCE, I'M PLANNING TO KILL WITHOUT MERCY.
ARE THERE ANY PROBLEMS WITH THAT?
WE'RE OUT-NUMBERED, SO SOME CASUALTIES CAN'T BE HELPED...

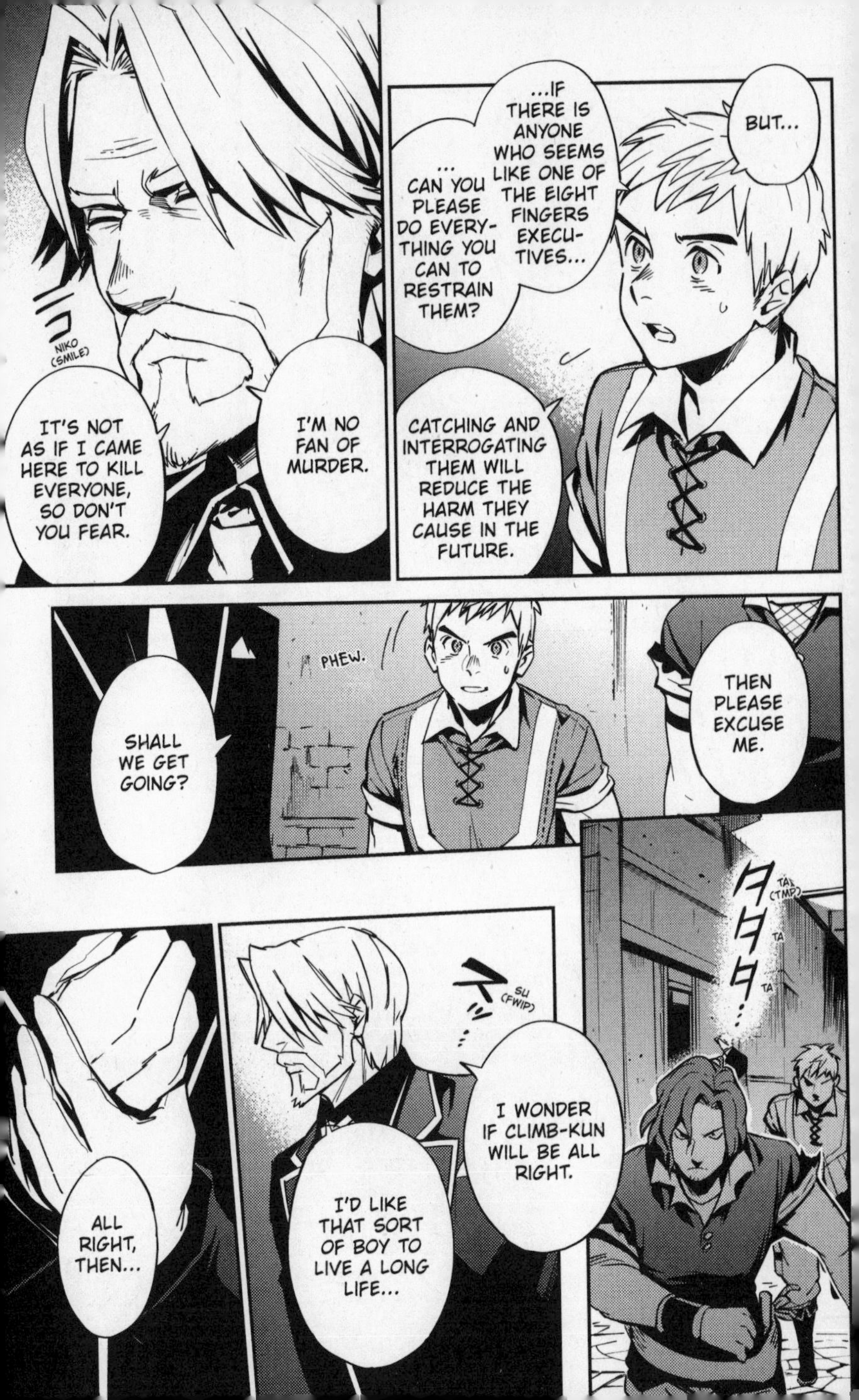
BUT...
...IF THERE IS ANYONE WHO SEEMS LIKE ONE OF THE EIGHT FINGERS EXECUTIVES...
...CAN YOU PLEASE DO EVERYTHING YOU CAN TO RESTRAIN THEM?
CATCHING AND INTERROGATING THEM WILL REDUCE THE HARM THEY CAUSE IN THE FUTURE.
NIKO (SMILE)
I'M NO FAN OF MURDER.
IT'S NOT AS IF I CAME HERE TO KILL EVERYONE, SO DON'T YOU FEAR.
THEN PLEASE EXCUSE ME.
PHEW.
SHALL WE GET GOING?
TA (TMP) TA TA
SU (FWIP)
I WONDER IF CLIMB-KUN WILL BE ALL RIGHT.
I'D LIKE THAT SORT OF BOY TO LIVE A LONG LIFE...
ALL RIGHT, THEN...

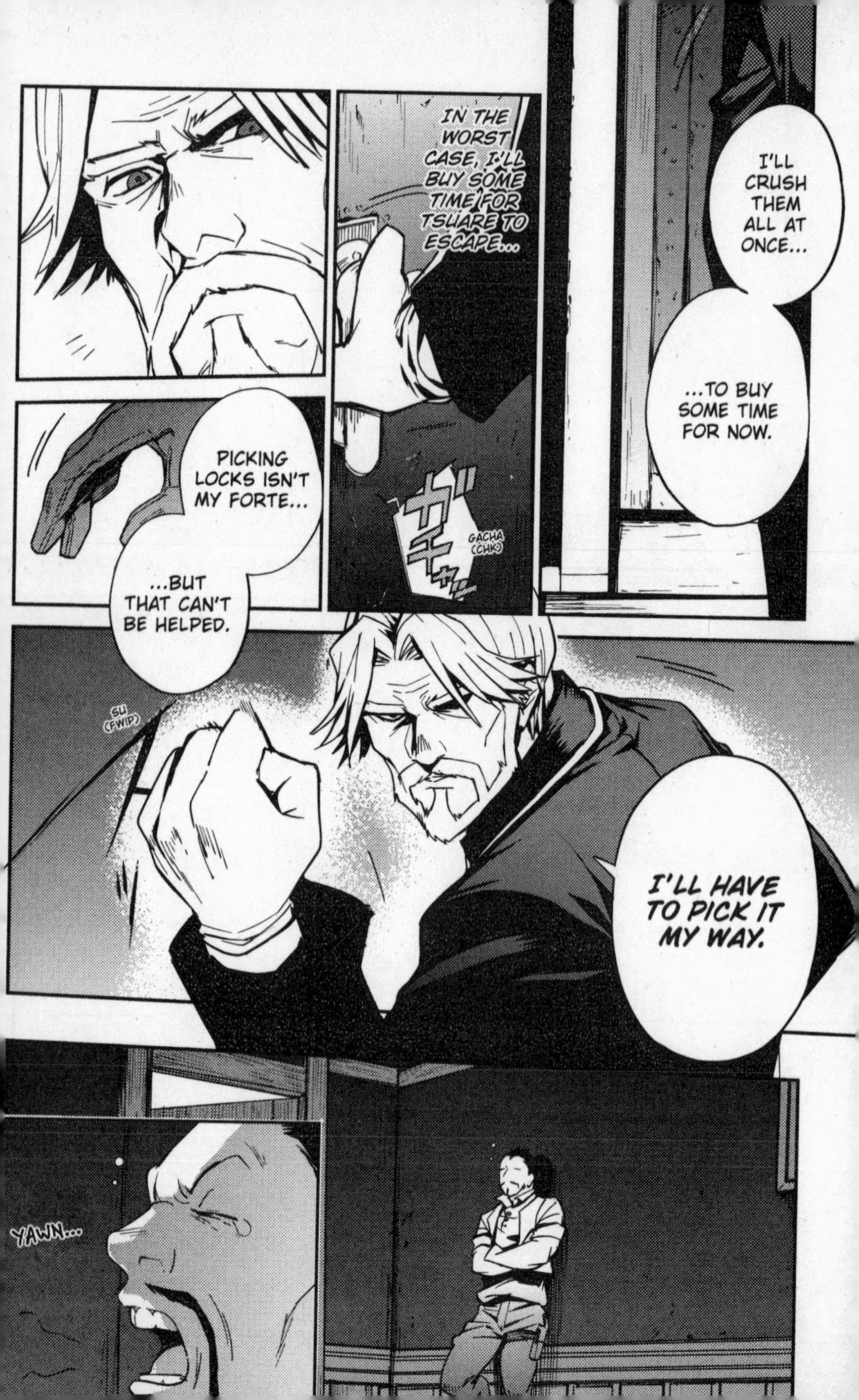

I'LL CRUSH THEM ALL AT ONCE...
...TO BUY SOME TIME FOR NOW.
IN THE WORST CASE, I'LL BUY SOME TIME FOR TSUARE TO ESCAPE...
GACHA (CHK)
PICKING LOCKS ISN'T MY FORTE...
...BUT THAT CAN'T BE HELPED.
SU (FWIP)
I'LL HAVE TO PICK IT MY WAY.
YAWN...

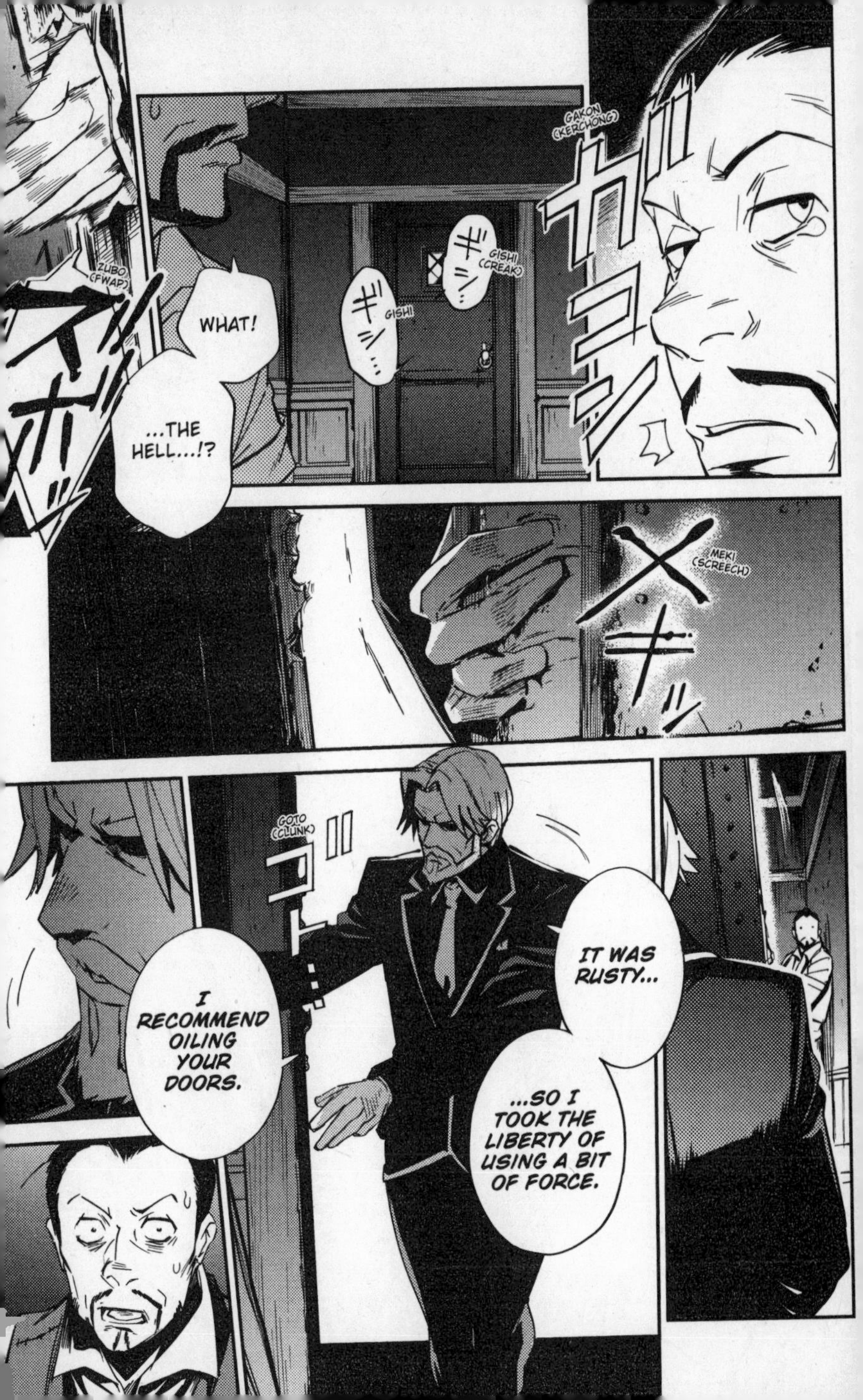
GAKON (KERCHONG)
GISHI (CREAK)
GISHI
WHAT!
...THE HELL...!?
ZUBO (FWAP)
MEKI (SCREECH)
GOTO (CLUNK)
IT WAS RUSTY...
...SO I TOOK THE LIBERTY OF USING A BIT OF FORCE.
I RECOMMEND OILING YOUR DOORS.

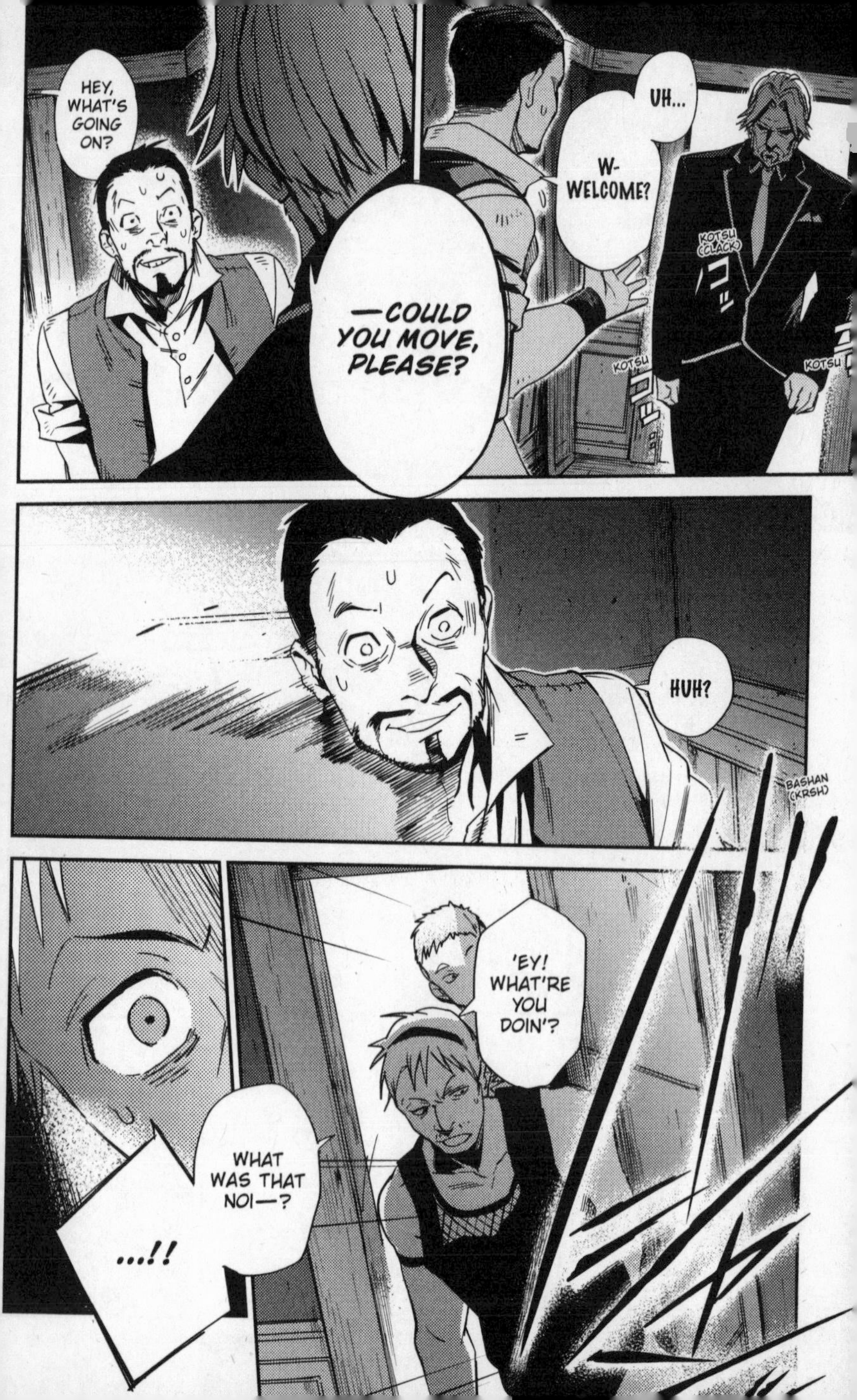
UH...
W-WELCOME?
KOTSU (CLACK)
KOTSU
KOTSU
—COULD YOU MOVE, PLEASE?
HEY, WHAT'S GOING ON?
HUH?
BASHAN (KRSH)
'EY! WHAT'RE YOU DOIN'?
WHAT WAS THAT NOI—?
...!!

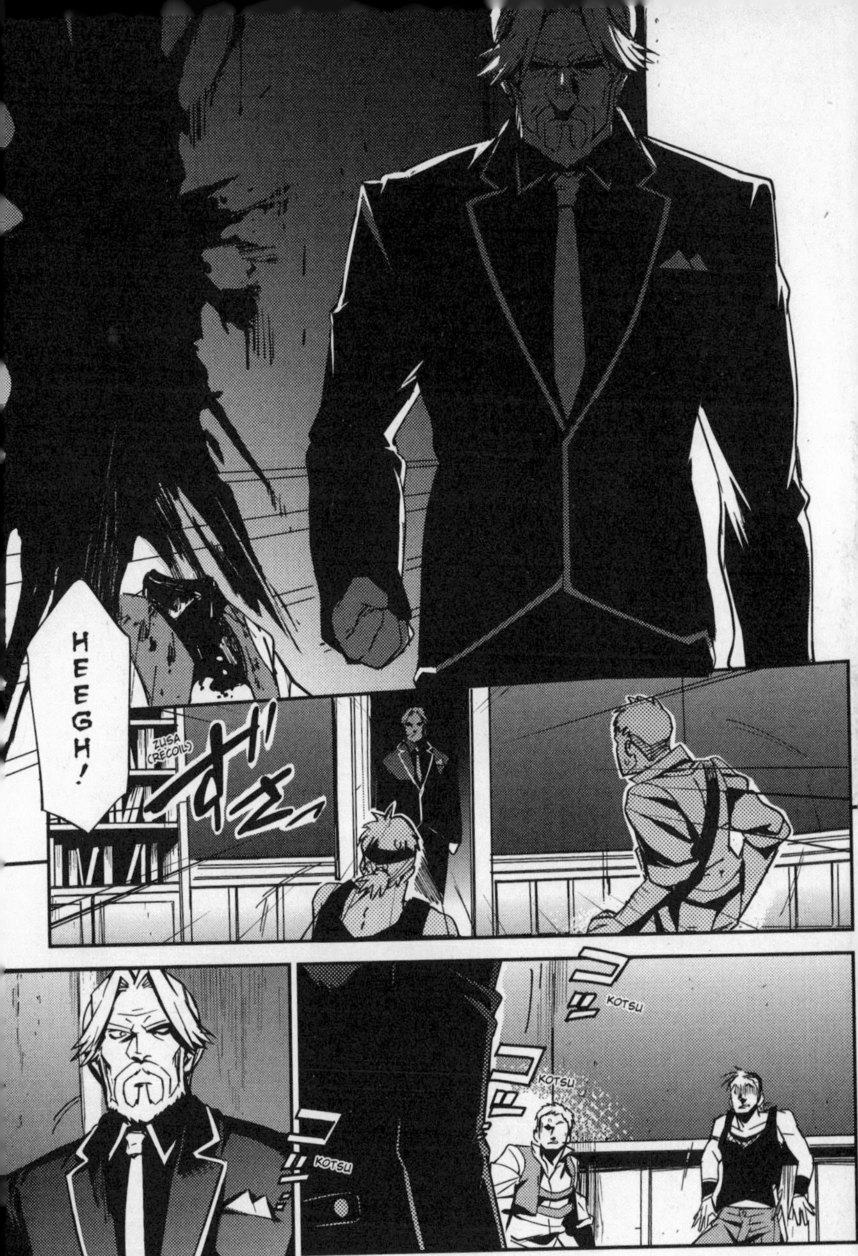
HEEGH!
ZUSA (RECOIL)
KOTSU
KOTSU
KOTSU

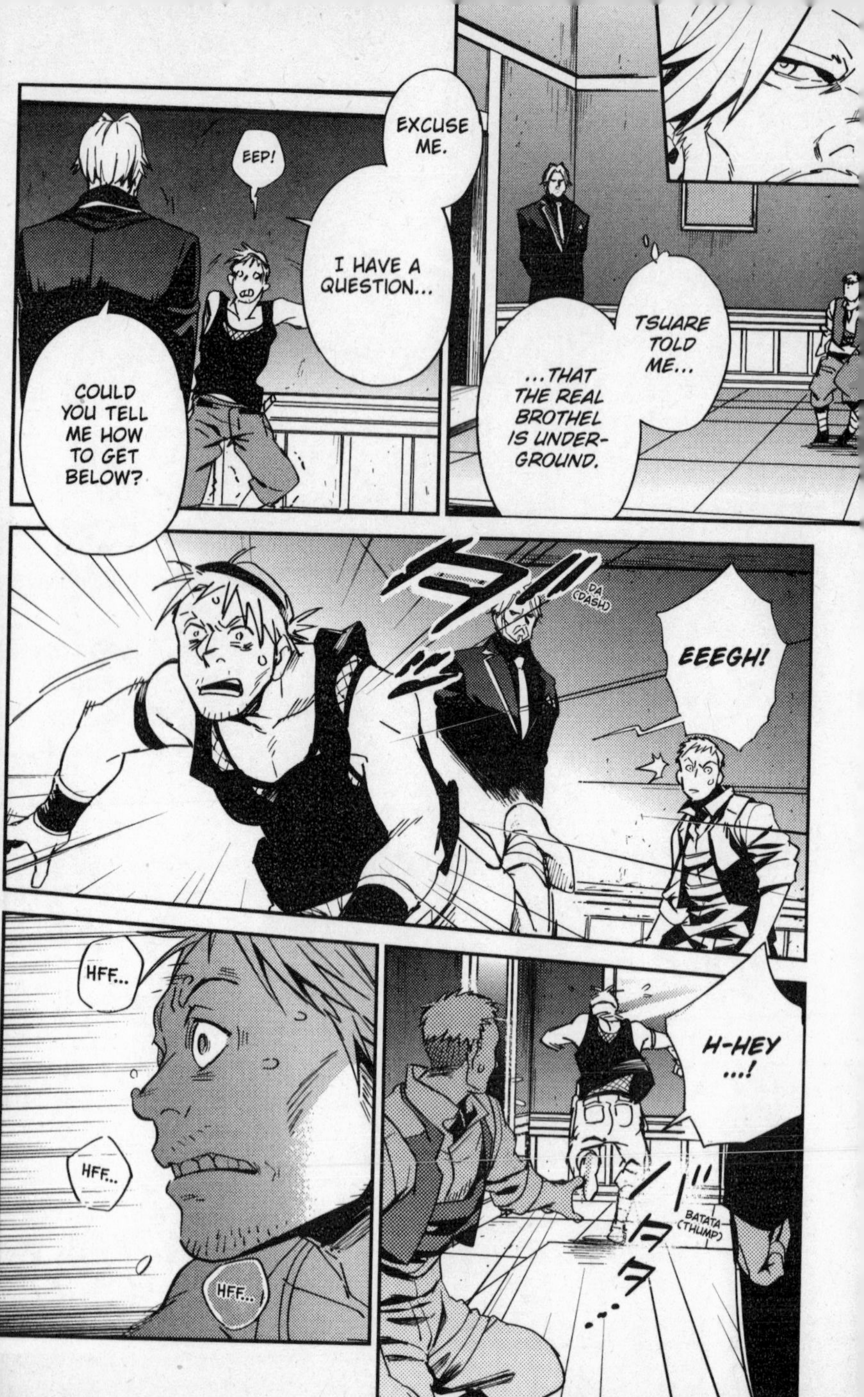
EXCUSE ME.
I HAVE A QUESTION...
TSUARE TOLD ME...
...THAT THE REAL BROTHEL IS UNDERGROUND.
COULD YOU TELL ME HOW TO GET BELOW?
EEP!
DA (DASH)
EEEGH!
H-HEY ...!
BATATA (THUMP)
HFF...
HFF...
HFF...

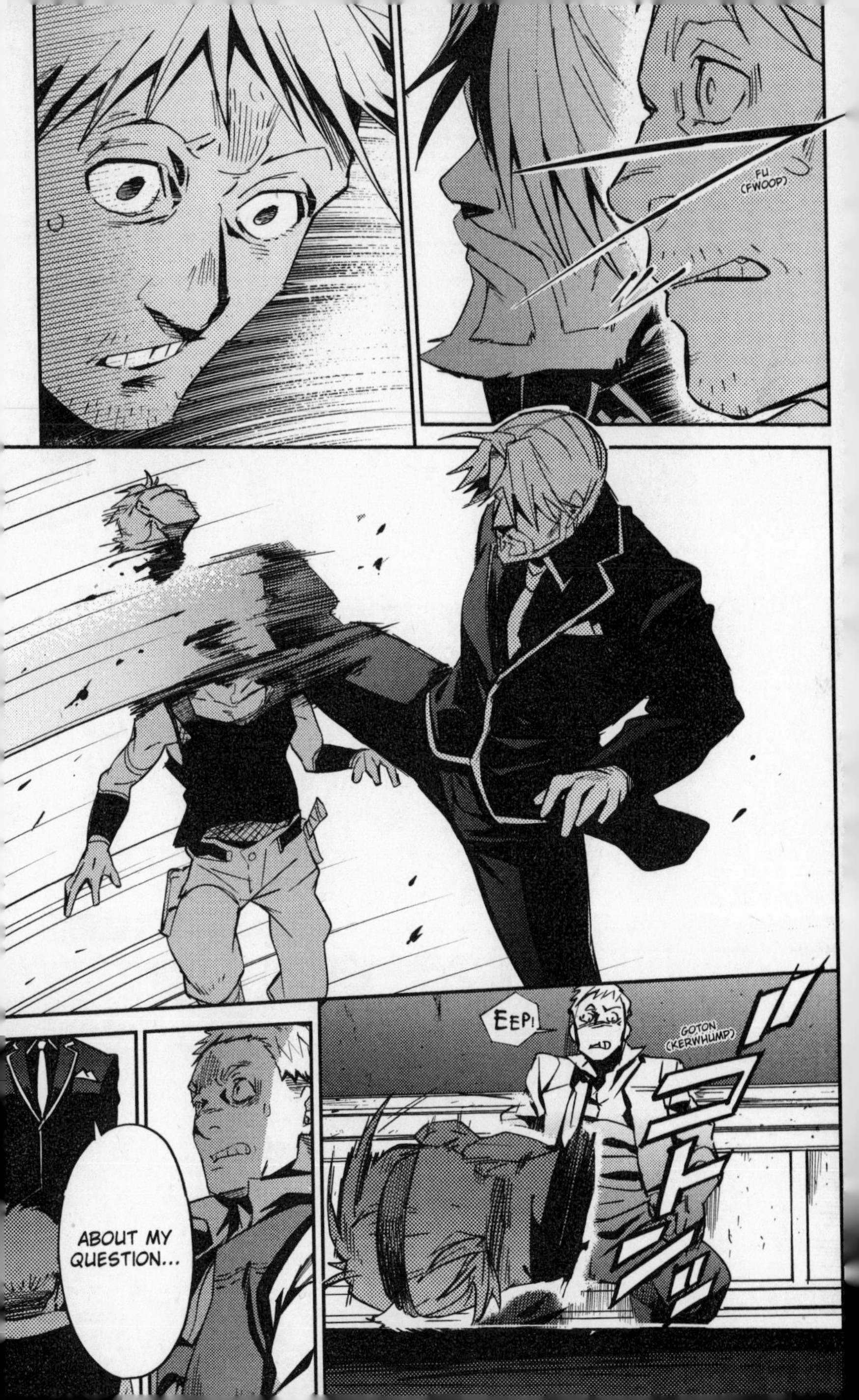
FU
(FWOOP)
EEP!
GOTON
(KERWHUMP)
ABOUT MY QUESTION...

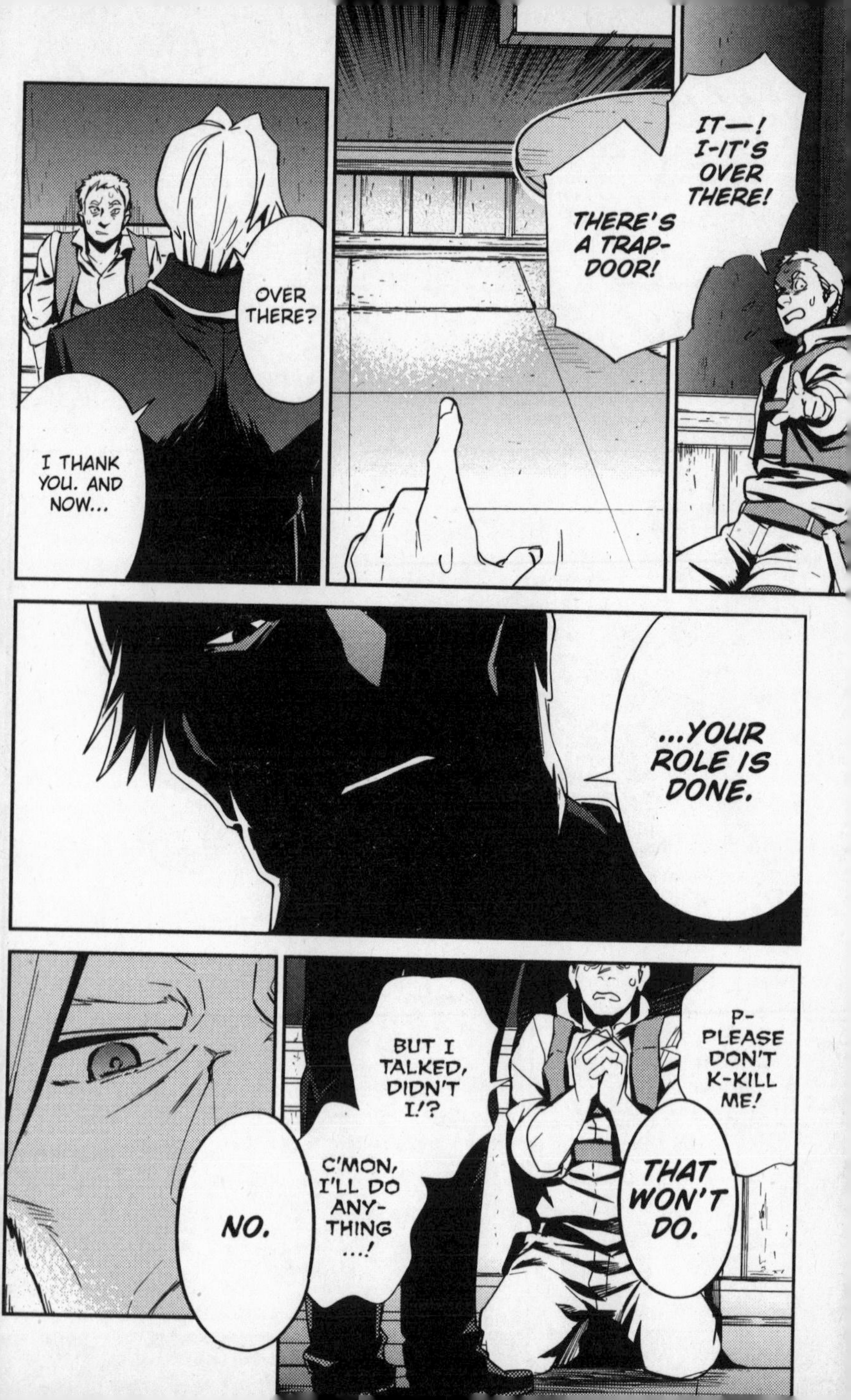
IT—! I-IT'S OVER THERE!
THERE'S A TRAP-DOOR!
OVER THERE?
I THANK YOU. AND NOW...
...YOUR ROLE IS DONE.
P-PLEASE DON'T K-KILL ME!
BUT I TALKED, DIDN'T I!?
THAT WON'T DO.
C'MON, I'LL DO ANY-THING...!
NO.

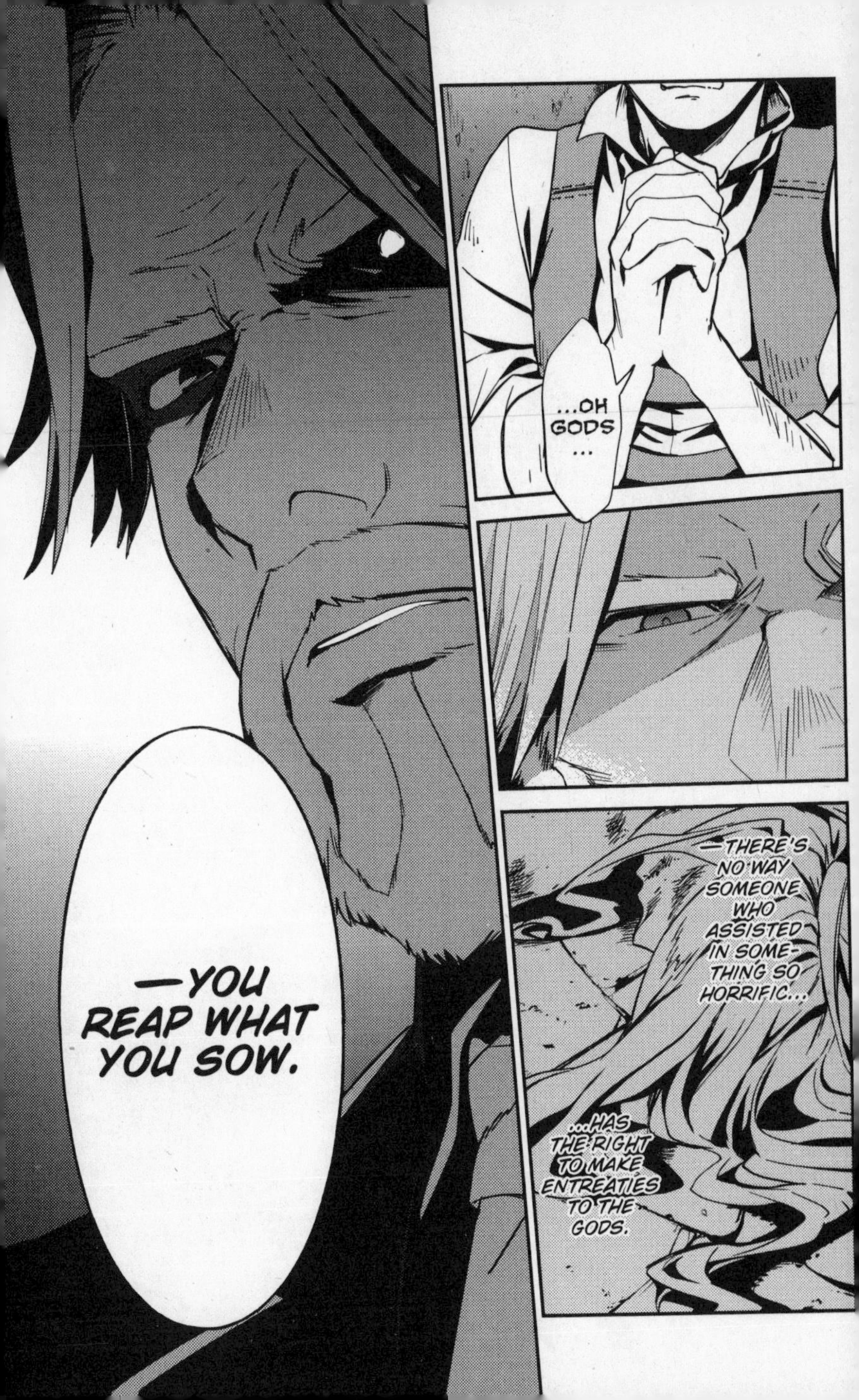
...OH GODS ...
—THERE'S NO WAY SOMEONE WHO ASSISTED IN SOME-THING SO HORRIFIC...
...HAS THE RIGHT TO MAKE ENTREATIES TO THE GODS.
—YOU REAP WHAT YOU SOW.

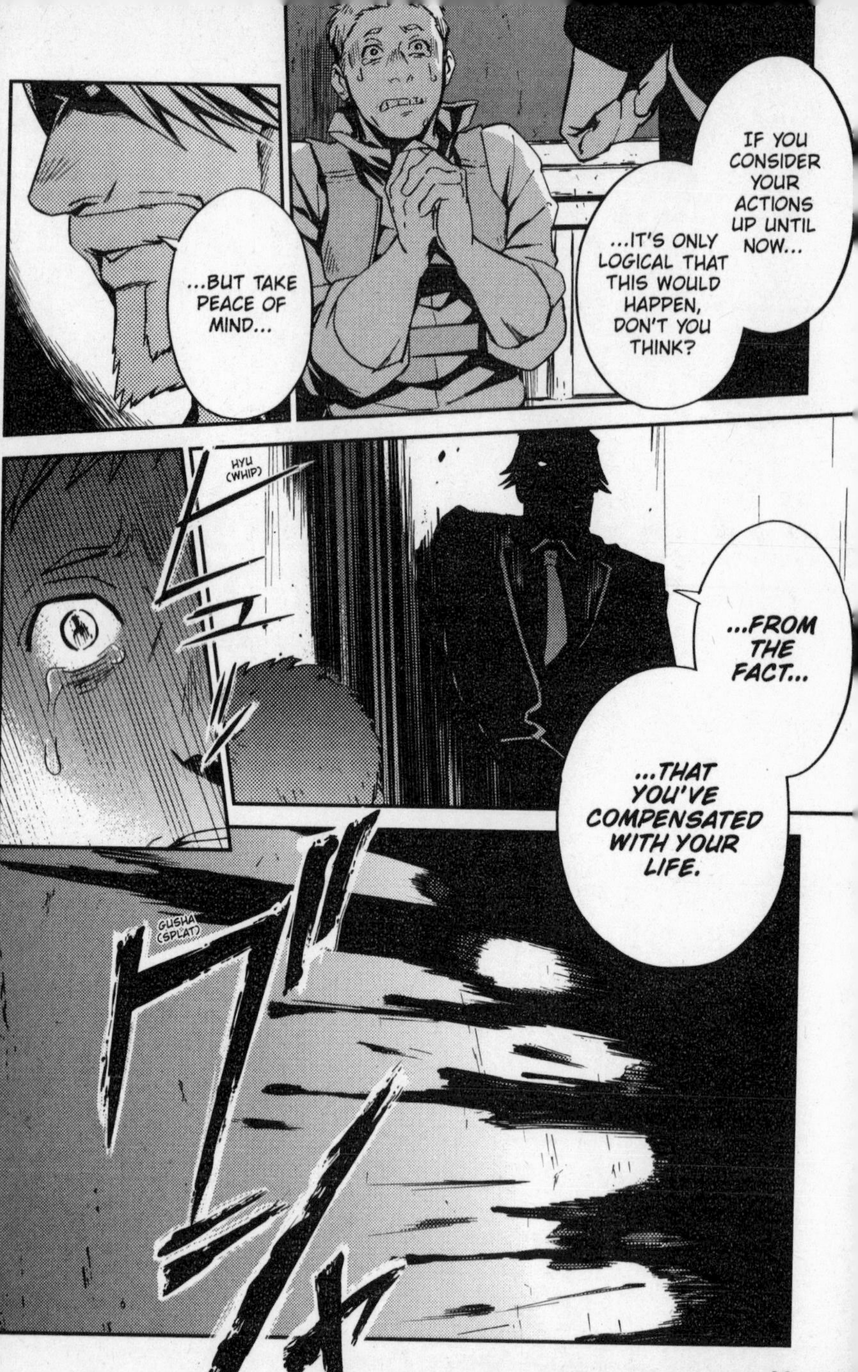
IF YOU CONSIDER YOUR ACTIONS UP UNTIL NOW...
...IT'S ONLY LOGICAL THAT THIS WOULD HAPPEN, DON'T YOU THINK?
...BUT TAKE PEACE OF MIND...
...FROM THE FACT...
...THAT YOU'VE COMPENSATED WITH YOUR LIFE.
HYU (WHIP)
GUSHA (SPLAT)

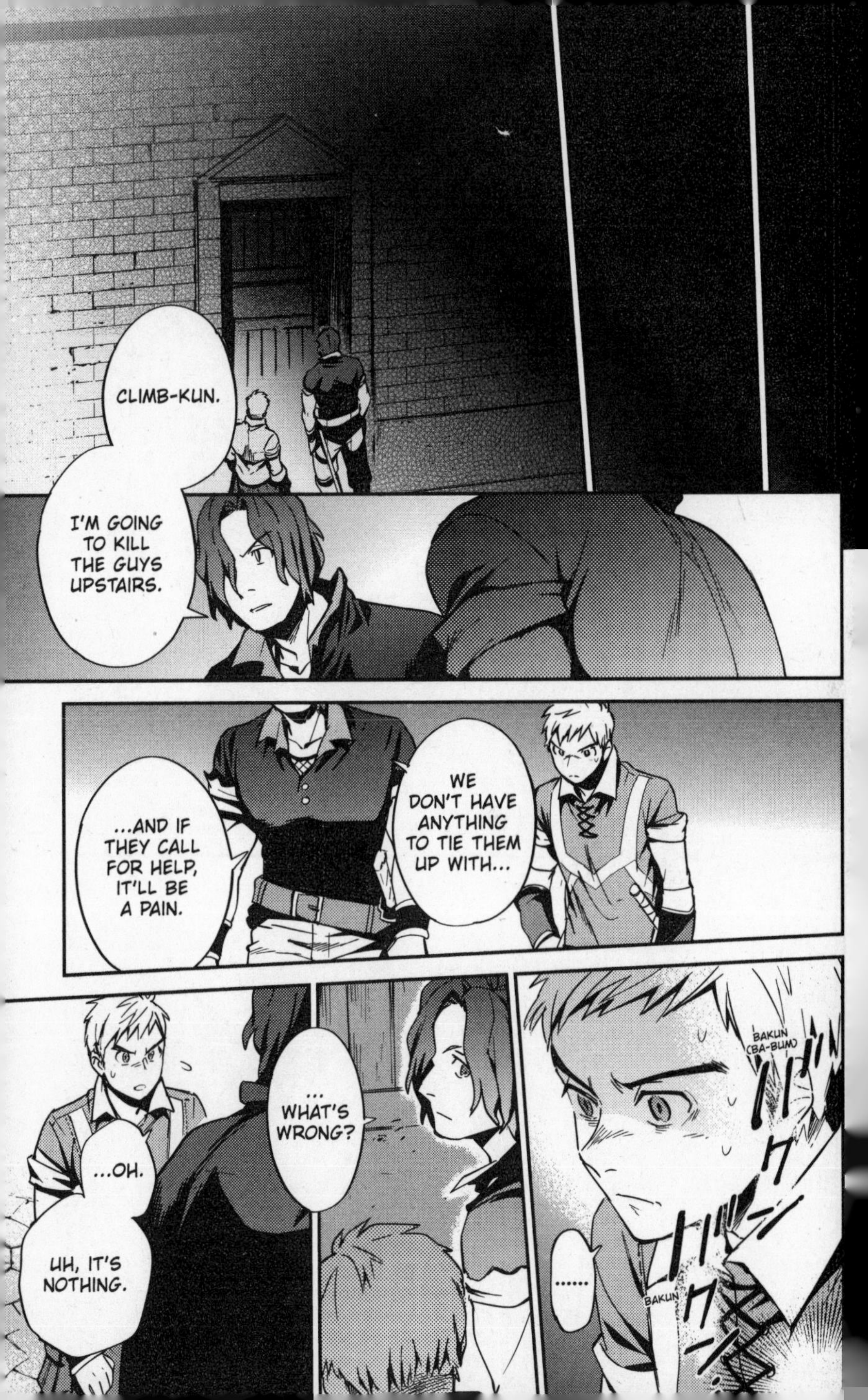
CLIMB-KUN.
I'M GOING TO KILL THE GUYS UPSTAIRS.
WE DON'T HAVE ANYTHING TO TIE THEM UP WITH...
...AND IF THEY CALL FOR HELP, IT'LL BE A PAIN.
BAKUN (BA-BUM)
......
BAKUN
... WHAT'S WRONG?
...OH.
UH, IT'S NOTHING.

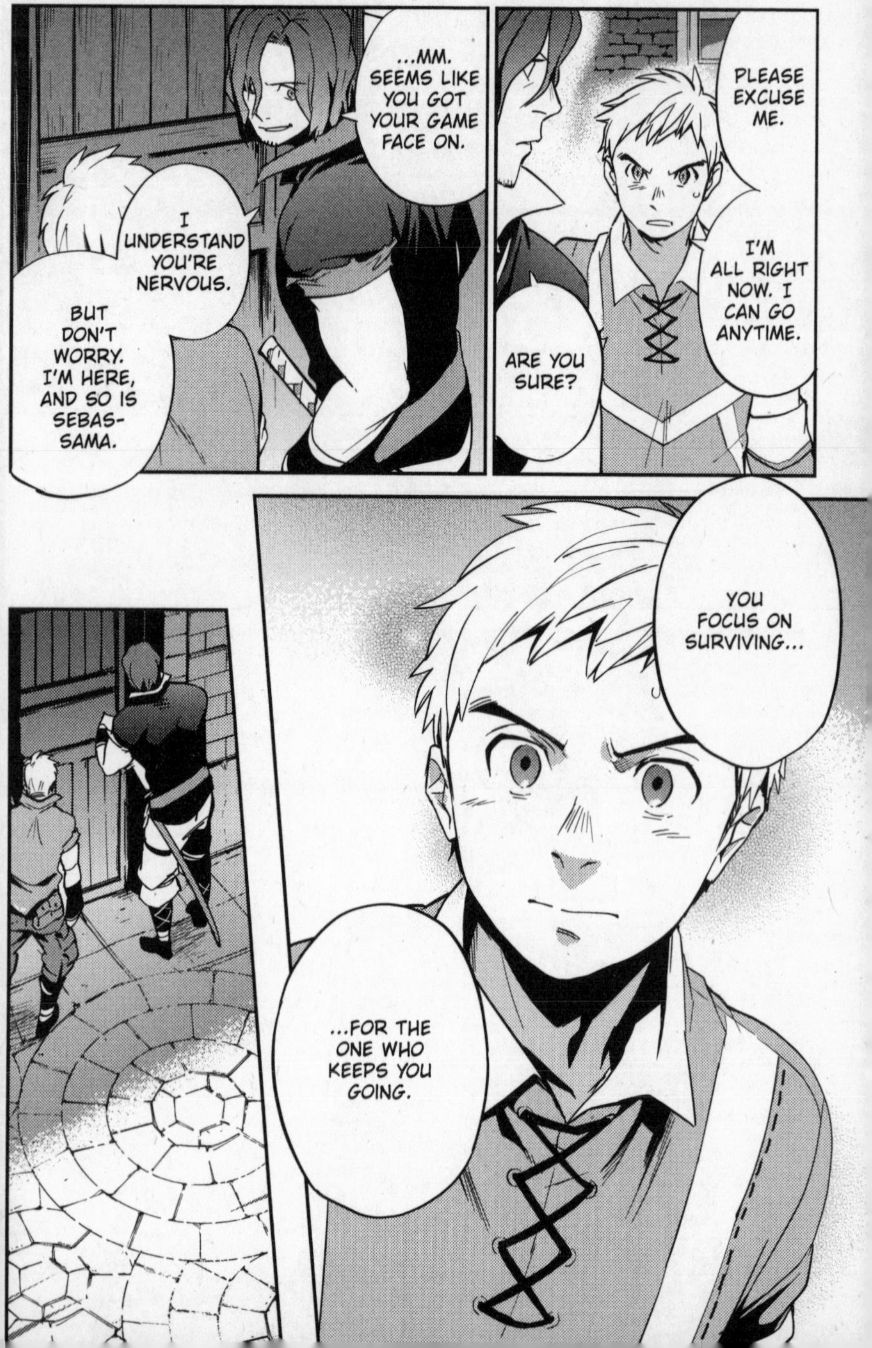
PLEASE EXCUSE ME.
I'M ALL RIGHT NOW. I CAN GO ANYTIME.
ARE YOU SURE?
...MM. SEEMS LIKE YOU GOT YOUR GAME FACE ON.
I UNDERSTAND YOU'RE NERVOUS.
BUT DON'T WORRY. I'M HERE, AND SO IS SEBAS-SAMA.
YOU FOCUS ON SURVIVING...
...FOR THE ONE WHO KEEPS YOU GOING.

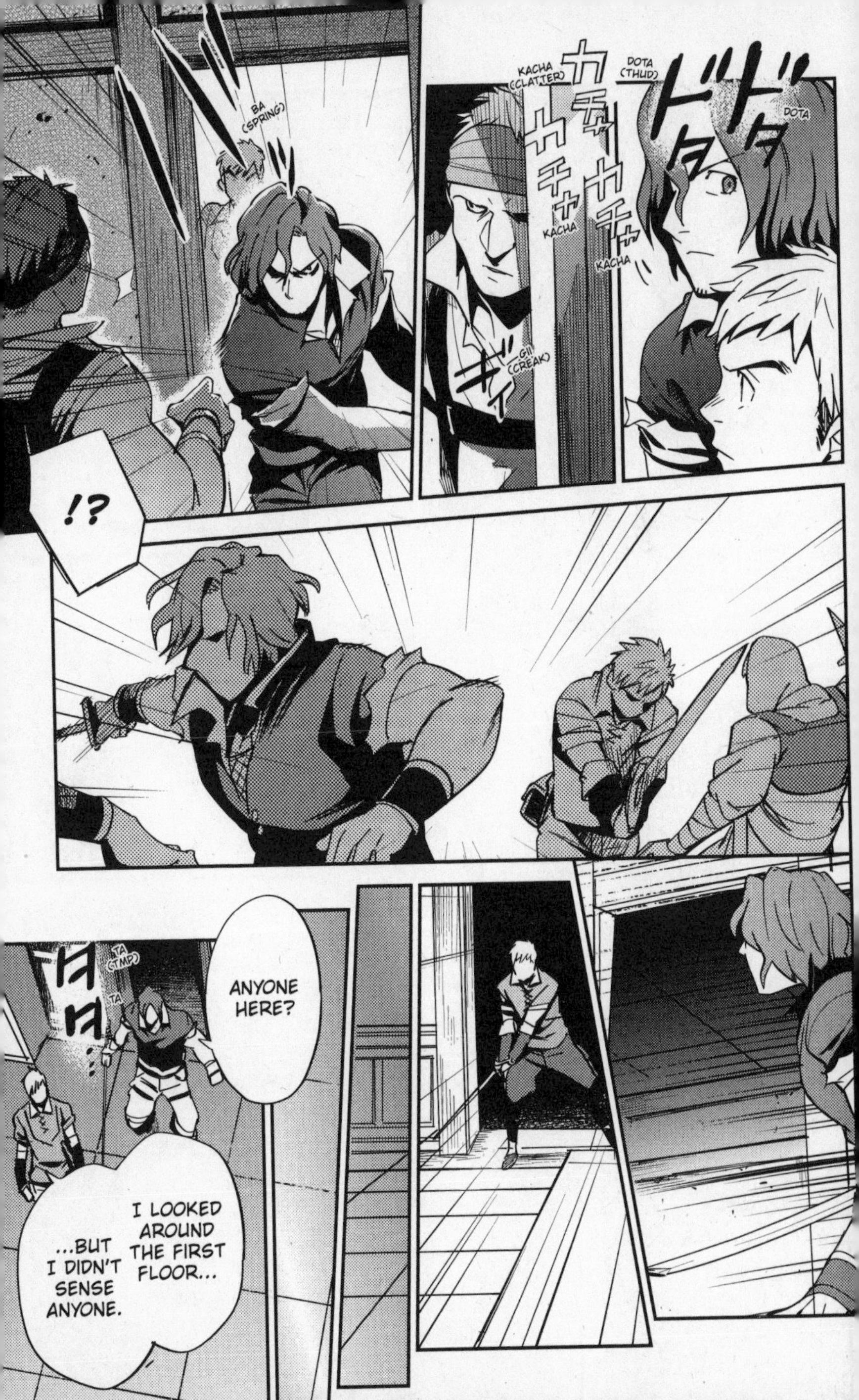
DOTA (THUD)
DOTA
KACHA (CLATTER)
KACHA
KACHA
GII (CREAK)
BA (SPRING)
!?
TA (TMP)
TA
ANYONE HERE?
I LOOKED AROUND THE FIRST FLOOR...
...BUT I DIDN'T SENSE ANYONE.

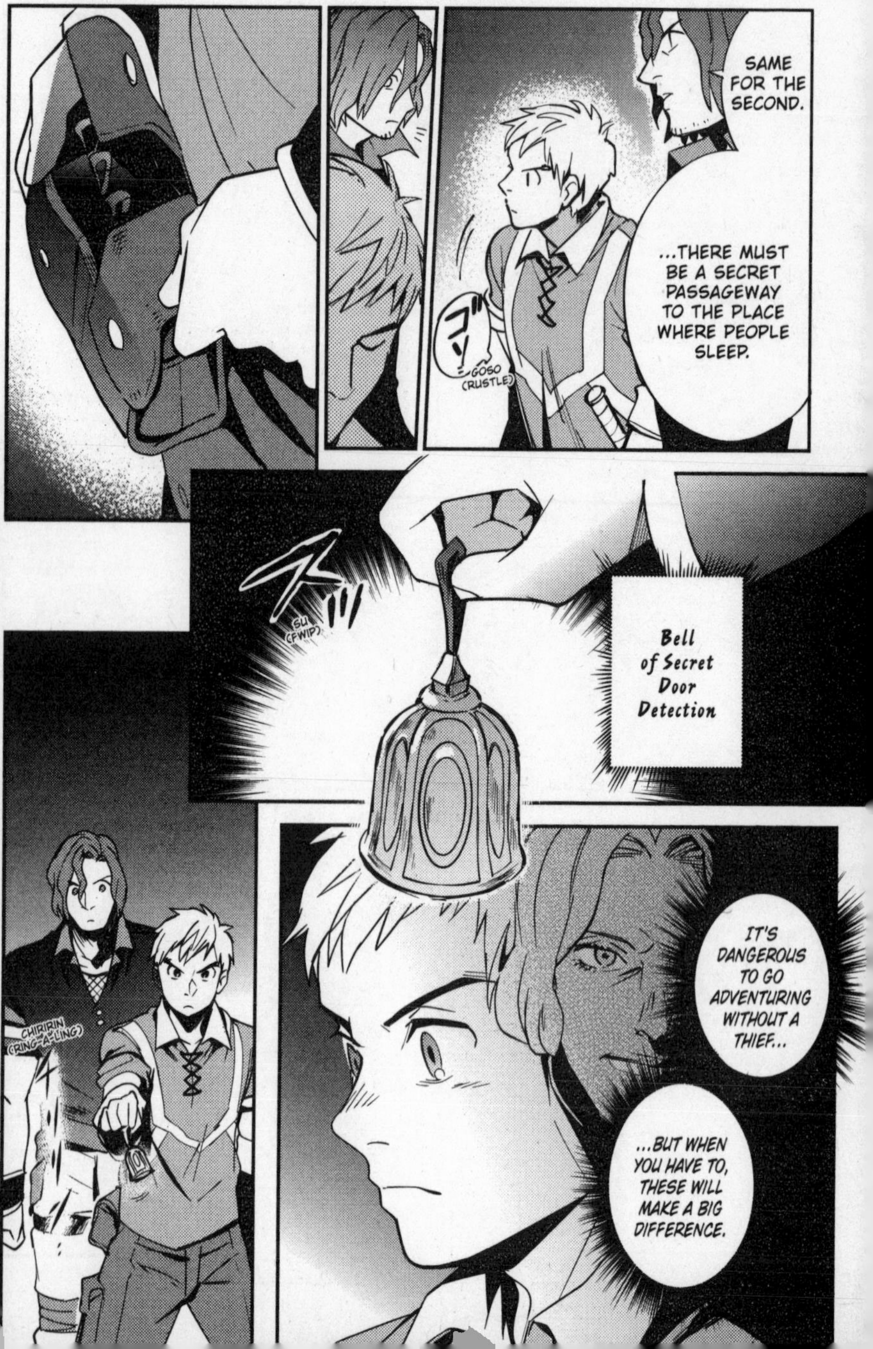

SAME FOR THE SECOND.
...THERE MUST BE A SECRET PASSAGEWAY TO THE PLACE WHERE PEOPLE SLEEP.
ゴソ
GOSO (RUSTLE)
スッ
SU (FWIP)
Bell of Secret Door Detection
IT'S DANGEROUS TO GO ADVENTURING WITHOUT A THIEF...
...BUT WHEN YOU HAVE TO, THESE WILL MAKE A BIG DIFFERENCE.
CHIRIRIN (RING-A-LING)

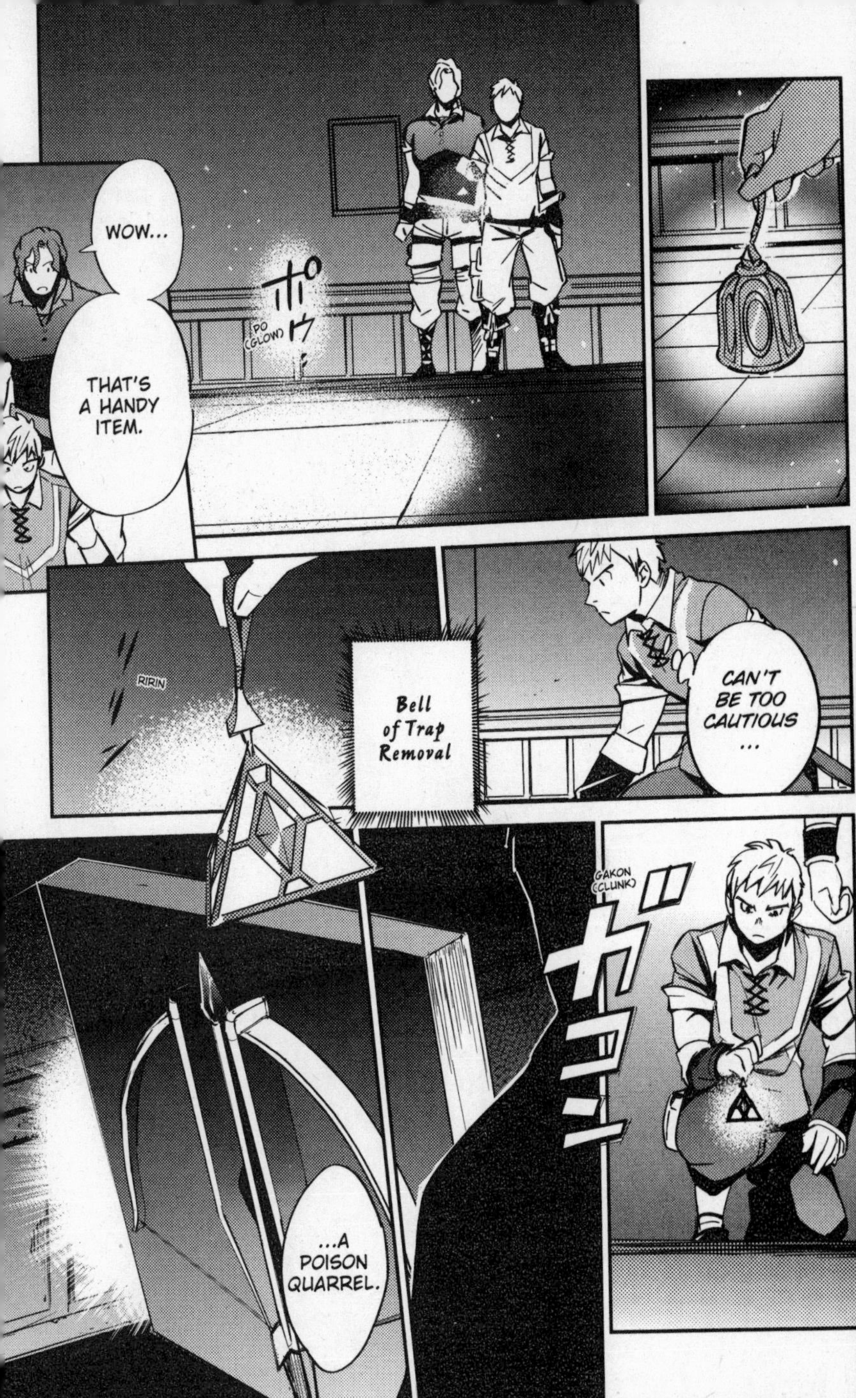
WOW...
THAT'S A HANDY ITEM.
PO (GLOW)
CAN'T BE TOO CAUTIOUS...
Bell of Trap Removal
RIRIN
GAKON (CLUNK)
...A POISON QUARREL.

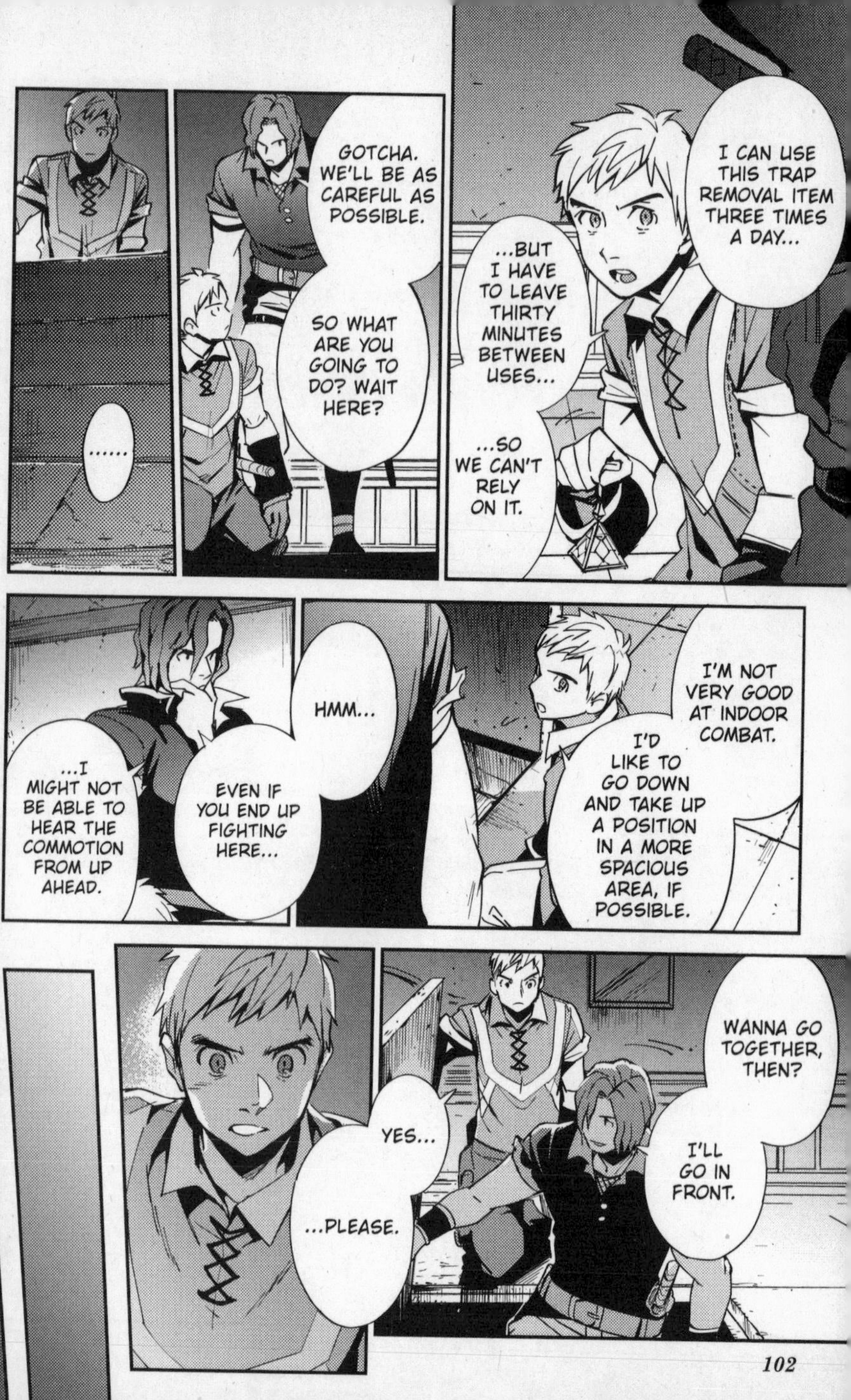
I CAN USE THIS TRAP REMOVAL ITEM THREE TIMES A DAY...
...BUT I HAVE TO LEAVE THIRTY MINUTES BETWEEN USES...
...SO WE CAN'T RELY ON IT.
GOTCHA. WE'LL BE AS CAREFUL AS POSSIBLE.
SO WHAT ARE YOU GOING TO DO? WAIT HERE?
......
I'M NOT VERY GOOD AT INDOOR COMBAT.
I'D LIKE TO GO DOWN AND TAKE UP A POSITION IN A MORE SPACIOUS AREA, IF POSSIBLE.
HMM...
EVEN IF YOU END UP FIGHTING HERE...
...I MIGHT NOT BE ABLE TO HEAR THE COMMOTION FROM UP AHEAD.
WANNA GO TOGETHER, THEN?
I'LL GO IN FRONT.
YES...
...PLEASE.

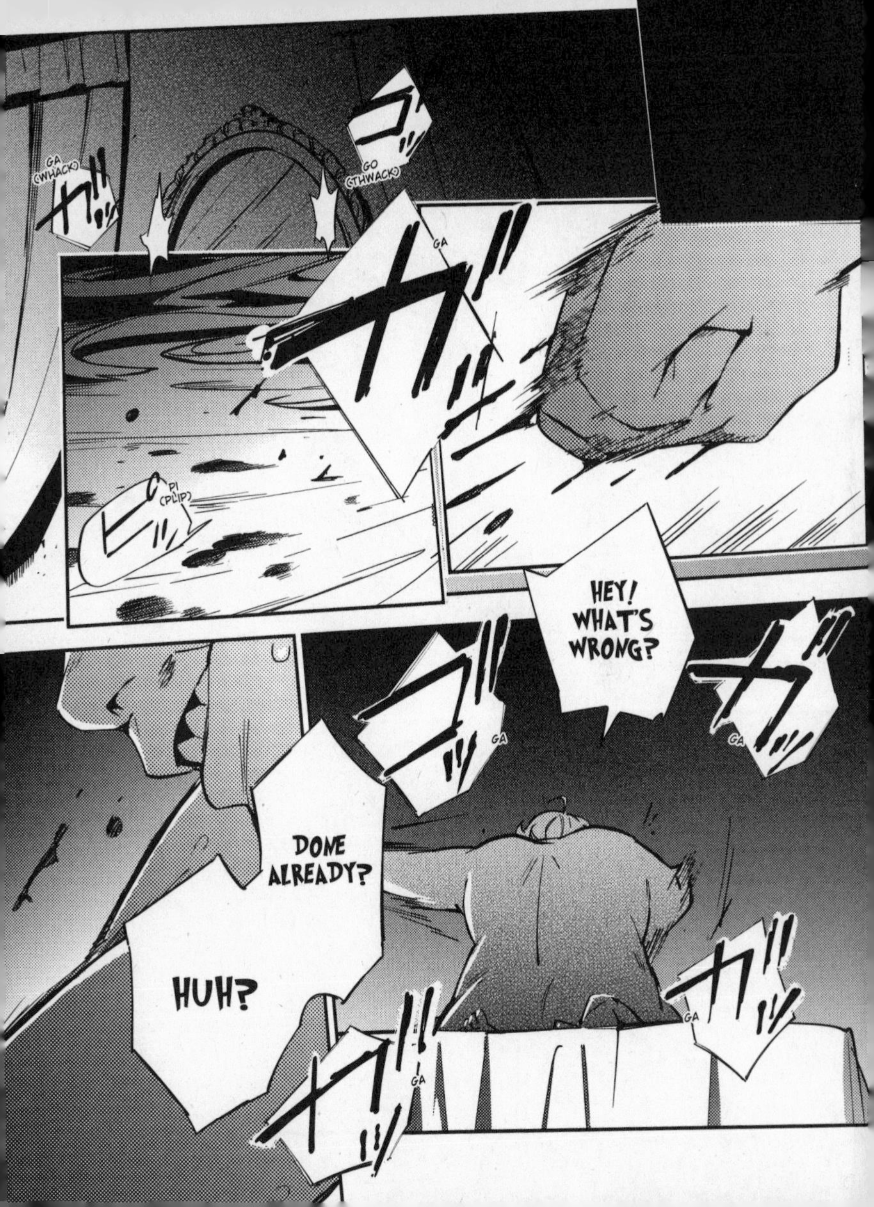
GO (THWACK)
GA (WHACK)
GA
PI (PLIP)
HEY! WHAT'S WRONG?
GA
GA
DONE ALREADY?
HUH?
GA
GA

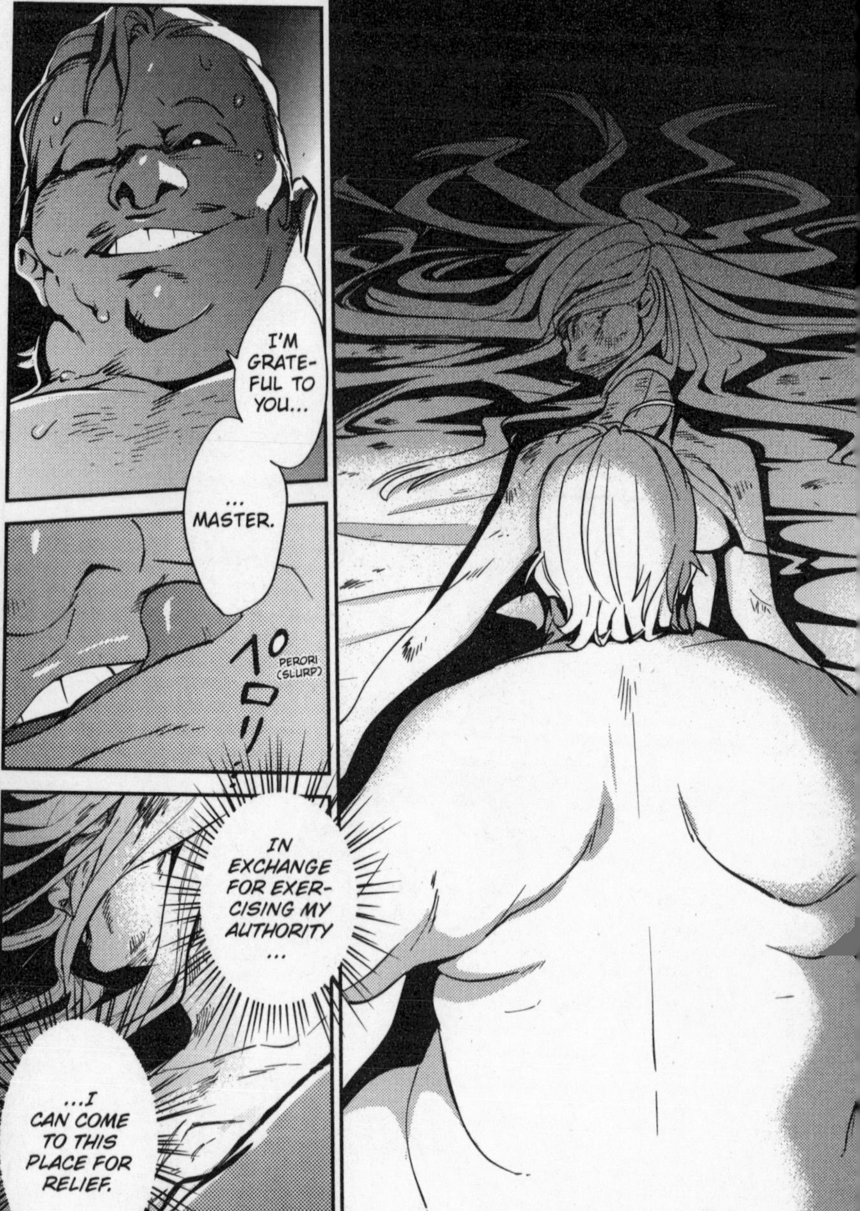
I'M GRATEFUL TO YOU...
...MASTER.
ペロリ
PERORI (SLURP)
IN EXCHANGE FOR EXERCISING MY AUTHORITY...
...I CAN COME TO THIS PLACE FOR RELIEF.

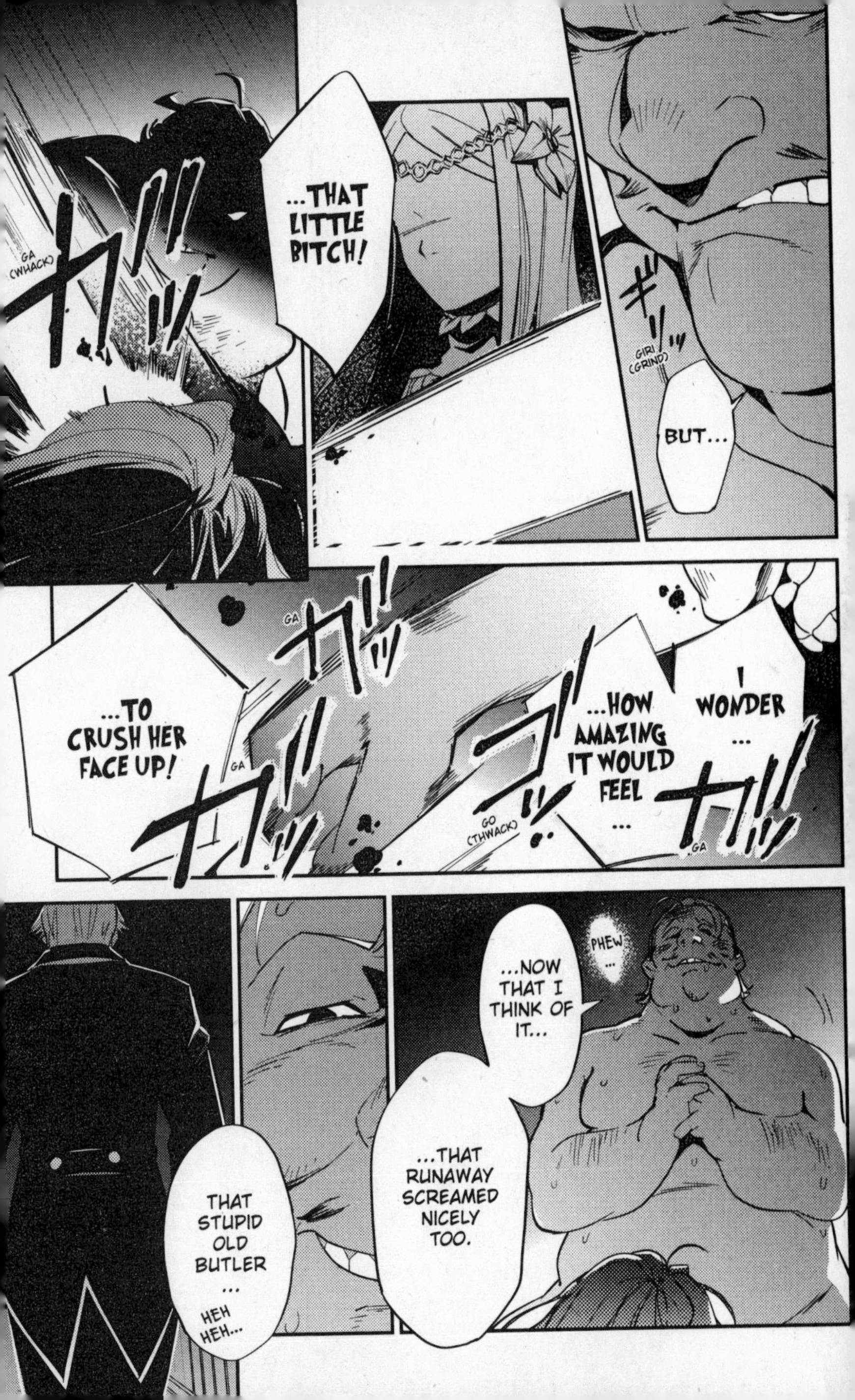
GIRI (GRIND)
BUT...
...THAT LITTLE BITCH!
GA (WHACK)
I WONDER...
GA
...HOW AMAZING IT WOULD FEEL...
GO (THWACK)
GA
GA
...TO CRUSH HER FACE UP!
PHEW...
...NOW THAT I THINK OF IT...
...THAT RUNAWAY SCREAMED NICELY TOO.
THAT STUPID OLD BUTLER...
HEH HEH...

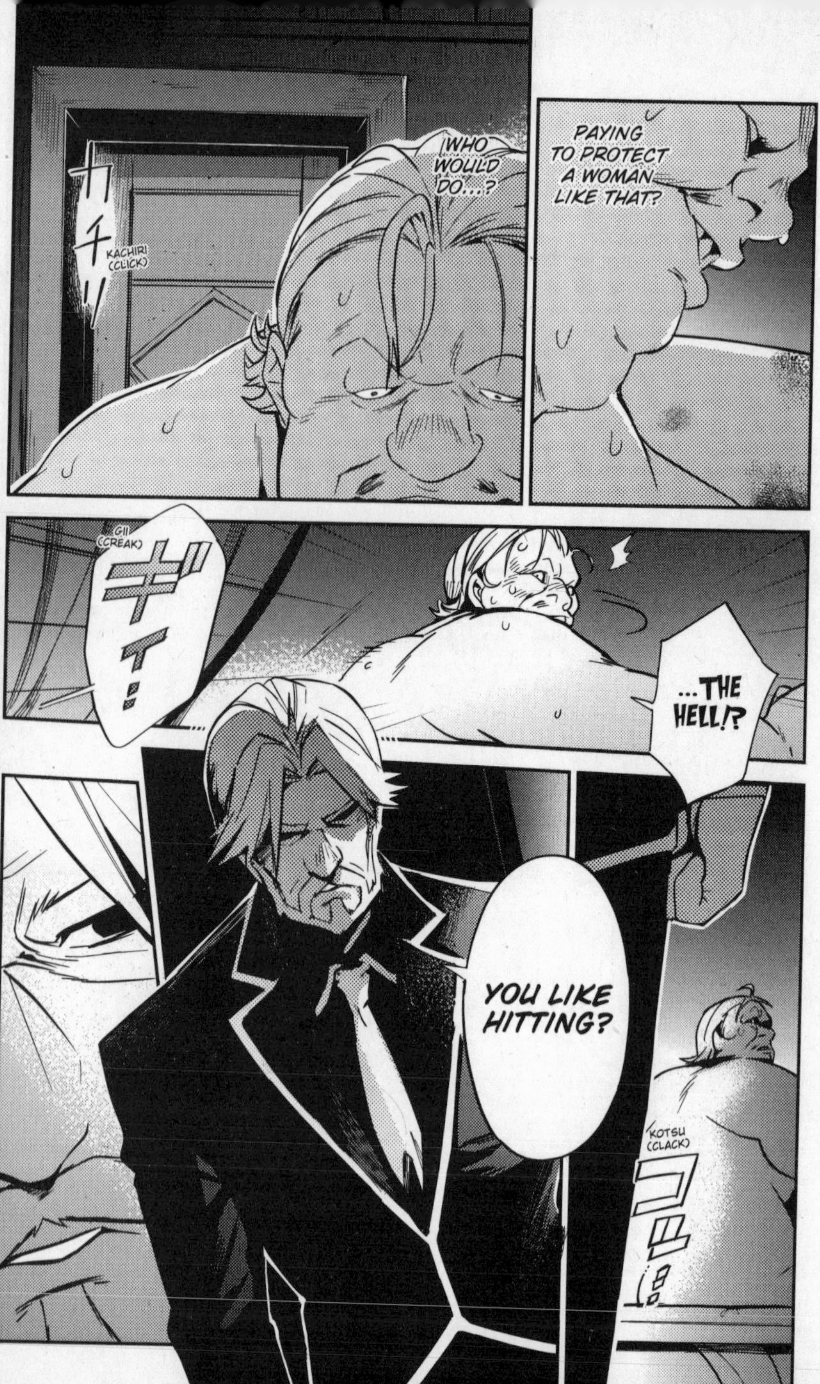
PAYING TO PROTECT A WOMAN LIKE THAT?
WHO WOULD DO...?
KACHIRI (CLICK)
...THE HELL!?
GII (CREAK)
YOU LIKE HITTING?
KOTSU (CLACK)

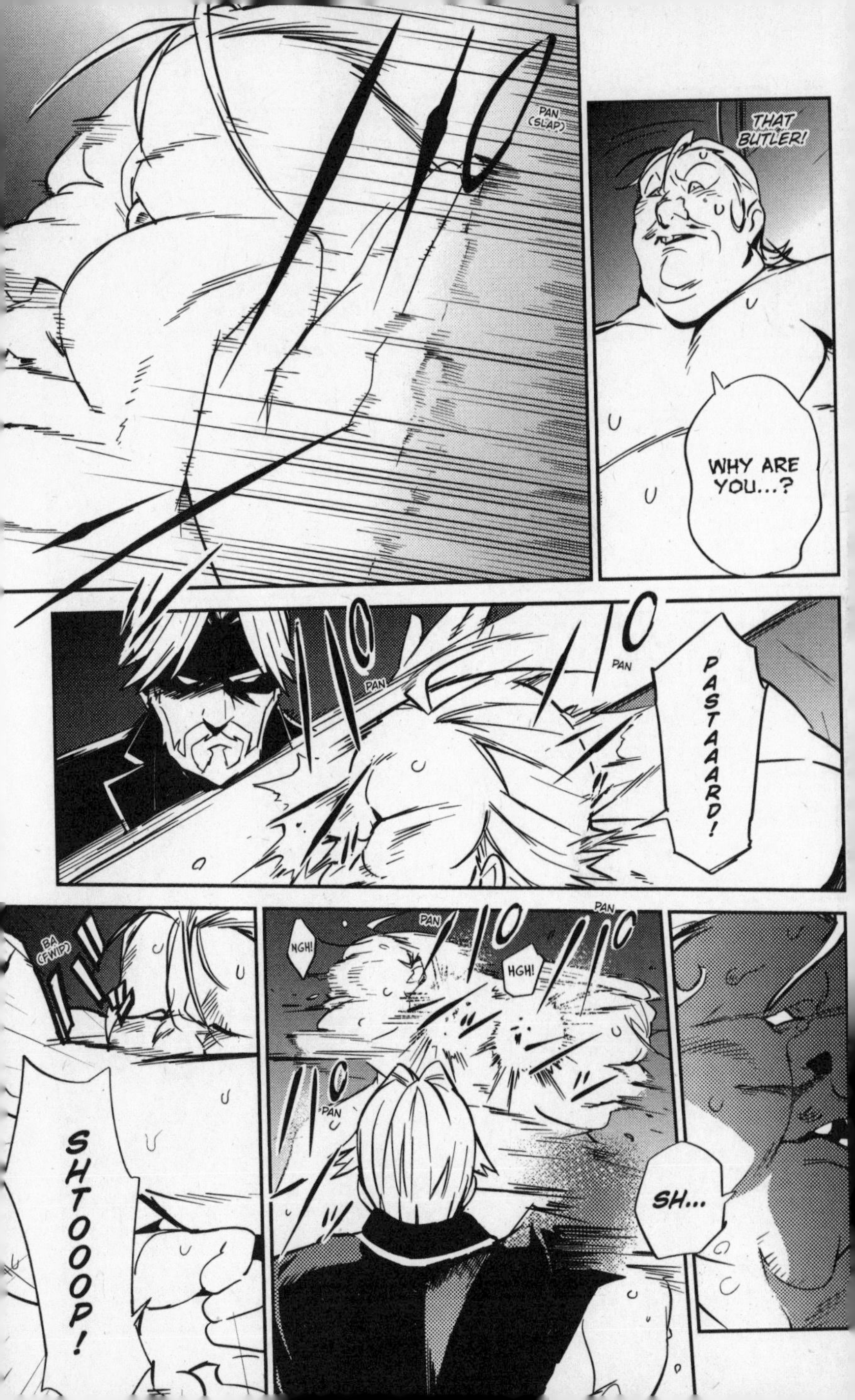
THAT BUTLER!
WHY ARE YOU...?
PAN (SLAP)
PASTAAARD!
PAN
PAN
SH...
PAN
PAN
HGH!
NGH!
PAN
BA (FWIP)
SHTOOOOP!

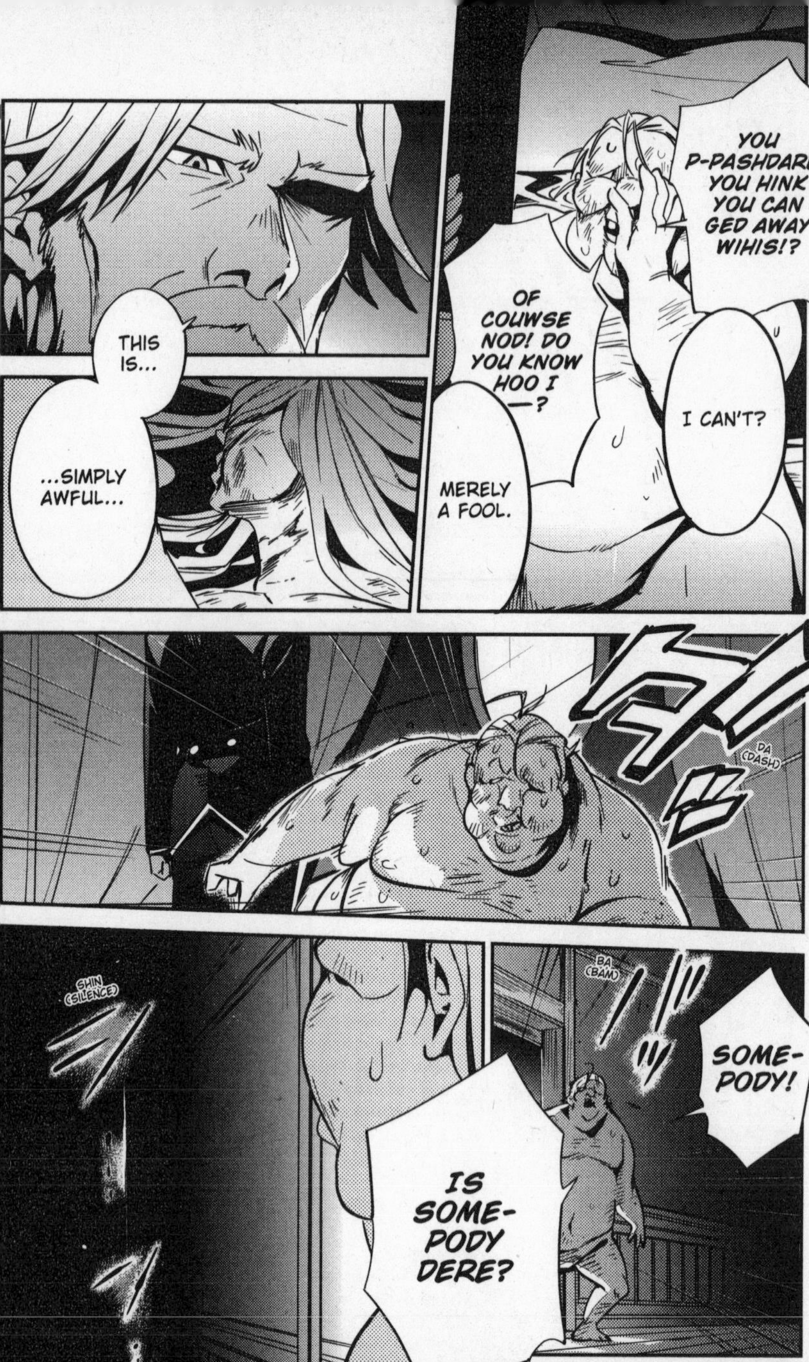
YOU P-PASHDARD! YOU HINK YOU CAN GED AWAY WIHIS!?
I CAN'T?
OF COUWSE NOD! DO YOU KNOW HOO I —?
MERELY A FOOL.
THIS IS...
...SIMPLY AWFUL...
DA (DASH)
BA (BAM)
SOME-PODY!
IS SOME-PODY DERE?
SHIN (SILENCE)

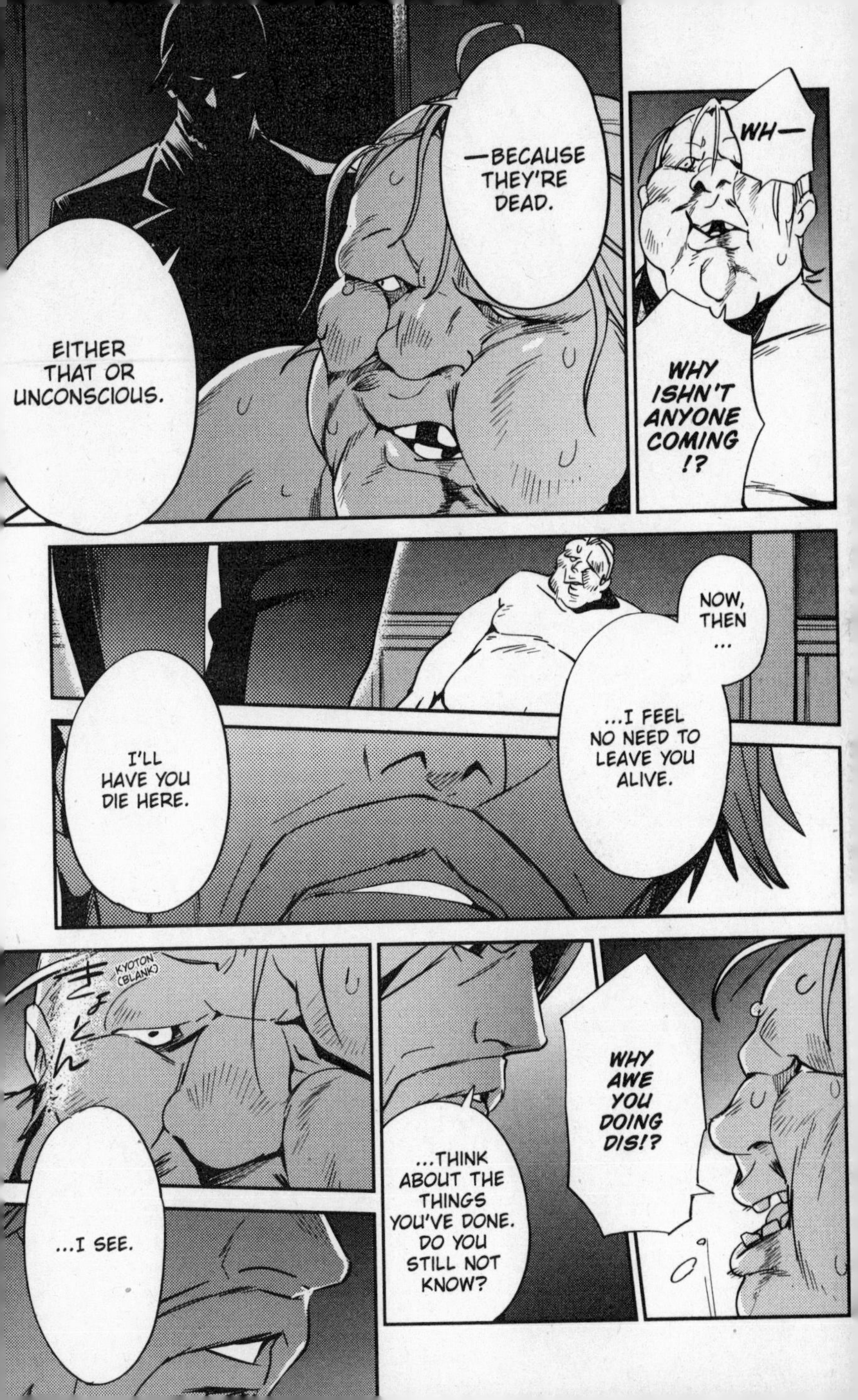
WH—
WHY ISHN'T ANYONE COMING!?
—BECAUSE THEY'RE DEAD.
EITHER THAT OR UNCONSCIOUS.
NOW, THEN...
...I FEEL NO NEED TO LEAVE YOU ALIVE.
I'LL HAVE YOU DIE HERE.
WHY AWE YOU DOING DIS!?
...THINK ABOUT THE THINGS YOU'VE DONE. DO YOU STILL NOT KNOW?
きょとん
KYOTON (BLANK)
...I SEE.

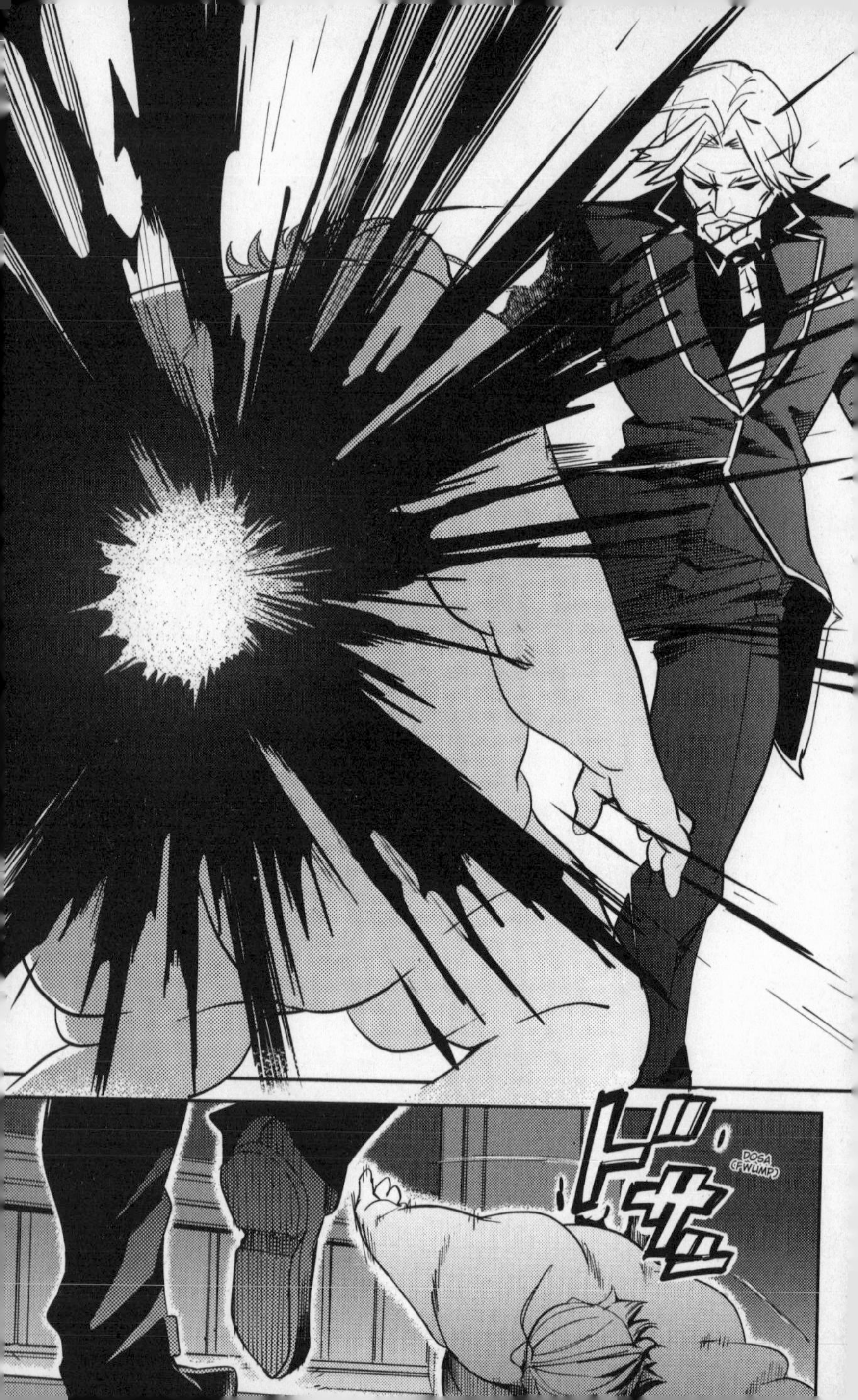
ドサッ
DOSA (FWUMP)

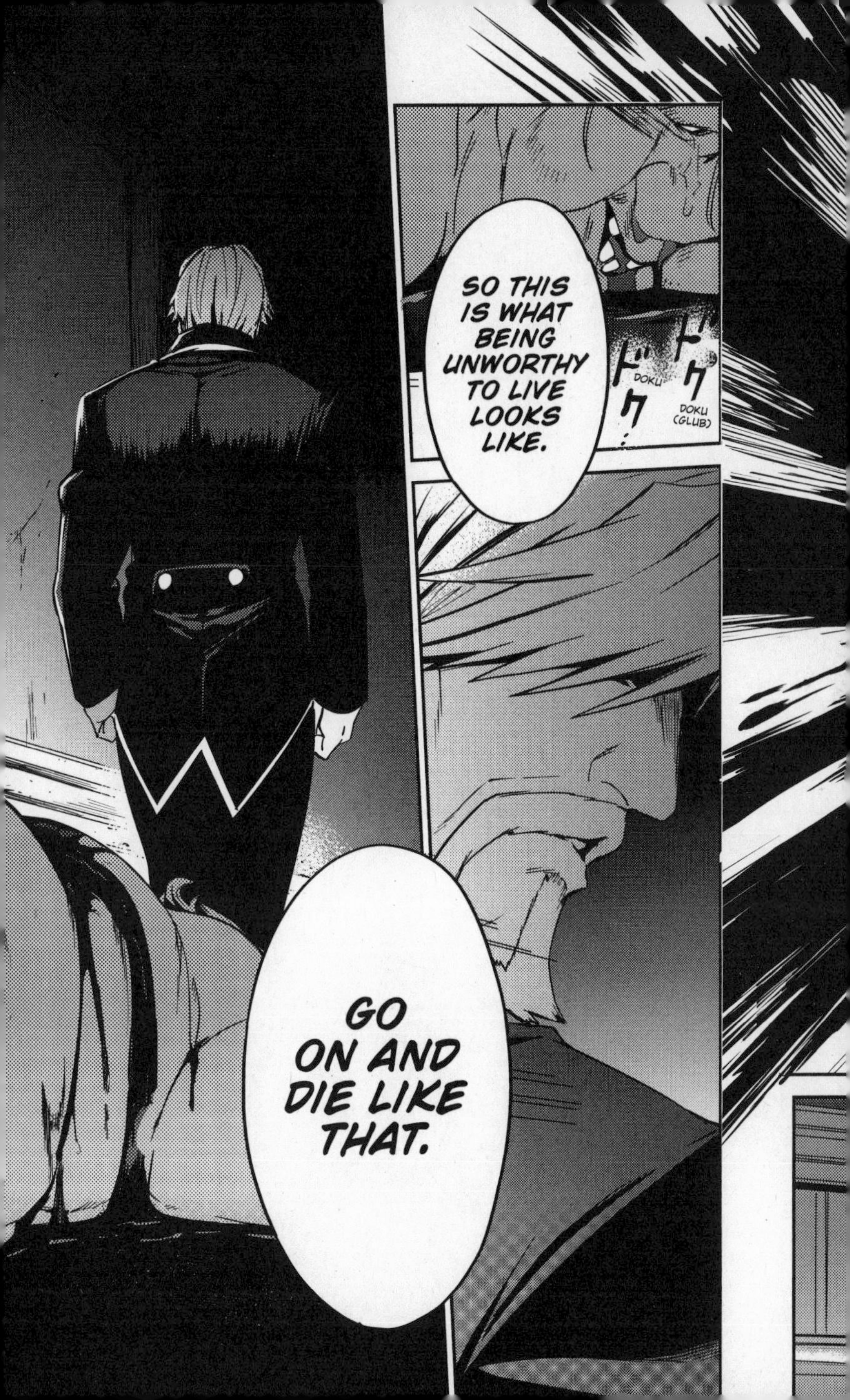
SO THIS IS WHAT BEING UNWORTHY TO LIVE LOOKS LIKE.
ドク ドク
DOKU
DOKU (GLUB)
GO ON AND DIE LIKE THAT.

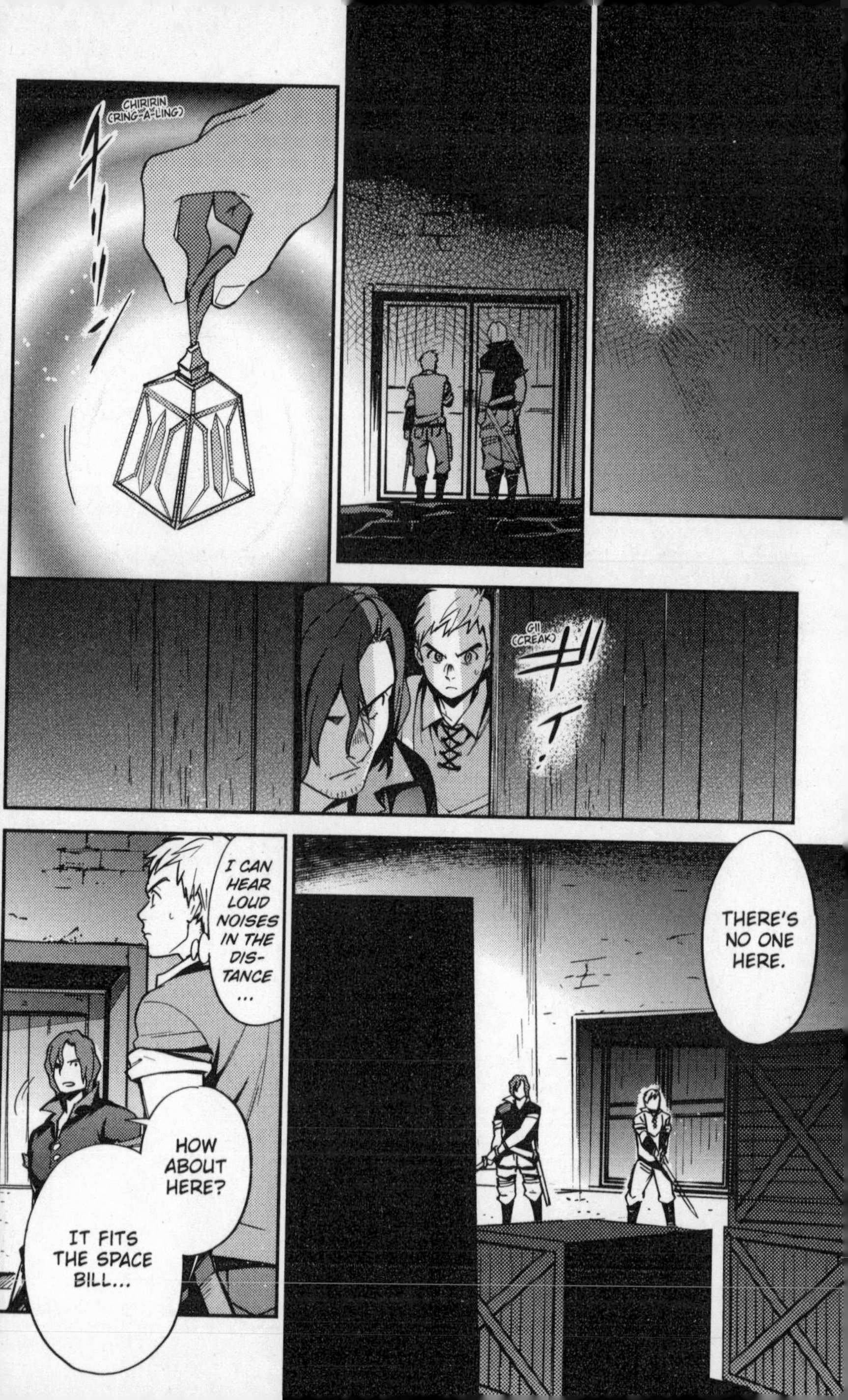
CHIRIRIN (RING-A-LING)
GII (CREAK)
THERE'S NO ONE HERE.
I CAN HEAR LOUD NOISES IN THE DIS-TANCE...
HOW ABOUT HERE?
IT FITS THE SPACE BILL...

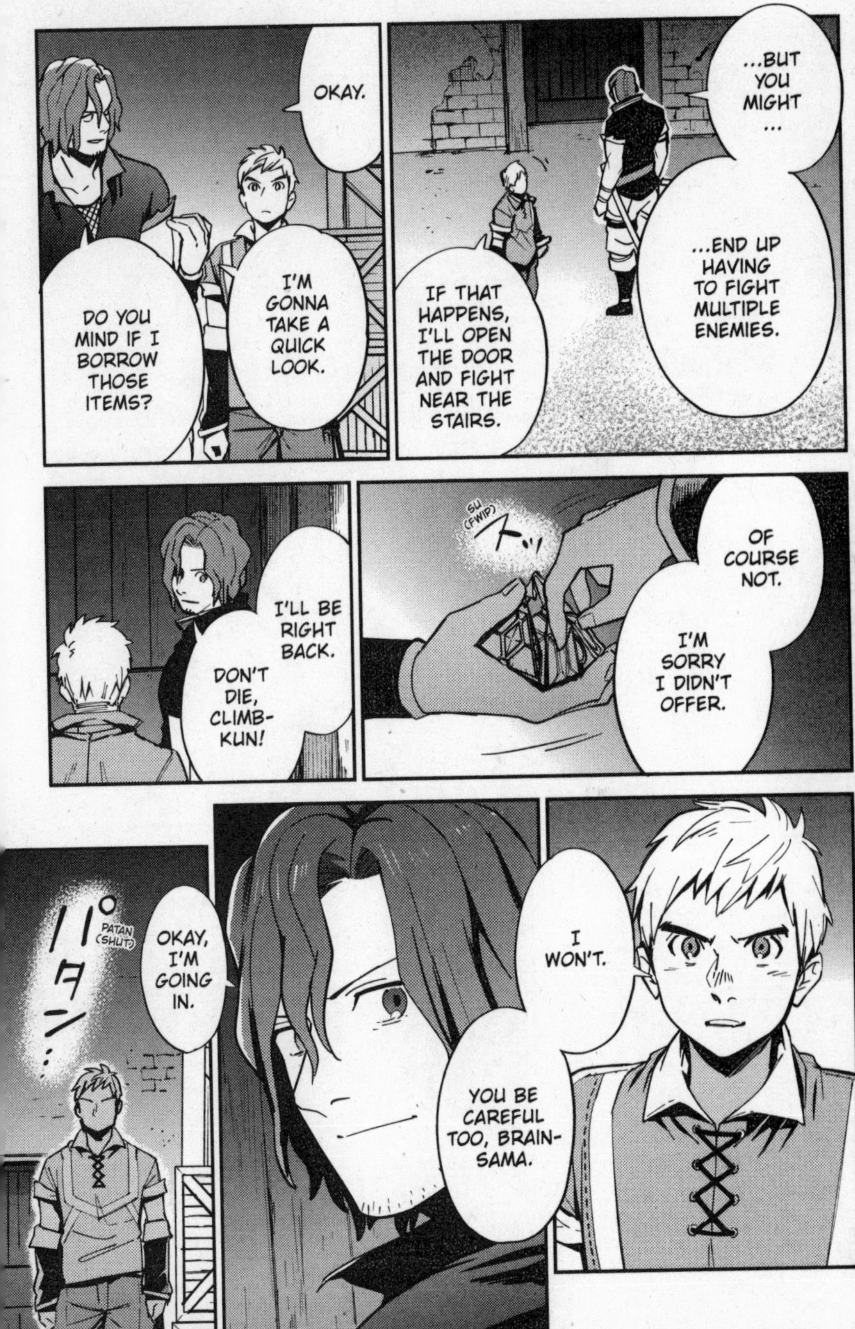
...BUT YOU MIGHT ...
...END UP HAVING TO FIGHT MULTIPLE ENEMIES.
IF THAT HAPPENS, I'LL OPEN THE DOOR AND FIGHT NEAR THE STAIRS.
OKAY.
I'M GONNA TAKE A QUICK LOOK.
DO YOU MIND IF I BORROW THOSE ITEMS?
SU (FWIP)
OF COURSE NOT.
I'M SORRY I DIDN'T OFFER.
I'LL BE RIGHT BACK.
DON'T DIE, CLIMB-KUN!
I WON'T.
YOU BE CAREFUL TOO, BRAIN-SAMA.
OKAY, I'M GOING IN.
PATAN (SHUT)

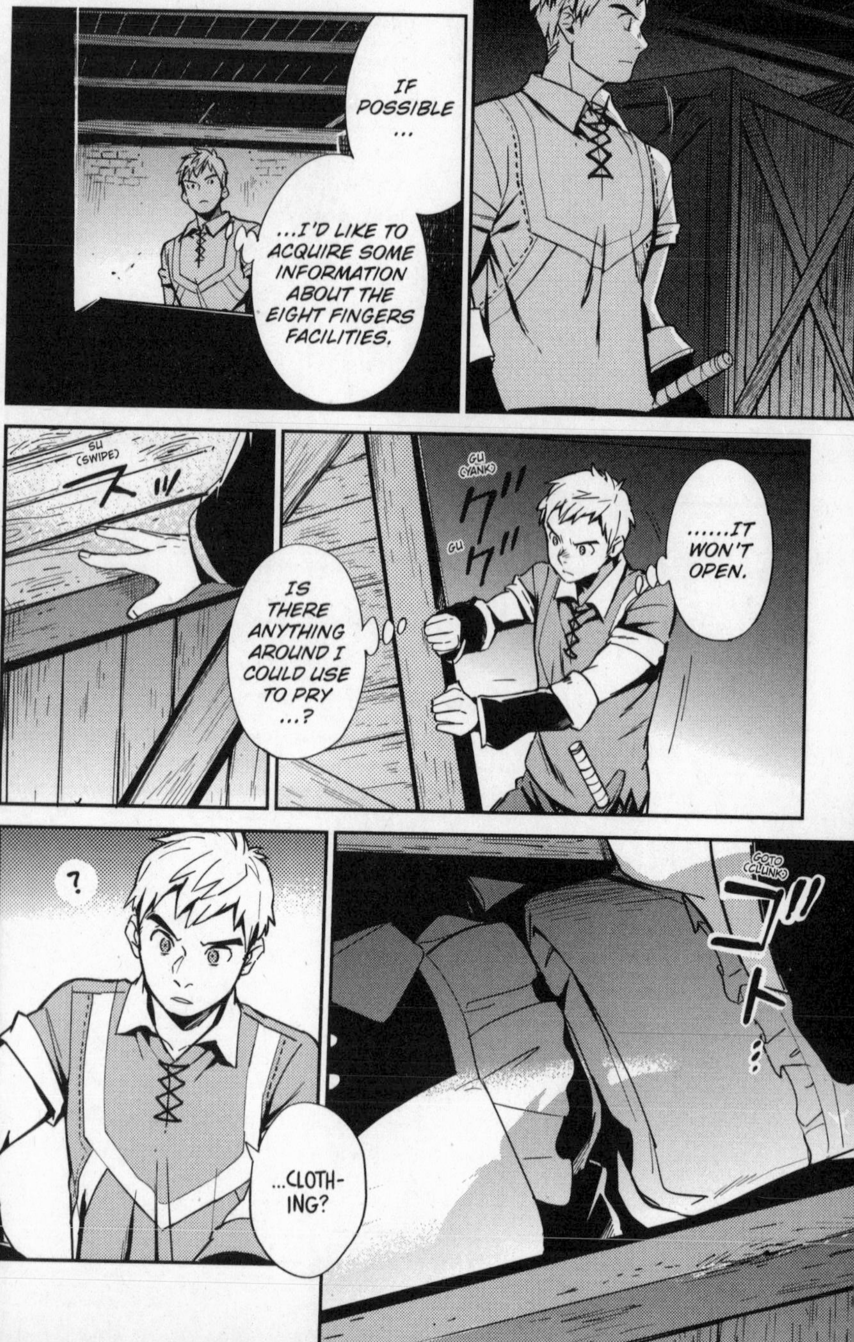
IF POSSIBLE ...
...I'D LIKE TO ACQUIRE SOME INFORMATION ABOUT THE EIGHT FINGERS FACILITIES.
GU (YANK)
グッ
GU
グッ
......IT WON'T OPEN.
IS THERE ANYTHING AROUND I COULD USE TO PRY ...?
SU (SWIPE)
スッ
GOTO (CLUNK)
ゴトッ...
?
...CLOTH-ING?

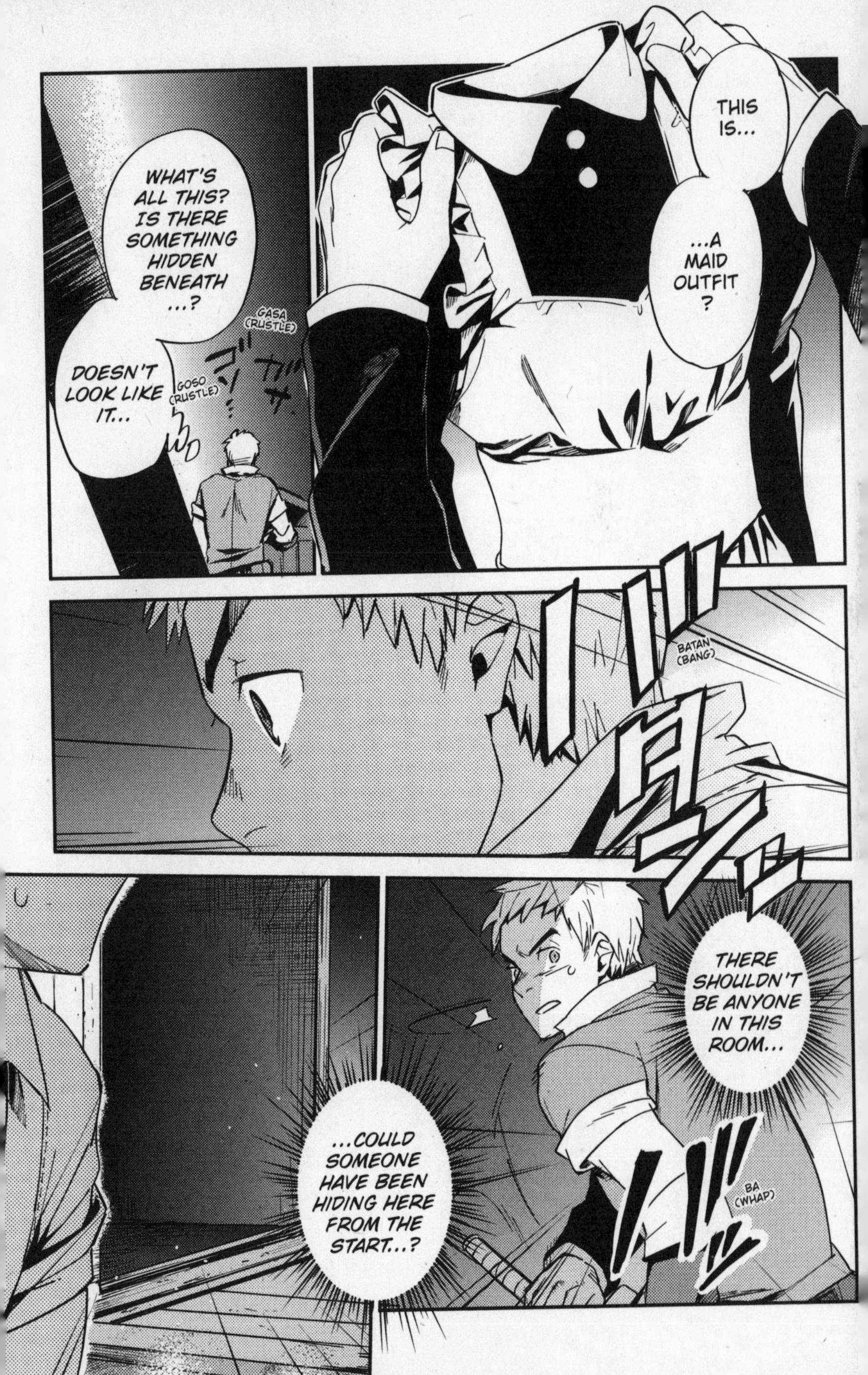
THIS IS...
...A MAID OUTFIT?
WHAT'S ALL THIS? IS THERE SOMETHING HIDDEN BENEATH...?
GASA (RUSTLE)
DOESN'T LOOK LIKE IT...
GOSO (RUSTLE)
BATAN (BANG)
THERE SHOULDN'T BE ANYONE IN THIS ROOM...
...COULD SOMEONE HAVE BEEN HIDING HERE FROM THE START...?
BA (WHAP)

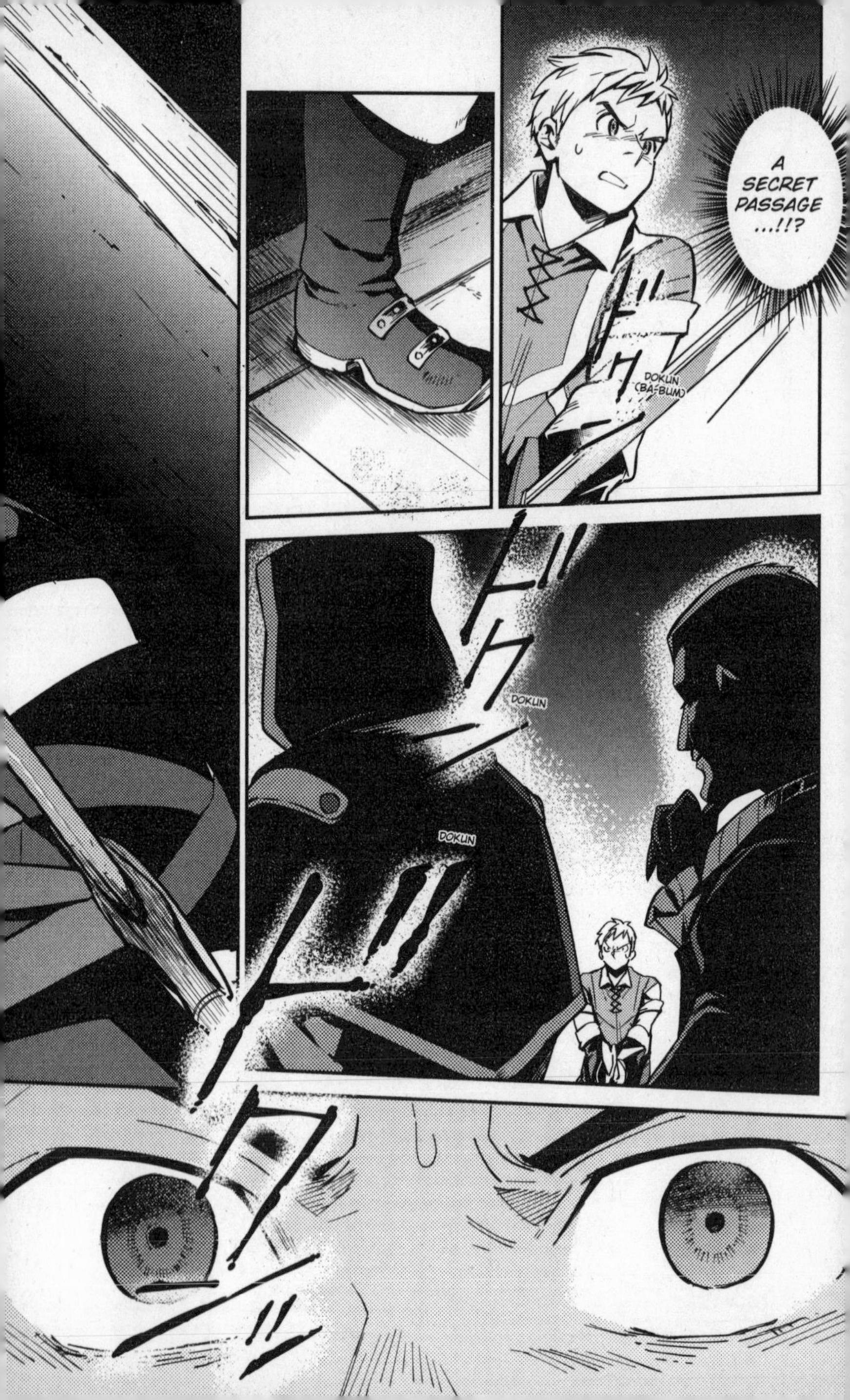
A SECRET PASSAGE ...!!?
DOKUN (BA-BUM)
DOKUN
DOKUN

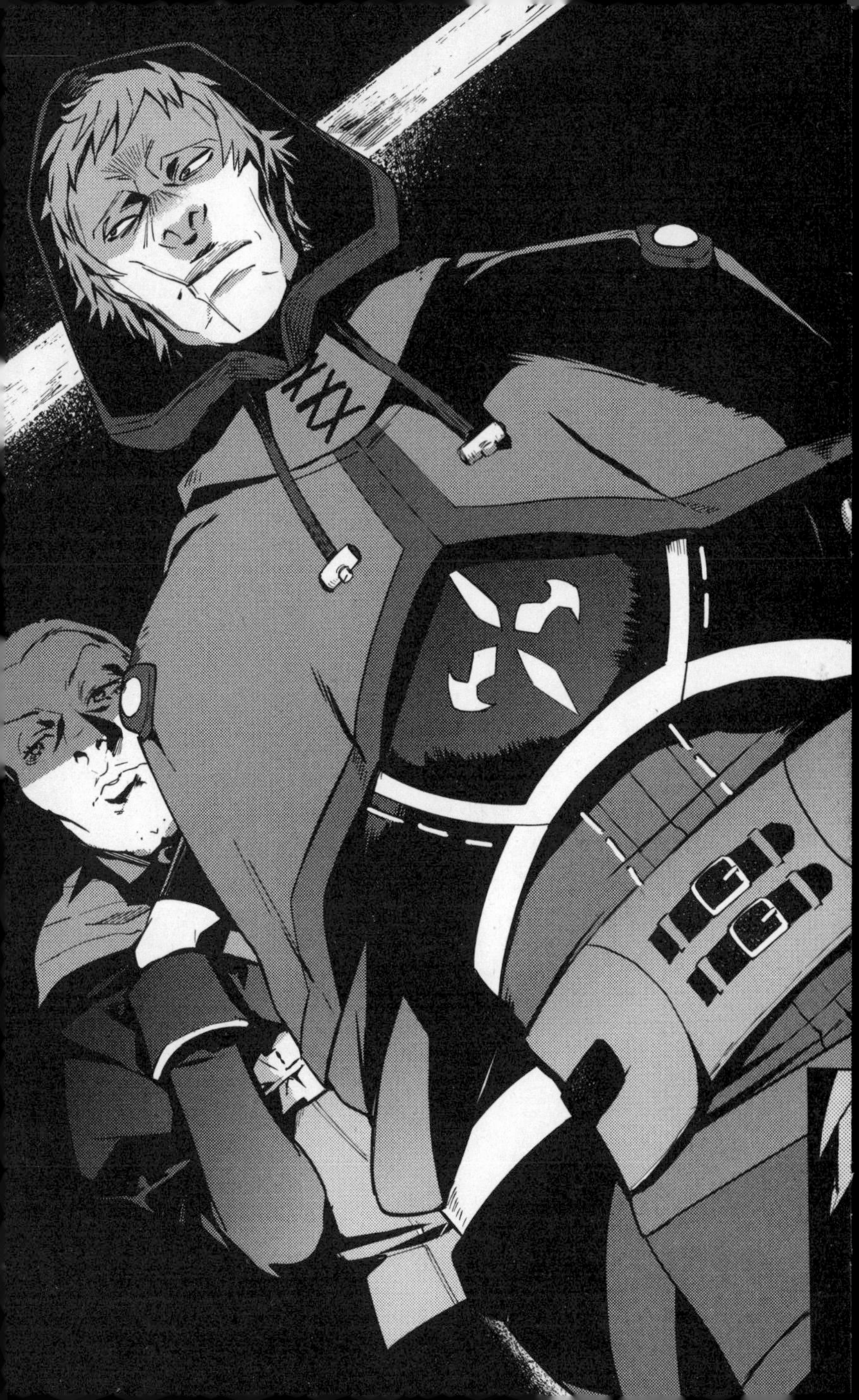

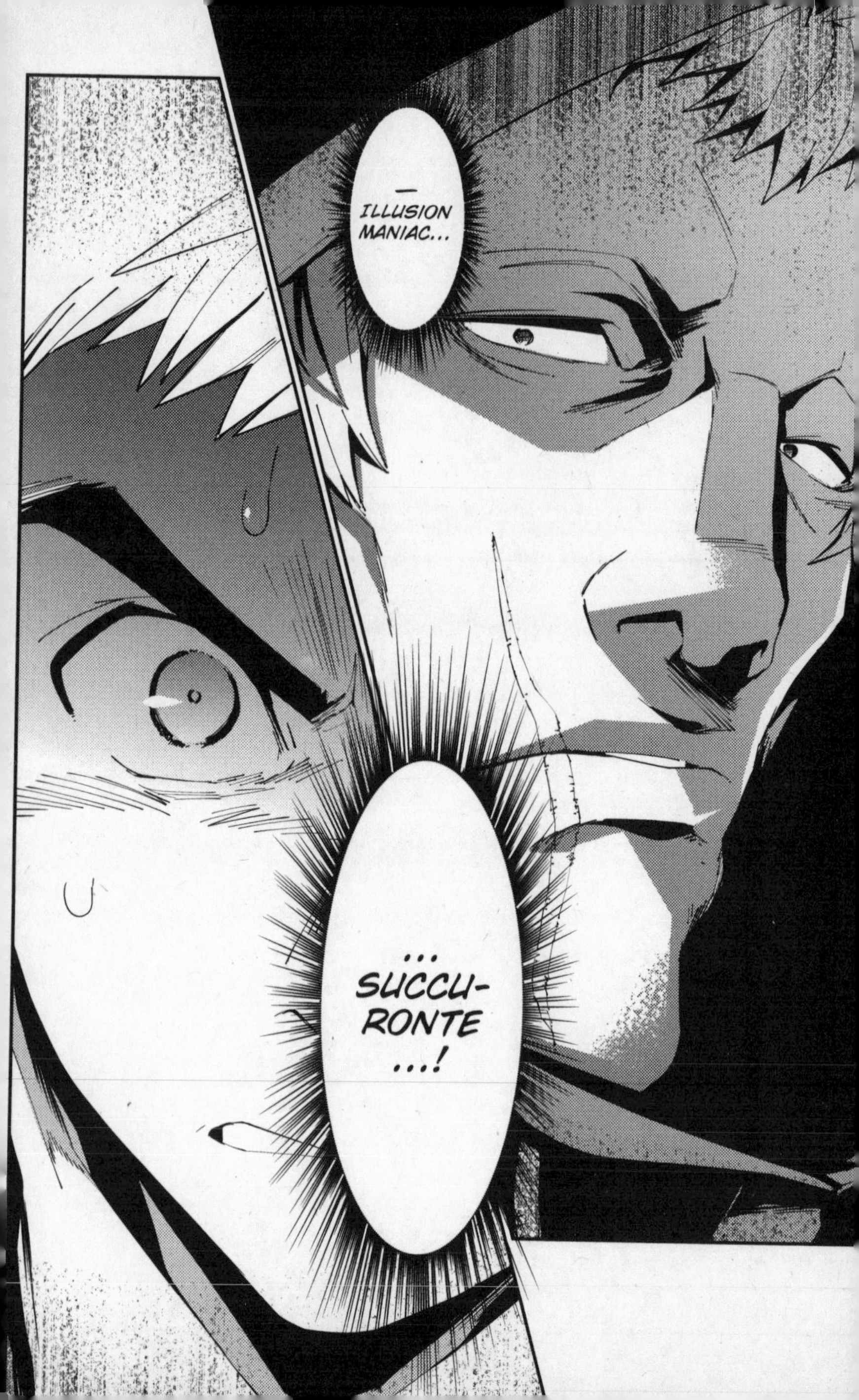
—ILLUSION MANIAC...
...SUCCU-RONTE ...!

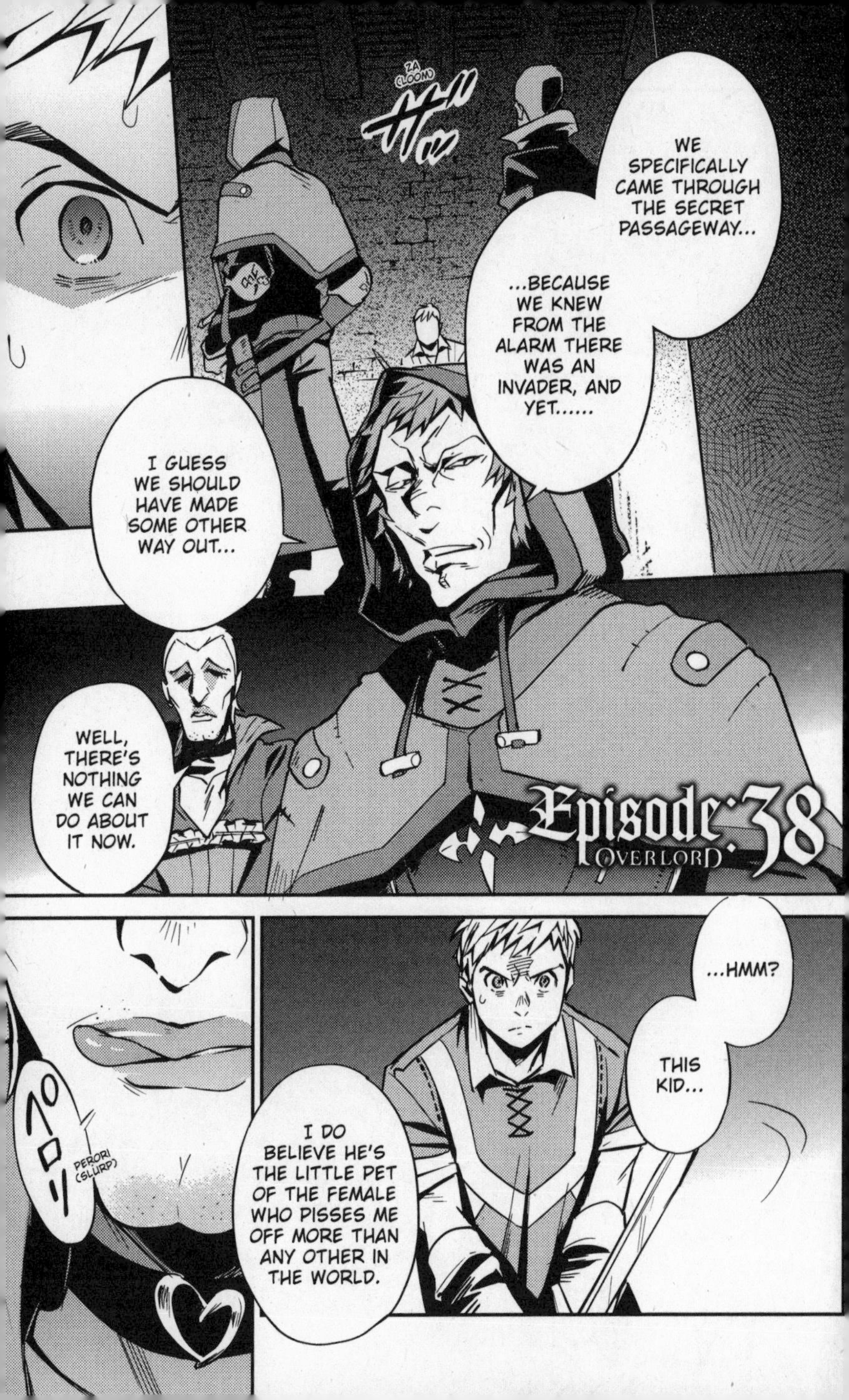

WE SPECIFICALLY CAME THROUGH THE SECRET PASSAGEWAY...
ZA (LOOM)
...BECAUSE WE KNEW FROM THE ALARM THERE WAS AN INVADER, AND YET......
I GUESS WE SHOULD HAVE MADE SOME OTHER WAY OUT...
WELL, THERE'S NOTHING WE CAN DO ABOUT IT NOW.
Episode:38
OVERLORD
...HMM?
THIS KID...
I DO BELIEVE HE'S THE LITTLE PET OF THE FEMALE WHO PISSES ME OFF MORE THAN ANY OTHER IN THE WORLD.
ペロリ
PERORI (SLURP)

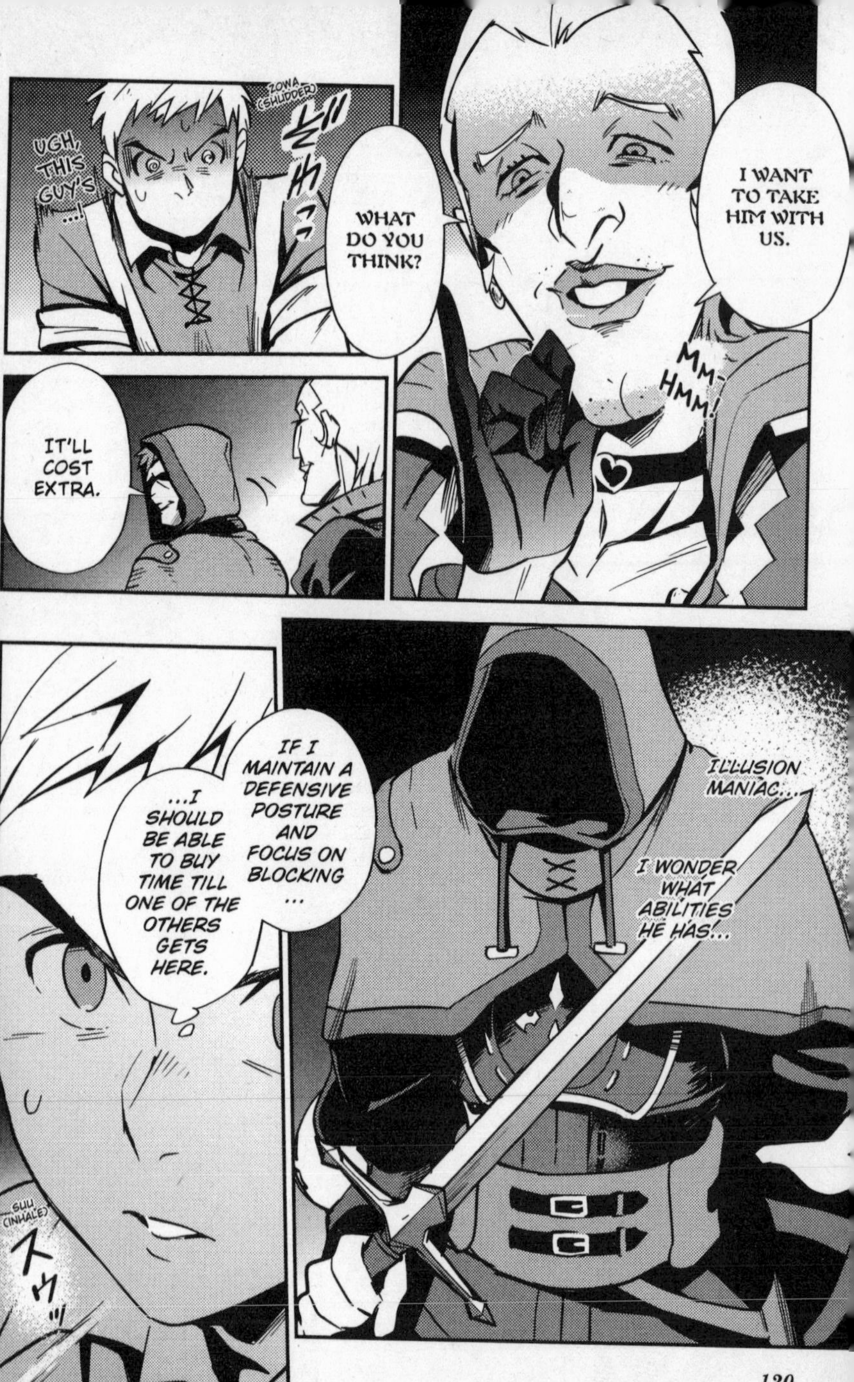
I WANT TO TAKE HIM WITH US.
WHAT DO YOU THINK?
MM-HMM!
ZOWA (SHUDDER)
UGH, THIS GUY'S ...!
IT'LL COST EXTRA.
ILLUSION MANIAC...
I WONDER WHAT ABILITIES HE HAS...
IF I MAINTAIN A DEFENSIVE POSTURE AND FOCUS ON BLOCKING ...
...I SHOULD BE ABLE TO BUY TIME TILL ONE OF THE OTHERS GETS HERE.
SUU (INHALE)

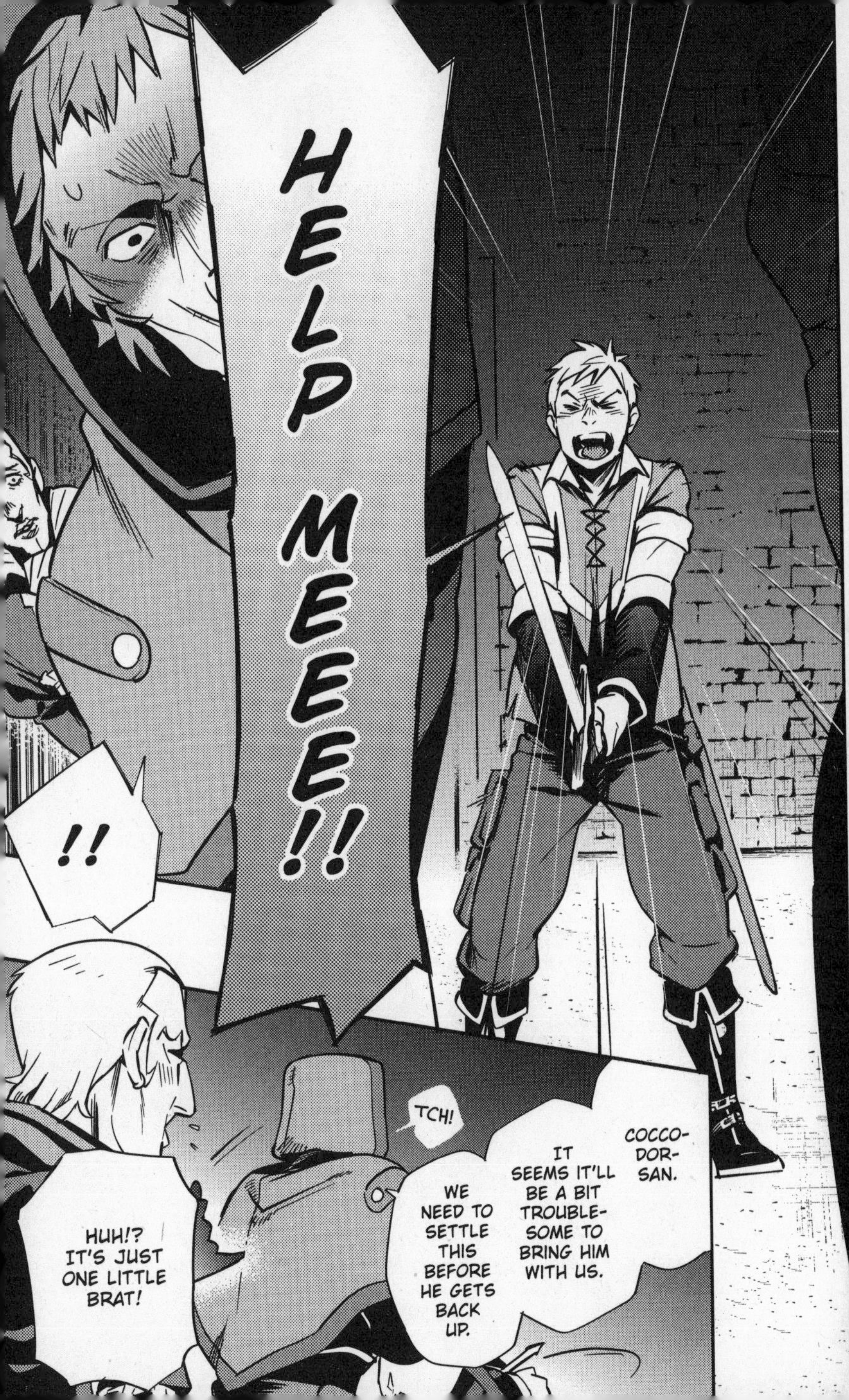
HELP MEEE!!
!!
COCCO-DOR-SAN.
IT SEEMS IT'LL BE A BIT TROUBLE-SOME TO BRING HIM WITH US.
WE NEED TO SETTLE THIS BEFORE HE GETS BACK UP.
TCH!
HUH!? IT'S JUST ONE LITTLE BRAT!

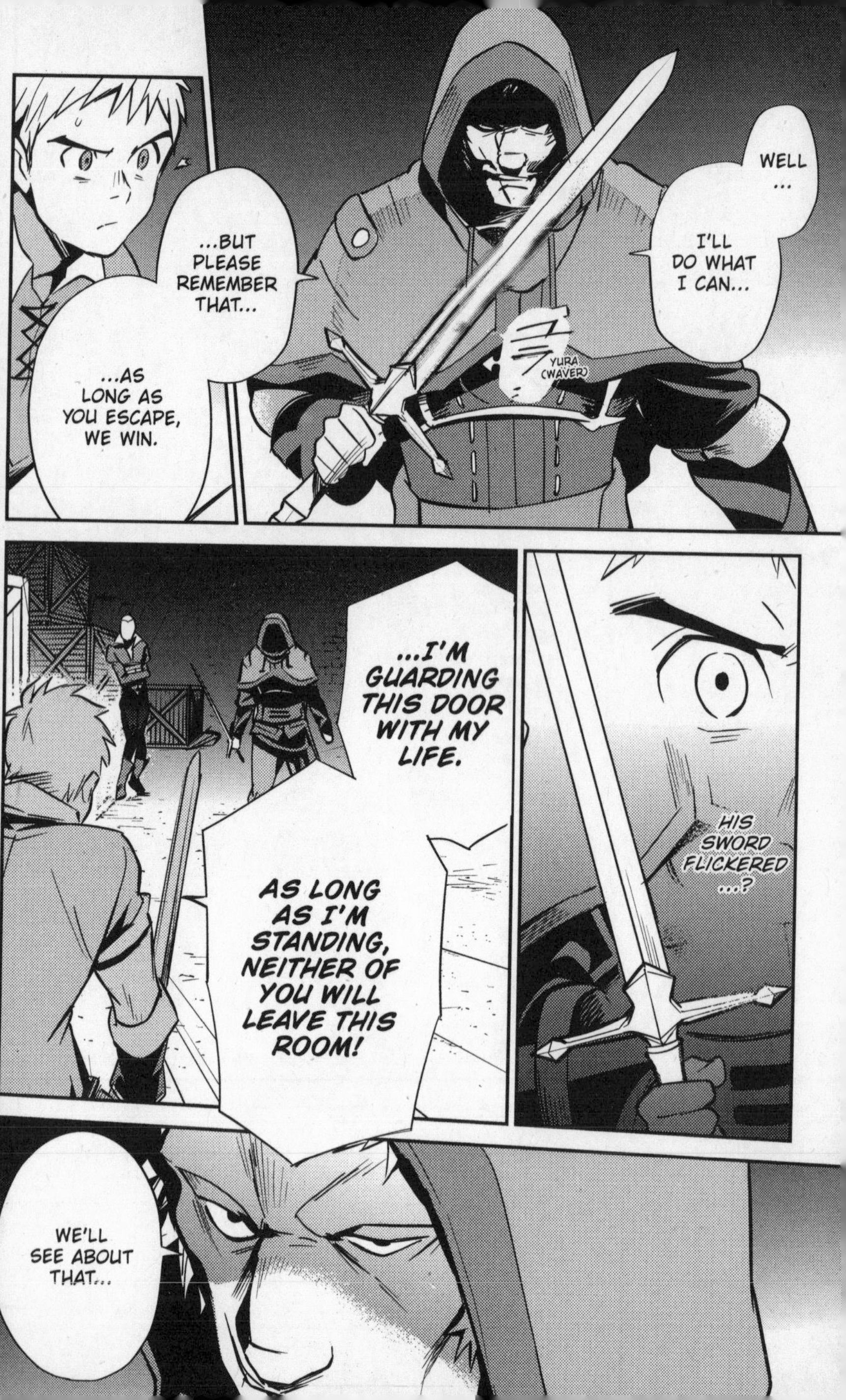
WELL ...
I'LL DO WHAT I CAN...
YURA (WAVER)
...BUT PLEASE REMEMBER THAT...
...AS LONG AS YOU ESCAPE, WE WIN.
HIS SWORD FLICKERED ...?
...I'M GUARDING THIS DOOR WITH MY LIFE.
AS LONG AS I'M STANDING, NEITHER OF YOU WILL LEAVE THIS ROOM!
WE'LL SEE ABOUT THAT...

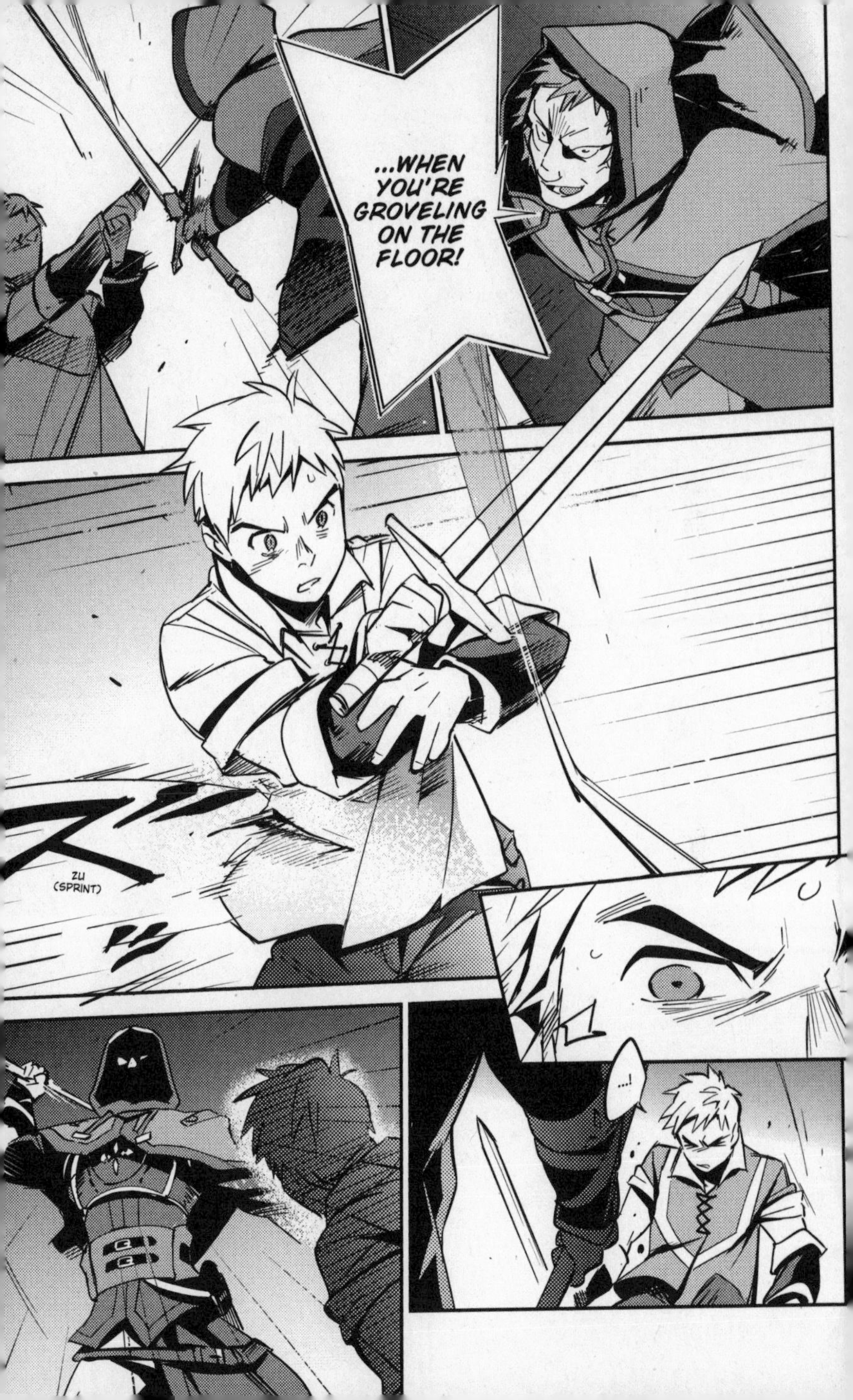
...WHEN YOU'RE GROVELING ON THE FLOOR!
ZU (SPRINT)
...!

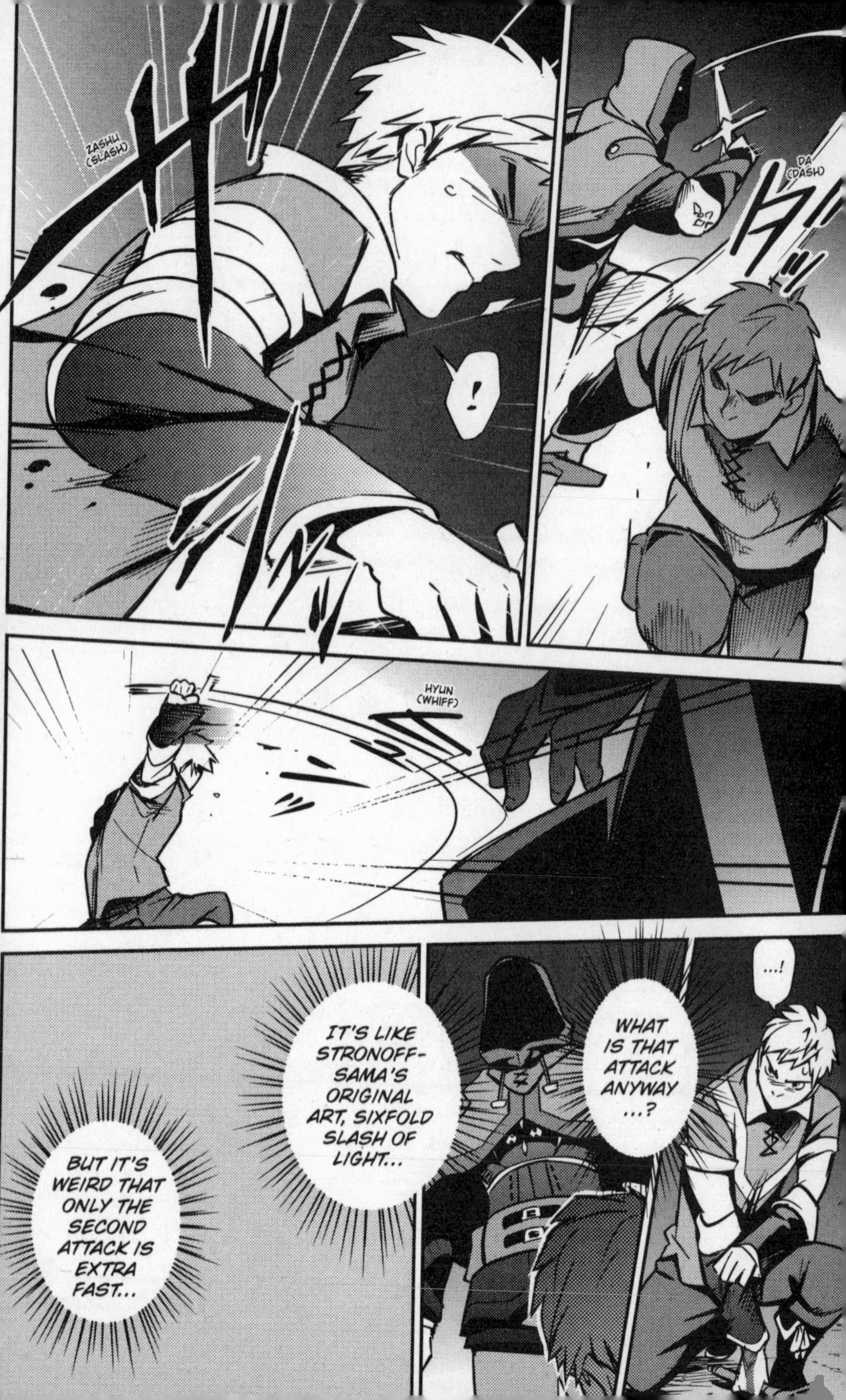
DA (DASH)
ZASHU (SLASH)
!
HYUN (WHIFF)
...!
WHAT IS THAT ATTACK ANYWAY...?
IT'S LIKE STRONOFF-SAMA'S ORIGINAL ART, SIXFOLD SLASH OF LIGHT...
BUT IT'S WEIRD THAT ONLY THE SECOND ATTACK IS EXTRA FAST...

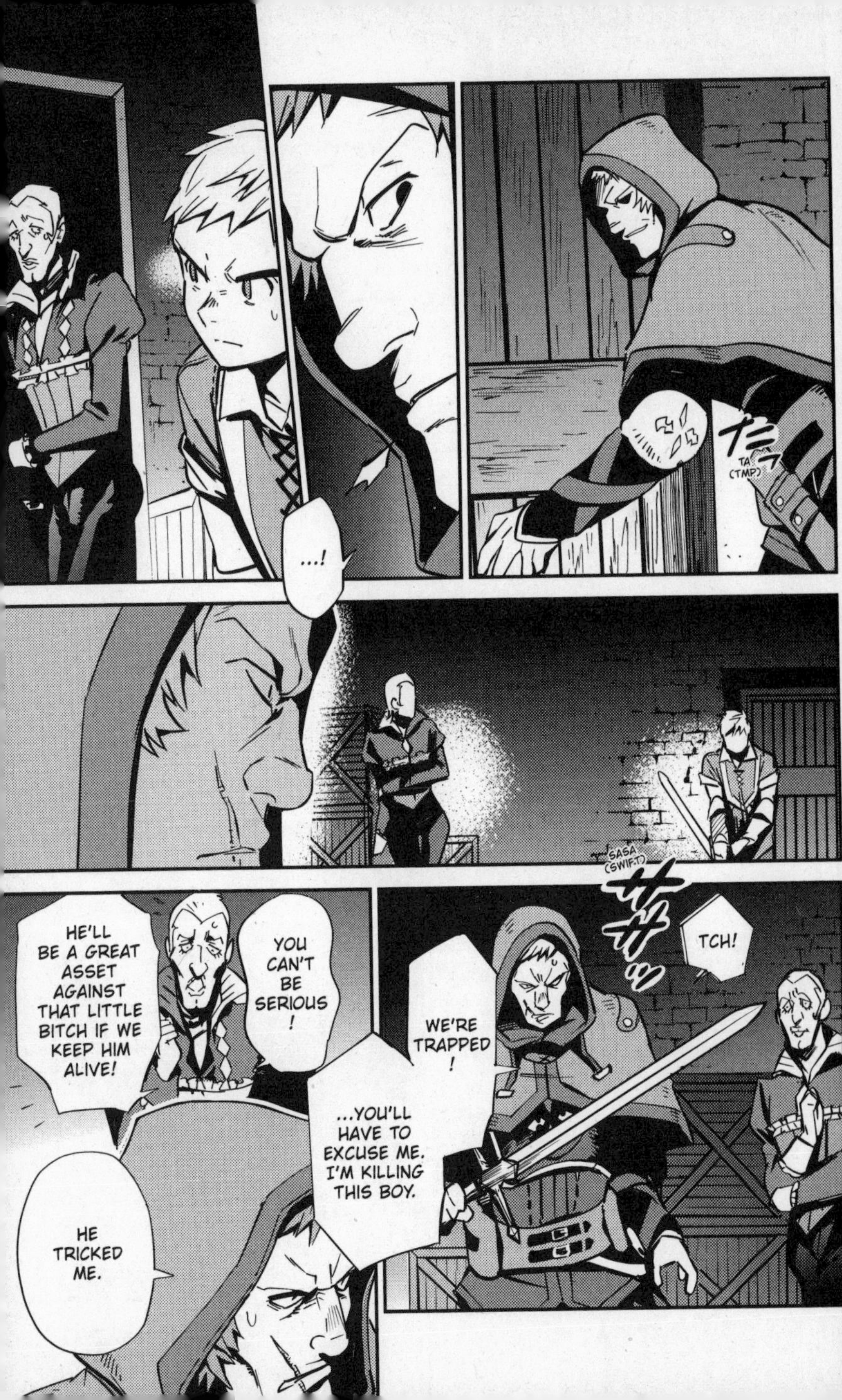
TA (TMP)
...!
SASA (SWIFT)
TCH!
WE'RE TRAPPED!
YOU CAN'T BE SERIOUS!
HE'LL BE A GREAT ASSET AGAINST THAT LITTLE BITCH IF WE KEEP HIM ALIVE!
...YOU'LL HAVE TO EXCUSE ME. I'M KILLING THIS BOY.
HE TRICKED ME.

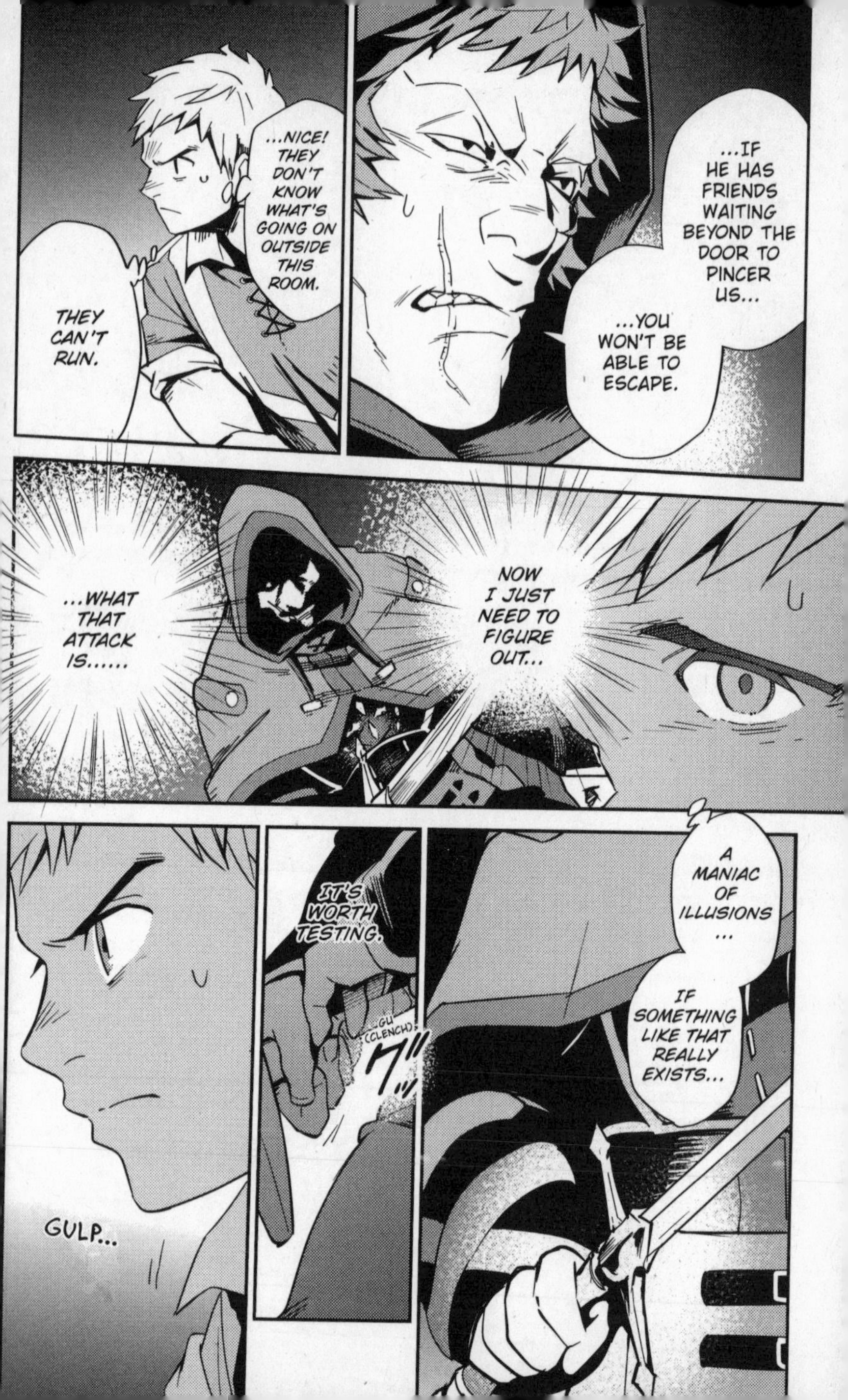
...IF HE HAS FRIENDS WAITING BEYOND THE DOOR TO PINCER US...
...YOU WON'T BE ABLE TO ESCAPE.
...NICE! THEY DON'T KNOW WHAT'S GOING ON OUTSIDE THIS ROOM.
THEY CAN'T RUN.
NOW I JUST NEED TO FIGURE OUT...
...WHAT THAT ATTACK IS......
A MANIAC OF ILLUSIONS ...
IF SOMETHING LIKE THAT REALLY EXISTS...
IT'S WORTH TESTING.
GU (CLENCH)
GULP...

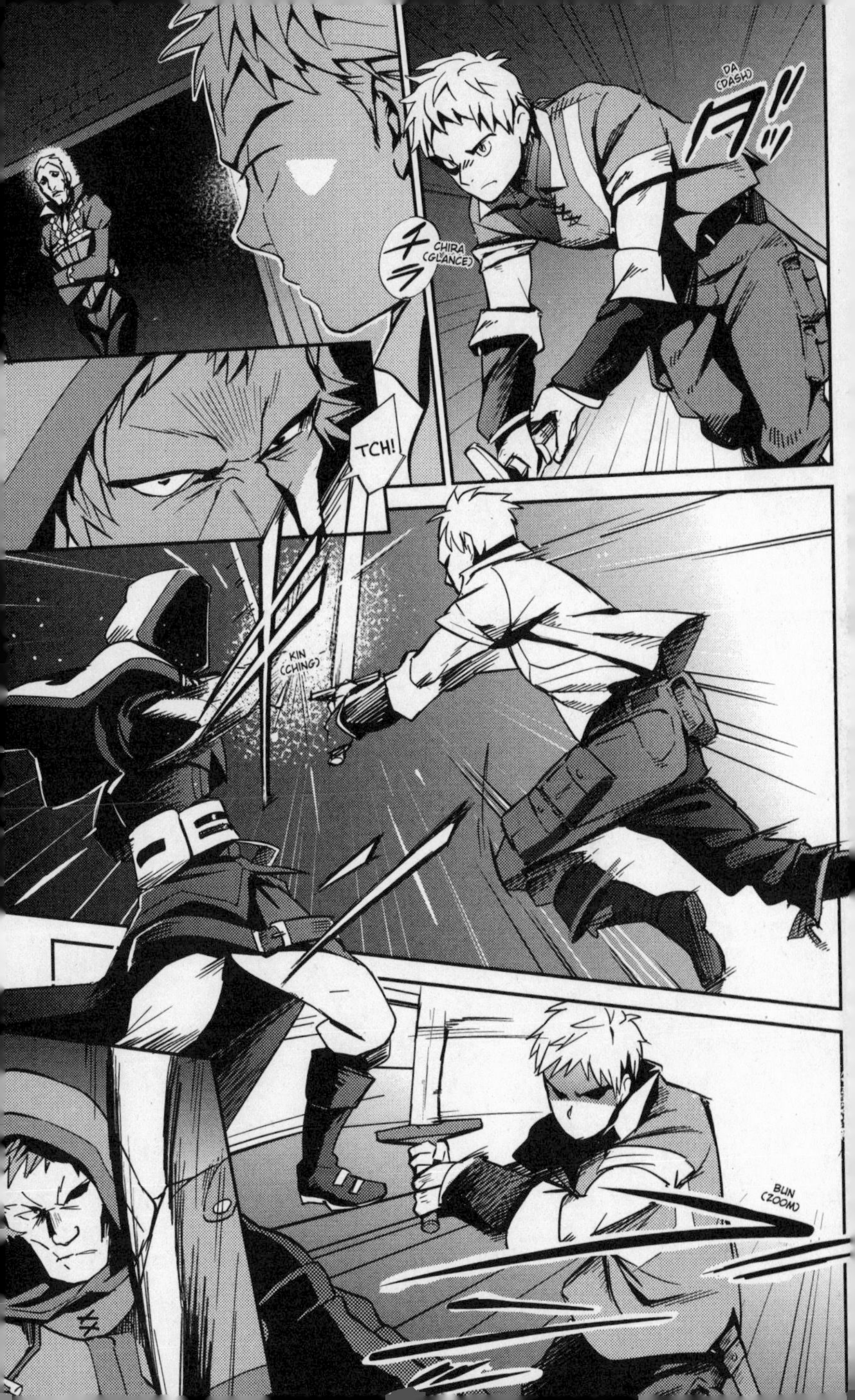
DA (DASH)
ダッ
チラ
CHIRA (GLANCE)
TCH!
KIN (CHING)
BUN (ZOOM)

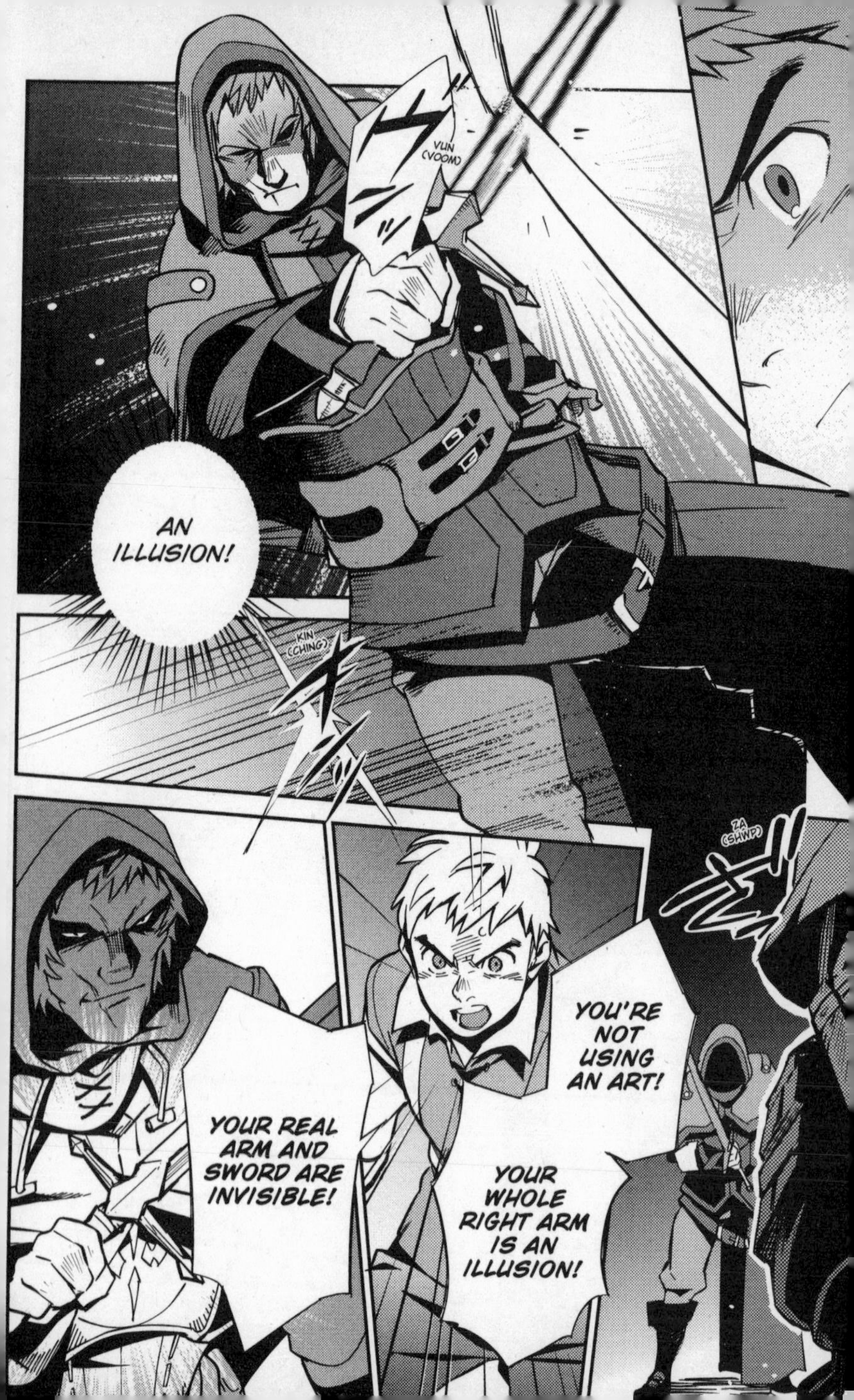
VUN (VOOM)
AN ILLUSION!
KIN (CHING)
ZA (SHWP)
YOU'RE NOT USING AN ART!
YOUR WHOLE RIGHT ARM IS AN ILLUSION!
YOUR REAL ARM AND SWORD ARE INVISIBLE!

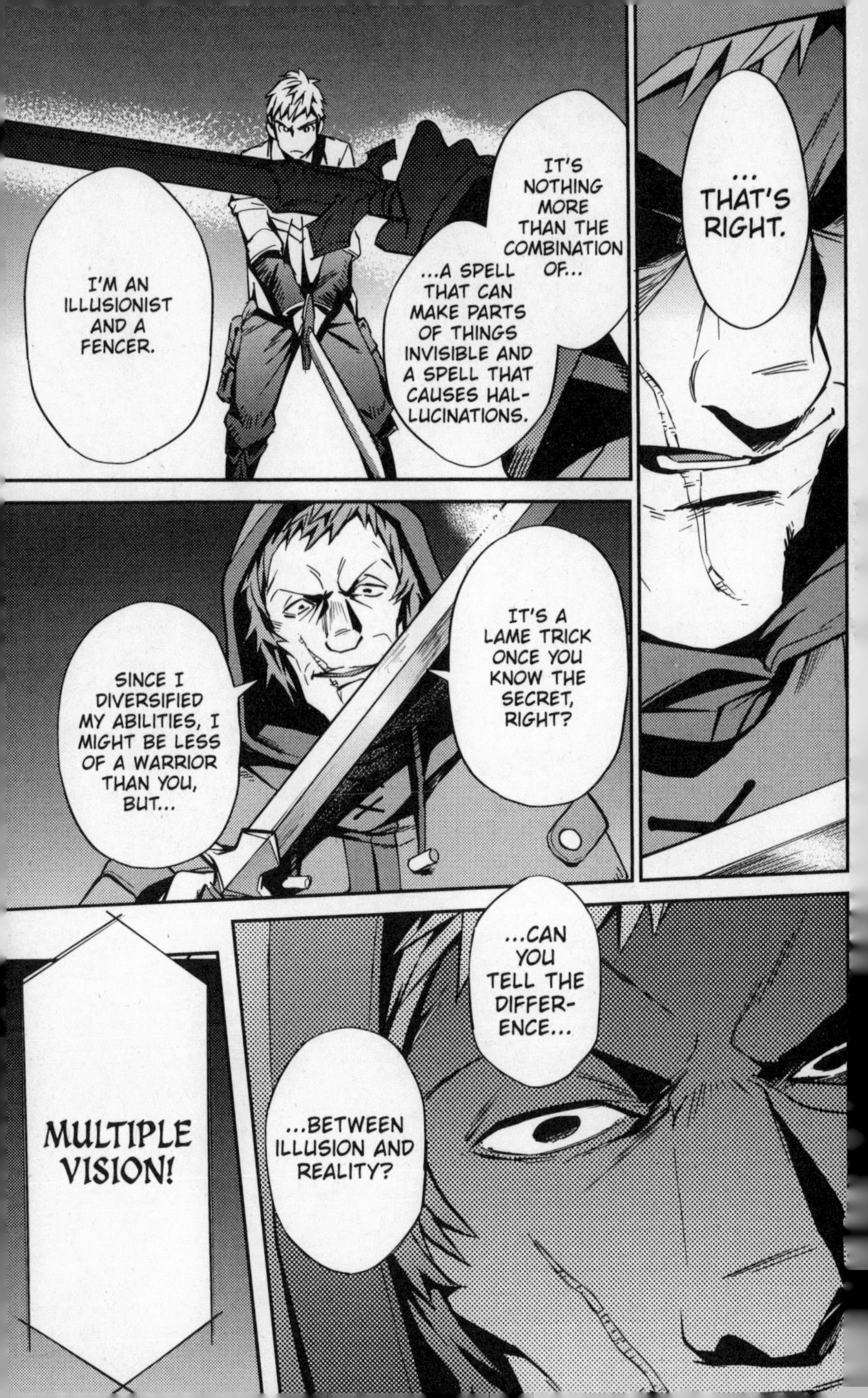
...THAT'S RIGHT.
IT'S NOTHING MORE THAN THE COMBINATION OF...
...A SPELL THAT CAN MAKE PARTS OF THINGS INVISIBLE AND A SPELL THAT CAUSES HAL-LUCINATIONS.
I'M AN ILLUSIONIST AND A FENCER.
IT'S A LAME TRICK ONCE YOU KNOW THE SECRET, RIGHT?
SINCE I DIVERSIFIED MY ABILITIES, I MIGHT BE LESS OF A WARRIOR THAN YOU, BUT...
...CAN YOU TELL THE DIFFER-ENCE...
...BETWEEN ILLUSION AND REALITY?
MULTIPLE VISION!

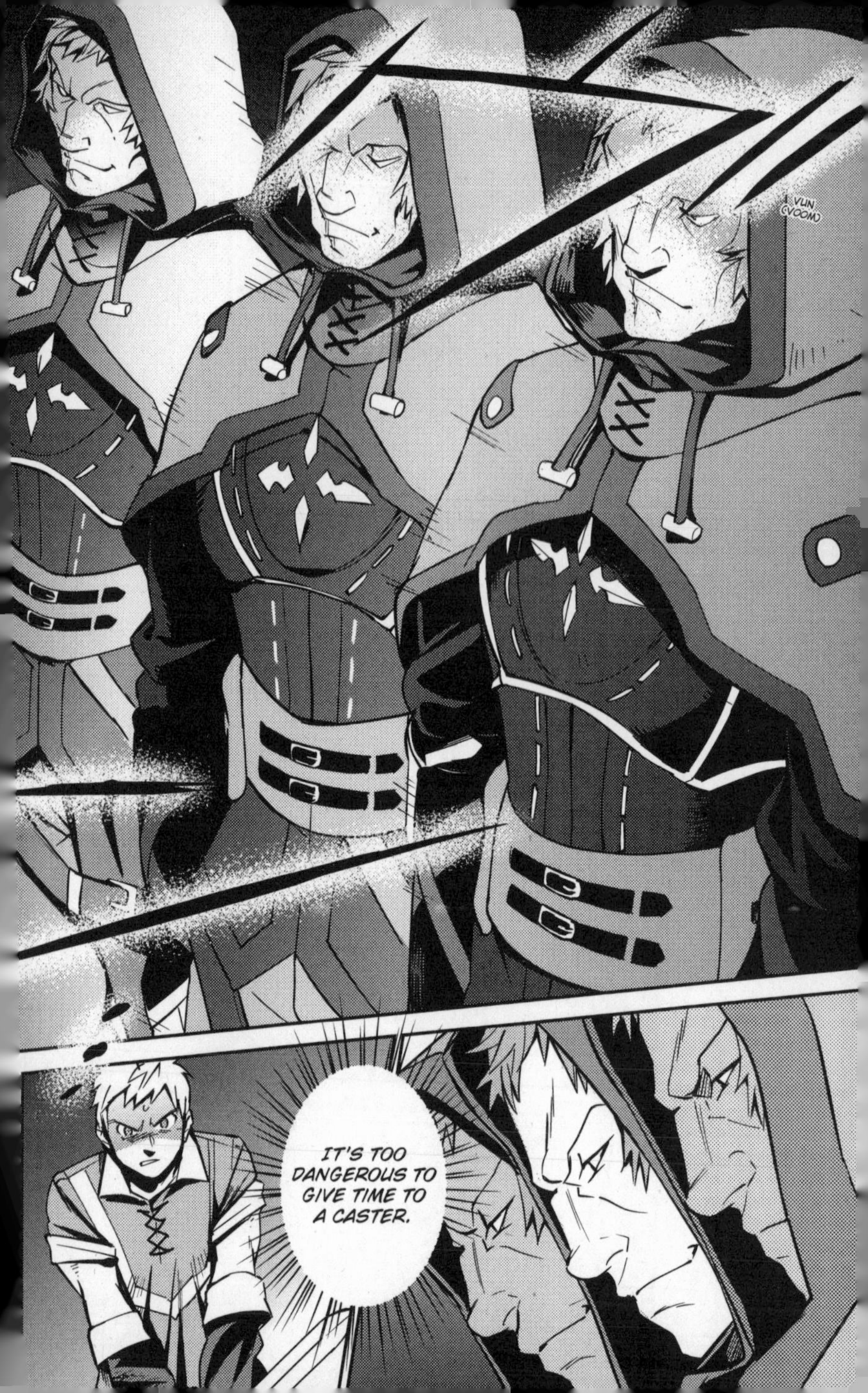
VUN (VOOM)
IT'S TOO DANGEROUS TO GIVE TIME TO A CASTER.

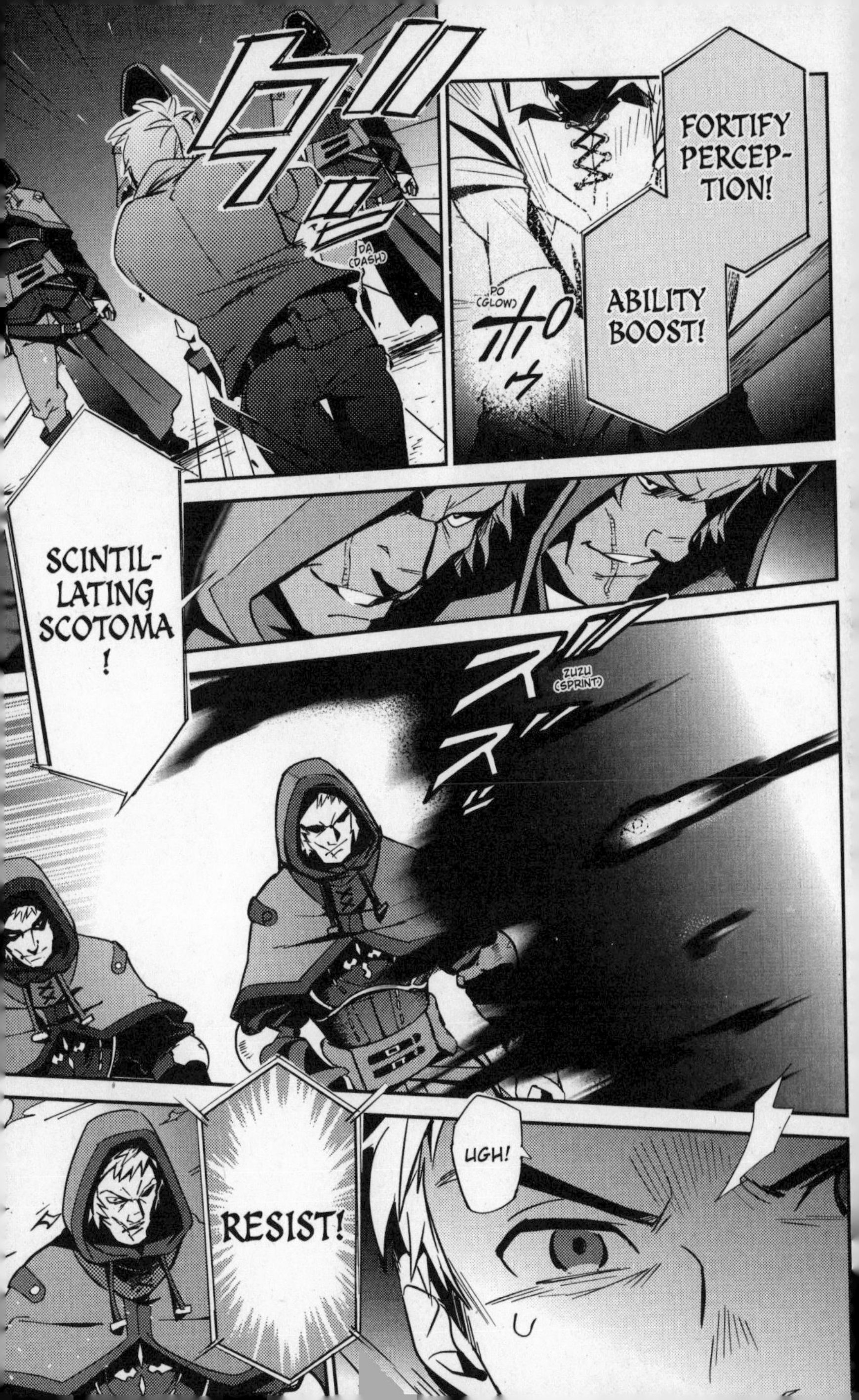
FORTIFY PERCEPTION!
ABILITY BOOST!
PO (GLOW)
DA (DASH)
SCINTILLATING SCOTOMA!
ZUZU (SPRINT)
UGH!
RESIST!

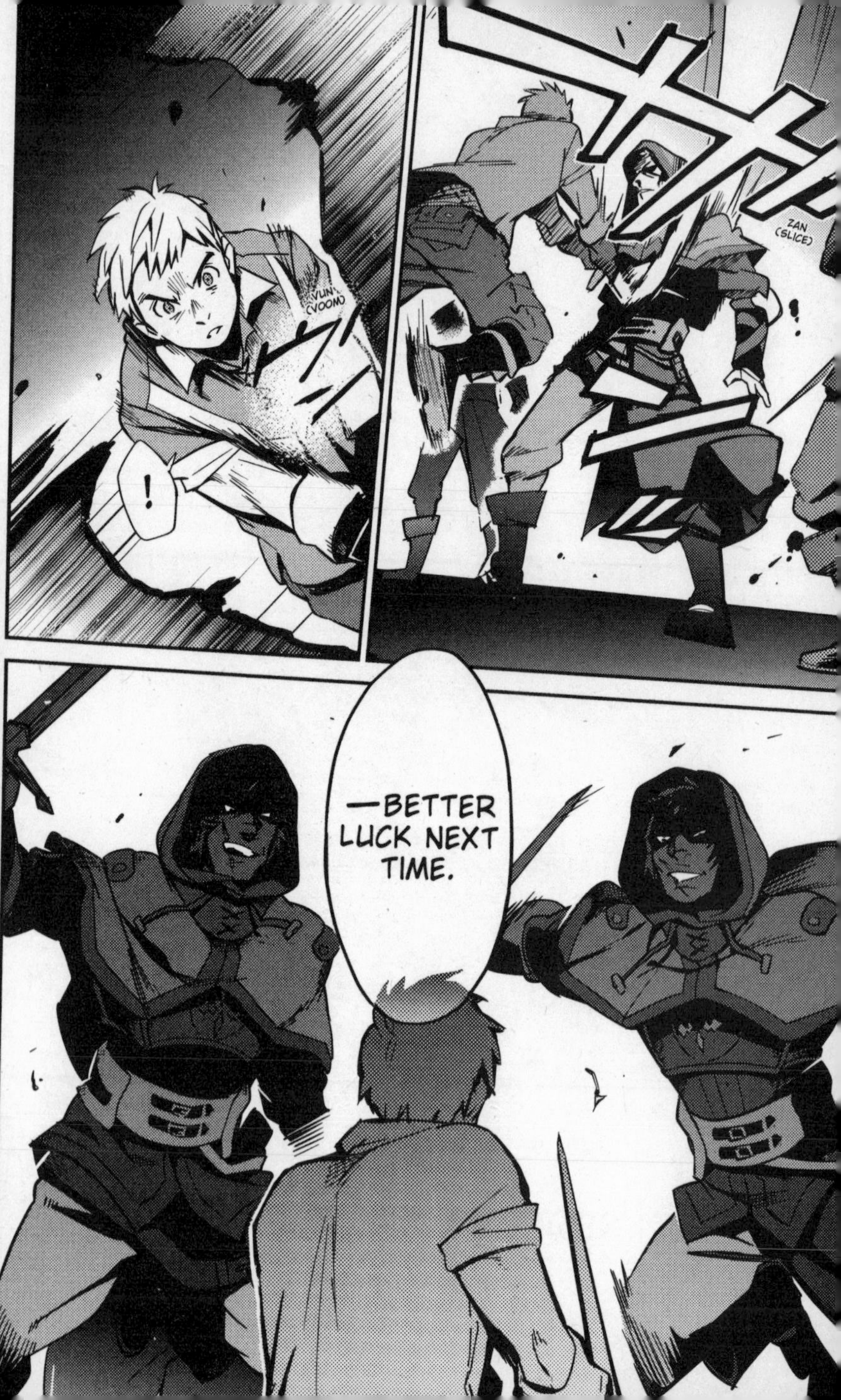
ZAN
(SLICE)
VUN
(VOOM)
!
—BETTER LUCK NEXT TIME.

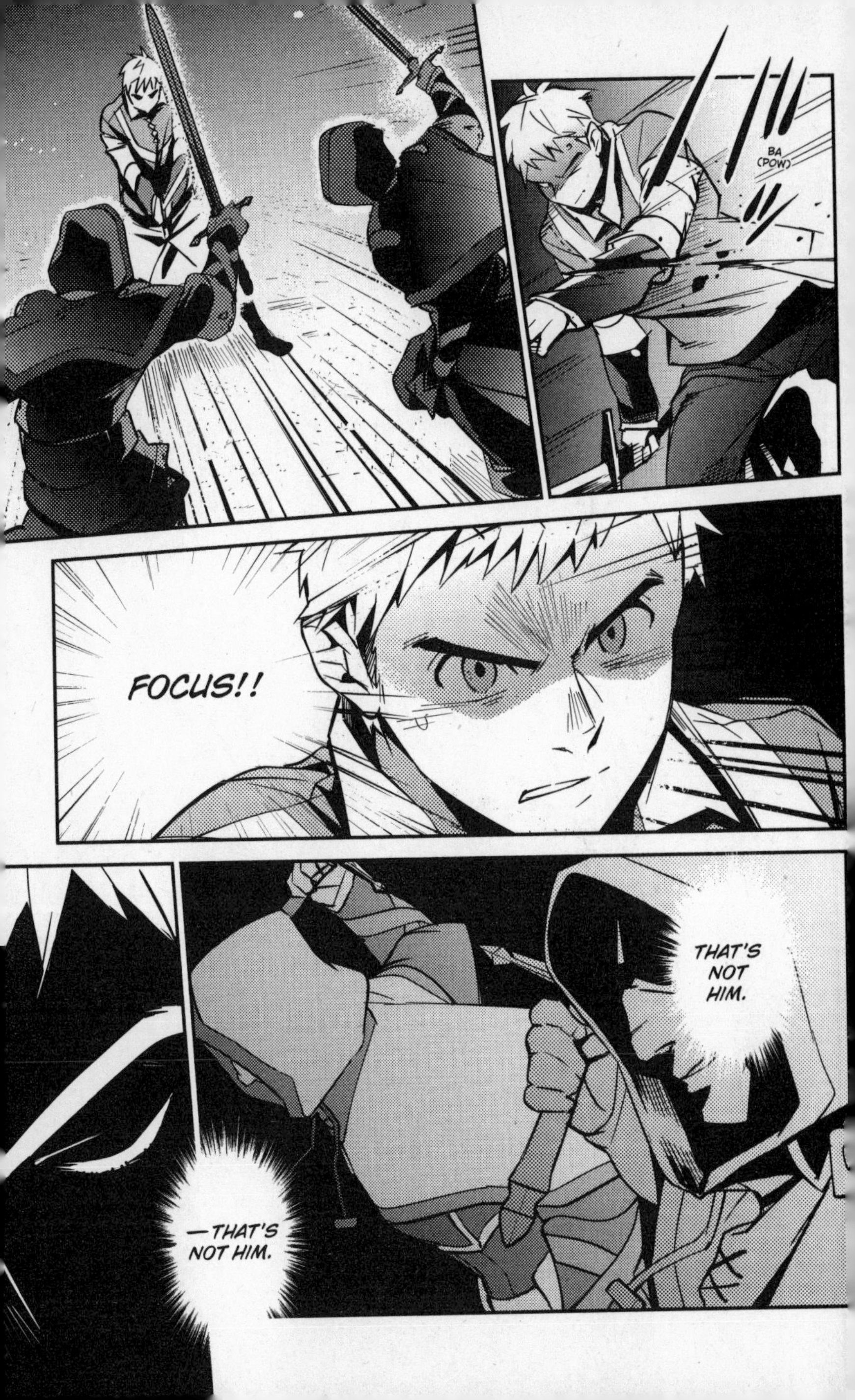
BA
(POW)
FOCUS!!
THAT'S NOT HIM.
—THAT'S NOT HIM.

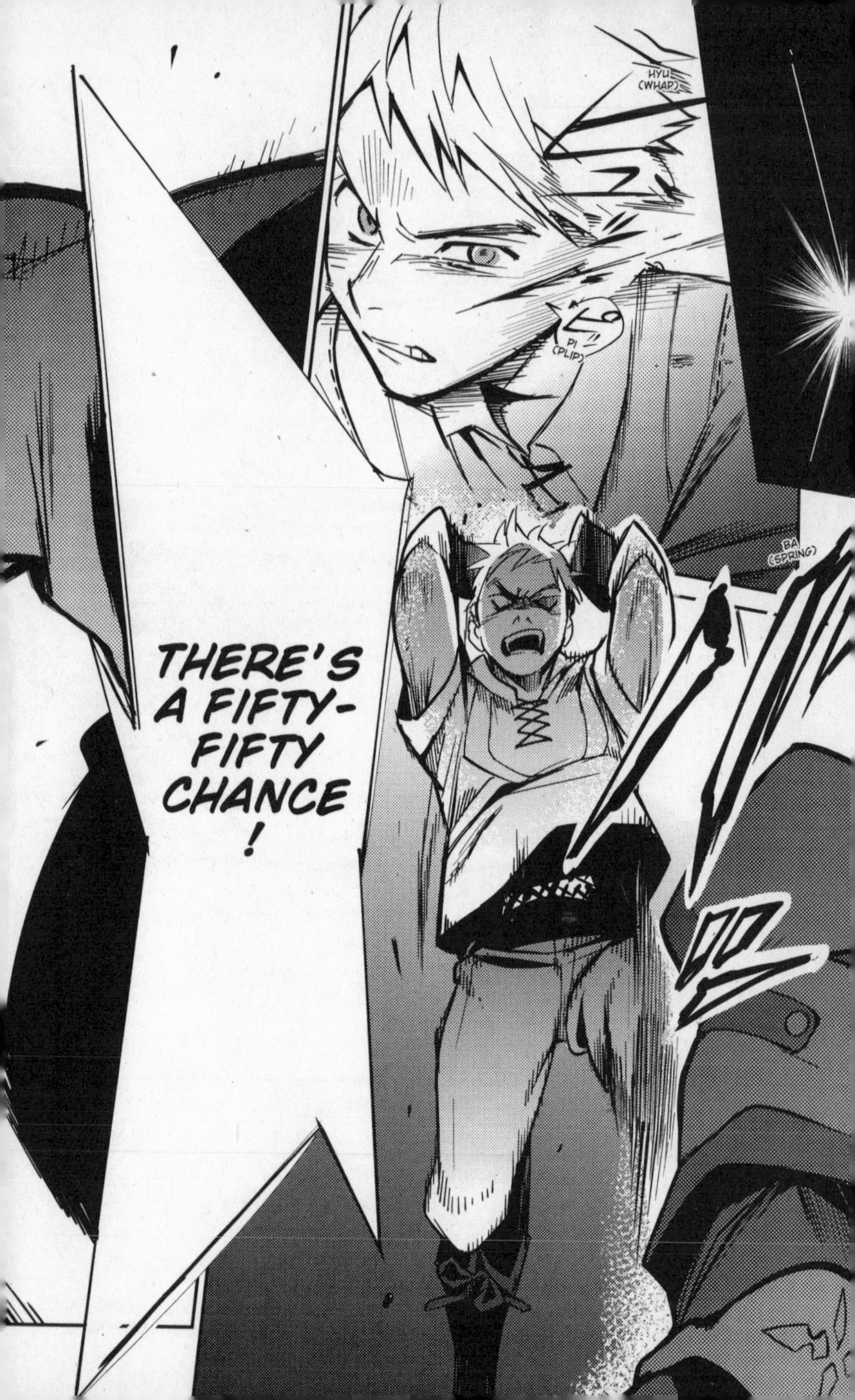
HYU
(WHAP)
PI
(PLIP)
BA
(SPRING)
THERE'S A FIFTY-FIFTY CHANCE!

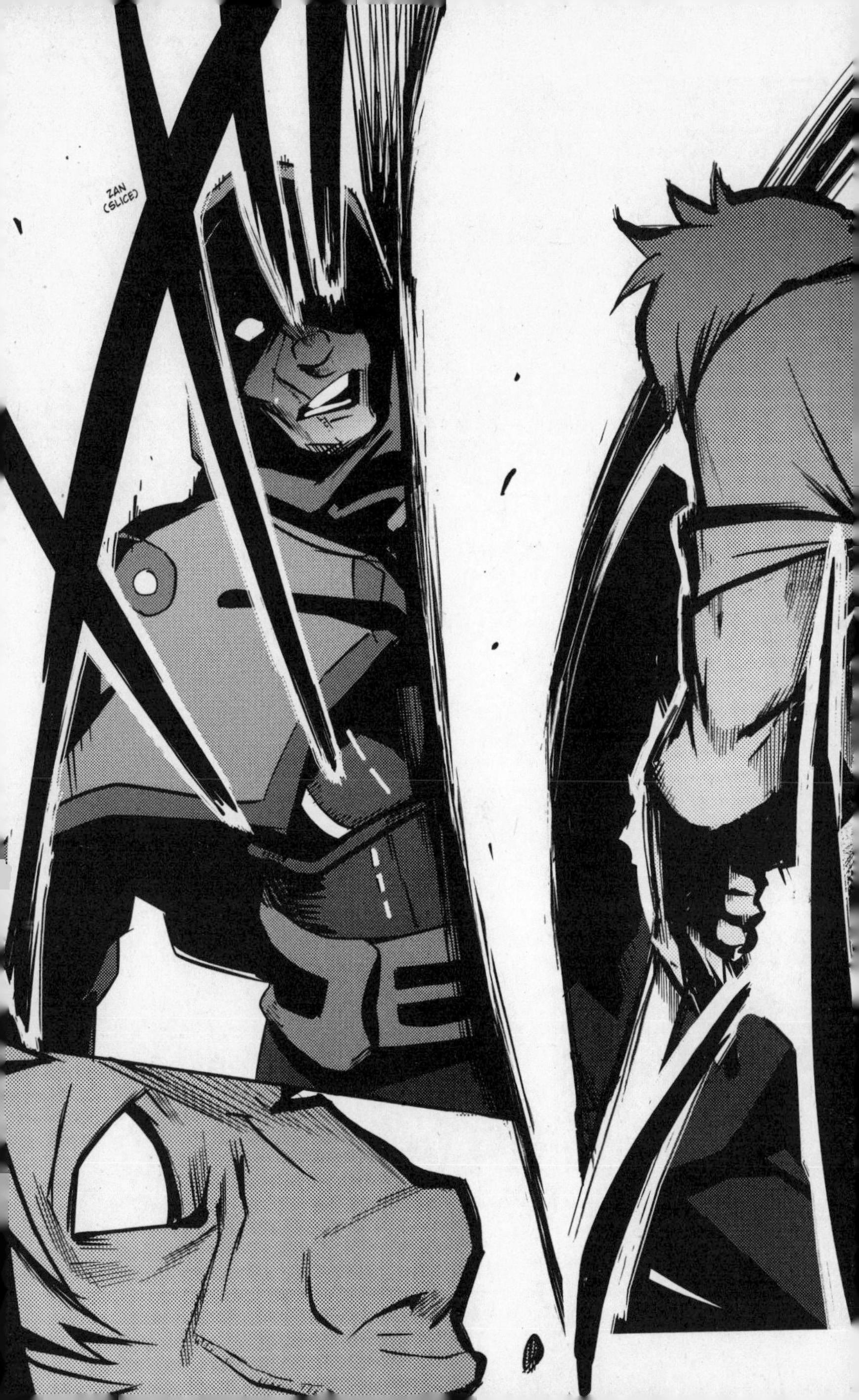
ZAN
(SLICE)

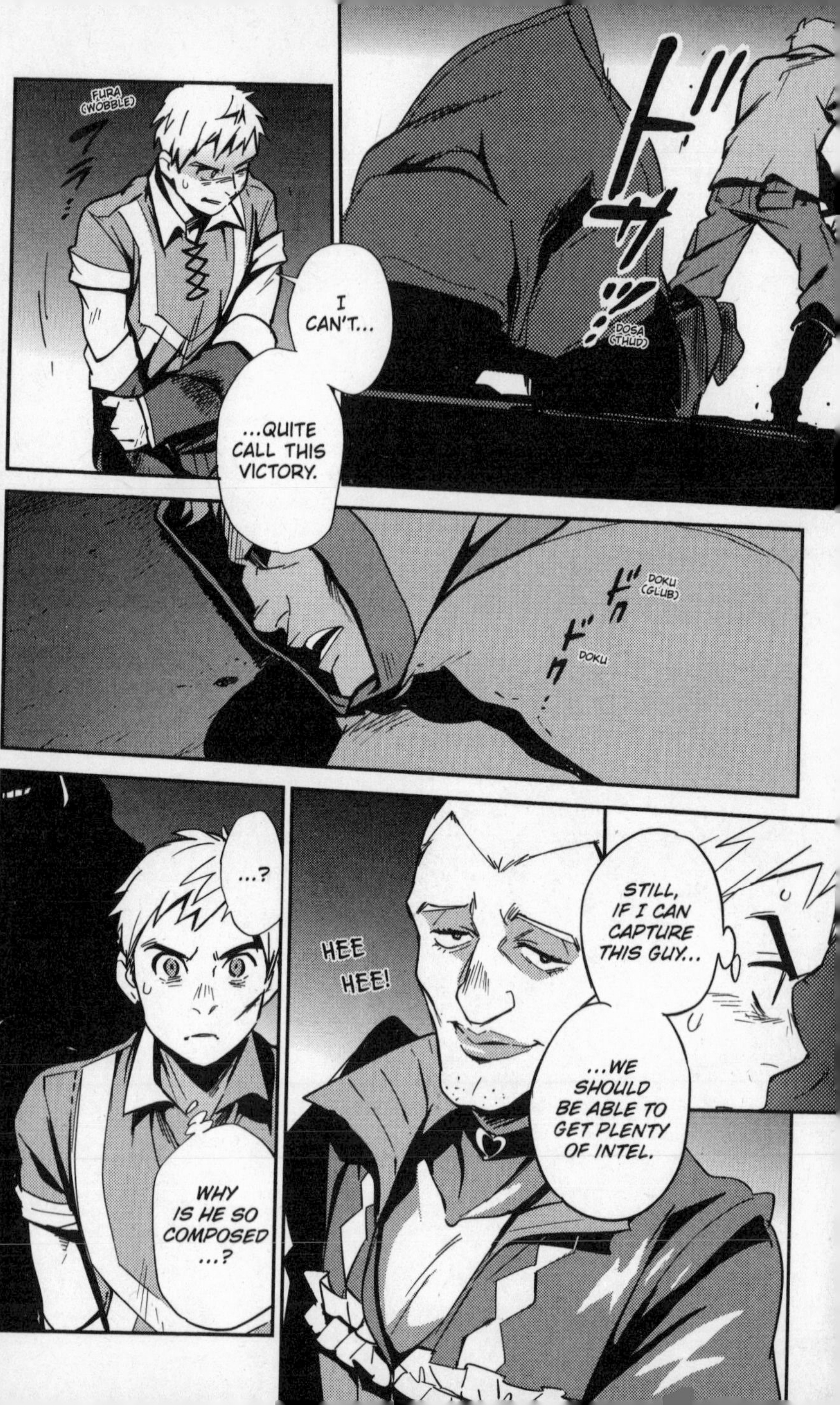
DOSA (THUD)
FURA (WOBBLE)
I CAN'T...
...QUITE CALL THIS VICTORY.
DOKU (GLUB)
DOKU
STILL, IF I CAN CAPTURE THIS GUY...
...WE SHOULD BE ABLE TO GET PLENTY OF INTEL.
HEE HEE!
...?
WHY IS HE SO COMPOSED ...?

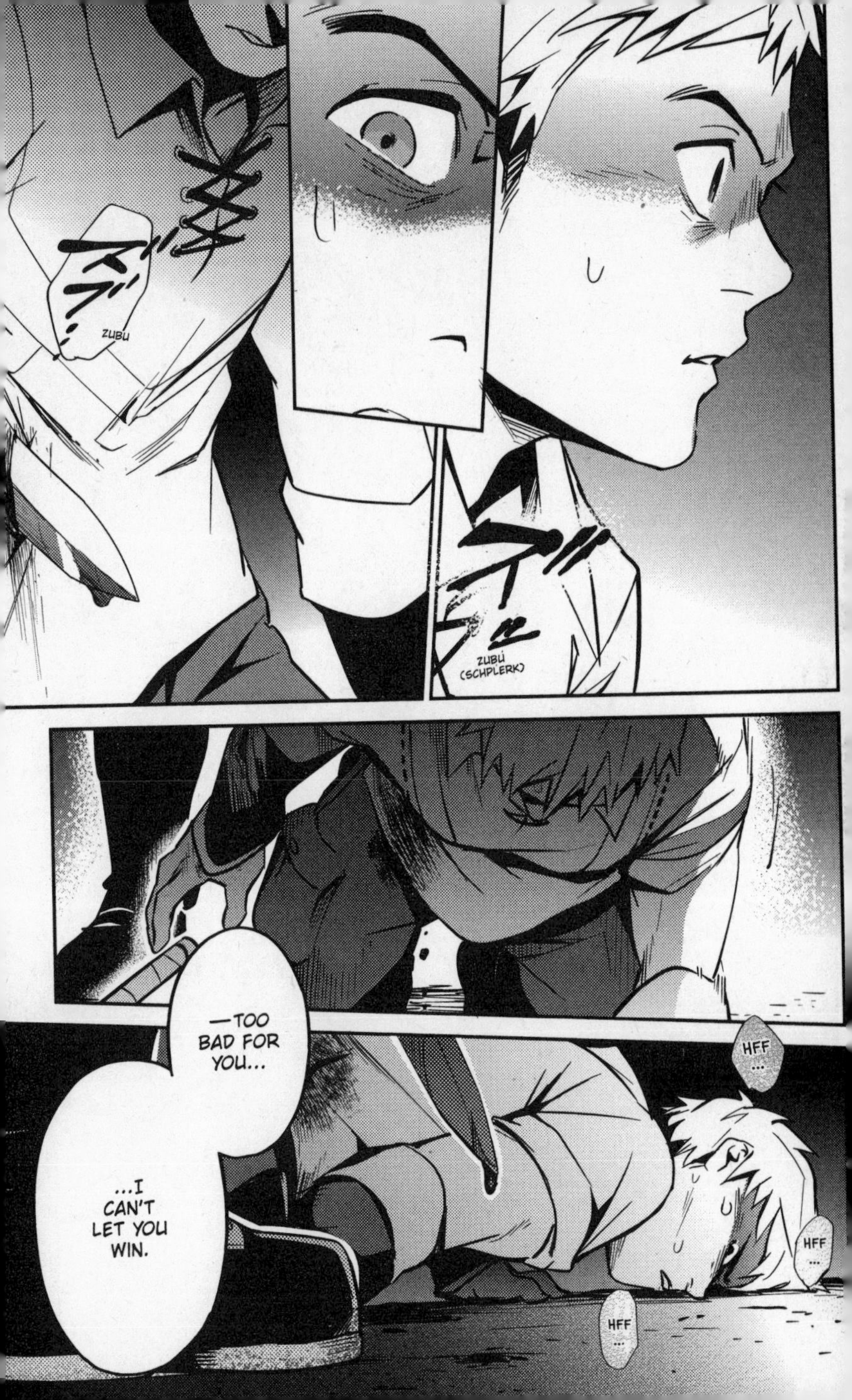
ZUBU (SCHPLERK)
ZUBU
HFF...
—TOO BAD FOR YOU...
...I CAN'T LET YOU WIN.
HFF...
HFF...

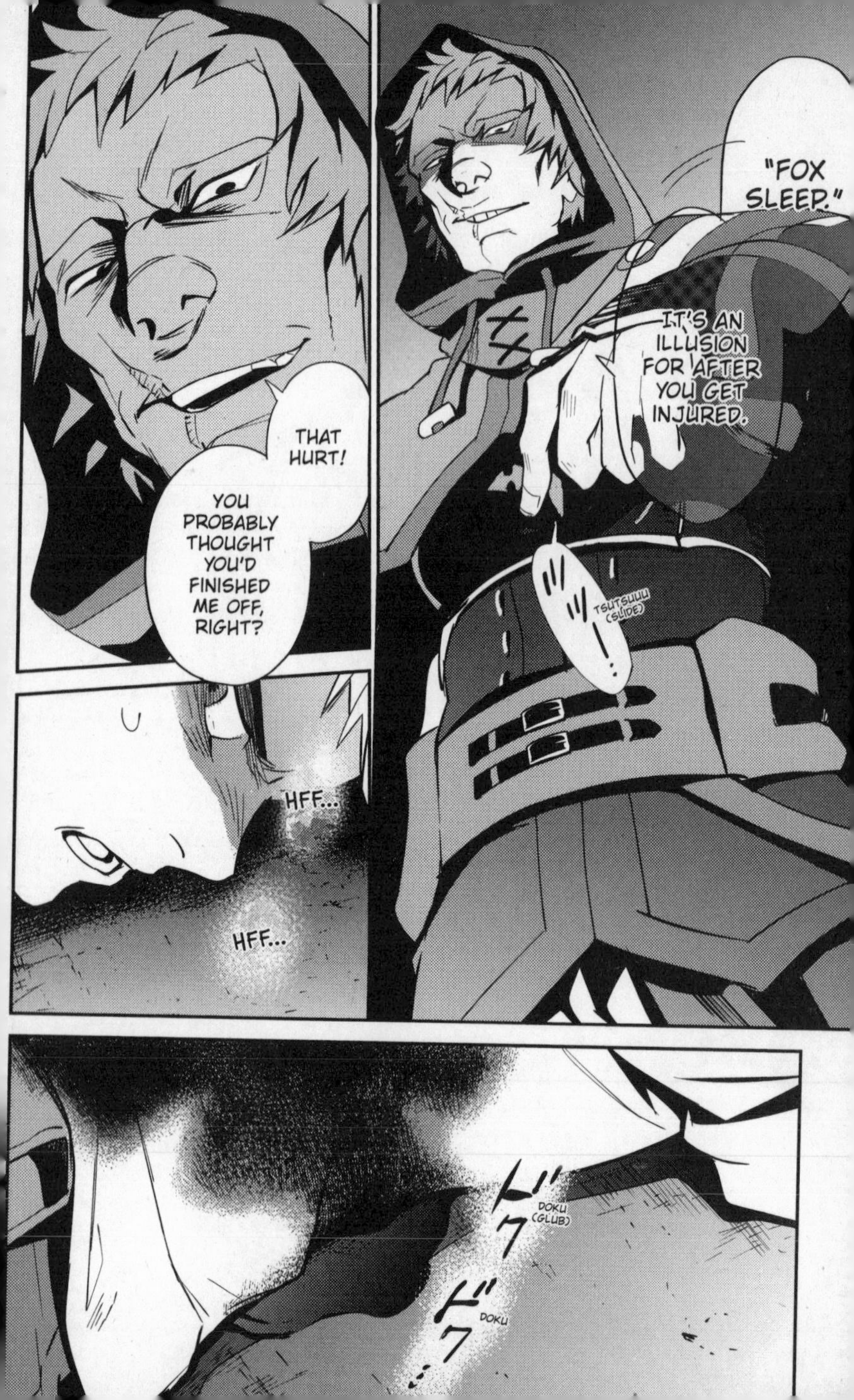
"FOX SLEEP."
IT'S AN ILLUSION FOR AFTER YOU GET INJURED.
TSUTSUUU (SLIDE)
THAT HURT!
YOU PROBABLY THOUGHT YOU'D FINISHED ME OFF, RIGHT?
HFF...
HFF...
DOKU (GLUB)
DOKU

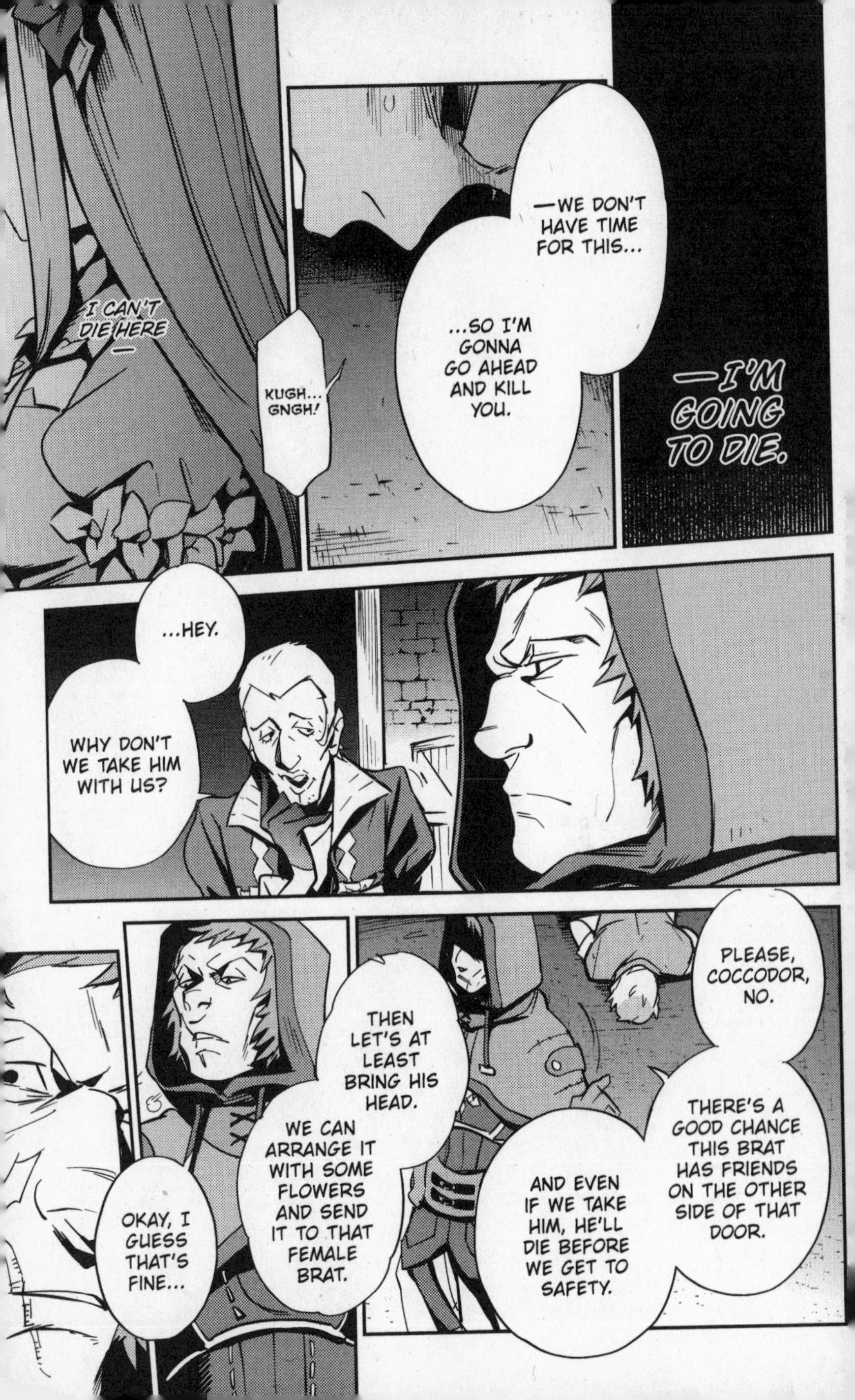
—I'M GOING TO DIE.
—WE DON'T HAVE TIME FOR THIS...
...SO I'M GONNA GO AHEAD AND KILL YOU.
KUGH... GNGH!
I CAN'T DIE HERE—
...HEY.
WHY DON'T WE TAKE HIM WITH US?
PLEASE, COCCODOR, NO.
THERE'S A GOOD CHANCE THIS BRAT HAS FRIENDS ON THE OTHER SIDE OF THAT DOOR.
AND EVEN IF WE TAKE HIM, HE'LL DIE BEFORE WE GET TO SAFETY.
THEN LET'S AT LEAST BRING HIS HEAD.
WE CAN ARRANGE IT WITH SOME FLOWERS AND SEND IT TO THAT FEMALE BRAT.
OKAY, I GUESS THAT'S FINE...

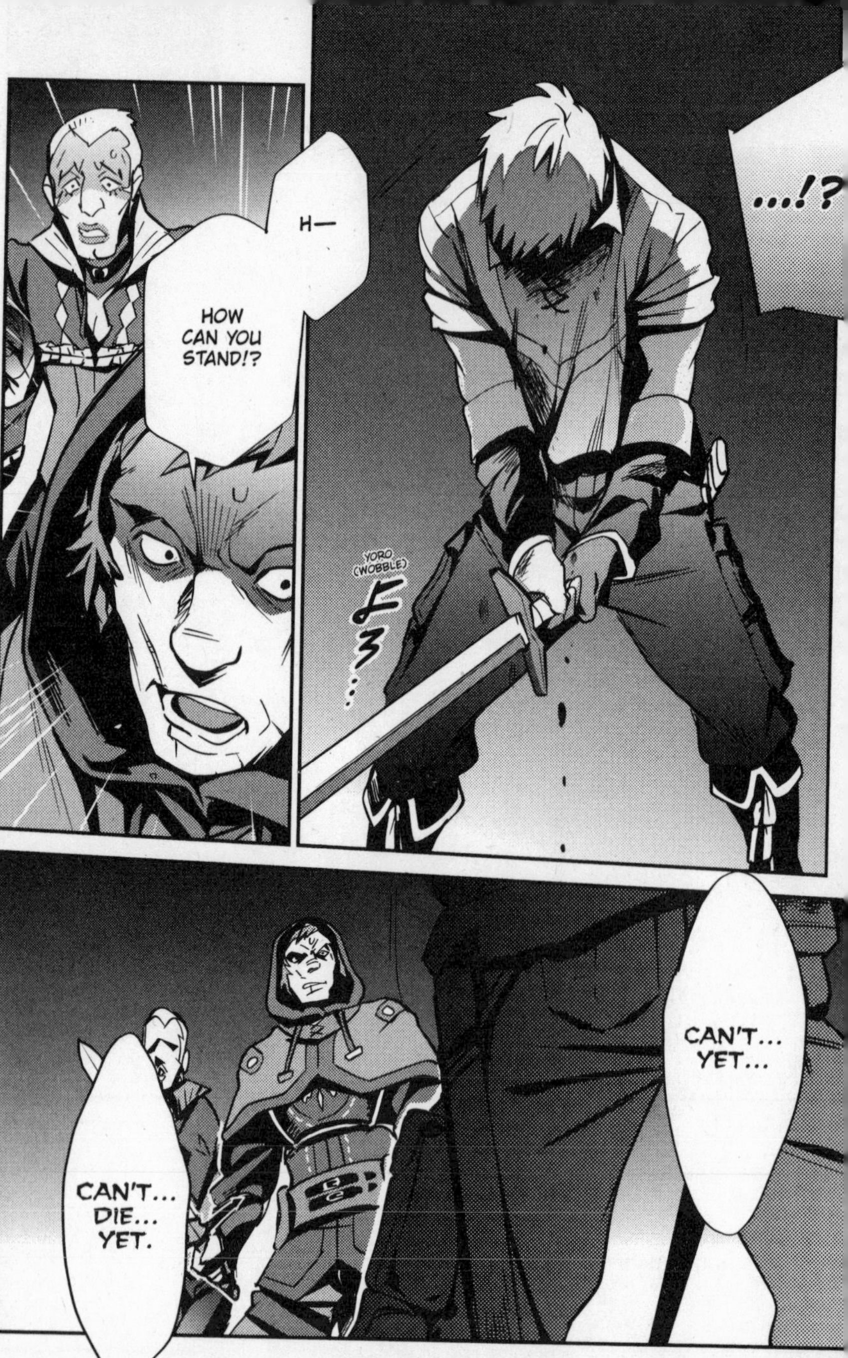

...!?
YORO (WOBBLE)
よろ…
H—
HOW CAN YOU STAND!?
CAN'T... YET...
CAN'T... DIE... YET.

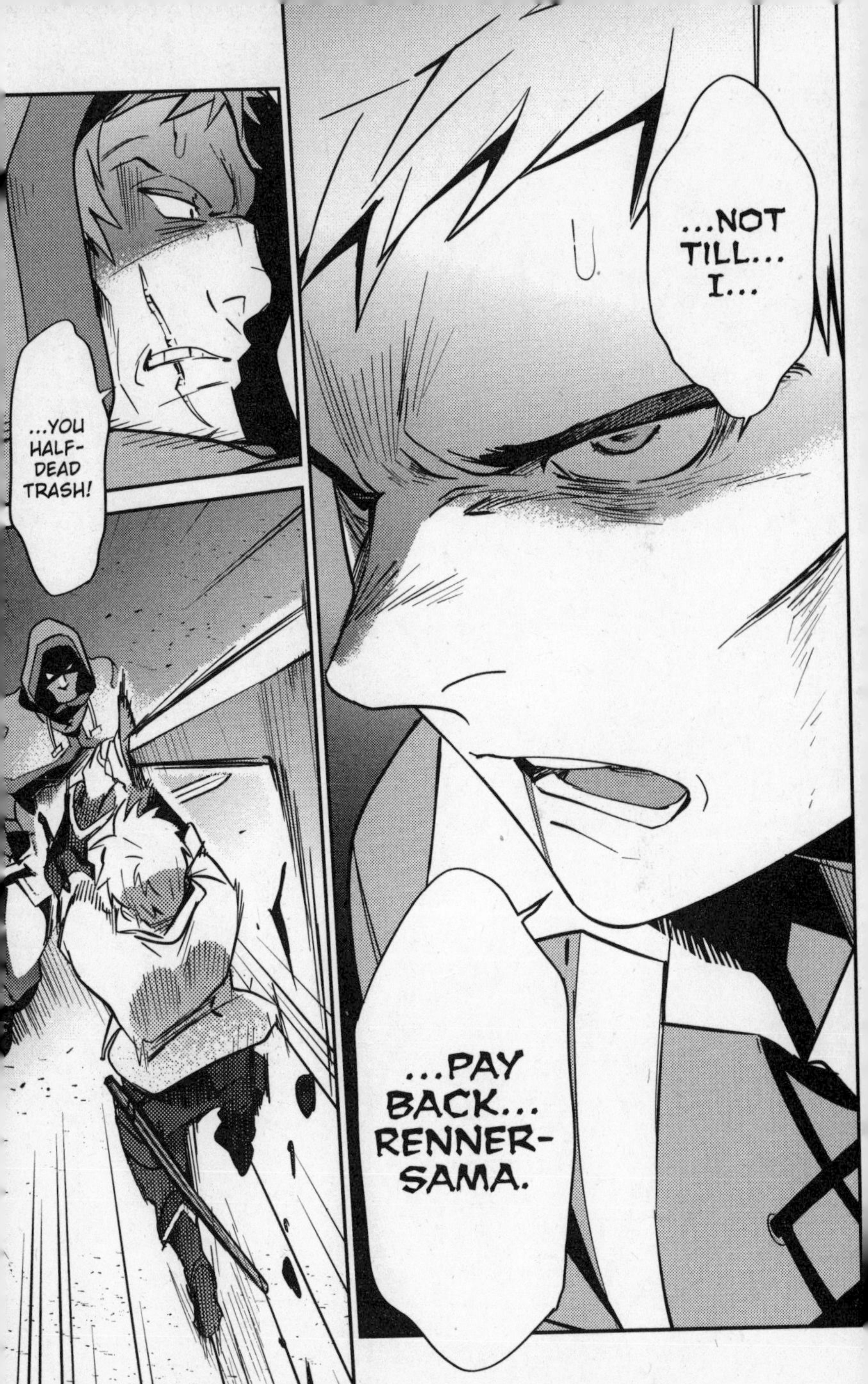
...NOT TILL... I...
...PAY BACK... RENNER-SAMA.
...YOU HALF-DEAD TRASH!

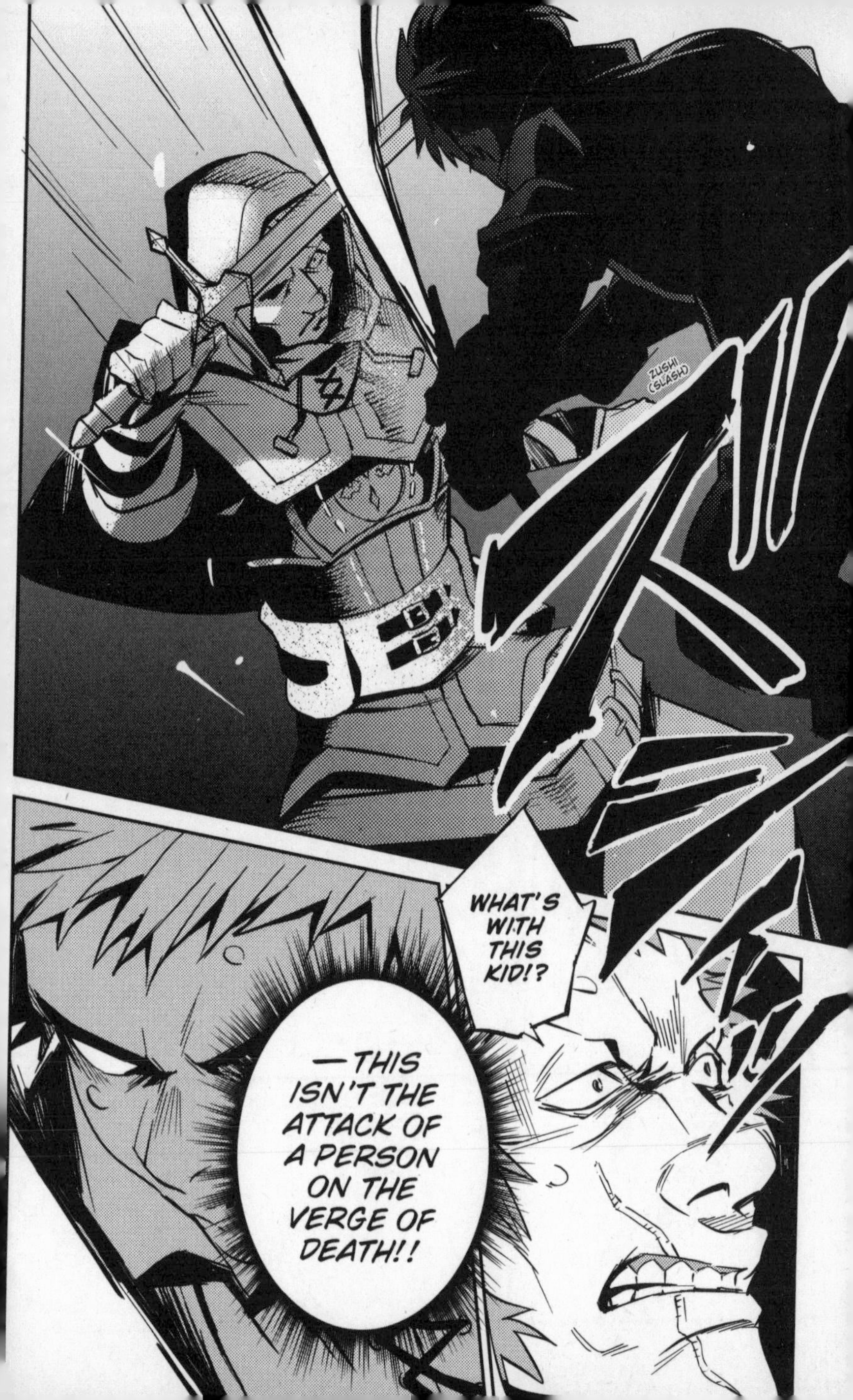
ZUSHI (SLASH)
WHAT'S WITH THIS KID!?
—THIS ISN'T THE ATTACK OF A PERSON ON THE VERGE OF DEATH!!

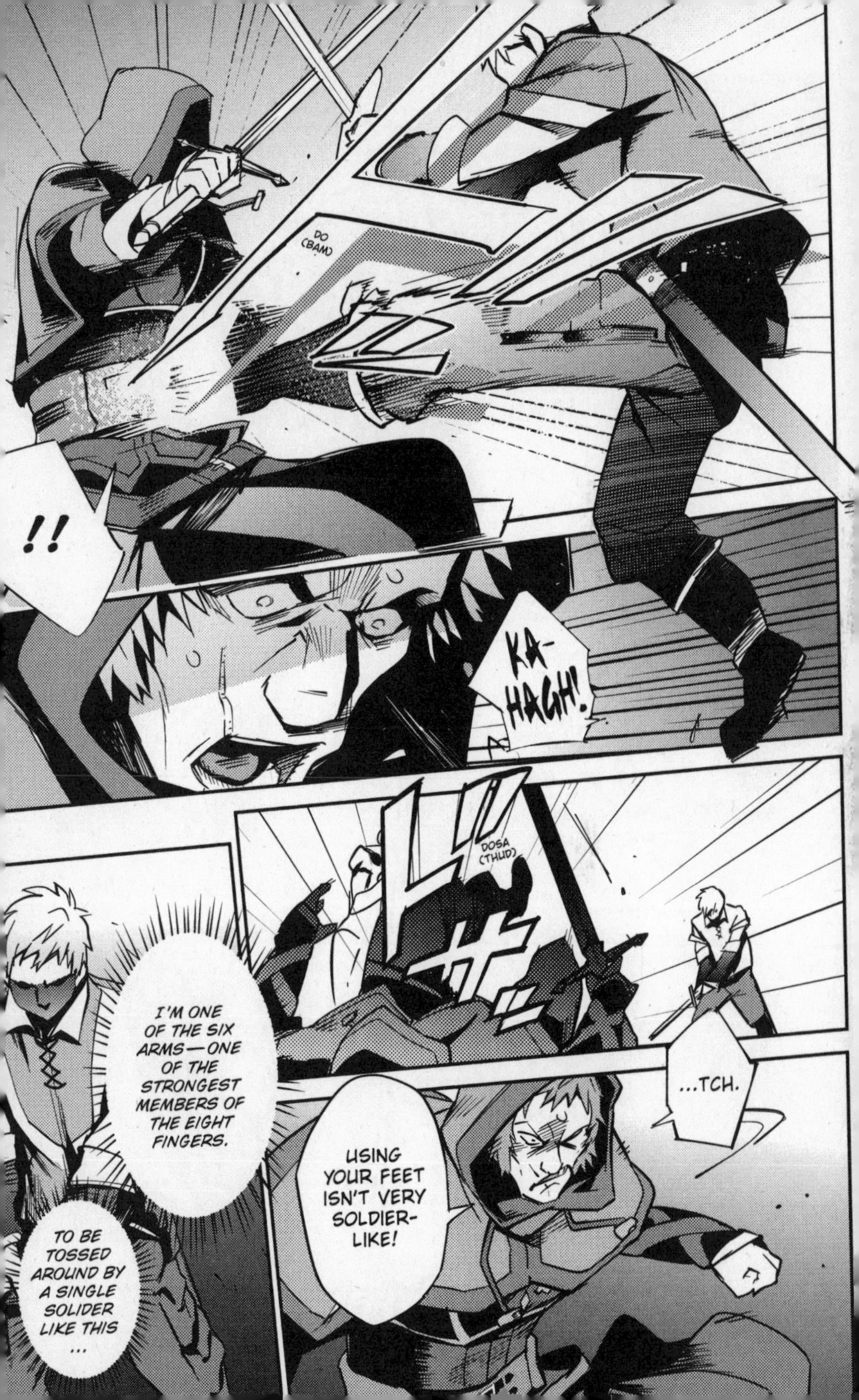
DO (BAM)
KA-HAGH!
!!
DOSA (THUD)
...TCH.
USING YOUR FEET ISN'T VERY SOLDIER-LIKE!
I'M ONE OF THE SIX ARMS—ONE OF THE STRONGEST MEMBERS OF THE EIGHT FINGERS.
TO BE TOSSED AROUND BY A SINGLE SOLIDER LIKE THIS ...

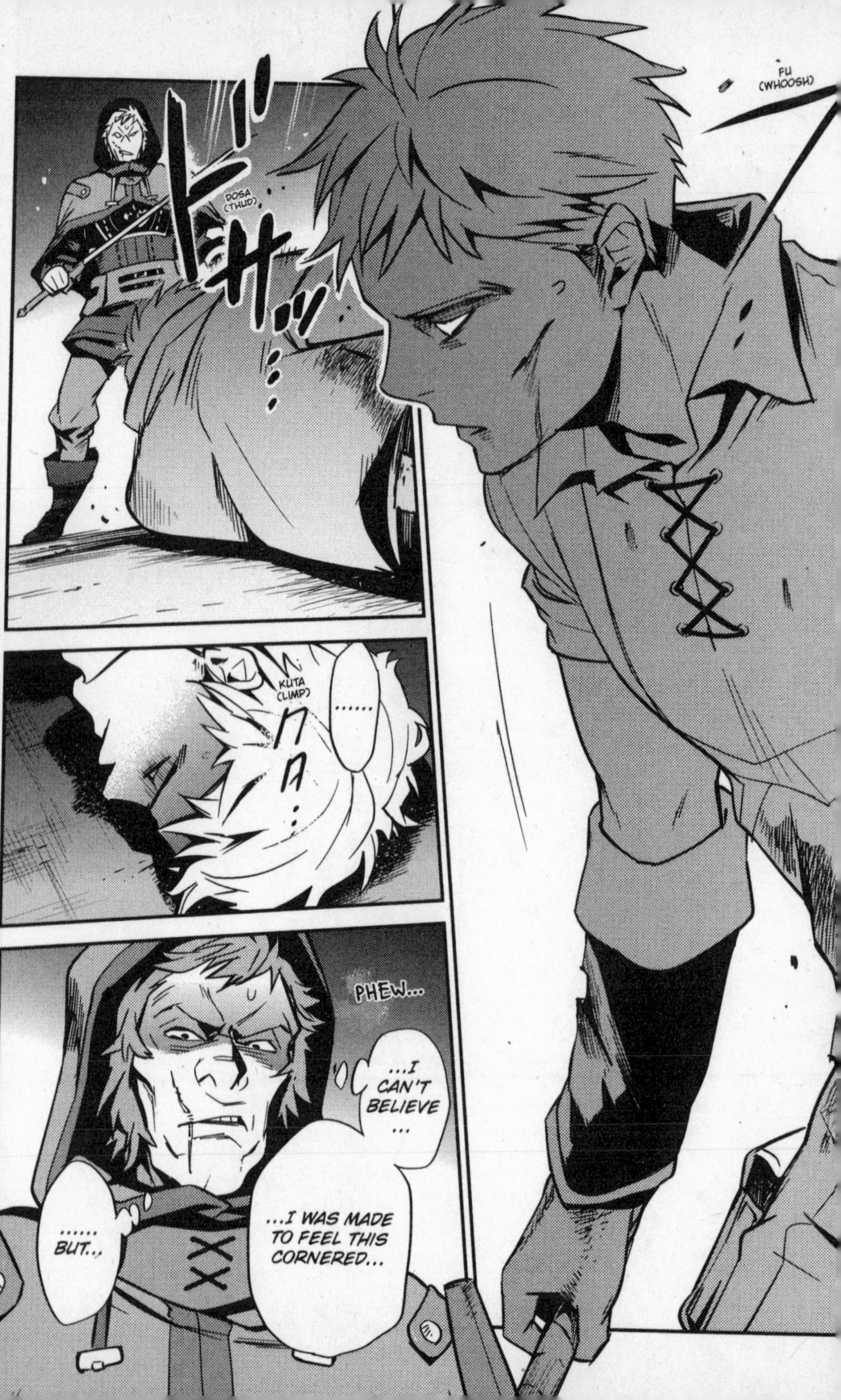
FU (WHOOSH)
DOSA (THUD)
KUTA (LIMP)
......
PHEW...
...I CAN'T BELIEVE ...
...I WAS MADE TO FEEL THIS CORNERED...
...... BUT..,

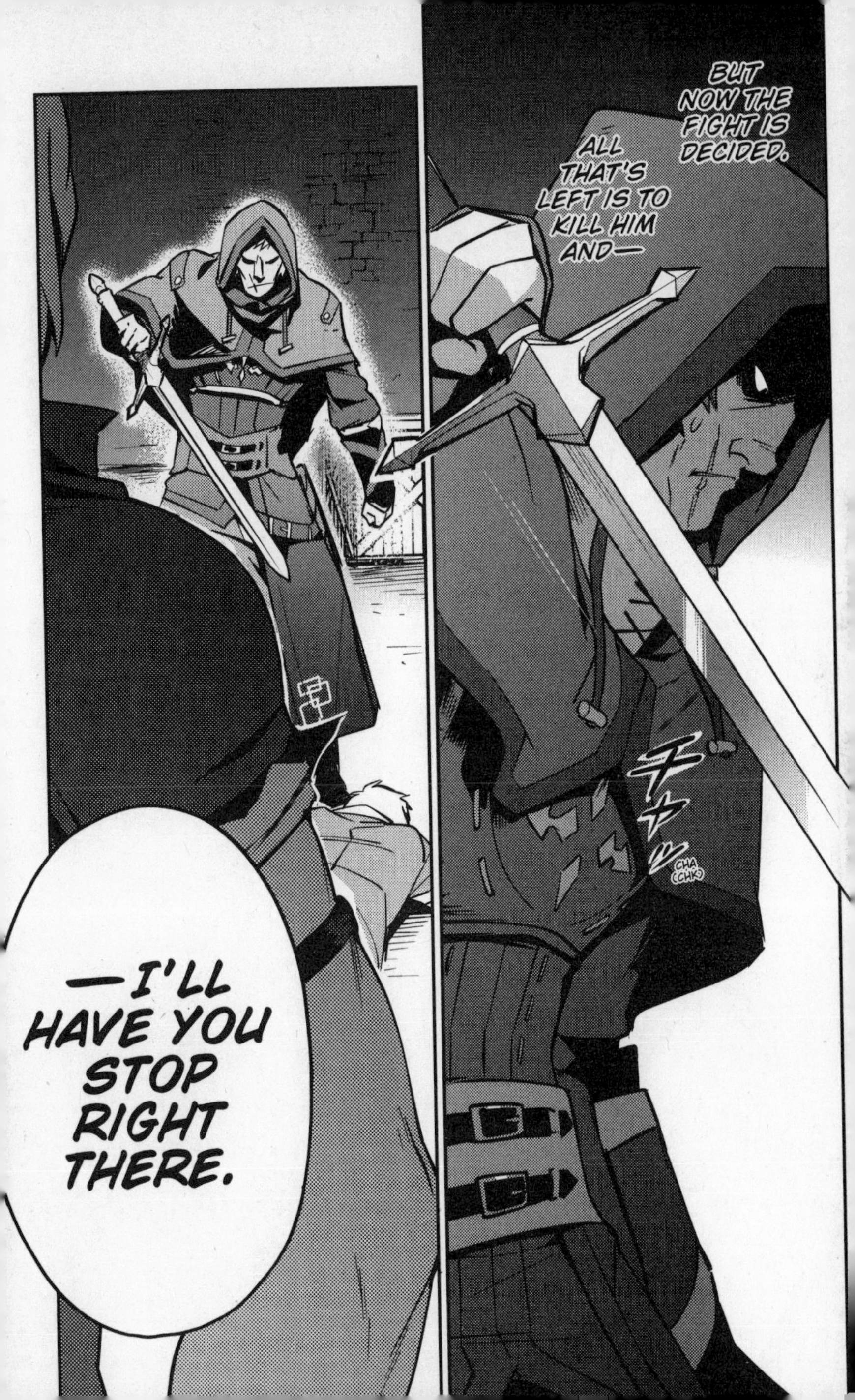
BUT NOW THE FIGHT IS DECIDED.
ALL THAT'S LEFT IS TO KILL HIM AND—
チャッ
CHA (CHK)
—I'LL HAVE YOU STOP RIGHT THERE.

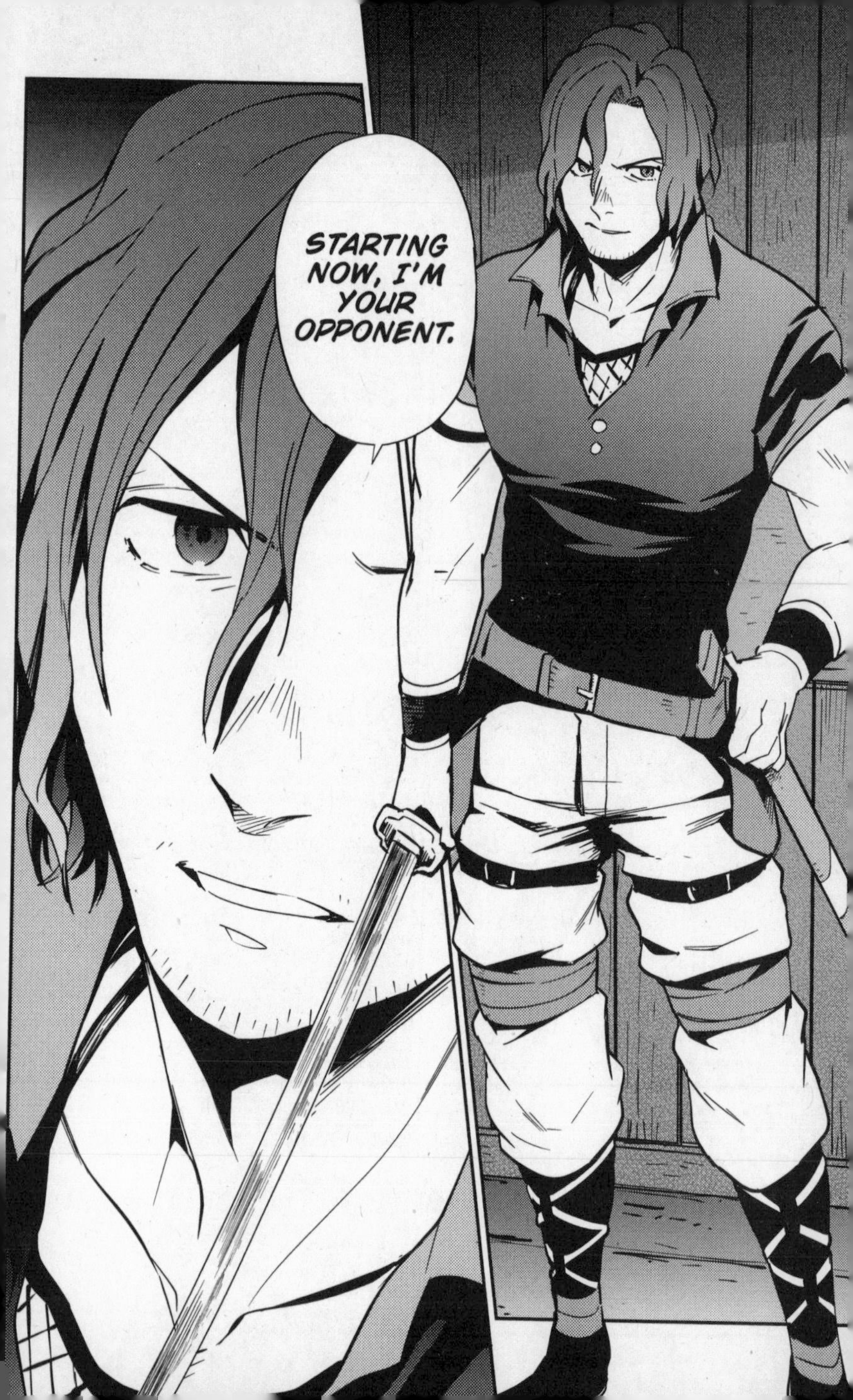
STARTING NOW, I'M YOUR OPPONENT.

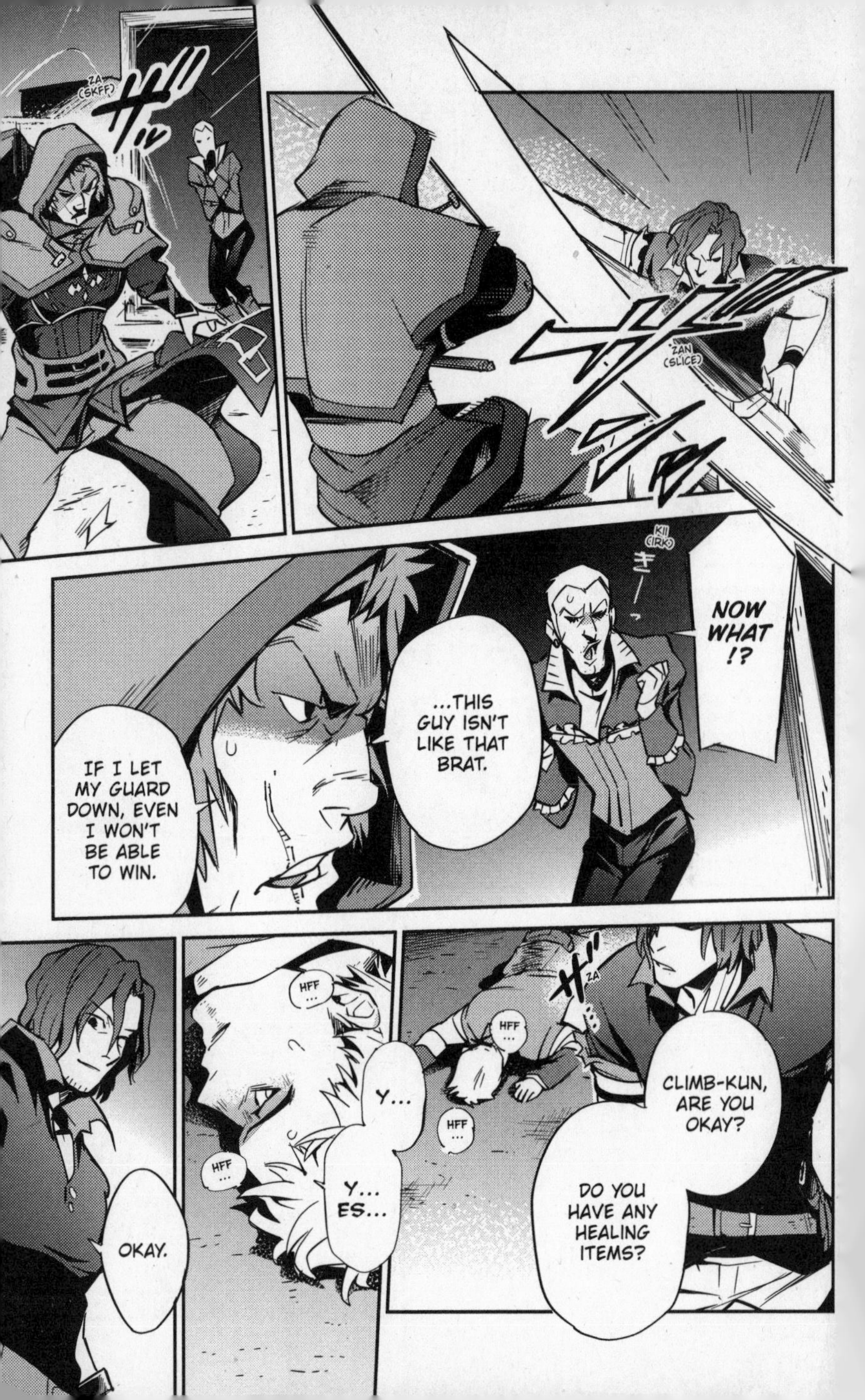
ZAN (SLICE)
ZA (SKFF)
KII (IRK)
NOW WHAT!?
...THIS GUY ISN'T LIKE THAT BRAT.
IF I LET MY GUARD DOWN, EVEN I WON'T BE ABLE TO WIN.
ZA
HFF...
CLIMB-KUN, ARE YOU OKAY?
DO YOU HAVE ANY HEALING ITEMS?
HFF...
Y...
HFF...
HFF...
Y... ES...
OKAY.

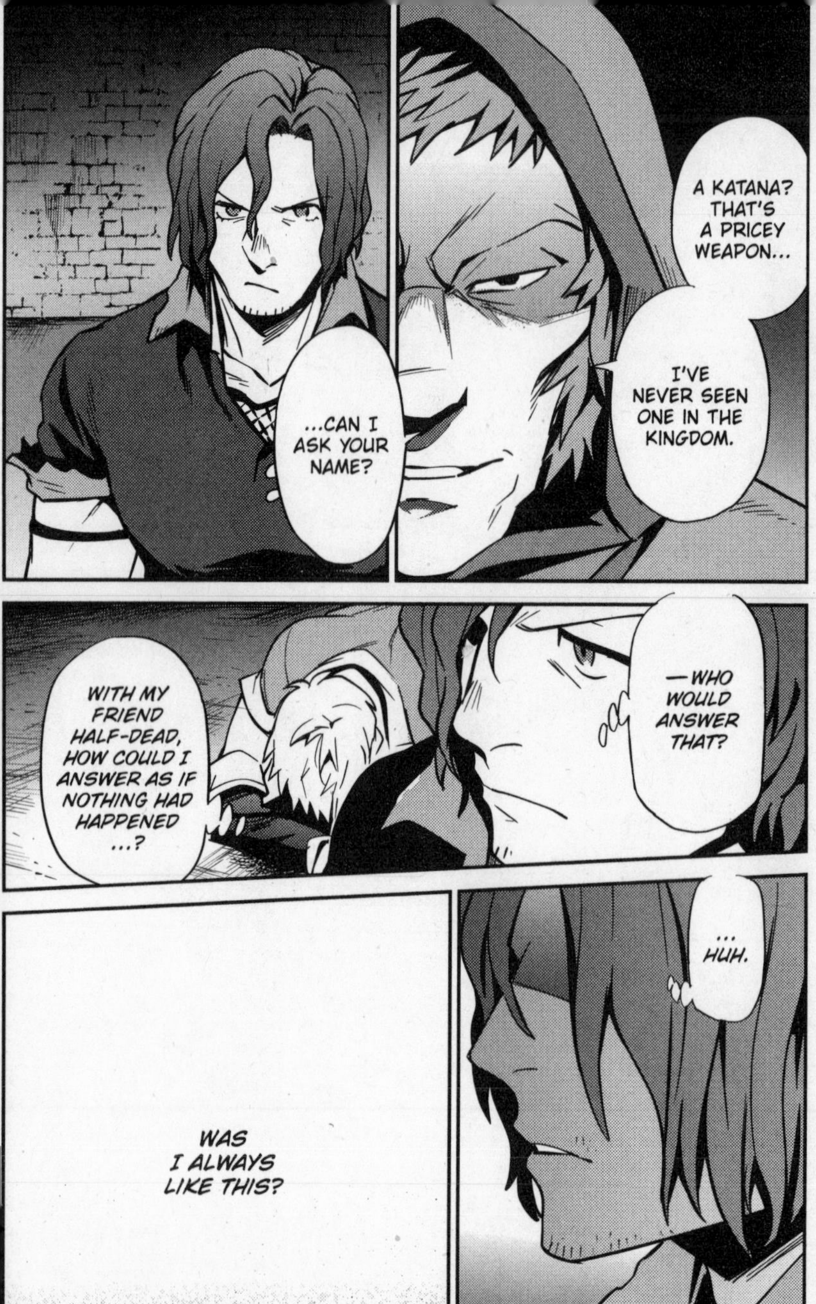
A KATANA? THAT'S A PRICEY WEAPON...
I'VE NEVER SEEN ONE IN THE KINGDOM.
...CAN I ASK YOUR NAME?
—WHO WOULD ANSWER THAT?
WITH MY FRIEND HALF-DEAD, HOW COULD I ANSWER AS IF NOTHING HAD HAPPENED...?
... HUH.
WAS I ALWAYS LIKE THIS?

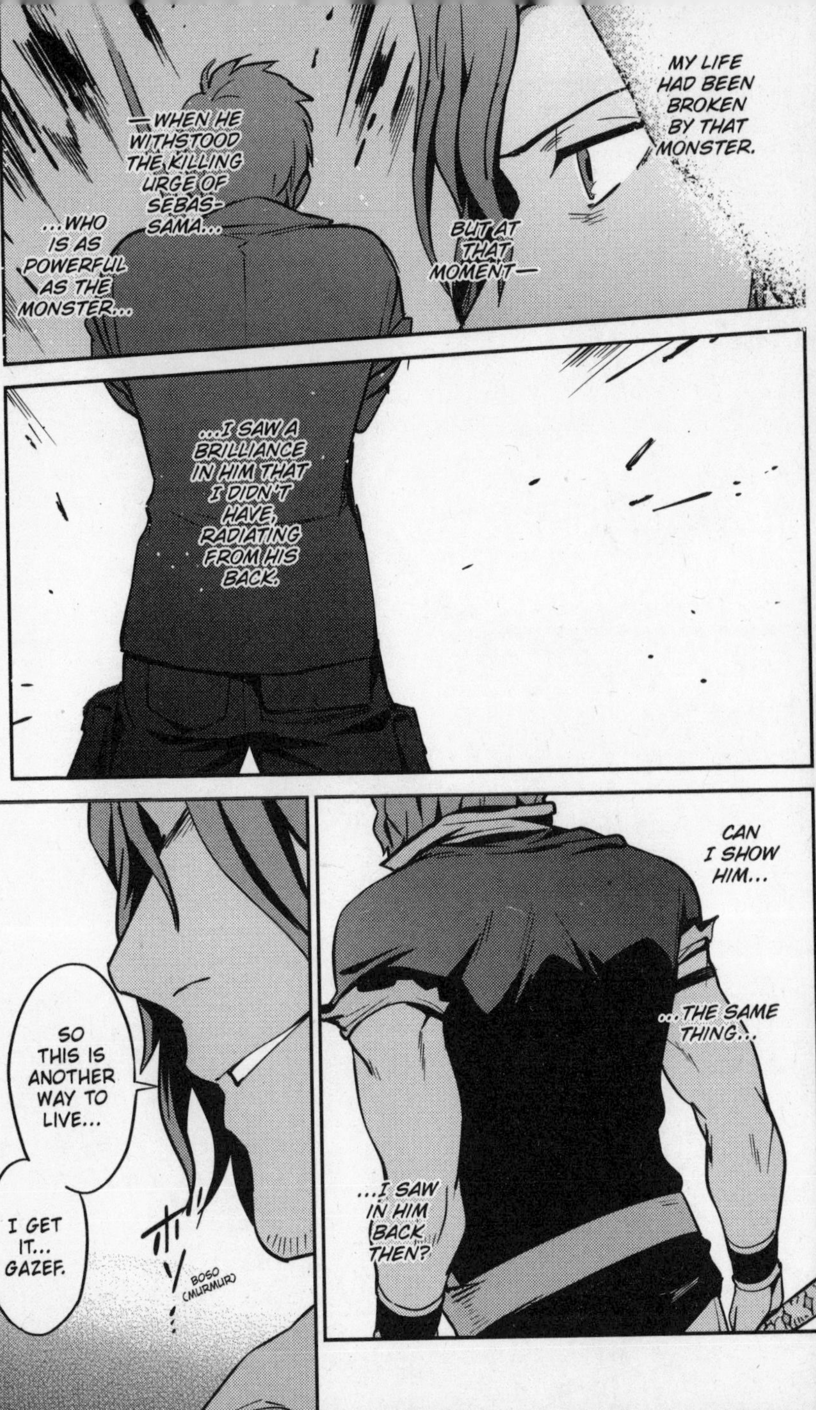
MY LIFE HAD BEEN BROKEN BY THAT MONSTER.
BUT AT THAT MOMENT—
—WHEN HE WITHSTOOD THE KILLING URGE OF SEBAS-SAMA...
...WHO IS AS POWERFUL AS THE MONSTER...
...I SAW A BRILLIANCE IN HIM THAT I DIDN'T HAVE, RADIATING FROM HIS BACK.
CAN I SHOW HIM...
...THE SAME THING...
...I SAW IN HIM BACK THEN?
SO THIS IS ANOTHER WAY TO LIVE...
I GET IT... GAZEF.
BOSO (MURMUR)

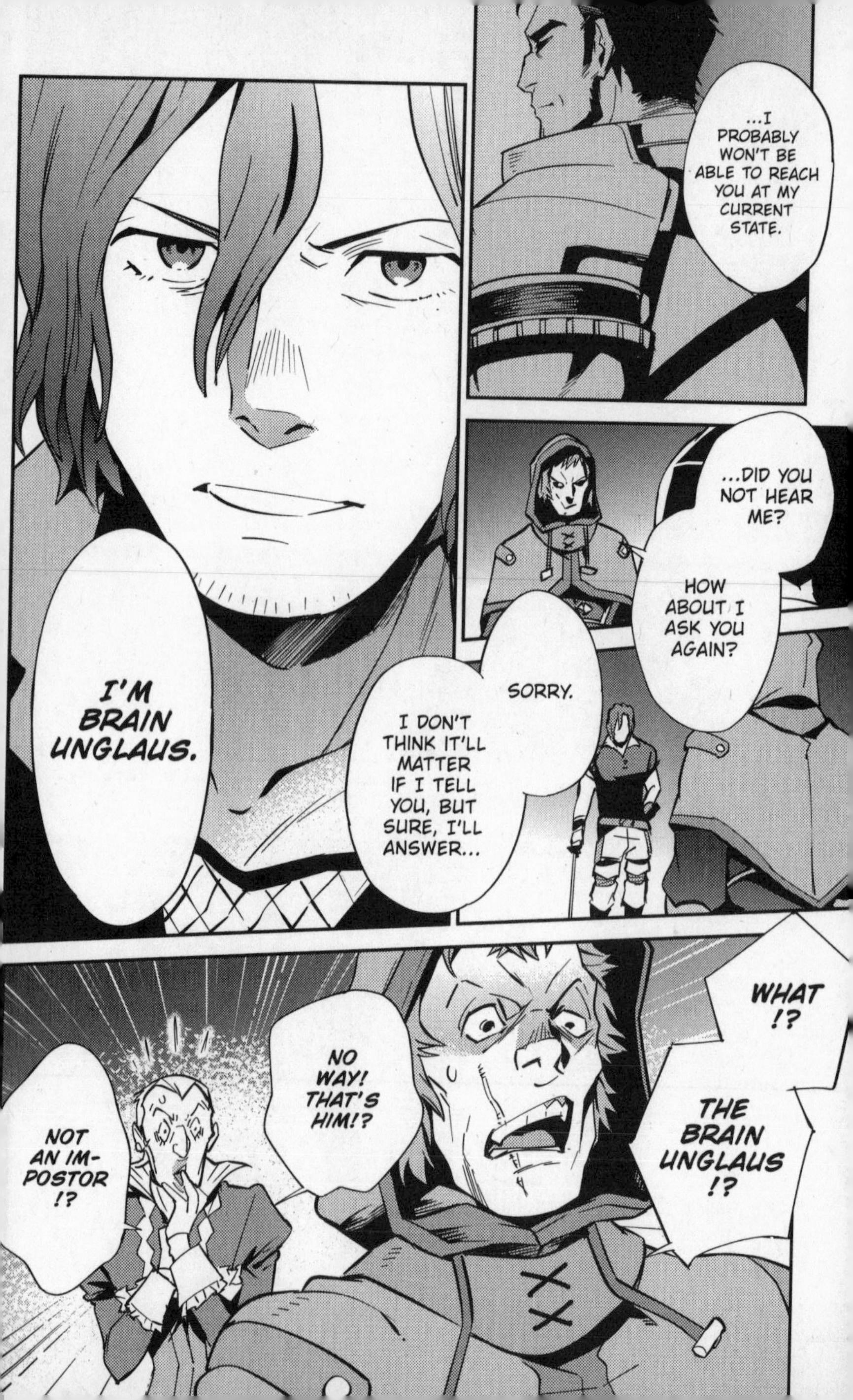
...I PROBABLY WON'T BE ABLE TO REACH YOU AT MY CURRENT STATE.
...DID YOU NOT HEAR ME?
HOW ABOUT I ASK YOU AGAIN?
SORRY.
I DON'T THINK IT'LL MATTER IF I TELL YOU, BUT SURE, I'LL ANSWER...
I'M BRAIN UNGLAUS.
WHAT!?
THE BRAIN UNGLAUS!?
NO WAY! THAT'S HIM!?
NOT AN IM-POSTOR!?

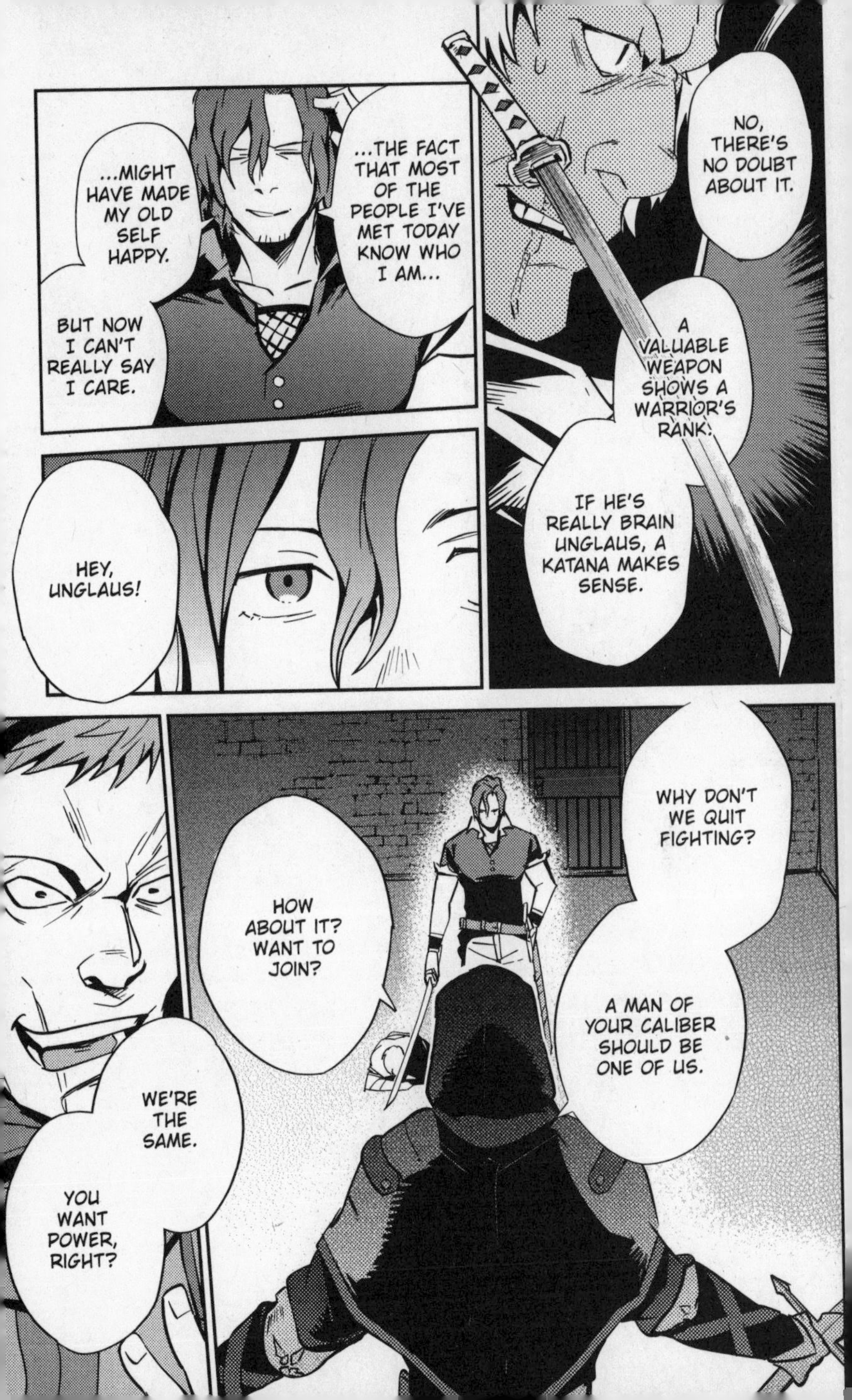
NO, THERE'S NO DOUBT ABOUT IT.
A VALUABLE WEAPON SHOWS A WARRIOR'S RANK.
IF HE'S REALLY BRAIN UNGLAUS, A KATANA MAKES SENSE.
...THE FACT THAT MOST OF THE PEOPLE I'VE MET TODAY KNOW WHO I AM...
...MIGHT HAVE MADE MY OLD SELF HAPPY.
BUT NOW I CAN'T REALLY SAY I CARE.
HEY, UNGLAUS!
WHY DON'T WE QUIT FIGHTING?
A MAN OF YOUR CALIBER SHOULD BE ONE OF US.
HOW ABOUT IT? WANT TO JOIN?
WE'RE THE SAME.
YOU WANT POWER, RIGHT?

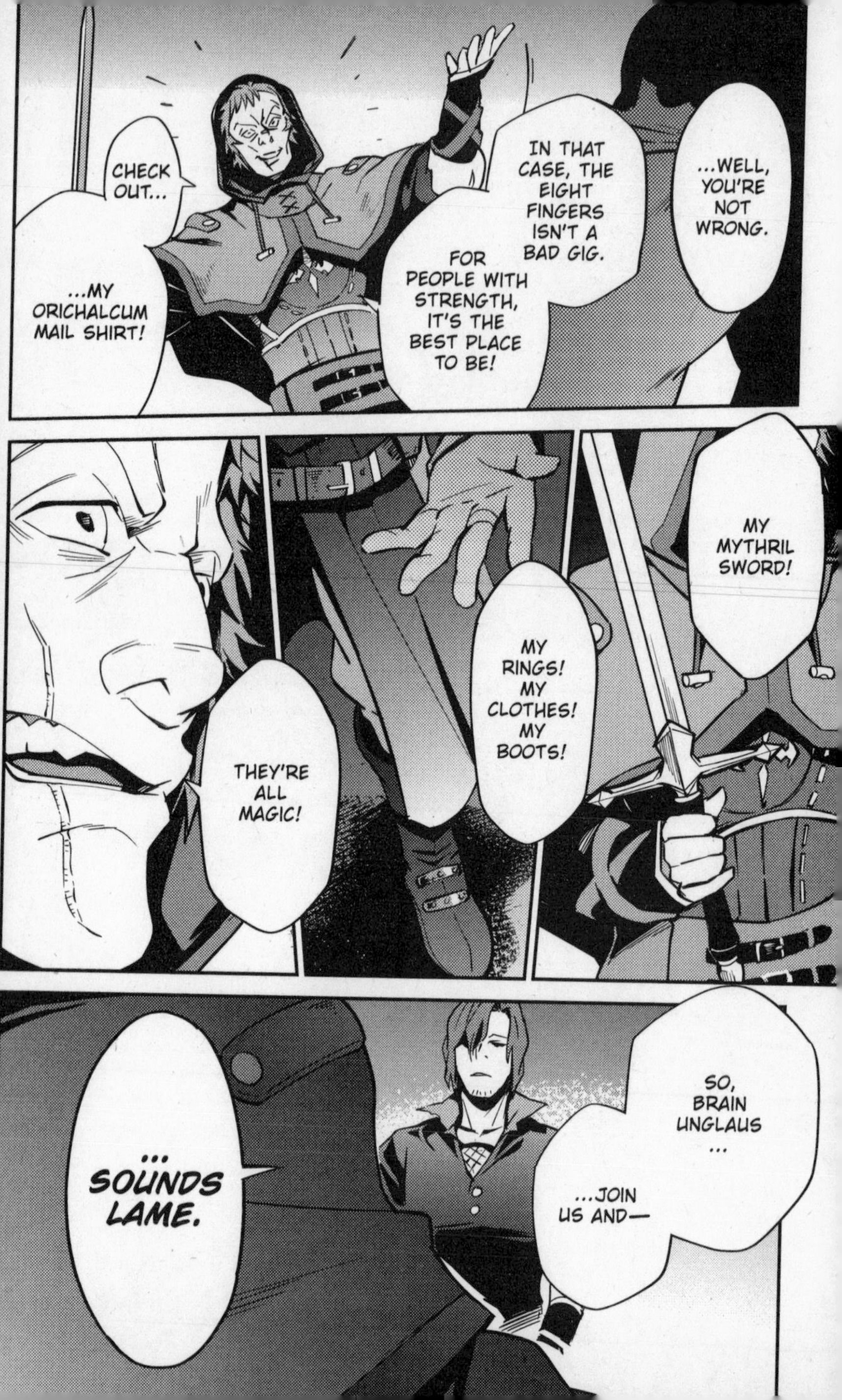
...WELL, YOU'RE NOT WRONG.
IN THAT CASE, THE EIGHT FINGERS ISN'T A BAD GIG.
FOR PEOPLE WITH STRENGTH, IT'S THE BEST PLACE TO BE!
CHECK OUT...
...MY ORICHALCUM MAIL SHIRT!
MY MYTHRIL SWORD!
MY RINGS! MY CLOTHES! MY BOOTS!
THEY'RE ALL MAGIC!
SO, BRAIN UNGLAUS ...
...JOIN US AND—
...SOUNDS LAME.

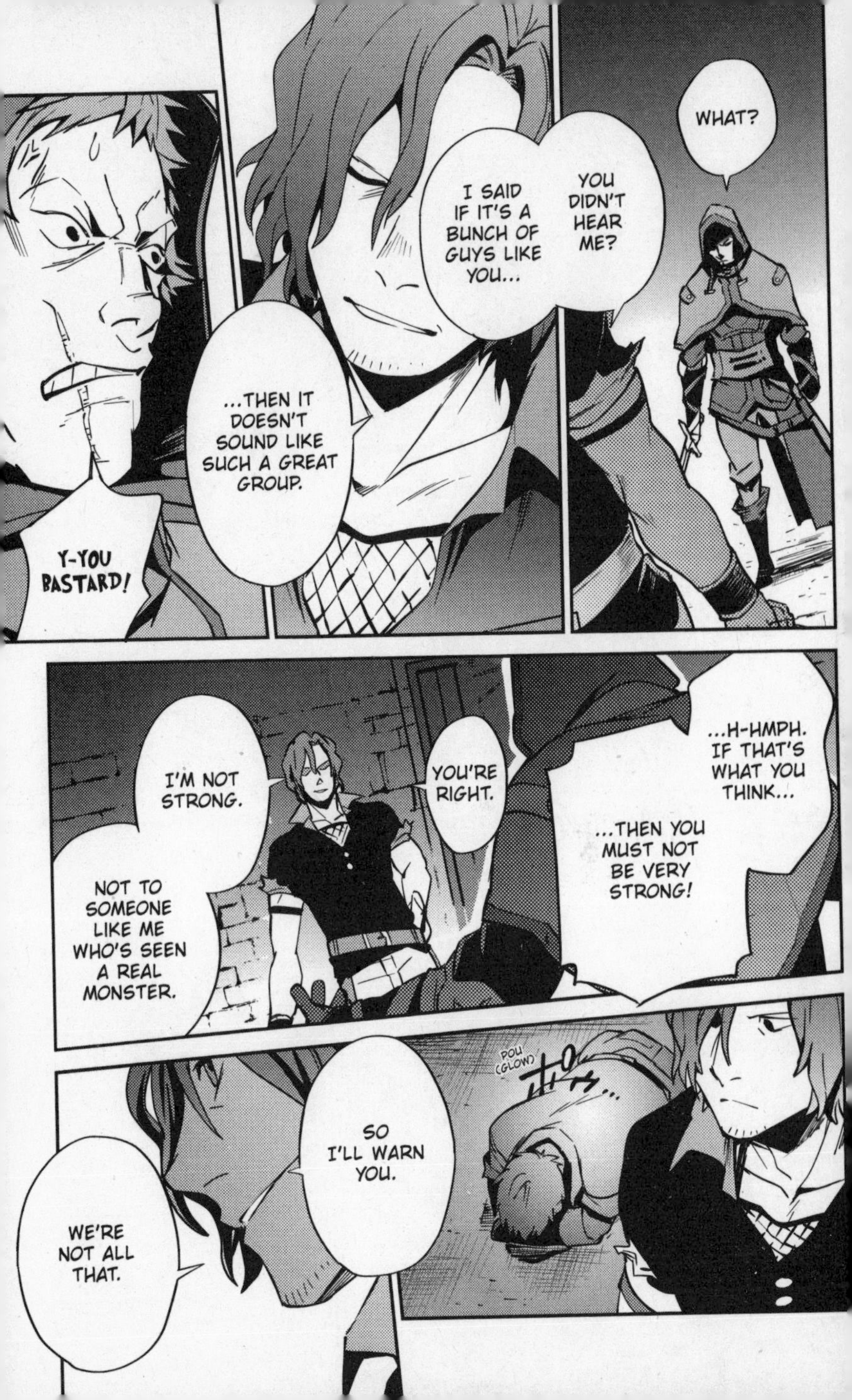
WHAT?
YOU DIDN'T HEAR ME?
I SAID IF IT'S A BUNCH OF GUYS LIKE YOU...
...THEN IT DOESN'T SOUND LIKE SUCH A GREAT GROUP.
Y-YOU BASTARD!
...H-HMPH. IF THAT'S WHAT YOU THINK...
...THEN YOU MUST NOT BE VERY STRONG!
YOU'RE RIGHT.
I'M NOT STRONG.
NOT TO SOMEONE LIKE ME WHO'S SEEN A REAL MONSTER.
POU (GLOW)
SO I'LL WARN YOU.
WE'RE NOT ALL THAT.

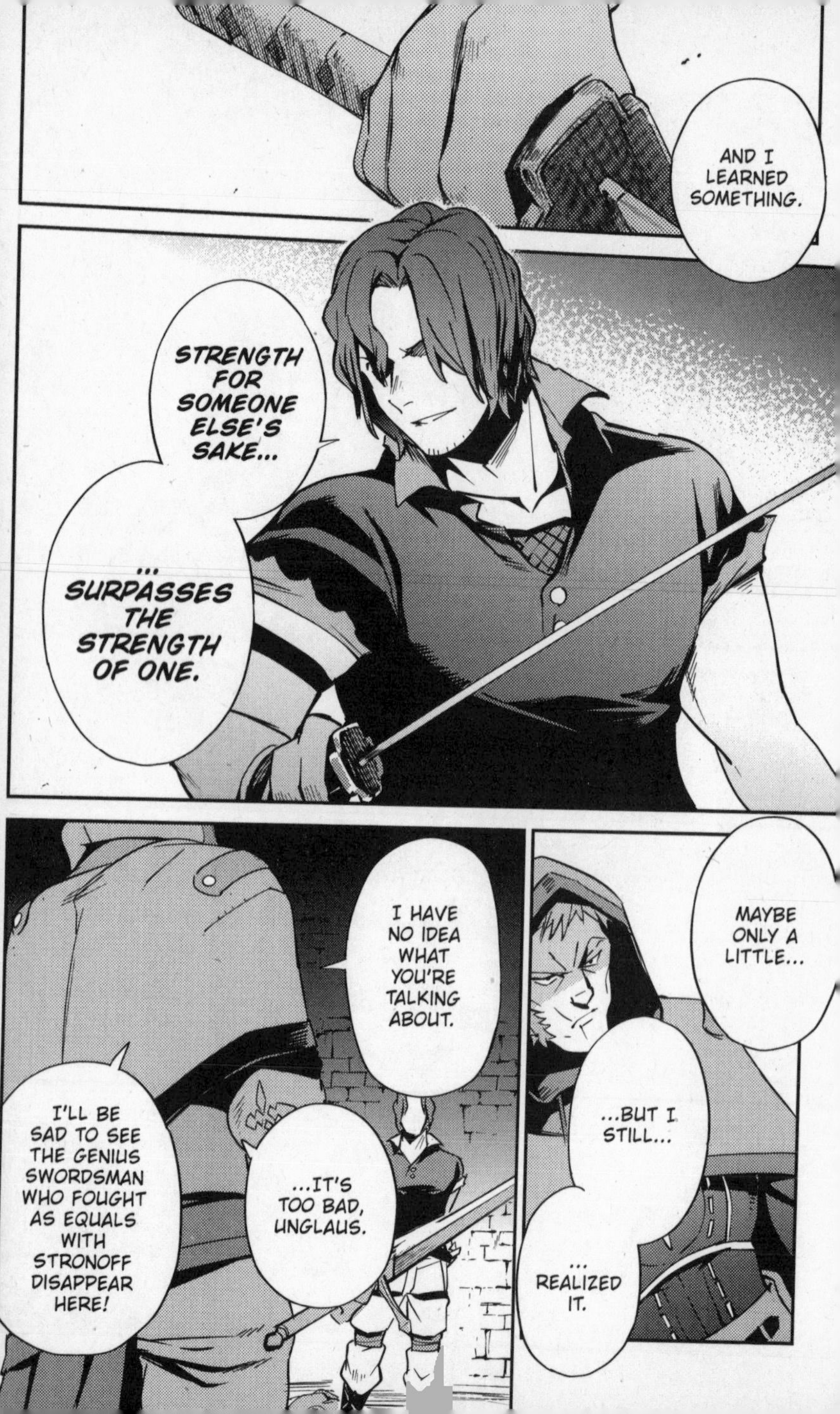
AND I LEARNED SOMETHING.
STRENGTH FOR SOMEONE ELSE'S SAKE...
...SURPASSES THE STRENGTH OF ONE.
MAYBE ONLY A LITTLE...
...BUT I STILL...
...REALIZED IT.
I HAVE NO IDEA WHAT YOU'RE TALKING ABOUT.
...IT'S TOO BAD, UNGLAUS.
I'LL BE SAD TO SEE THE GENIUS SWORDSMAN WHO FOUGHT AS EQUALS WITH STRONOFF DISAPPEAR HERE!

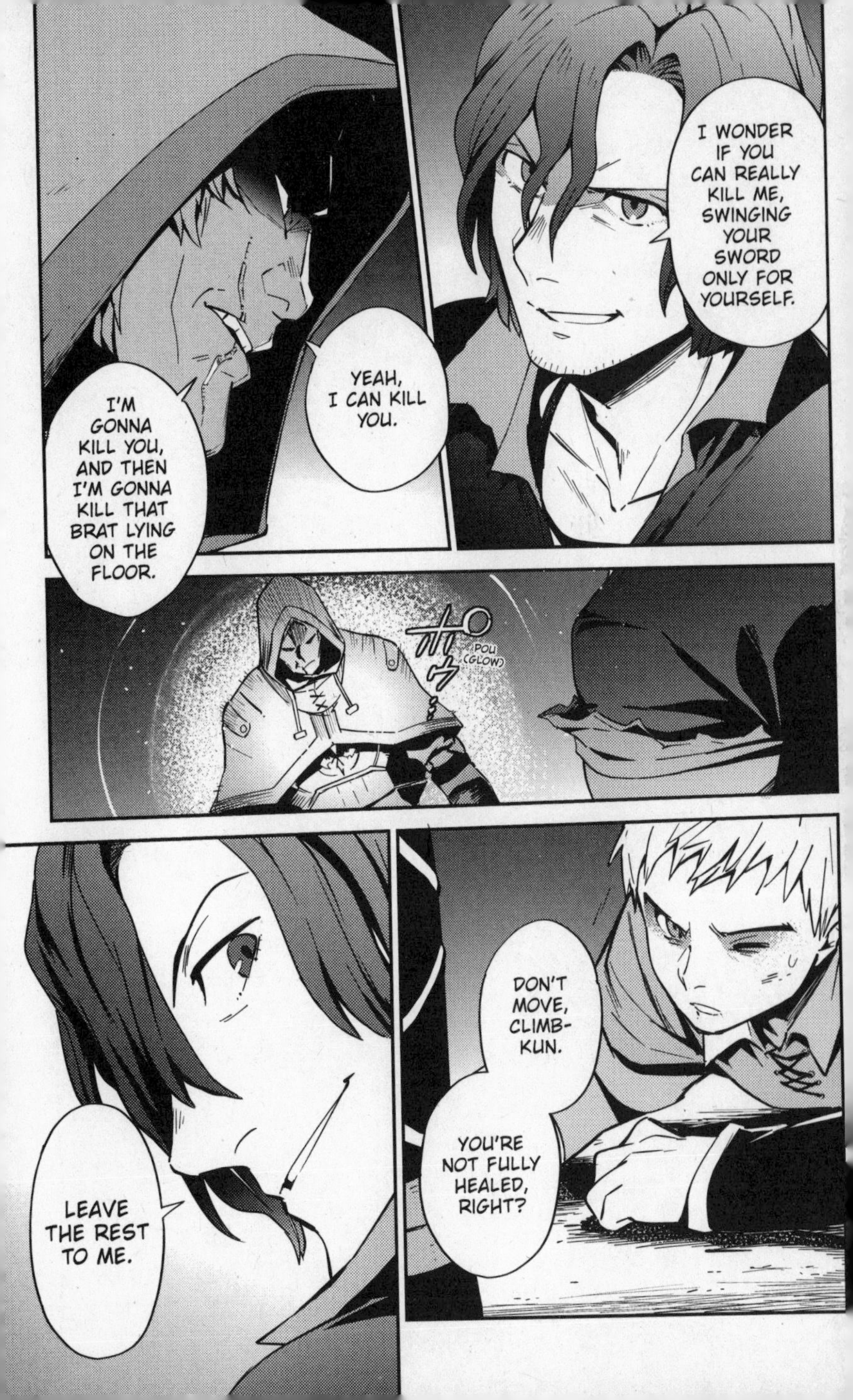

I WONDER IF YOU CAN REALLY KILL ME, SWINGING YOUR SWORD ONLY FOR YOURSELF.
YEAH, I CAN KILL YOU.
I'M GONNA KILL YOU, AND THEN I'M GONNA KILL THAT BRAT LYING ON THE FLOOR.
POU (GLOW)
DON'T MOVE, CLIMB-KUN.
YOU'RE NOT FULLY HEALED, RIGHT?
LEAVE THE REST TO ME.

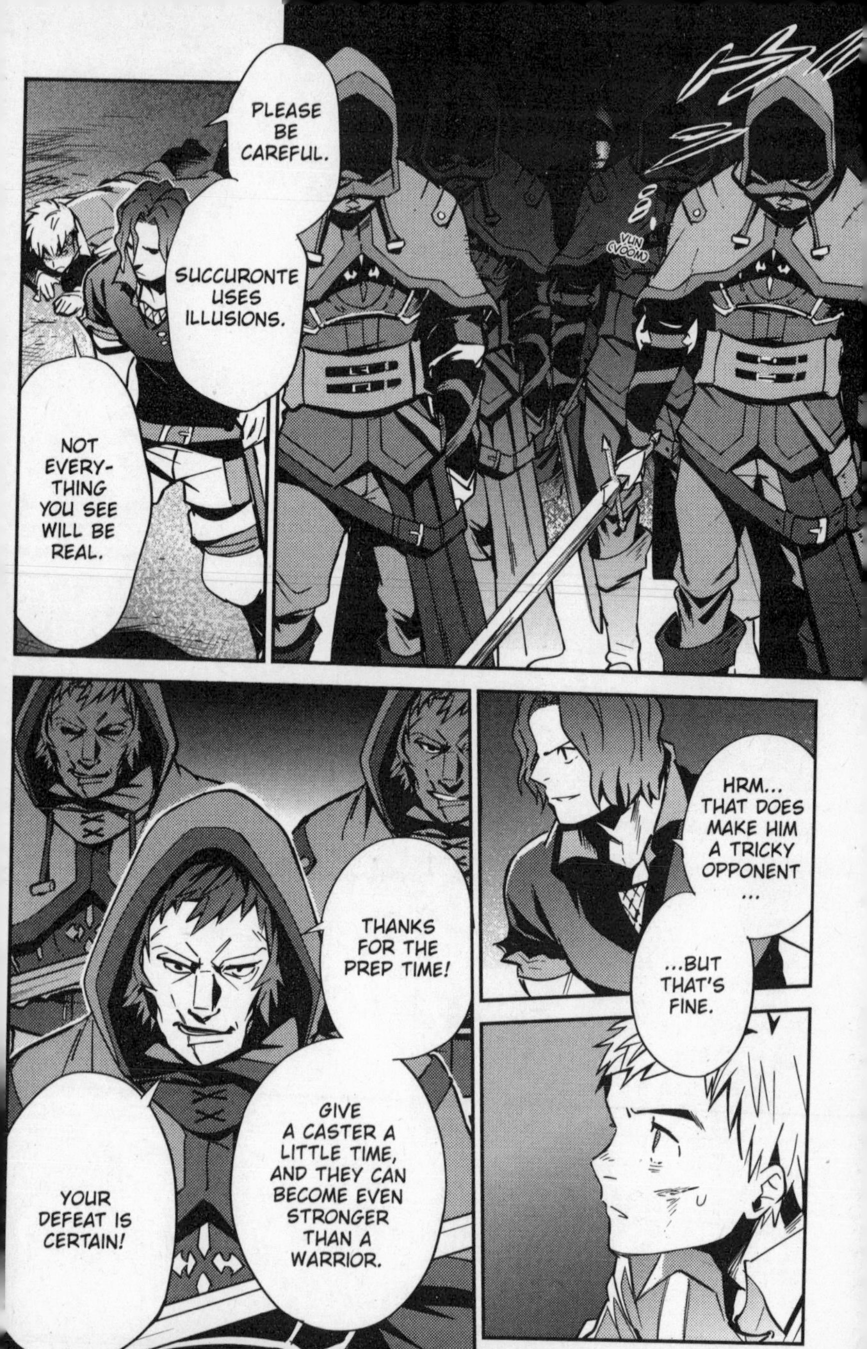
VUN (VOOM)
PLEASE BE CAREFUL.
SUCCURONTE USES ILLUSIONS.
NOT EVERYTHING YOU SEE WILL BE REAL.
HRM... THAT DOES MAKE HIM A TRICKY OPPONENT ...
...BUT THAT'S FINE.
THANKS FOR THE PREP TIME!
GIVE A CASTER A LITTLE TIME, AND THEY CAN BECOME EVEN STRONGER THAN A WARRIOR.
YOUR DEFEAT IS CERTAIN!

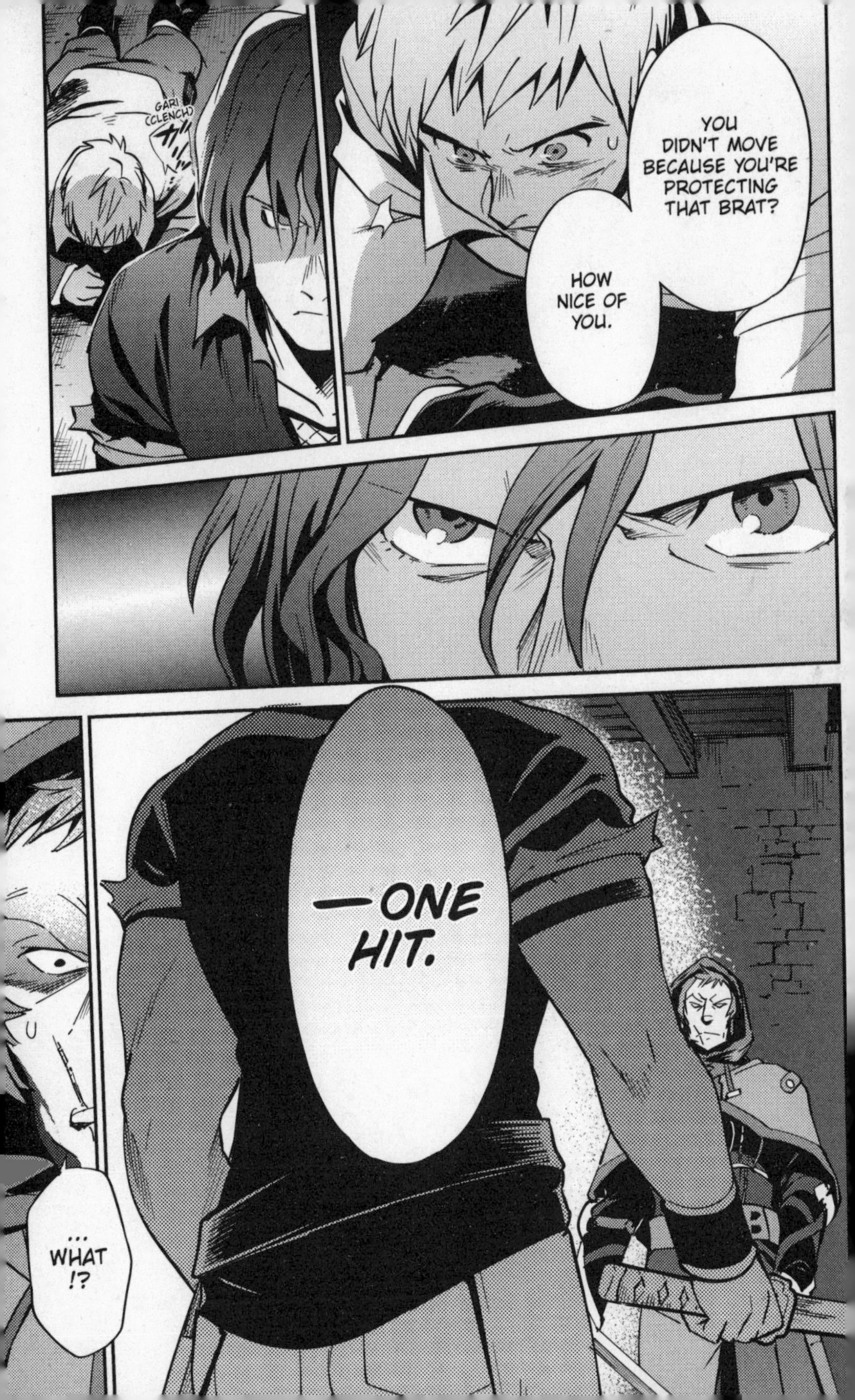
YOU DIDN'T MOVE BECAUSE YOU'RE PROTECTING THAT BRAT?
HOW NICE OF YOU.
GARI (CLENCH)
—ONE HIT.
... WHAT !?

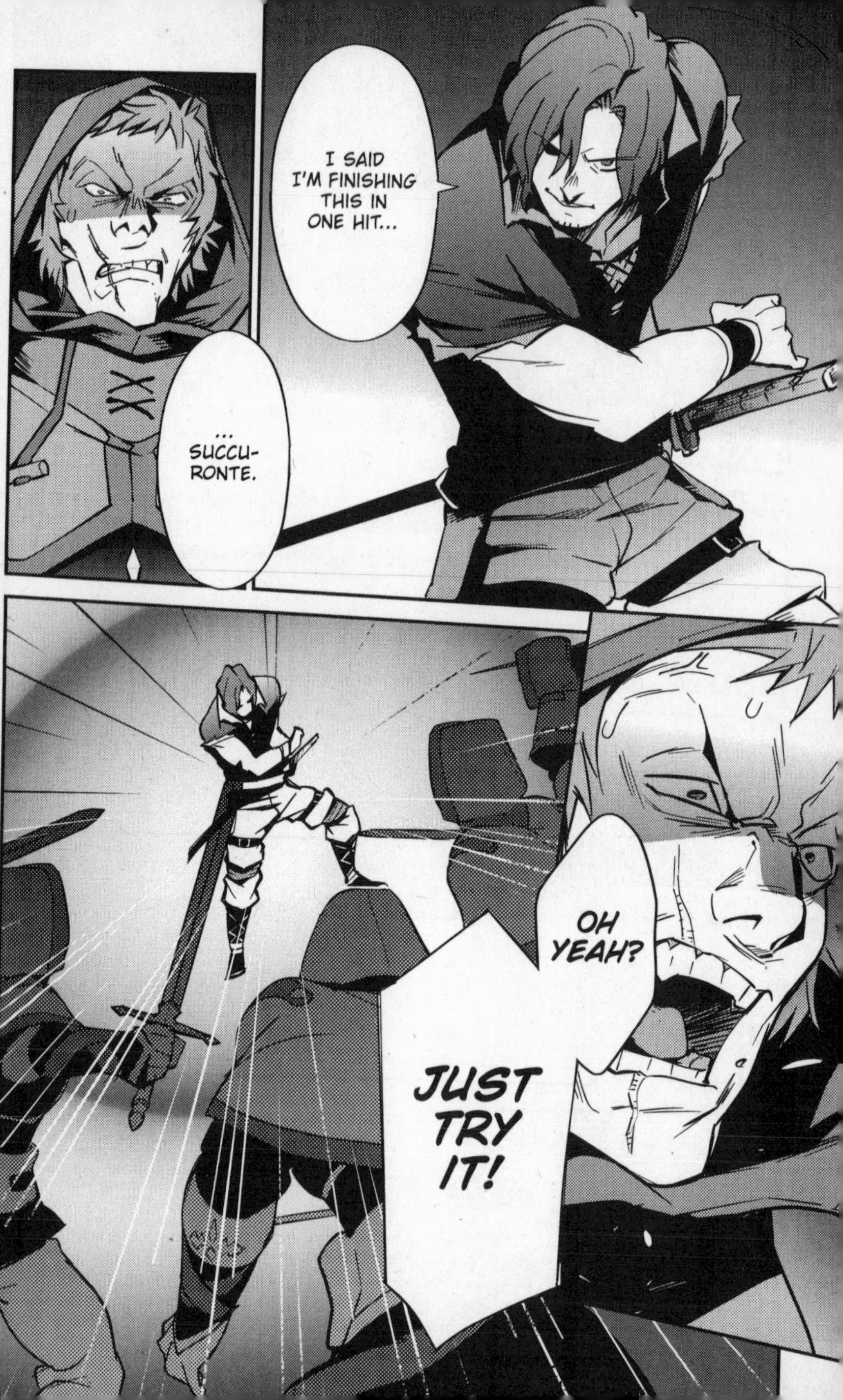
I SAID I'M FINISHING THIS IN ONE HIT...
...SUCCU-RONTE.
OH YEAH?
JUST TRY IT!

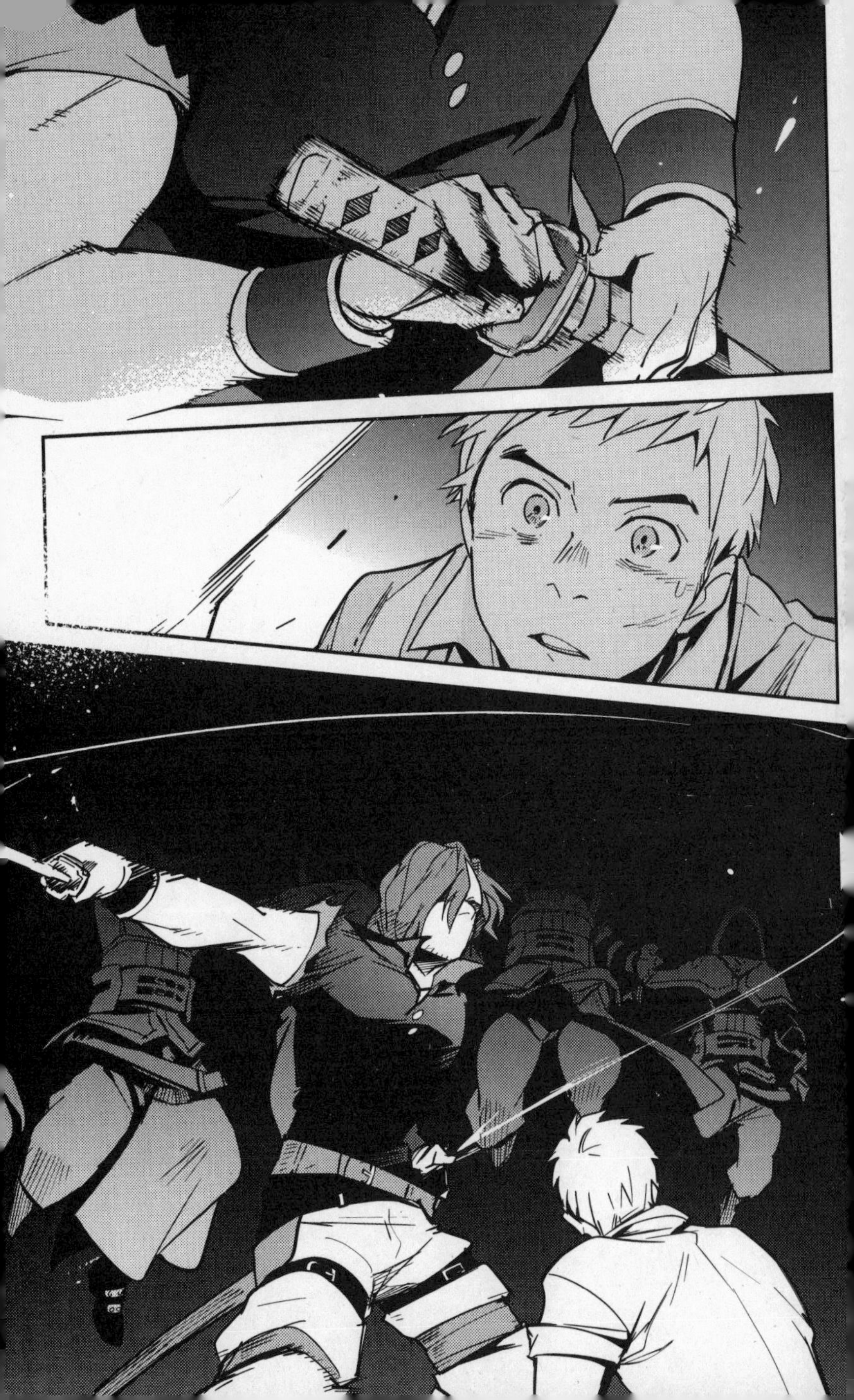

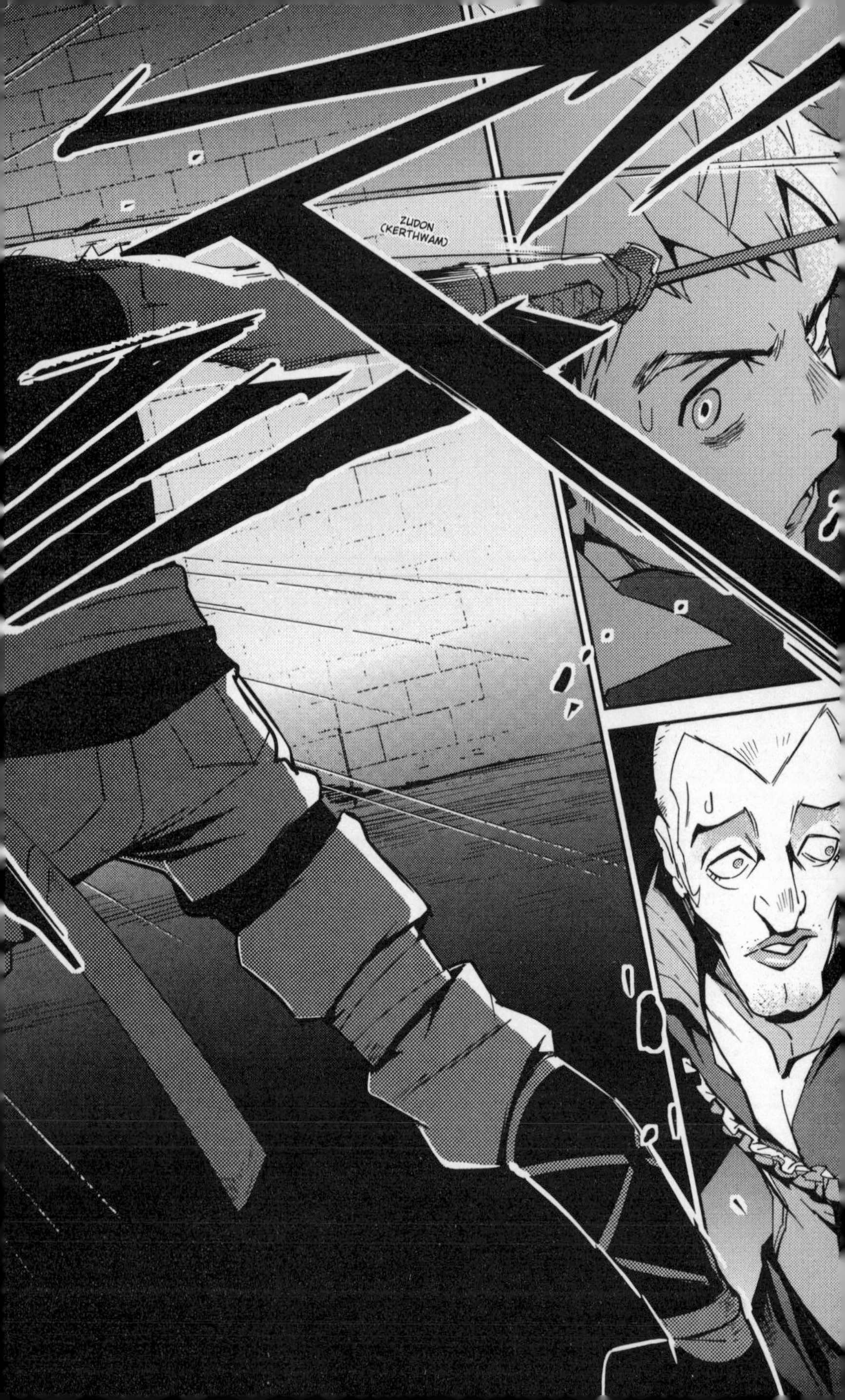
ZUDON
(KERTHWAM)

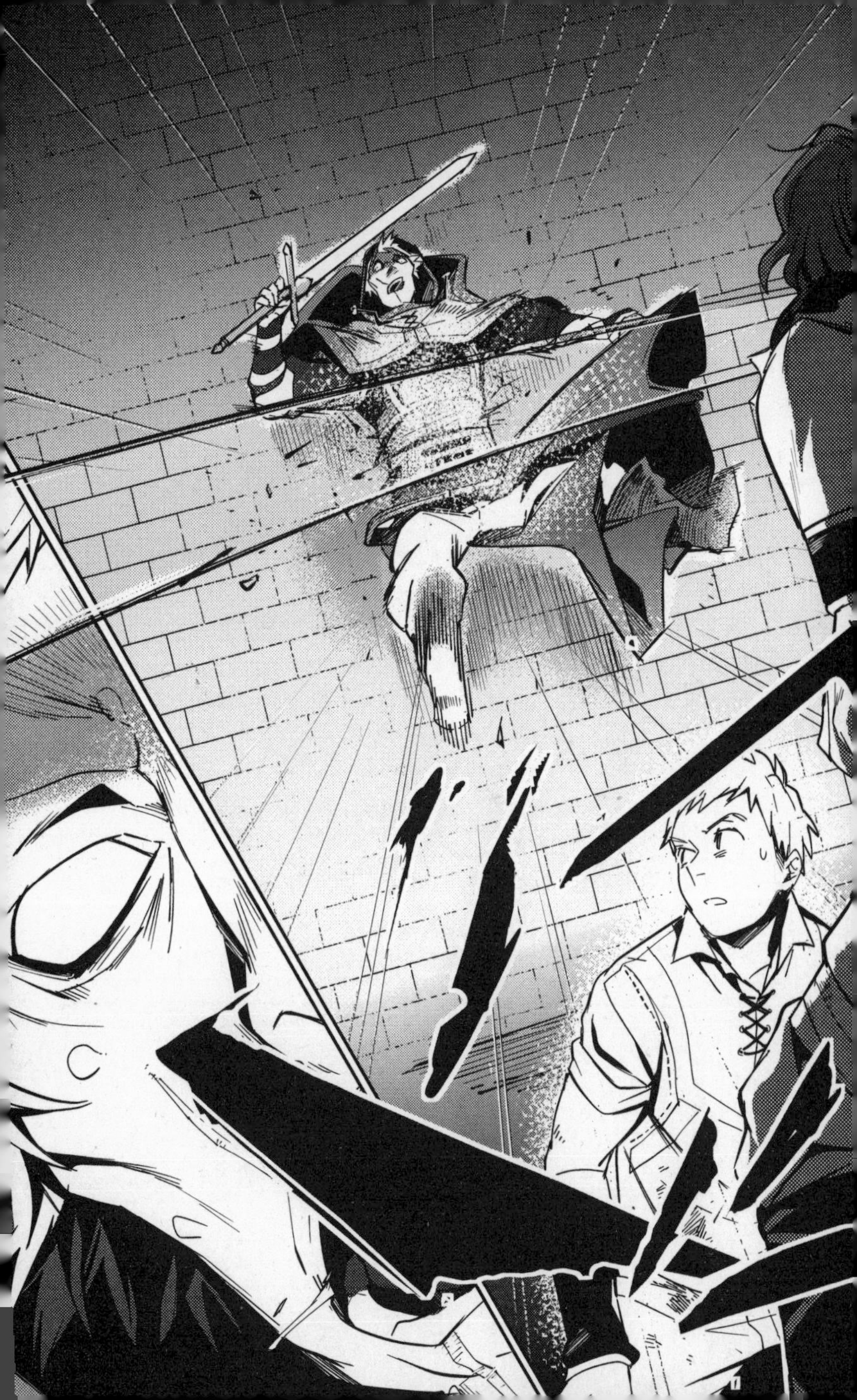

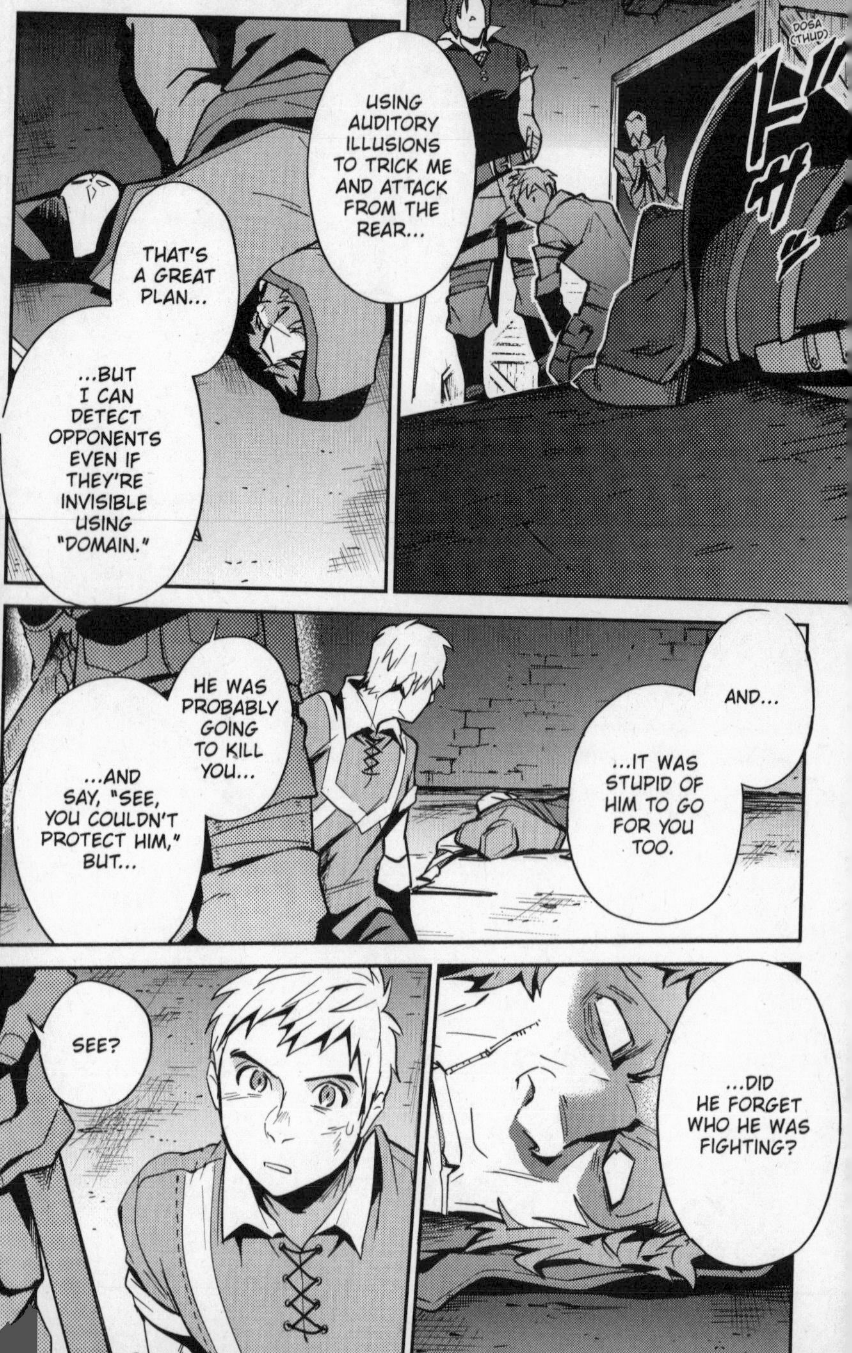
DOSA (THUD)
USING AUDITORY ILLUSIONS TO TRICK ME AND ATTACK FROM THE REAR...
THAT'S A GREAT PLAN...
...BUT I CAN DETECT OPPONENTS EVEN IF THEY'RE INVISIBLE USING "DOMAIN."
AND...
...IT WAS STUPID OF HIM TO GO FOR YOU TOO.
HE WAS PROBABLY GOING TO KILL YOU...
...AND SAY, "SEE, YOU COULDN'T PROTECT HIM," BUT...
...DID HE FORGET WHO HE WAS FIGHTING?
SEE?

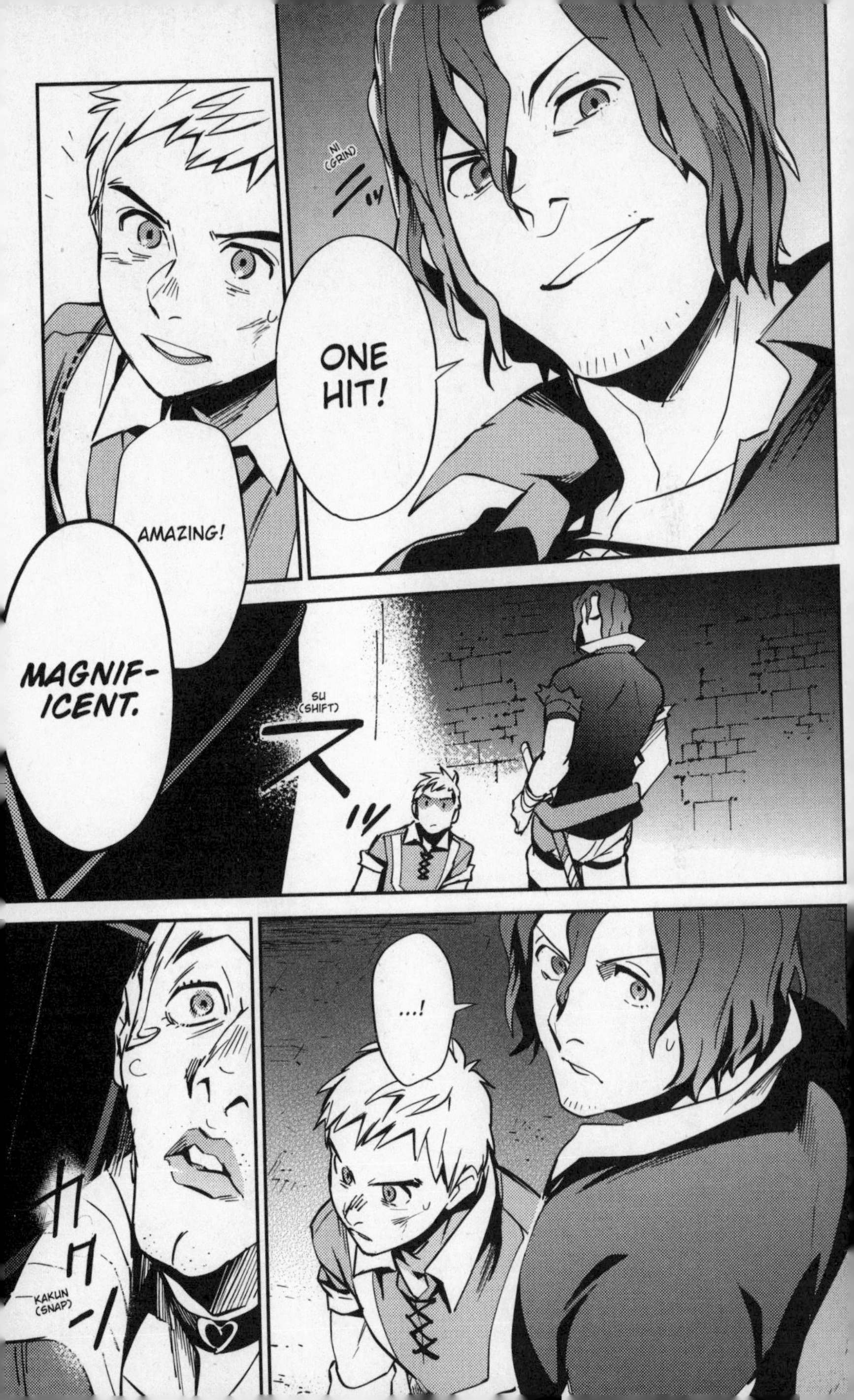
NI (GRIN)
ONE HIT!
AMAZING!
MAGNIF-ICENT.
SU (SHIFT)
...!
KAKUN (SNAP)

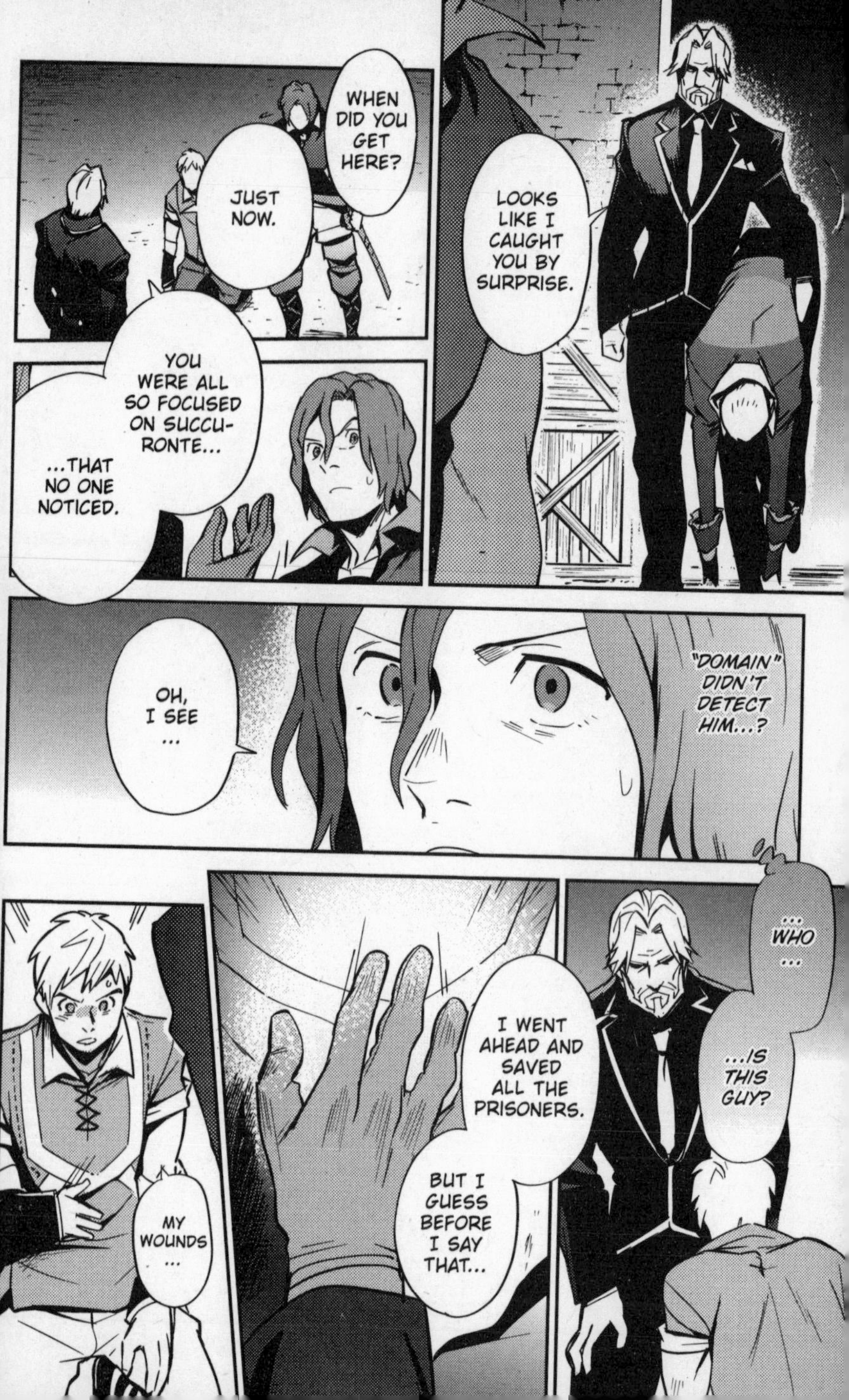

LOOKS LIKE I CAUGHT YOU BY SURPRISE.
WHEN DID YOU GET HERE?
JUST NOW.
YOU WERE ALL SO FOCUSED ON SUCCU-RONTE...
...THAT NO ONE NOTICED.
"DOMAIN" DIDN'T DETECT HIM...?
OH, I SEE...
...WHO...
...IS THIS GUY?
I WENT AHEAD AND SAVED ALL THE PRISONERS.
BUT I GUESS BEFORE I SAY THAT...
MY WOUNDS...

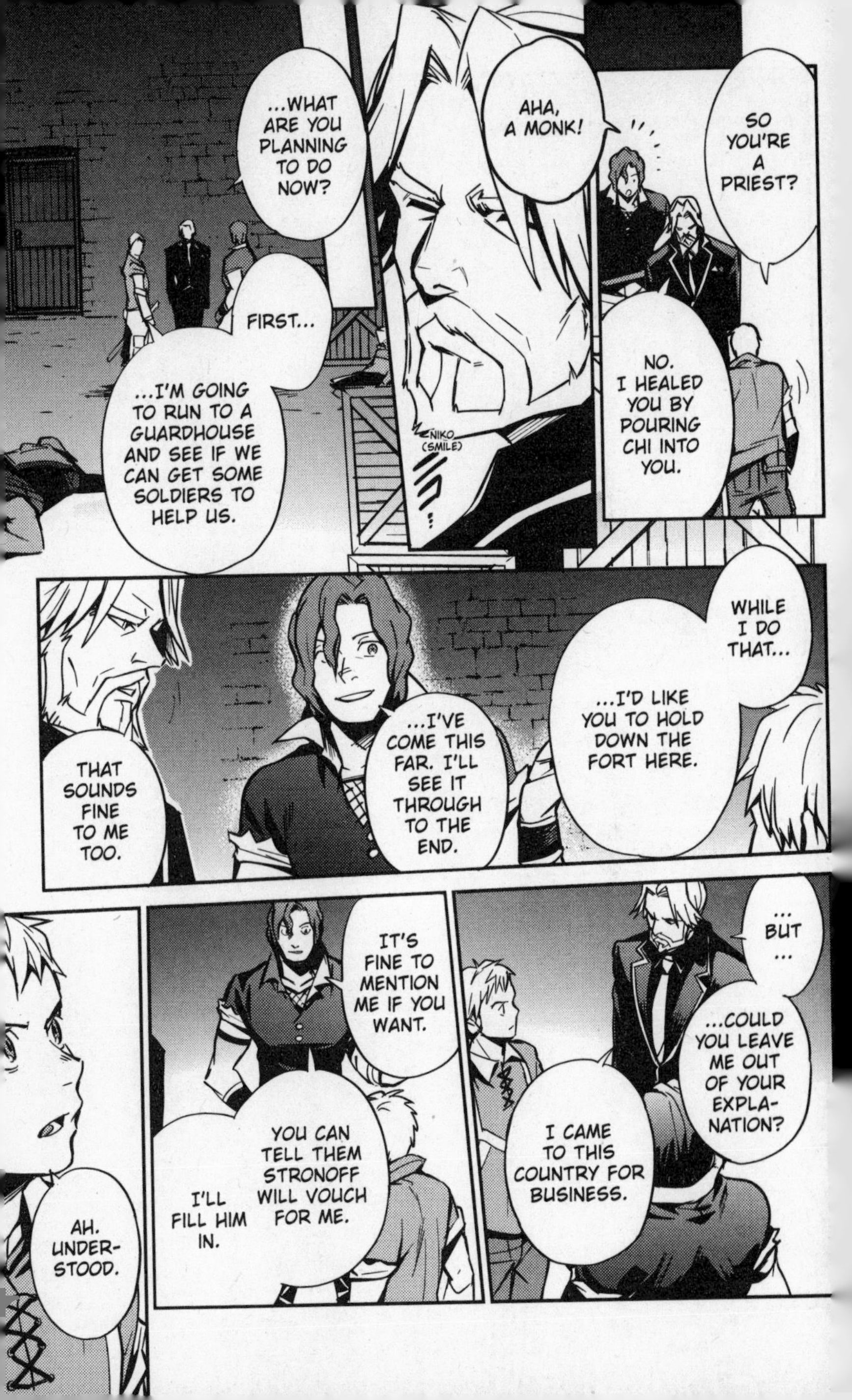
SO YOU'RE A PRIEST?
NO. I HEALED YOU BY POURING CHI INTO YOU.
AHA, A MONK!
NIKO (SMILE)
...WHAT ARE YOU PLANNING TO DO NOW?
FIRST...
...I'M GOING TO RUN TO A GUARDHOUSE AND SEE IF WE CAN GET SOME SOLDIERS TO HELP US.
WHILE I DO THAT...
...I'D LIKE YOU TO HOLD DOWN THE FORT HERE.
...I'VE COME THIS FAR. I'LL SEE IT THROUGH TO THE END.
THAT SOUNDS FINE TO ME TOO.
...BUT...
...COULD YOU LEAVE ME OUT OF YOUR EXPLA-NATION?
I CAME TO THIS COUNTRY FOR BUSINESS.
IT'S FINE TO MENTION ME IF YOU WANT.
YOU CAN TELL THEM STRONOFF WILL VOUCH FOR ME.
I'LL FILL HIM IN.
AH. UNDER-STOOD.

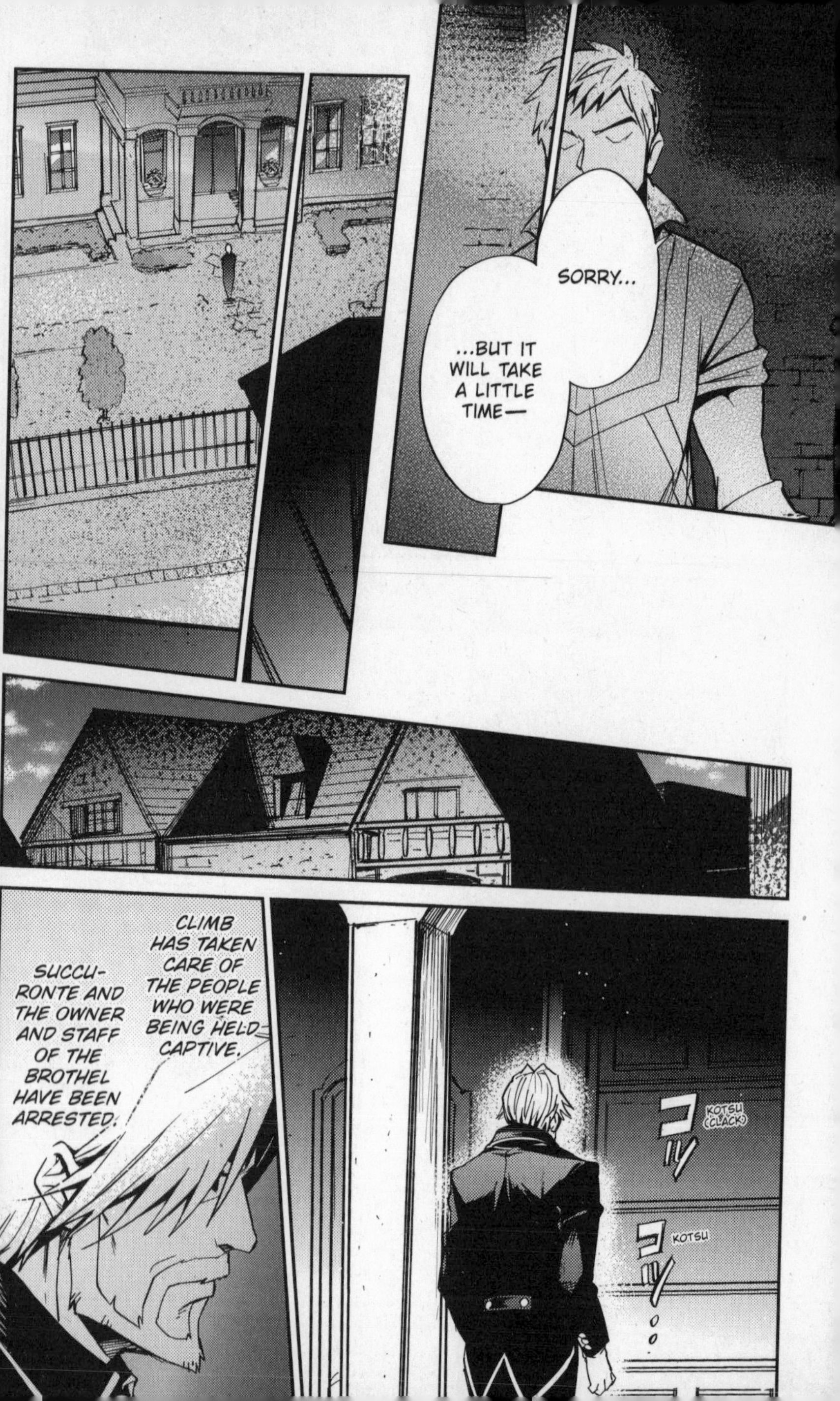
SORRY...
...BUT IT WILL TAKE A LITTLE TIME—
KOTSU (CLACK)
KOTSU
CLIMB HAS TAKEN CARE OF THE PEOPLE WHO WERE BEING HELD CAPTIVE.
SUCCU-RONTE AND THE OWNER AND STAFF OF THE BROTHEL HAVE BEEN ARRESTED.

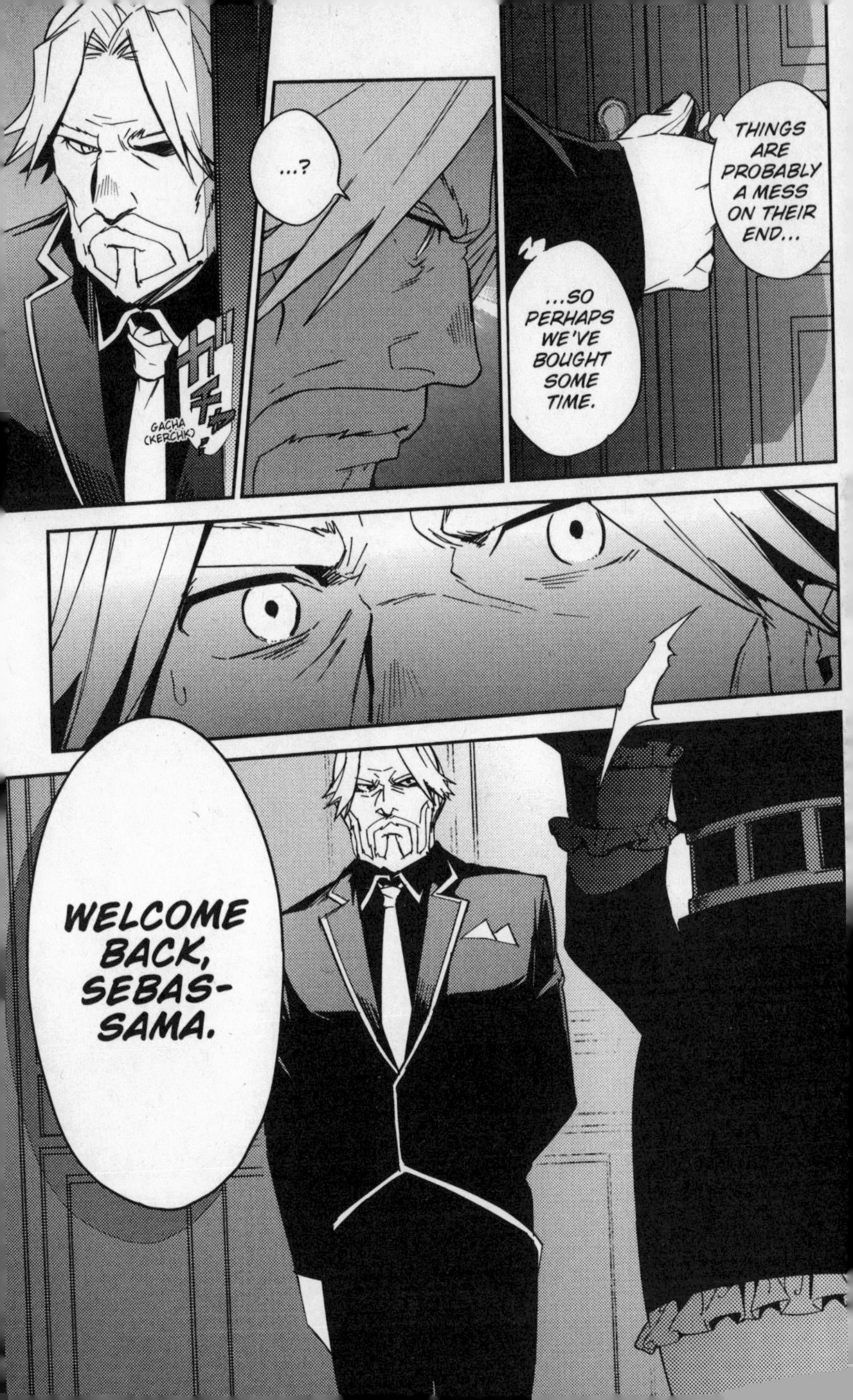
THINGS ARE PROBABLY A MESS ON THEIR END...
...SO PERHAPS WE'VE BOUGHT SOME TIME.
...?
GACHA (KERCHK)
WELCOME BACK, SEBAS-SAMA.

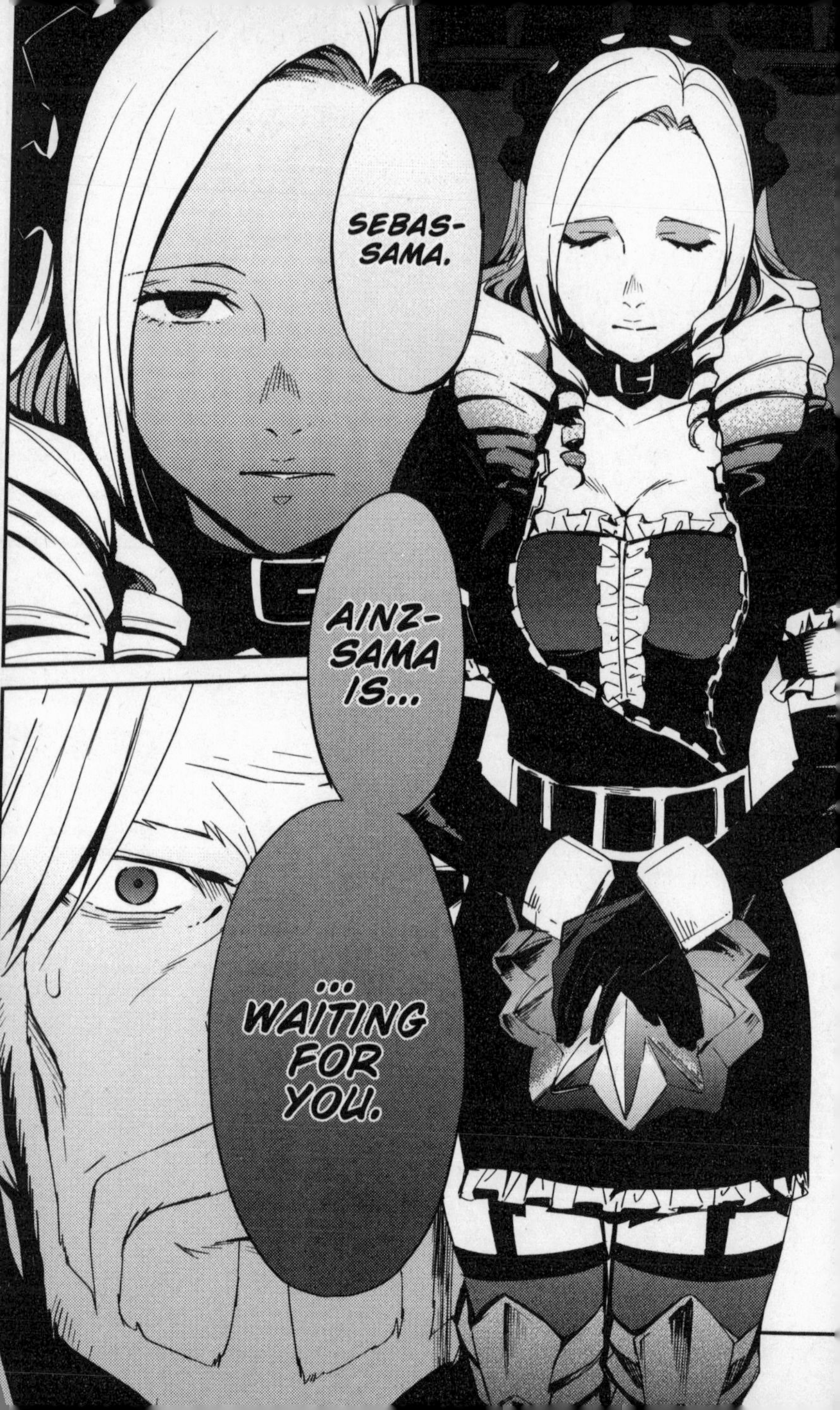
SEBAS-SAMA.
AINZ-SAMA IS...
...WAITING FOR YOU.

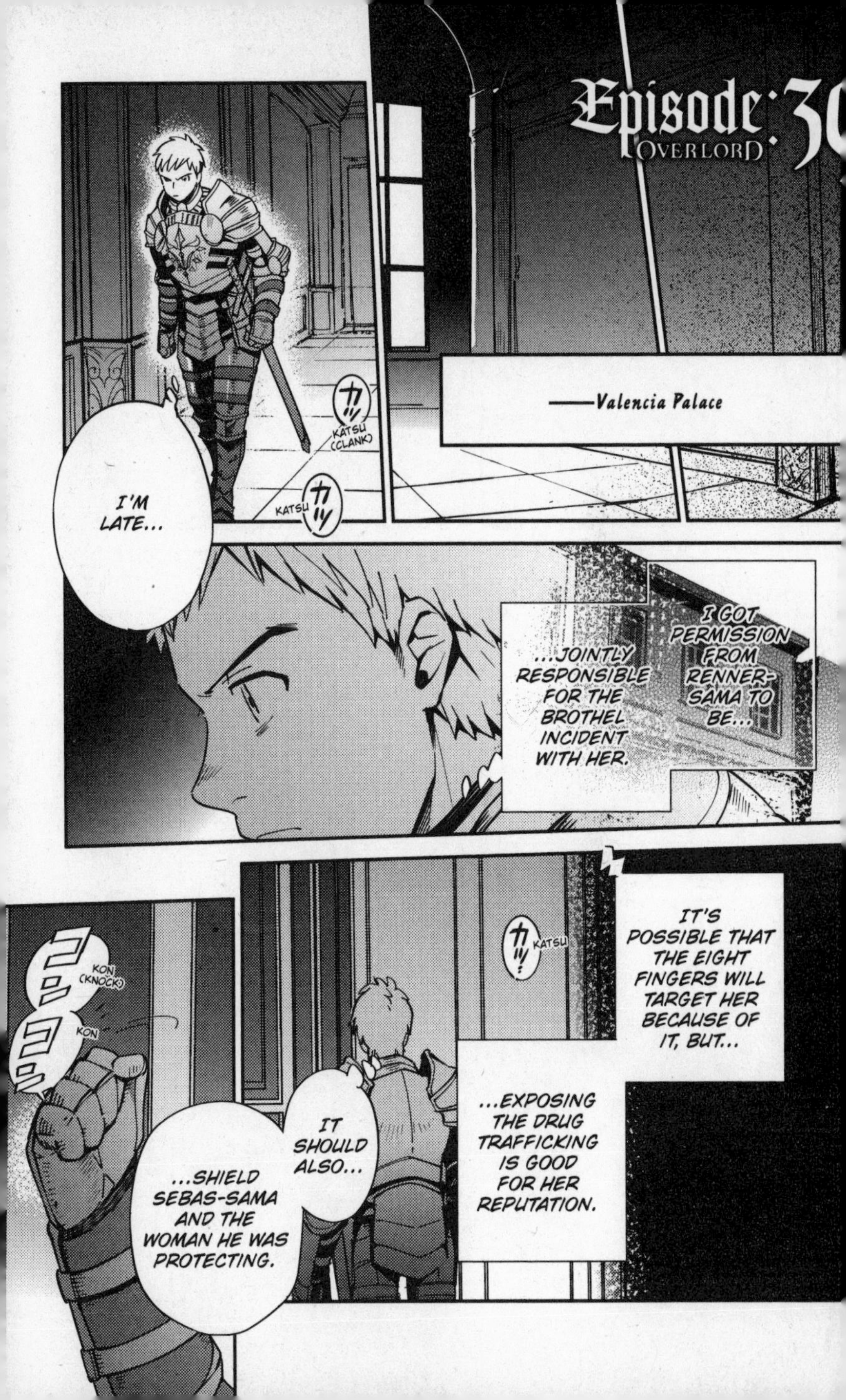
Episode: 30
OVERLORD
—Valencia Palace
カッ
KATSU (CLANK)
カッ
KATSU
I'M LATE...
I GOT PERMISSION FROM RENNER-SAMA TO BE...
...JOINTLY RESPONSIBLE FOR THE BROTHEL INCIDENT WITH HER.
カッ
KATSU
IT'S POSSIBLE THAT THE EIGHT FINGERS WILL TARGET HER BECAUSE OF IT, BUT...
...EXPOSING THE DRUG TRAFFICKING IS GOOD FOR HER REPUTATION.
コン
KON (KNOCK)
コン
KON
IT SHOULD ALSO...
...SHIELD SEBAS-SAMA AND THE WOMAN HE WAS PROTECTING.

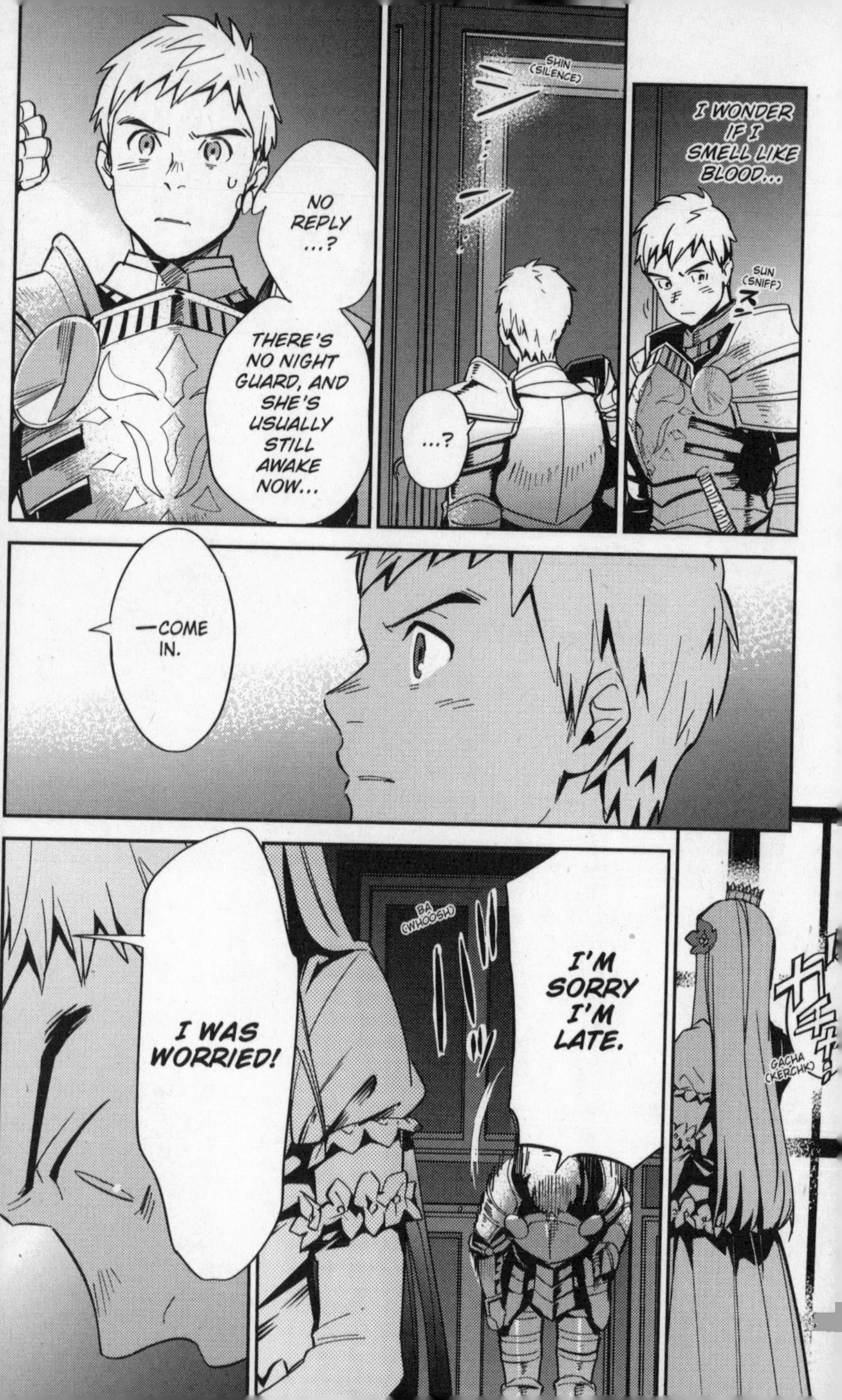
I WONDER IF I SMELL LIKE BLOOD...
SUN (SNIFF)
SHIN (SILENCE)
...?
NO REPLY ...?
THERE'S NO NIGHT GUARD, AND SHE'S USUALLY STILL AWAKE NOW...
—COME IN.
GACHA (KERCHK)
BA (WHOOSH)
I'M SORRY I'M LATE.
I WAS WORRIED!

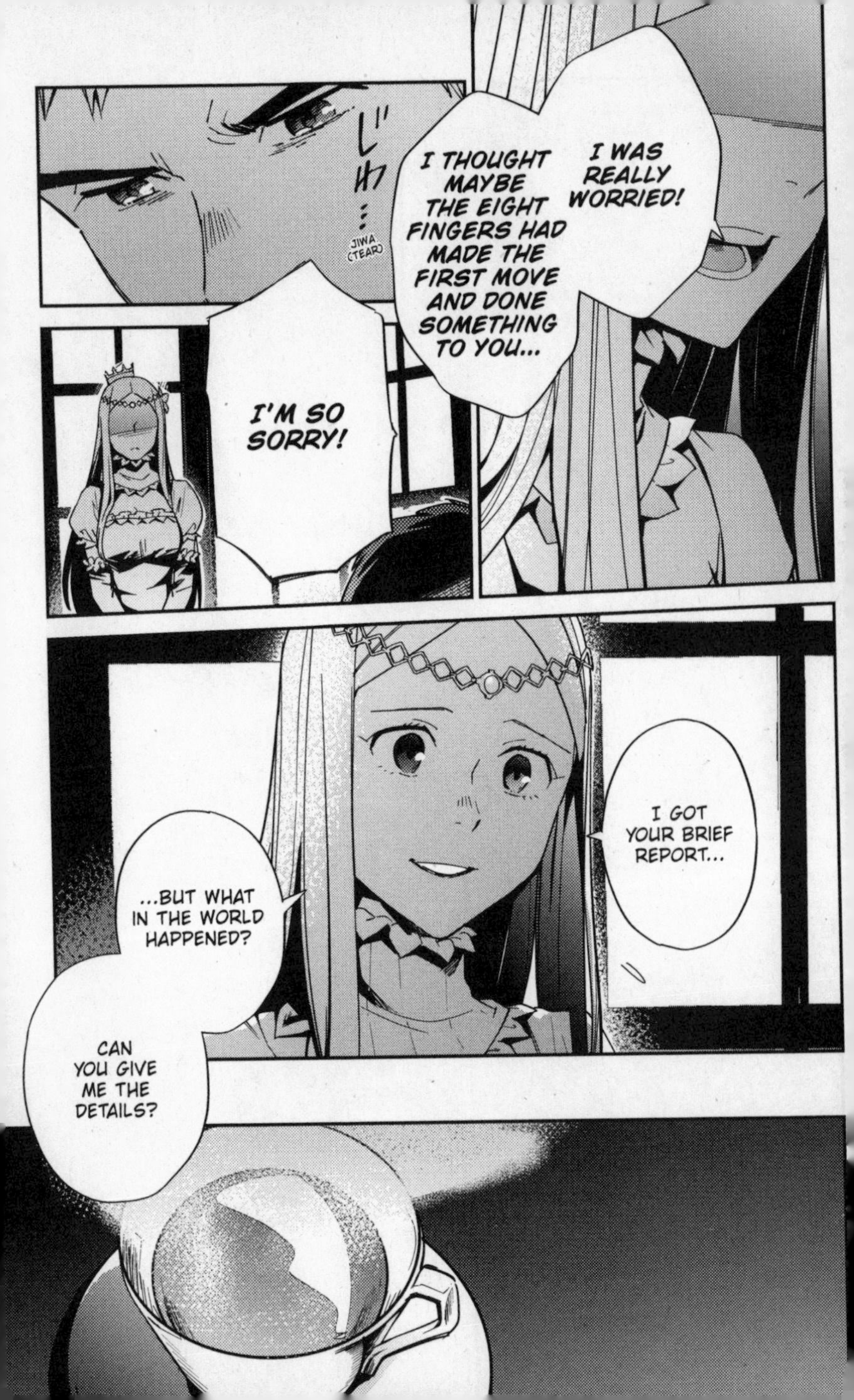
I WAS REALLY WORRIED!
I THOUGHT MAYBE THE EIGHT FINGERS HAD MADE THE FIRST MOVE AND DONE SOMETHING TO YOU...
JIWA (TEAR)
I'M SO SORRY!
I GOT YOUR BRIEF REPORT...
...BUT WHAT IN THE WORLD HAPPENED?
CAN YOU GIVE ME THE DETAILS?

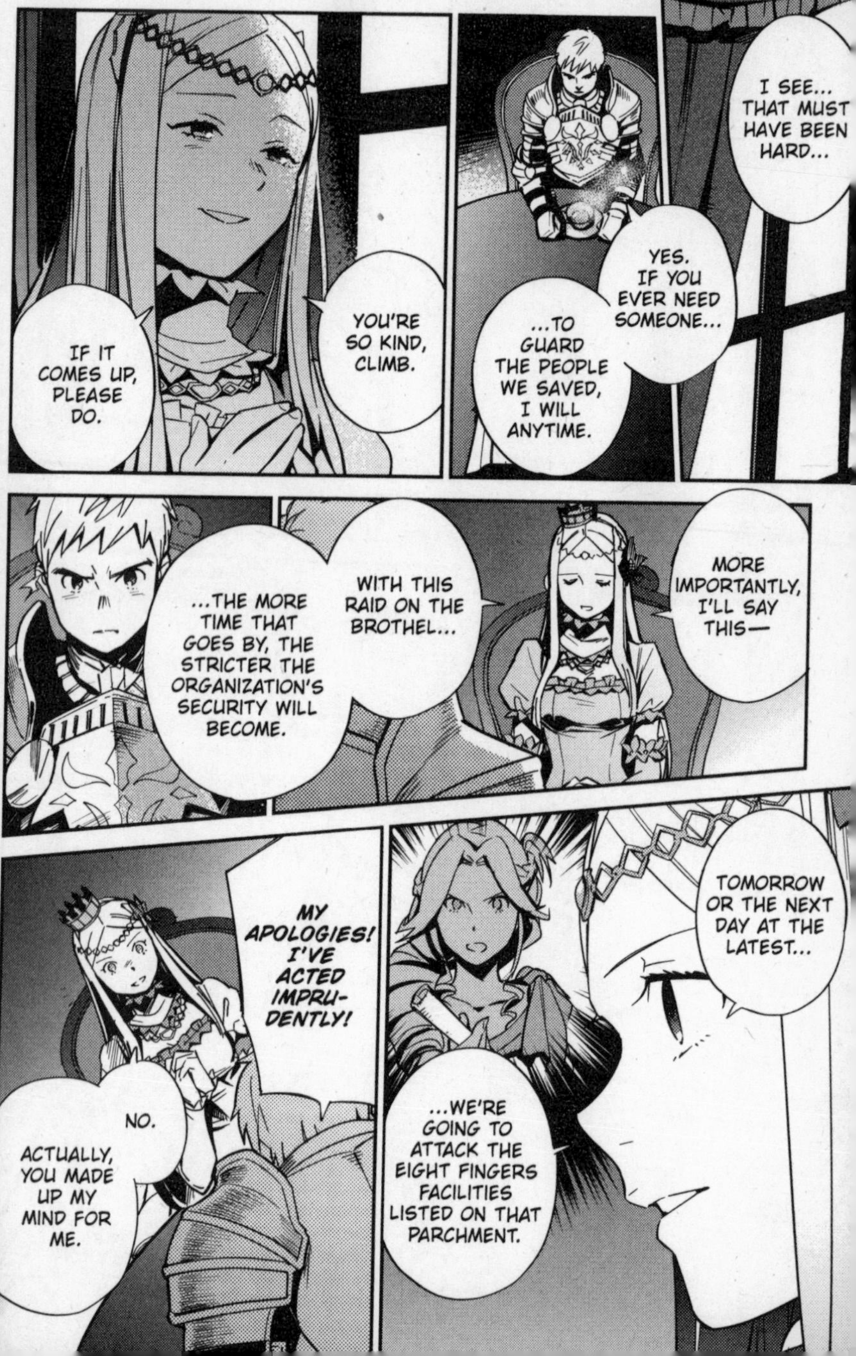
I SEE... THAT MUST HAVE BEEN HARD...
YES. IF YOU EVER NEED SOMEONE...
...TO GUARD THE PEOPLE WE SAVED, I WILL ANYTIME.
YOU'RE SO KIND, CLIMB.
IF IT COMES UP, PLEASE DO.
MORE IMPORTANTLY, I'LL SAY THIS—
WITH THIS RAID ON THE BROTHEL...
...THE MORE TIME THAT GOES BY, THE STRICTER THE ORGANIZATION'S SECURITY WILL BECOME.
TOMORROW OR THE NEXT DAY AT THE LATEST...
...WE'RE GOING TO ATTACK THE EIGHT FINGERS FACILITIES LISTED ON THAT PARCHMENT.
MY APOLOGIES! I'VE ACTED IMPRU-DENTLY!
NO.
ACTUALLY, YOU MADE UP MY MIND FOR ME.

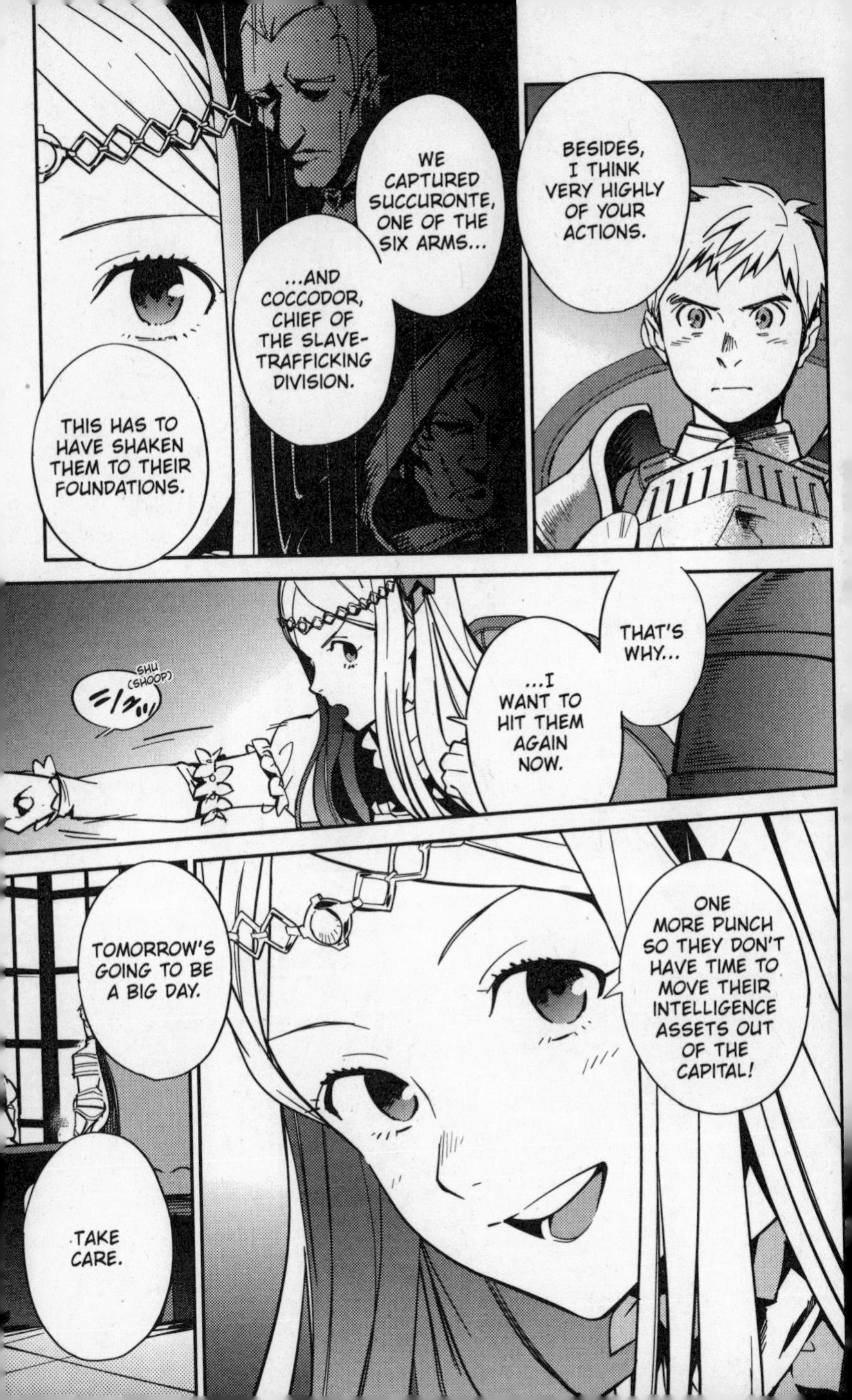
BESIDES, I THINK VERY HIGHLY OF YOUR ACTIONS.
WE CAPTURED SUCCURONTE, ONE OF THE SIX ARMS...
...AND COCCODOR, CHIEF OF THE SLAVE-TRAFFICKING DIVISION.
THIS HAS TO HAVE SHAKEN THEM TO THEIR FOUNDATIONS.
THAT'S WHY...
...I WANT TO HIT THEM AGAIN NOW.
SHU (SHOOP)
ONE MORE PUNCH SO THEY DON'T HAVE TIME TO MOVE THEIR INTELLIGENCE ASSETS OUT OF THE CAPITAL!
TOMORROW'S GOING TO BE A BIG DAY.
TAKE CARE.

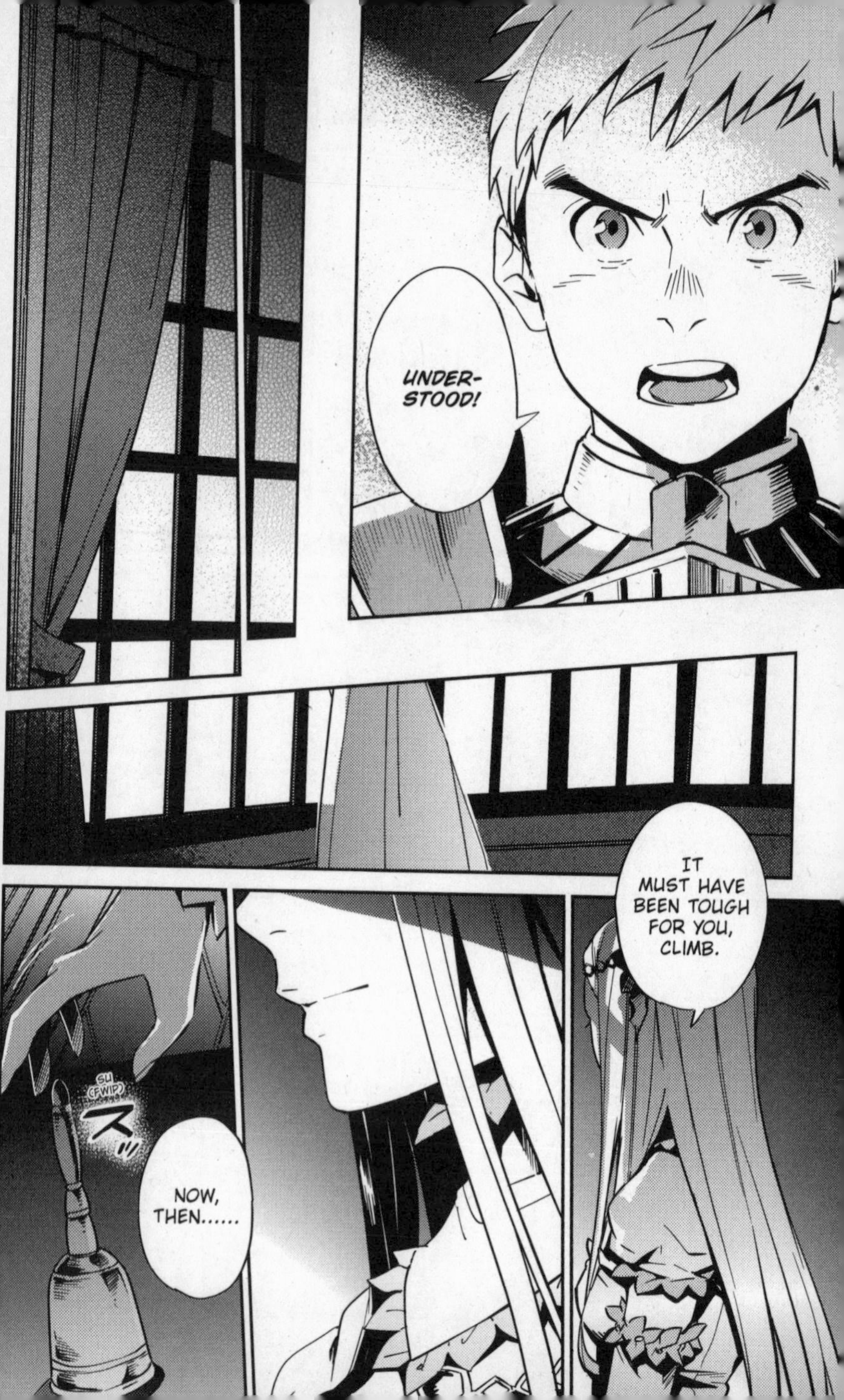
UNDER-STOOD!
IT MUST HAVE BEEN TOUGH FOR YOU, CLIMB.
SU (FWIP)
ス
NOW, THEN......

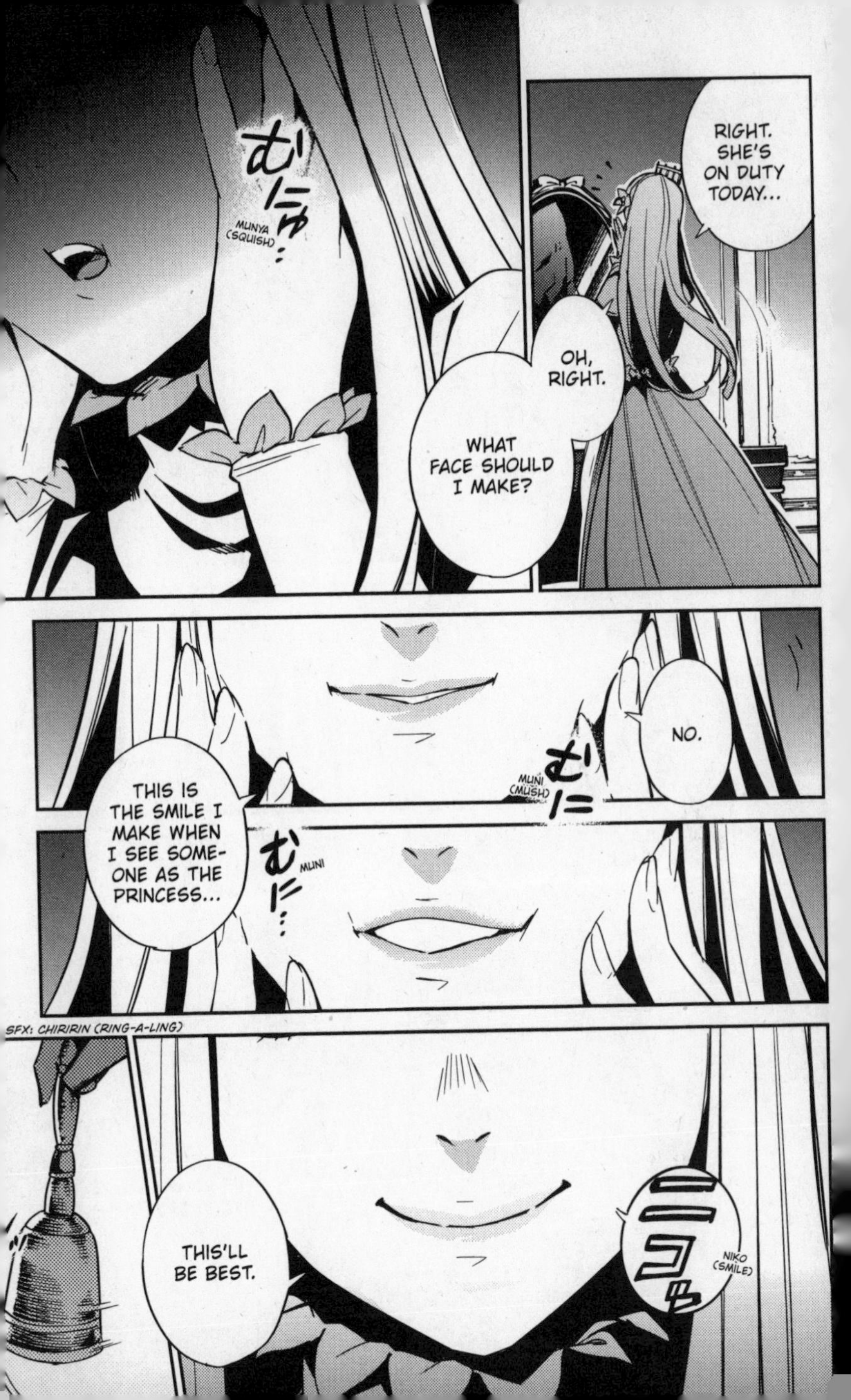
RIGHT. SHE'S ON DUTY TODAY...
OH, RIGHT.
WHAT FACE SHOULD I MAKE?
MUNYA (SQUISH)
NO.
MUNI (MUSH)
THIS IS THE SMILE I MAKE WHEN I SEE SOME-ONE AS THE PRINCESS...
MUNI
SFX: CHIRIRIN (RING-A-LING)
NIKO (SMILE)
THIS'LL BE BEST.

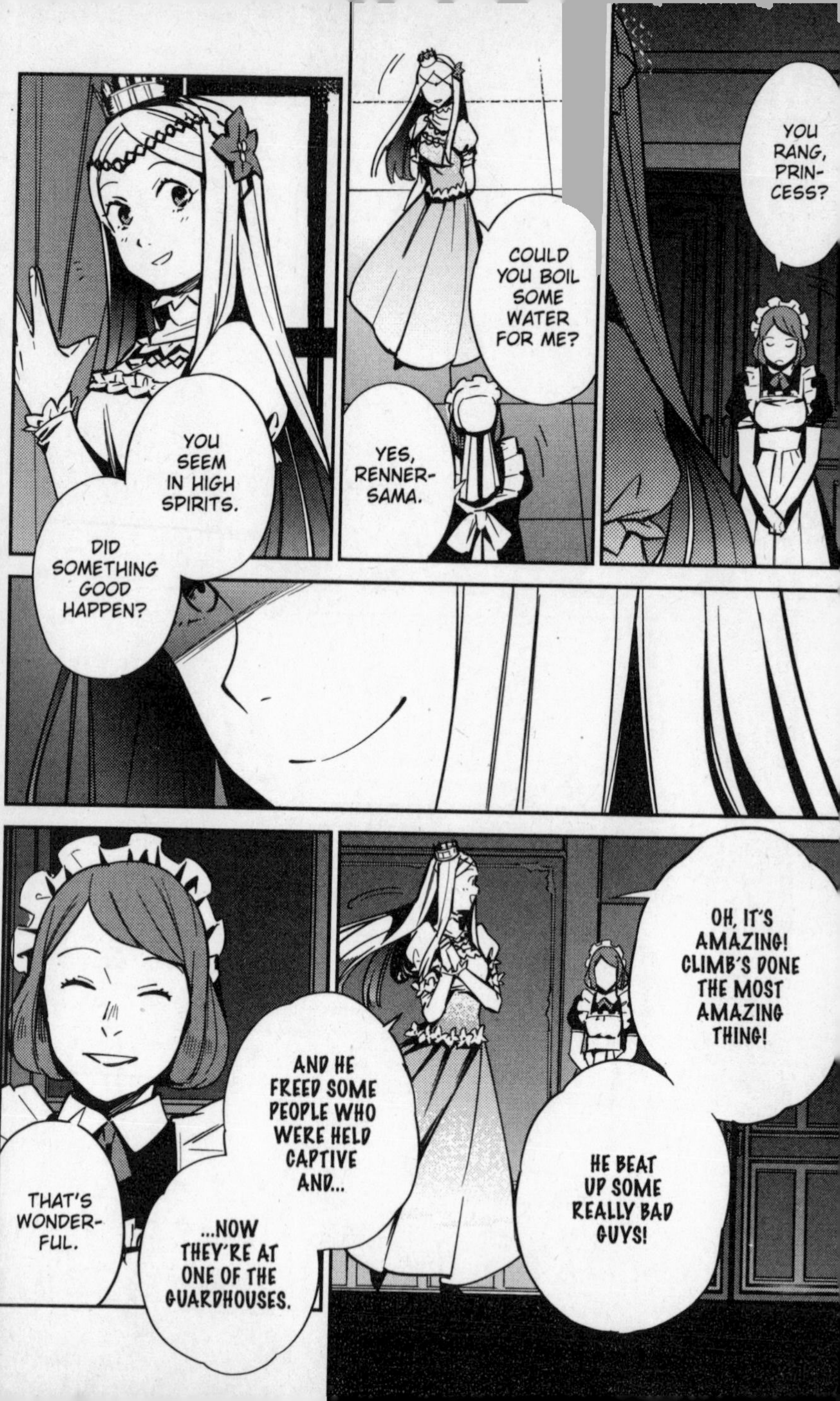
YOU RANG, PRINCESS?
COULD YOU BOIL SOME WATER FOR ME?
YES, RENNER-SAMA.
YOU SEEM IN HIGH SPIRITS.
DID SOMETHING GOOD HAPPEN?
OH, IT'S AMAZING! CLIMB'S DONE THE MOST AMAZING THING!
HE BEAT UP SOME REALLY BAD GUYS!
AND HE FREED SOME PEOPLE WHO WERE HELD CAPTIVE AND...
...NOW THEY'RE AT ONE OF THE GUARDHOUSES.
THAT'S WONDERFUL.

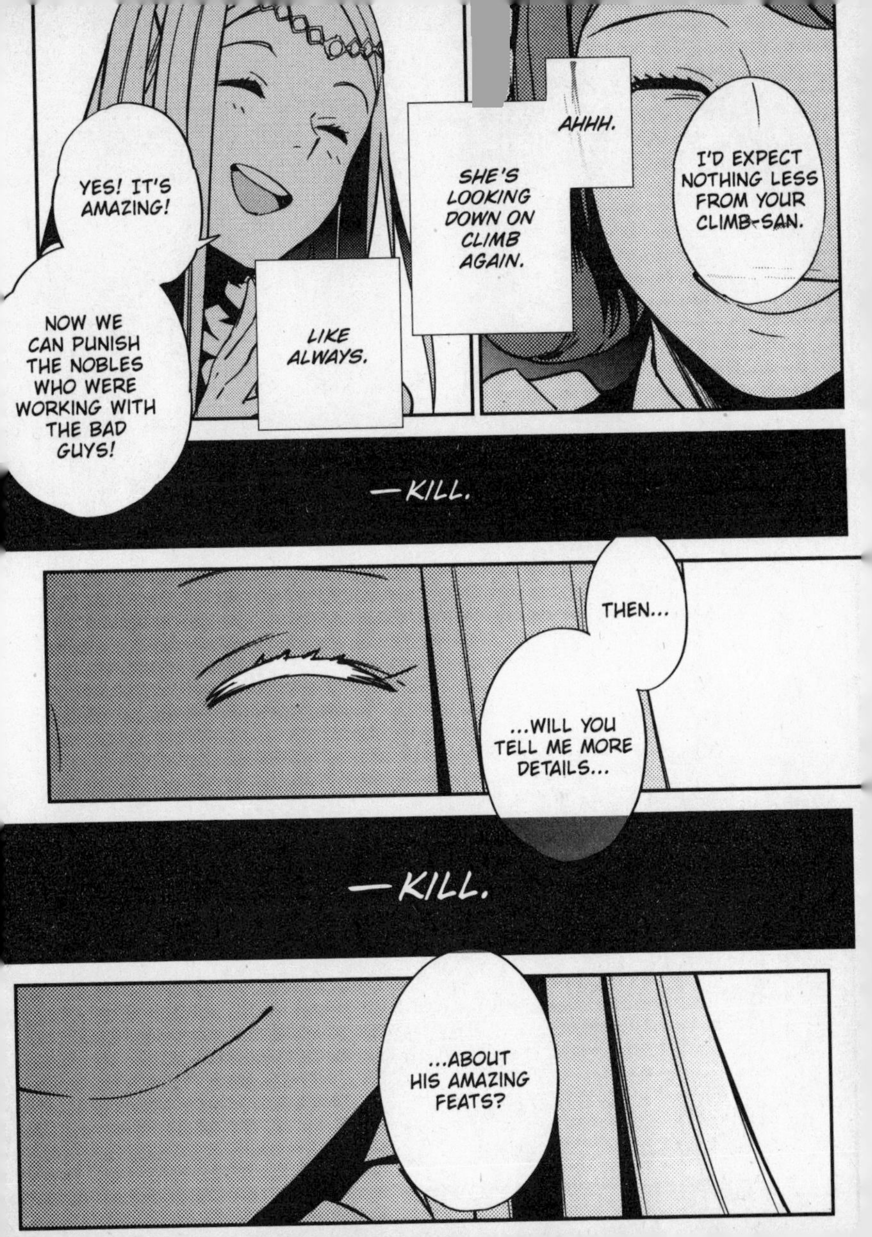
I'D EXPECT NOTHING LESS FROM YOUR CLIMB-SAN.
AHHH.
SHE'S LOOKING DOWN ON CLIMB AGAIN.
YES! IT'S AMAZING!
NOW WE CAN PUNISH THE NOBLES WHO WERE WORKING WITH THE BAD GUYS!
LIKE ALWAYS.
—KILL.
THEN...
...WILL YOU TELL ME MORE DETAILS...
—KILL.
...ABOUT HIS AMAZING FEATS?

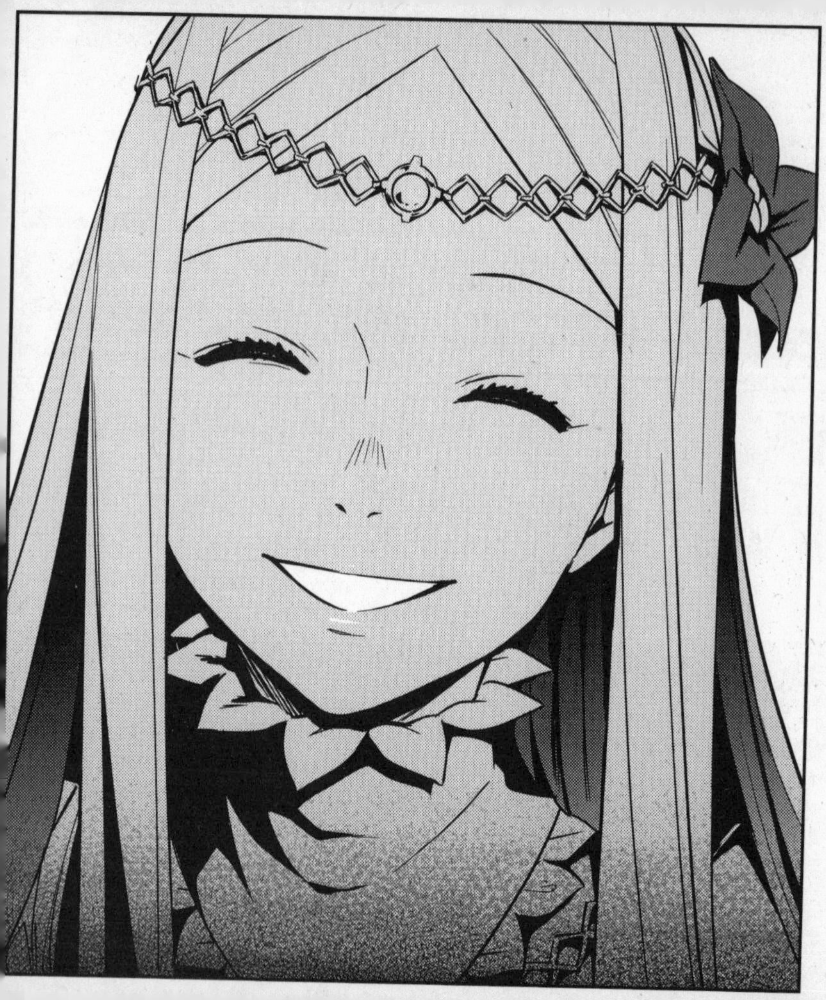

Renner Theiere Chardelon Ryle Vaiself

Third daughter of King Ramposa III of the Re-Estize Kingdom. Younger sister of first prince Barbro and second prince Zanac. Has two older sisters who have been married off. Also known as the "Golden Princess." Having received her mother's looks, she's so beautiful, a portrait can't do her justice. She was called Golden not only for her beauty but also for her work helping the people by establishing organizations and enacting laws, as well as her superior wisdom and intellect. She's sixteen years old, and no small number of nobles are aiming for her hand in marriage.

Relationships

Adored by her father, Ramposa III, as his youngest daughter. Meets often with the members of the Blue Roses, and they cooperate on solving the kingdom's issues. She gave the boy she plucked off the street, Climb, a post higher than appropriate for his status; he's very important to her.

Achievements

Nobles are always warring for power in the feudal Re-Estize Kingdom, so even those aligned with the king can't get their way very easily. In that climate, Renner has realized a few policies despite opposition.

Highway security

The kingdom's roads (traveled by merchants, adventurers, and others) are critical infrastructure, yet there is a risk of bandit and monster attacks. Highway security was provided by the nobles who lived on the estates through which the roads ran, but the nobles were only in it to charge tolls, leaving the security they provided often unreliable. In order to ameliorate the issue, Renner organized patrols for the areas directly under the king's jurisdiction. Due to noble opposition, though, she was unable to implement enough, making it a stretch to say that the highways were being protected.

Pavement

In addition to the highway patrols, stone pavement maintenance was also initiated due to a proposal from Renner. The area under the jurisdiction of the king (as well as part of the nobles' domains) had been paved, but as stated previously, the nobles considered the roads a source of income. Loath to let maintenance costs eat into their profits, they opposed the upkeep, so the project didn't go according to plan. The result is the current heavily potholed state of the roads.

Abolishment of slavery

Abducted children and people bought and paid for were being forced into slavery, so Renner promoted the abolishment of the slave trade. As a result, brothels using slaves were forced underground, which was a huge blow to the Eight Fingers, who had run a profitable prostitution business.

Renner is adored by many for her looks, character, and intelligence, but some people, like Zanac, call her a monster. Climb doesn't know why.

OVERLORD ⑩

Art: Hugin Miyama
Original Story: Kugane Maruyama
Character Design: so-bin
Scenario: Satoshi Oshio

Translation: Emily Balistrieri   •   **Lettering: Liz Kolkman**

OVERLORD Volume 10
© Hugin MIYAMA 2018
© Satoshi OSHIO 2018
© 2012 Kugane Maruyama
First published in Japan in 2018 by KADOKAWA CORPORATION, Tokyo
English translation rights arranged with KADOKAWA CORPORATION, Tokyo
through Tuttle-Mori Agency, Inc.

English translation © 2019 by Yen Press, LLC

Yen Press
1290 Avenue of the Americas
New York, NY 10104

Visit us at yenpress.com
facebook.com/yenpress
twitter.com/yenpress
yenpress.tumblr.com
instagram.com/yenpress

First Yen Press Edition: May 2019

Yen Press is an imprint of Yen Press, LLC.
The Yen Press name and logo are trademarks of Yen Press, LLC.

Library of Congress Control Number: 2016932688

ISBNs: 978-1-9753-5739-9 (paperback)
        978-1-9753-5740-5 (ebook)

10 9 8 7 6 5 4 3 2 1

WOR

Printed in the United States of America